D1222550

Washington Brotherhood

CIVIL WAR AMERICA

Gary W. Gallagher, Peter S. Carmichael, Caroline E. Janney,
and Aaron Sheehan-Dean, editors

Washington
BROTHERHOOD

Politics, Social Life, and the Coming of the Civil War

RACHEL A. SHELDEN

The University of North Carolina Press CHAPEL HILL

This book was published with the assistance of the Thornton H. Brooks Fund
of the University of North Carolina Press.

Set in Galliard by Tseng Information Systems, Inc.
Manufactured in the United States of America

The paper in this book meets the guidelines for permanence and durability of
the Committee on Production Guidelines for Book Longevity of the Council on Library Resources. The University of North Carolina Press has been a
member of the Green Press Initiative since 2003.

Library of Congress Cataloging-in-Publication Data
Shelden, Rachel A., 1981–
Washington brotherhood : politics, social life, and the coming of the
Civil War / Rachel A. Shelden.
pages cm. — (Civil War America)
Includes bibliographical references and index.
ISBN 978-1-4696-1085-6 (hardback)
ISBN 978-1-4696-1086-3 (ebook)
1. United States—Social life and customs—1783–1865. 2. Washington
(D.C.)—Social life and customs—19th century. 3. Politicians—United
States—Social life and customs—19th century. 4. Statesmen—United States—
Social life and customs—19th century. 5. Political culture—United States—
History—19th century. 6. Political culture—Washington (D.C.)—History—
19th century. 7. United States—Politics and government—1815–1861. I. Title.
E166.S55 2013
973.7—dc23
2013022516

17 16 15 14 13 5 4 3 2 1

For Andy

CONTENTS

TABLES AND ILLUSTRATIONS

ACKNOWLEDGMENTS

Perhaps the most satisfying part of finishing this book is the opportunity to thank all of the important people who helped in making it possible. This project started during my graduate years at the University of Virginia, a truly special place to study history. My adviser, Michael F. Holt, offered endless wisdom and guidance. As his last student, I can only hope to live up to his reputation for meticulous research. Anyone who has worked with Michael also knows that he is a relentlessly thorough reader, and I am certain that I would have made many more mistakes without his close eye on the details of antebellum politics. Beginning with my first day in graduate school, I relished every opportunity to converse with Gary W. Gallagher about this project and a variety of other topics, from Civil War scholarship to steroids in baseball. Gary is a wonderful mentor and friend, and undoubtedly I am a better historian for knowing him.

I was lucky enough to work with Elizabeth Varon in the short time we overlapped at Virginia. Her professionalism and dedication have served as an inspiration to me. As an early reader of the project, Liz also offered the single most important suggestion I received for framing and refining my approach to the antebellum Washington community. Charles W. McCurdy has always challenged me to think more clearly and carefully. I also want to thank Peter Onuf, Sophie Rosenfeld, and especially Ed Ayers, who supported my project early on and who taught me about the power of drama in history.

Writing a book may be a solitary experience in some ways, but I could not have done it without the encouragement of terrific friends and colleagues. I owe an enormous debt of gratitude to Laura Kolar, who read every word of my early drafts and offered more good cheer than I could ever ask for. Chris Childers, Katy Meier, and Sean Nalty each read several chapters and gave invaluable critiques. Lauren Acker, Erik Alexander, Nathan Buman, Philip Herrington, Cynthia Nicoletti, Carl and Sarah Paulus, and Adam Pratt provided important suggestions and support. Sunday night dinners with Andy Shelden, Justin Pront, David Katz, Brian Alvo, and Jori Lambert challenged me to think in more general terms about Washington as both a social and political place. And more recently my colleagues at Georgia College, particularly Mark Huddle and Bob Wilson, have enthusiastically supported my work.

Early on in my research, members of the vibrant Civil War–era scholarly community generously welcomed me into their ranks; conversations with Bill Blair, Steve Berry, Russ McClintock, Yonatan Eyal, Bill Freehling, Jim Huston, Matt Mason, Mark Neely, Paul Quigley, Michael Perman, Aaron Sheehan-Dean, Andrew Torget, Frank Towers, Eric Walther, and Joan Waugh helped shape and refine my thinking. Steve Maizlish and Mark Stegmaier both sent collections of papers and articles they thought I would find useful, and Steve took the time to give thoughtful comments and suggestions on an earlier draft. Dan Crofts has supported my project in its various iterations for several years. In addition to pointing me in the direction of a number of useful primary sources, Dan twice read the manuscript for the University of North Carolina Press with a careful eye and offered insightful additions and subtractions.

At the University of North Carolina Press, I have been lucky to work with David Perry, who believed in my work from day one. His skill and professionalism helped shape the book in innumerable ways; I could not have asked for a better editor. In addition to Dan Crofts, a second anonymous reader took the time to offer critical changes that greatly improved the book. I also want to thank Caitlin Bell-Butterfield, who has helped keep my project moving, as well as Ron Maner and Brian MacDonald.

A number of organizations and archives supported my research, including the North Caroliniana Society Archie K. Davis Fund, the University of Michigan Bentley Historical Library, the White House Historical Association, the Everett M. Dirksen Congressional Center, the University of Chicago Special Collections Research Center, the Filson Historical Society, the Massachusetts Historical Society Andrew Mellon fund, the W. M. Keck Foundation at the Huntington Library, the William and Madeline Welder Smith Research fund at the University of Texas at Austin Briscoe Center for American History, and the Virginia Historical Society Andrew Mellon fund. In addition, the University of Virginia and the Doris G. Quinn foundation both offered financial assistance during the writing process.

Several friends and family members offered me housing while I conducted my research. Kristin and Matt Acocella, Peter and Marsha Pront, Enid Shapiro, and Katie Shapiro were all generous in their hospitality. Both of my families—the Shapiros and the Sheldens—have offered constant love and support. I especially want to thank my parents, Susan and Rob Shapiro, who gave me my passion for history and encouraged me to follow that passion wherever it took me. Most important, this book would not exist without my husband, Andy Shelden. Andy listened to every story, helped me tackle every challenge, read every word, and supported me every day of this project. For those reasons, and so many more, I dedicate this book to him.

The Washington Fraternity in the Mid-Nineteenth Century

This is a book about the coming of the Civil War. Historians will recognize the typical antebellum story of political events associated with growing sectionalism and conflict, from the Wilmot Proviso through the secession winter of 1860–61. But this is also a book about Americans' personal experiences and social community; it is about how one community, in particular, understood the events of the 1840s and 1850s. It just so happens that this community was made up of most of the key players in the political decision making of this period. In the pages that follow, I retell the coming of the Civil War from the perspective of Washington politicians.

For generations, historians have portrayed Washington's politicians as emblematic of a larger social and cultural divide throughout the United States. Scholars frequently describe the capital city as a violent and divisive place, pointing to angry rants in the *Congressional Globe* and particularly Preston Brooks's caning of Charles Sumner in 1856. By the 1850s, so the story goes, politicians from the North and South could barely look one another in the eye in the halls of Congress and carried bowie knives and pistols when they dared leave the comforts of their Washington homes.[1]

As this book demonstrates, the violent and divisive interpretation of the capital city overlooks the degree to which Washington was, itself, an important social community in the mid-nineteenth century. It can be easy to forget that federal politicians were more than the political parties, sections, or ideas that they represented. Most of what we know about these men comes from sectional and partisan newspaper reports of their speeches and actions in the Capitol Building and the White House. Yet these men were more than just politicians representing varied constituents. They were *real* people who worked and lived in a tight-knit Washington community that included a vibrant social and cultural life in the mid-nineteenth century. Most important, this social and cultural life was a critical part of the way that politicians engaged with the sectional and ideological struggles of the antebellum era.

While in the capital city, politicians from different sections of the country could hardly avoid interacting in a variety of day-to-day activities, inside and outside the halls of Congress and the various executive departments. Some met each other for religious worship. Others gathered together in local philanthropic organizations, clubs, or chapters like the Washington, D.C., Freemasons. Lavish parties, state banquets, and intimate dinners provided other opportunities for cross-sectional interaction. Men from all parts of the country boarded together at local hotels or houses or shared a street in the same neighborhood. At taverns and temperance meetings, concert halls and gambling houses, federal politicians found themselves interacting with men who hailed from states all over the Union. Through these experiences and activities, many lawmakers got to know one another on a personal level. Soon, a Southerner was more than a slaveholder; he was also a colleague. And a Northerner may have opposed slavery, but he was also a drinking buddy or an expert card player. To a large degree, then, these men came to see each other as part of a fraternity of Washington politicians.

Washington society did more than just provide an environment where men from different sections could interact. It also gave politicians the opportunity to discuss political issues outside the traditional structures of lawmaking. Congressmen, cabinet members, Supreme Court justices, and other federal politicians did not leave their work behind at the office; they brought their arguments, ideas, and solutions to the church pew, the dinner table, the boardinghouse parlor, and the hotel bar. Furthermore, because the Capitol itself was extremely public—particularly when it was full of partisan reporters and visitors in the galleries—many found that it was more effective to make political deals away from the Capitol, in a more private setting. As a result, these men blurred the line between Washington's social and political spaces, creating what one might call the "unofficial" political arena.[2]

The "unofficial" arena that existed in the private spaces of the capital is critical to understanding the nature of federal politics in the antebellum era.

Politicians had two different roles while serving in the capital. First, they had to attend to the needs of their constituents. Senators and representatives generally did this by making congressional speeches. Yet federal politicians did not necessarily direct their public words toward each other. Instead, congressmen frequently delivered speeches designed to please their constituents that were otherwise ignored by their colleagues. Such speechmaking was a well-accepted part of the Washington political experience, even if it had a tendency to make congressional sessions long and tedious.

Federal lawmakers' second role in Washington was to participate in actual policy making, engaging in issues of national importance and making one's mark through bills, amendments, and backroom dealings. By the 1840s and 1850s, this second role had become increasingly separate from speechmaking, as sectional issues involving slavery often dominated the halls of Congress. As a result, in order to fully understand this second role, historians must move beyond lawmakers' public words in congressional debate, political pamphlets, and newspaper articles and instead dig deeper into what happened behind the scenes in the unofficial setting of the Washington community.[3]

The tension between constituent demands and unofficial policy making was not new in the antebellum period. The distinctive nature of the capital city—and particularly its living arrangements—helped to define federal policy making from the earliest days of the new nation.[4] Politicians who came to Washington throughout the nineteenth century had to make strategic choices about their level of participation in their roles as both representatives and policy makers. By the 1840s, the number of federal politicians in Washington had grown considerably, and exercising influence proved more difficult. Interacting in the unofficial social atmosphere, then, became the critical means for gaining political power; a group of socially inclined policy makers was more likely to have an impact on political decisions than one senator or congressman could acting on his own.

Ultimately, this sociable Washington political environment had important consequences for how lawmakers engaged with the sectional disputes that plagued the country during the 1840s and 1850s. First, sociability helped to forge political deals involving slavery in the territories. Lawmakers used social spaces to recruit others to their cause, most notably during the run-up to the Compromise of 1850 and the Kansas-Nebraska Act of 1854. In these examples and others, Washington's social atmosphere created the circumstances in which political negotiation was possible. Second, participating in Washington's social life gave lawmakers a more nuanced view of what was happening in the city itself. While the introduction of the Wilmot Proviso in 1846 and the caning of Massachusetts senator Charles Sumner in 1856 enraged Northerners and Southerners outside of the capital, fueling sectional political movements, these events were far less polarizing among Washington politicians who understood them in the context of their city's culture.

Finally, while working through these political battles, Washington's social environment gave federal politicians a unique view of the American Union. As Paul Quigley has recently argued, nineteenth-century Americans connected with the Union in deeply personal ways. They saw the Union in relationship to other loyalties and interests, such as those of family, city, state, and section. Unlike most of their constituents, Washington politicians had a strong personal connection both to the federal government itself and to many of their colleagues from the other section. Such ties complicated their perception of what the Union was and what it stood for.[5] While in 1860 most Northerners saw the Union as synonymous with Northern society and Southerners equated it with Southern values, Washington politicians held a more nuanced view.[6] A Washington reporter for *Harper's New Monthly Magazine* observed about Washington in 1852 that, "in this social collision, sectional prejudices wear off, and the East and West, the South and North thus brought into closer intimacy, become cemented by more enduring ties."[7]

The point here is not that all federal politicians were strong unionists or that their cross-sectional bonds trumped all other loyalties.[8] Like their constituents across the North and South, politicians weighed their attachment to the Union against other relationships. But their distinctive view of the Union does help to explain lawmakers' behavior during the winter of 1860–61, when seven Deep South states seceded from the Union. During that time, many Washington politicians, and particularly Southern Democrats, found themselves surprised by the speed at which secession took hold. Once they saw that the crisis was real, a number of them fought to find a settlement that would keep the Upper South in the country and bring back the seceded states, thereby preserving their cherished Union. Washington's sociability, therefore, defined both the successes and the failures of federal policy making.[9]

Any investigation of this kind must engage with the complicated debates over what caused the Civil War. In particular, historians may wonder what the sociability of Washington does to the "blundering generation" thesis of sectional conflict. In 1940 James G. Randall coined the phrase in arguing that the politicians of the antebellum era helped breed fanaticism in the North and South primarily through "emotional unreason and overbold leadership." In essence, he explained, it was the incompetence of prewar politicians that created a needless war. Few scholars in the twenty-first century would call the Civil War "needless," as the emancipation of 4 million slaves hinged on Union victory. Yet questions about the role of blundering politicians remain, particularly: How much responsibility do politicians have for the conflict?[10]

Washington's politicians did fan the flames of sectional discord through contentious speeches and violent outbursts. Furthermore, the network of mass newspapers facilitated by politically inclined editors helped carry negative rhetoric throughout the nation. Yet the move toward secession must be considered, above all, a rejection of federal politics. In letters, newspaper editorials, and speeches during the secession winter, men and women throughout the South evinced a loss of faith in their representatives in Washington, insisting these federal politicians could not be trusted. From the perspective of many Southerners back home, secession was the only answer to an unresponsive, corrupt federal government. Rather than creating disunion, therefore, the bubble of Washington often shielded federal politicians from the difficulties of sectionalism and ultimately rendered many of them unprepared for the disunion movement.[11]

The "blundering generation" thesis highlights a second aspect of Civil War–era historiography: the problem of inevitability. As recent books by William W. Freehling and Marc Egnal suggest, 150 years after the conflict began, scholars still disagree as to whether the Civil War was destined to come and why.[12] Such debates hinge in part on the question of what caused secession: was there an irrepressible conflict over slavery that portended violent conflict, or was the war contingent on political events? Slavery *and* politics are important to understanding how individuals felt in the 1840s and 1850s. Indeed, Abraham Lincoln's pronouncement in his second inaugural address that "all knew" that the Southern interest in slavery "was, somehow, the cause of the war" is compatible with the power of contingency during the secession winter of 1860–61. As a result, I follow the lead of scholars like Elizabeth Varon and Edward Ayers in moving beyond these debates to look at personal connections to union and disunion.[13]

My intent is not to minimize the importance of sectional identity, economic differences, slavery, or party politics. Each of these issues played a role in the lives of federal politicians. Rather, I emphasize that men with wide-ranging backgrounds, beliefs, affiliations, habits, and allegiances interacted in the social and political spaces of Washington. Some came from north of the Mason-Dixon line and others from the South. They hailed from large cities and small towns, from coastal states and the frontier. Lutherans, Methodists, Presbyterians, and nonbelievers came to Washington, as did Masons, Odd Fellows, and temperance advocates. Doctors, ministers, farmers, and a large number of lawyers graced the halls of the Capitol and the cabinet departments. There were Whigs, Democrats, Free-Soilers, Americans, Republicans, and Opposition men. Some were slaveholders and some were not. Drinkers, gamblers, and womanizers populated every rank. Most arrived without their families, while others brought wives and children with them to the capital city. Together, these men made up the complex and textured political community of Washington, with its myriad relationships, behavior, and loyalties. And because of this community, federal politicians had a unique connection to the political events of the antebellum era.[14]

I have organized this book both chronologically and thematically. In each chapter I begin with an important political event or issue in the antebellum period and then analyze it in the context of one aspect of Washington's social and political community. Chapter 1 illustrates how the city's political life did not operate, reexamining the Wilmot Proviso controversy through the lens of congressional culture inside the Capitol. I highlight the limitations of the *Congressional Globe* and document the reasons why much politicking happened outside the halls of Congress.

Chapters 2 through 6 focus on social and political spaces outside the Capitol as events unfolded from 1846 to 1860. The second chapter revisits Abraham Lincoln's short tenure as a representative in the Thirtieth Congress and his involvement with a group called the Young Indian Club. As I show, the Young Indians were one of many cross-sectional organizations that included Washington politicians among their membership. Chapter 3 takes another look at the Compromise of 1850 through the context of parties, balls, dinners, and other social events. In addition to federal politicians, it highlights the role prominent Washington socialites like local banker William W. Corcoran had in promoting cross-sectional conciliation. Chapter 4 documents the importance of Washington's temporary housing arrangements in formulating the Kansas-Nebraska Act of 1854. Historians have often credited a single congressional boardinghouse—the F Street Mess—with designing that bill. I show how living together could provide opportunities to negotiate the details for a piece of legislation such as the Kansas-Nebraska Act and that, unlike the F Street messmates, most politicians in Washington lived in cross-sectional housing.

In chapter 5, I explore Washington politicians' reactions to the caning of

Charles Sumner in the context of vice and violence in the capital city. I argue that although the caning raised sectional tensions outside of Washington, federal politicians reacted in a more moderate way because of their familiarity with the culture of Washington. Chapter 6 looks at the consequences of the Lecompton Constitution battle in Congress in early 1858. During that fight, Illinois Democrat Stephen Douglas and Kentuckian John J. Crittenden of the American Party developed an important cross-partisan relationship. As I demonstrate, Washington's political fraternity helped forge many surprising friendships that crossed both partisan and sectional boundaries. Finally, chapter 7 reexamines the winter of 1860–61, when politicians faced the possibility of disunion. During those months, Washington lawmakers continued to interact in the cross-sectional sociable atmosphere of Washington. Many made efforts toward conciliation and compromise. Their efforts failed primarily because the ability to prevent Civil War was not in their hands.

Readers will note that this work focuses primarily on the perspectives and actions of elite white men. I have taken this approach, in part, because these men were the movers and shakers in the national political arena during the antebellum period. Yet I also focus on these men because of the decidedly masculine nature of Washington's political society. Many of the politicians who came to Washington had little daily interaction with women after leaving their wives and daughters back home. Instead, they found themselves in a fraternal network of male ritual and interaction. The decidedly male dominance of Washington's political society played an important role in defining the way that federal politicians operated in the capital itself.[15]

There were, however, many others who lived in the Washington community, including women, free and enslaved African Americans, and poor whites. Many of these community members played critical roles in the day-to-day life of the capital city. Some tried—and a few even succeeded—to influence political events. While I have occasionally documented their efforts as part of the overall picture of political Washington, they are not the primary characters in my story. That said, I would not have been able to complete this project without the existence of politicians' wives. The many letters that these women wrote and received during the antebellum period opened doors that would have been otherwise locked.

Through these doors I came to understand that the Washington fraternity produced an insulated and sometimes odd assortment of relationships among men from different backgrounds and beliefs. These relationships at times even dismayed politicians and activists living outside the capital city. Perhaps this oddity can best be demonstrated by the correspondence between antislavery preacher Theodore Parker and a friend named Joseph Allen, who was visiting Washington in the spring of 1848. Tempers had been running high throughout the country, as politicians struggled to determine the slave or nonslave status of territory acquired during the recently ended Mexican War. Parker and others hoped that antislavery congressmen like New Hampshire senator John P. Hale would push their free-soil agenda, regardless of Southern threats of disunion. But Allen would disappoint him. Parker's friend reported from Washington that, although disunion talk was ubiquitous throughout the United States, in the nation's capital such threats were "constantly being neutralized by the practical operation at the Seat of Government." The day-to-day interactions of congressmen who lived and worked in Washington served as a buffer for sectional prejudices. As Allen reported, "Men who would have shot Hale with a rifle if they had met him at the South, part with him on good terms, inviting him cordially to make them a visit."[16]

The Politician's Landscape in Antebellum Washington

In the 1840s and 1850s, Washington city was far from a vacation destination. Most of the streets were unpaved, leaving them muddy in wet weather and caked in dust when dry. One resident later remembered that "horses, cattle and swine roamed about the streets, no city ordinance being then in force to keep them within stableyard bounds." Another described Washington in the early 1850s as "an overgrown tattered village which some late hurricane had scattered along the river's edge." The beautiful plan of city architect Pierre L'Enfant had, in actuality, resulted in a haphazard pattern of buildings and squares littered throughout the city. For most visitors, the only real attraction in Washington was the Capitol, with its imposing dome and elegant gardens. And even this building had cracking walls and rotting timbers. The mall was a "half developed park," while the president's mansion was "an ordinary country home, wanting in either taste or splendor." There was little to draw Americans to the capital city other than the political spectacle. "Few people would live in Washington, I take it, who were not obliged to reside there," quipped the English writer Charles Dickens after a trip to the capital city in 1842.[1]

Given all of this unpleasantness, who would choose to live in such a city? In 1850 the population reached 40,000 people. Of these residents, 26 percent were classified by the census as "colored" and 5 percent were African American slaves. In addition, there were hordes of temporary inhabitants in

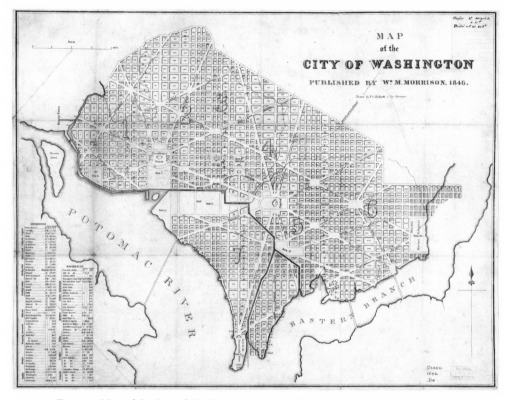

Figure 1. Map of the City of Washington by DeKrafft, 1846 (Washington, D.C.: William M. Morrison, 1846). Maps Division, Library of Congress.

the capital, most prominently the politicians who were, as Dickens put it, "obliged to reside there" during the congressional session. The influx of politicians every December made Washington something of a "winter resort" for fashionables, even though the city itself inspired little in the way of elegance. In the brutal summer heat, Washington, "presented a curious aspect," according to another resident. "In utter stagnation it awaited the return of Congress, and the strangers which December brought back to the hotels and boarding-houses."[2]

Partly as a result of these seasonal living patterns, there were really *two* Washingtons—two residential circles that occasionally could overlap but generally operated in different worlds. In one circle were the permanent residents, including the sizable African American population, along with the many tavern keepers, laborers, schoolteachers, and merchants. Permanent residents could be found in all of the city's nooks and crannies but, other than the most fashionable and wealthy families, they tended to congregate in neighborhoods away from the center of political action. One of the largest sets of inhabitants resided near the Navy Yard in the eastern branch of the city. According to one resident, this was "the oldest of the village communities," largely "rural and self contained." On the western side of the city, separated by Rock Creek, lay Georgetown, home to about 8,000 Washingtonians. The men and women of Georgetown included some fashionables lobbying Congress, but most of them were working class, involved in the fish or flouring business. On both ends, only a regular omnibus line connected these neighborhoods to the city's political center. Other, less inhabited parts of the city were notoriously dangerous; the neighborhood north of the Washington Canal was even known as "Murder Bay." In this area of the city, as in others, the police could not be counted on to protect citizens from "gangs of rowdies."[3]

While permanent residents spread out across all parts of Washington, the second circle, full of temporary residents, generally stuck to one long corridor in the capital, with Pennsylvania Avenue at its central line and the Capitol building and White House as its bookends. The "Avenue" was the epicenter of political traffic, but even this central area was "sparsely and irregularly built up," showcasing an array of buildings with shacks arranged next to mansions. The streets were unkempt as the city provided no garbage collection or street cleaning, and in the winter, when Congress was in session, the wind often swirled mercilessly through the Avenue. On particularly dry days, walkers could be seen holding handkerchiefs to their faces to avoid suffocation.[4]

In part because of its uncleanliness, the city was also rife with disease. Politicians consistently wrote home about their health and the dangers of not only dyspepsia but also cholera, typhoid fever, and small pox. Attempts to address the city's state of filth could be dangerous. According to one account, somewhere between twenty and thirty residents at one Avenue hotel were accidentally poisoned by arsenic once when the proprietors tried to root out a rat infestation. Fires were also a problem, sometimes set by hoodlums and other times by accident. In January 1857 a Supreme Court justice's wife was burned to death after her clothes caught on fire.[5]

This ugly, violent, dirty, and disease-ridden city was no place for a lady of class. While some wives braved the unpleasantness of the capital city's streets, temporary residents were typically men. The stretch of Pennsylvania Avenue, and particularly the Capitol itself, therefore, served as one large fraternity house with occasional female visitors and passers-through. "In no part of the republic is the social sway of woman so limited as it is in the

Figure 2. A bird's-eye view of Washington, 1856, looking west from the Capitol grounds up Pennsylvania Avenue. Prints and Photographs Division, Library of Congress.

Figure 3. Sketch of Buchanan's inaugural procession down Pennsylvania Avenue in 1857. *Frank Leslie's Illustrated Newspaper*, March 21, 1857. Prints and Photographs Division, Library of Congress.

capital," wrote one foreign visitor. "This does not arise from any inferiority in the Washington ladies, but from the absolute paucity of their numbers." Without female society to keep manners and dress in line, many federal politicians looked almost like beggars. Texas senator Sam Houston was particularly known for tying "his neckcloth in a very clumsy bow" and wearing "a tiger-skin vest, built as if for an Arctic expedition." Virginia senator Robert M. T. Hunter may have been a gallant speaker, but his dress was negligent. One observer wrote that "his clothes are so indefinitely cut, as to be an equally good fit for any other Senator in the chamber."[6]

Such was the Washington landscape for antebellum politicians. "The glories of politics!" Massachusetts Whig Robert Winthrop wrote to a friend in 1841. "To leave a quiet, comfortable home, wife, children and troops of friends, and come to a hot, dirty, dusty hole, to be shut up for six or eight hours a day with a couple of hundred savage fellows in an amphitheater lined with laughing or sneering spectators."[7]

CHAPTER ONE

A Perfect Tower of Babel

The Culture of Congress and the Wilmot Proviso

By Saturday, August 8, 1846, congressmen were getting rest-less. After braving a hot and sticky summer in Washington, members were anxious for the session's end. Both houses were wasting time on personal business when the House of Representatives recessed for dinner at three o'clock that after-noon. At five o'clock, the appointed hour for the House to re-convene, congressmen slowly shuffled back to their seats. But when the time for restarting debate began, the House found itself without a quorum.

To most of the members, the inability to maintain a quorum was unsurprising. Some congressmen had already left the city for their home states, rushing back to their families or trying to avoid the chaos of the end of a session. Because the Demo-cratic majority in Congress had finally passed the Tariff of 1846, a crucial piece of legislation that many considered the capstone of the session, some members believed they had no need to stay for the final days of the term.[1] Others simply had not yet returned from dinner or did not plan to return after a long week's work. A few members were in the building but not on the floor; they lurked in antechambers, in the congressional restaurant, or in the Senate. Even those who bothered to re-turn on time were not necessarily ready to proceed with con-gressional business; a few were drunk, others stretched out on the sofas lining the walls of the House chamber, and still more wrote letters to constituents and loved ones at their desks.

As congressmen began to trickle in, finally reaching critical mass, debate eventually resumed on a bill that President James K. Polk had submitted to the two houses of Congress shortly before they broke at three o'clock. Polk was hoping to raise $2 million to help fund negotiations to end the Mexican War. The war had begun after the United States annexed Texas in 1845. Texas was technically an independent republic in 1845, but Mexico had controlled the area until the mid-1830s, and rightly held the United States responsible for aiding Texas in its rebellion. As a result, once Congress proceeded with annexation deliberations, Mexico cut off all diplomatic communication with its neighbor. Over the next few months, a crisis began to brew, and both the United States and Mexico sent troops to the Rio Grande. In April 1846, tensions reached a boiling point when the Mexican army crossed the river and ambushed General Zachary Taylor's men. By August 1846, the war with Mexico was in full swing.[2]

The Whig Party both in and outside of Congress strongly opposed the war, often accusing Polk of provoking Mexican retaliation. Yet Democrats were generally behind the president. Northeastern merchants, northwestern farmers, and Southern slaveholders, in particular, advocated expansion westward. Thus, as the conflict opened in 1846, Polk hoped that a speedy decisive victory would result in negotiations to end the war and cede Mexican territory to the United States. On August 8, he expected the overwhelmingly Democratic Congress to push through the $2 million war appropriation bill in the waning hours of the congressional session.[3]

Yet Polk did not account for the actions of a small group of antislavery Democrats, all of whom belonged to a wing of the party headed by former president Martin Van Buren. This group was inordinately frustrated by the lack of power it held in the Polk administration. Polk not only failed to appoint representatives of Van Buren's faction to his cabinet but also denied them crucial patronage positions in their home states. Additionally, these men increasingly opposed slavery (most would become key organizers of the Free-Soil Party) and suspected that Polk intended to use the money to acquire more slave territory from Mexico.[4]

During the afternoon recess, the group had gathered over dinner and discussed the possibility of introducing an amendment to the president's proposal. When the House began its debate of the $2 million bill, David Wilmot, a short and corpulent Pennsylvania Democrat, rose and delivered a blow to the president's wishes: he intended to introduce an amendment, soon to be known as the "Wilmot Proviso," providing "against the establishment of slavery, or involuntary servitude, in any territory which may be acquired."[5]

Although the proviso became an intense topic of discussion in future congresses, immediate reaction in the House to Wilmot's amendment was minimal. Few of the speakers that followed (including several Southerners) even commented on the antislavery proposal. Rather than becoming enraged over the slavery issue, the only Southerner to directly refer to the amendment in the ensuing debate, Alexander Sims of South Carolina, merely "regretted that the gentleman from Pennsylvania . . . had chosen to mingle with the question the exciting topic of slavery," finding "the agitation of that subject . . . premature."[6]

Sims's use of the word "premature" is telling. Many Southerners expected some sort of slavery agitation to enter the debate eventually. Members of the Twenty-Ninth Congress were no strangers to speeches and amendments that dealt with the peculiar institution. Most had served in previous congresses, in which, for nearly ten years, House members had repeatedly battled over the right to introduce antislavery petitions on the floor of Congress. Disagreements over the "gag rule," which Southerners imposed on the petitions, would occasionally become heated, and the issue tended to split both parties along sectional lines. Everyone knew Northerners and Southerners were bound to disagree about slavery. The question was whether such agitation was necessary, before the United States had even acquired any territory.[7]

Thus, when Wilmot's amendment came to a vote, James Dobbin of North Carolina made a last-ditch effort to override the antislavery addition. He moved that Wilmot's amendment be excluded because "slavery has nothing to do with the appropriation." But the chair overruled him, explaining that the House was permitted to attach stipulations to any appropriation that the body granted to the president. Dobbin appealed the chair's decision, but the House voted to sustain the ruling 92 to 37. Finally, the proviso came to a vote, passing the House by an overwhelming majority, 83 to 64. The House then approved the $2 million appropriation, 87 to 64. Ohio Democrat Jacob Brinkerhoff asked for a reconsideration of the bill, but this was voted down by a majority of Northerners, 70 to 83. Still, nothing came of the appropriation, as the Senate did not take up the House measure, and instead let the $2 million bill lapse at the end of the session. Because the Senate did not pass the bill, Polk was left without his appropriation.[8]

The Wilmot Proviso eventually became one of the most polarizing pieces of legislation in Congress in the late 1840s. By 1847 and 1848, Northern state legislatures repeatedly instructed their senators to vote for the amendment, and Southerners frequently threatened disunion at the mere mention of Wilmot's provision. Some scholars have even identified the introduction of the proviso debate as the critical turning point on the road to Southern secession and civil war.[9]

Yet, as other historians have noted, immediate reaction to the Wilmot Proviso was limited among both congressmen and the voting public. Few politicians outside of Washington, in particular, foresaw how polarizing the amendment would become. In fact, not until the following summer would Southerners become fully agitated by the bill. Similarly, New Hampshire was the only state to instruct its senators to repeatedly vote for the anti-slavery provision in the fall of 1846. Even the Washington press made little note of the amendment; the administration's organ, the *Daily Union*, merely regretted that Congress had not passed the $2 million appropriation.[10]

What explains this gap between the initial introduction of Wilmot's amendment in 1846 and the eventual explosion that the proviso created in Congress throughout the rest of the decade? How did members of the House of Representatives allow the Wilmot attachment to be introduced and passed so easily, with little discussion and even less hoopla, in the waning days of the first session of the Twenty-Ninth Congress? The answers to these questions are found in the day-to-day workings of the antebellum Congress. The passage of and reaction to Wilmot's proviso in the House of Representatives and throughout Washington did not happen in a vacuum. Rather, Congress's modus operandi, particularly at the end of a long session, provided the critical backdrop in which the Wilmot Proviso could come to the floor, pass, and receive little attention.

Few members paid much attention to the Wilmot Proviso, both before and after the vote on the amendment, because in *every* meeting of Congress only a small amount of business of any consequence transpired during debate on the floor of the Senate and House of Representatives. This was particularly true in the final days of the session. As the behavior of senators and representatives in Congress throughout the 1840s and 1850s demonstrates, most of the real action—the *real* politicking and decision making—was happening elsewhere. Ultimately, in order to fully understand the circumstances in which the Wilmot Proviso could pass, we must have a better understanding of the culture of Congress in the mid-nineteenth century.

■ The scene in the House on August 8, 1846, was typical of the end of a congressional session in the antebellum era. To begin with, it was somewhat empty: out of 228 total representatives of the states elected to Congress at one time, no more than 153 were present for votes during the evening debate. At the end of a session, it could often be difficult for either the House or the Senate to maintain a quorum, and both operated with a substantially reduced number of attendees. In the summer of 1846, men like Mississippi representative Jefferson Davis had left their posts to join the army fighting in Mexico. Others had not been renominated for the fall elections and either left once Congress passed the tariff or, like Missouri congressman Sterling Price, simply resigned their seats.[11]

If it was common for the Capitol to be emptier near the end of the session, congressmen made finding a quorum difficult at other times by abandoning their posts for short periods during the middle of the term. Some members simply left Washington if they believed work was at a standstill and assumed they would not be missed. Congressional sessions could be long and tedious; the 1846 term itself had lasted from December 1845 to the following August. During these extended meetings, business in the halls of the House of Representatives and Senate could become woefully inefficient. Congressmen repeatedly remarked, as Michigan Democrat Kinsley S. Bingham did, that House members "have been very steadily engaged doing *nothing* this last week and that is probably all we shall do for the three weeks to come." A Senate colleague agreed: "*Talk* and not business is the order of the day."[12]

Part of the problem was that the first session of Congress was expected to be long—it always carried well into the summer. With the promise of eight or nine months to consider and pass legislation, members had few incentives to get started on their work. The first session of the Twenty-Ninth Congress was no exception. As President Polk pointed out to a cousin in January 1846, "Congress has been in session six weeks, but as is usual at the commencement of a long session, but little business of importance has been done." Another reason for inactivity had to do with the way that congressmen were compensated. Until 1856, each member received payment for every day that Congress met rather than a set salary. As a result, some of the men elected to serve in Washington did the best they could to prolong their experience in the capital city, enjoying higher pay, and, frequently, a more active social life. Such a questionable use of time and money frustrated some Washington residents, lobbyists, and even a few congressmen themselves. For example, one observer in the long 1852 term thought that although Congress had been in session for more than six months, "all the business which has been done could have been better done and better discussed by a body of sensible men, *not paid by the day*, in two weeks."[13]

An easy way for lazy members to prolong the session without doing much congressional business was to meet briefly and adjourn. Members quickly adjourned for a variety of reasons, from providing time for the Speaker of the House to organize committees to the simple inability to maintain a quorum. One of the more common reasons for the House of Representatives to quickly close the meeting for the day, however, was the announcement of the death of a member of the House, and sometimes even a member of the Senate. This practice made sense when Congress lost a popular man, as was the case when Louisiana senator Alexander Barrow died in late 1846. Barrow had become friendly with a large number of senators and representatives from around the country, and all mourned his death.[14]

Yet the practice of adjourning for a dead member could sometimes be more comical than melancholy. During one slow period, New Yorker James G. King mused, "We commence lazily in Congress—no work yet. . . . To day we eulogized Mr. Chester Butler [of Pennsylvania] and adjourned. [Tomorrow] we have another dead member from Ohio—to lament and adjourn upon." The practice of adjourning seemed particularly silly when the dead member had not even taken his seat in Congress. Massachusetts representative Horace Mann wrote to his wife during a long session in 1850 that "today a member from Virginia, announced the death [of] a Mr. Somebody, who had been elected . . . Whereupon the House adjourned tho' not one of the members, or almost [none] . . . saw him or knew any thing about him." Members in the first session of the Twenty-Ninth Congress did not actually lose many of their colleagues, but that did not stop congressmen from finding other reasons to quickly meet and postpone debate for another day.[15]

All of this adjourning meant that the House or Senate could occasionally go several days or even weeks without undertaking substantial business. During these lulls, members often decided to leave town in the middle of the session, hoping to see family or take care of other business outside of Washington. When North Carolina representative David Outlaw, a Whig, left the city on such a trip, however, he needed to find a Democrat willing to "pair off" with him. Pairing off was a common practice among congressmen in the mid-nineteenth century. Members who left town would find a "pair" from the opposite party, section, or position (depending upon the issues before Congress) who pledged not to participate if a vote came up during his time away from Washington. When the House discussed the Walker Tariff earlier in the 1846 session, for example, absent Democratic members who opposed the trade restrictions found Whigs to pair with them, in case the bill came to a vote while they were away. Similarly, during debates on the Compromise of 1850, pro-compromise men paired with anti-compromise men. Such was the case when Ohioan Salmon Chase, a compromise opponent, repeatedly paired off with Texas senator Sam Houston, who was actively pro-compromise.[16]

Sometimes members had important reasons to pair off. Senator John M. Clayton left town in January 1849 after learning of the death of his son. Similarly, Massachusetts senator Edward Everett returned to Massachusetts in 1854 upon becoming too ill to attend to political business. Everett asked his friend, Georgian William C. Dawson, to pair with him in case of a vote on the Kansas-Nebraska Act. Members would occasionally pair off to take care of pressing personal business in their home states. Senator Dixon H. Lewis left Washington for more than a week in 1847 when several of his slaves went missing from his Alabama home. Other times, members' personal reasons for being absent seemed less than sufficient to their peers. During the 1846 session, Sam Houston complained to his wife that the Senate was "not well attended" because "The *Races* are going on within two miles of the Capital."[17]

Some congressmen left Washington before the term was over for political reasons. This was particularly true for House members who hoped to confirm their renomination for the following session. Horace Mann described the problem: "In some states the elections will come on very soon & such of the members as are candidates, [are] feeling too anxious about their own private, political fortunes, to stay longer & attend to the public business."[18] Political conventions could also draw away a large portion of the members. In June 1856, a Washington resident described the city as unusually quiet, remarking that "the congressional wire-workers have not yet returned from the [Democratic] Convention, and there will not probably be a full Congress or any work done in the present week." Likewise, the Senate barely maintained a quorum during the Charleston Convention in April 1860.[19]

Members occasionally missed several days of a session on official congressional business. When a prominent senator or representative died while serving in Washington, a group of members escorted the body back to the congressman's home state. Such trips seemed more common in the late 1840s and early 1850s when Congress lost several of its most famous members, including John Quincy Adams, John C. Calhoun, Henry Clay, and Daniel Webster. A committee that included Michigan senator Lewis Cass accompanied Clay's body to Lexington, Kentucky, in July 1852. Cass was absent about two weeks while the funeral procession passed through Philadelphia, New York City, Albany, Buffalo, Cleveland and Cincinnati, and the Michigan senator was the first committee member to return to Washington. Others used the opportunity of serving on a funeral procession to see family or friends who lived somewhere along the committee's travel path. North Carolina congressman Daniel Barringer asked permission from the chairman leading John Quincy Adams's funeral procession for a short "leave of absence" on the way to Massachusetts to visit his sweetheart in Baltimore. Ultimately, such trips meant that congressmen would occasionally miss long stretches of debate and even important votes.[20]

Even if a majority of Congressmen remained in Washington, the House and Senate often struggled to maintain a quorum. Senators and representatives frequently arrived late to the Capitol, a practice that the majority seemed to accept. As one former member complained about the Senate, "The President instead of taking his seat at the time for opening the session waits until enough of his lazy associates come in to make a quorum—often half an hour." Furthermore, if the agenda looked unappealing for the day, some senators "felt no haste to get to the Capitol."[21]

Others left in the afternoon for dinner since local boardinghouses did not necessarily cater to the congressional schedule when serving meals. Dinner typically took place between four and six, when Congress would temporarily adjourn. But Ann Sprigg, one of the local proprietors, served the meal at two o'clock, leaving her boarders to choose between debate or dinner. An invitation to dine with a cabinet member or diplomat could also compel a congressman to leave in the midst of debate. During the heated arguments over the Kansas-Nebraska Act, Edward Everett left to dine with the secretary of the Navy during a speech by New Hampshire Democrat Moses Norris at about six o'clock. Everett clearly did not miss much, recording in his diary: "Went back to the Senate at 9. [Isaac] Toucey of Conn. who had followed Norris was still speaking." The three to five o'clock dinner break on August 8, 1846, was timed well for some members, but others were still eating when the House was scheduled to reassemble.[22]

Aside from missing the speeches, leaving for an hour or two in the middle of congressional debate typically did not influence the course of Congress. Leaving early, on the other hand, sometimes meant not being present for important votes. This was particularly true at the end of a session, when Congress sat up until the wee hours of the morning trying to pass final bills before the exodus from Washington. Not everyone was willing to stay, though, until four or five in the morning. For example, on the final evening of the first session of the Thirtieth Congress, Missouri bigwig Thomas Hart Benton "left about bed-time, after announcing to the Senate that he would sit 'dog days' but not 'dog-nights.'" Benton was not alone. As day turned to night, congressmen had a much more difficult time seeing each other in candlelight. Those who dutifully remained in the chamber during their dinner hours could become cross and hungry, itching to adjourn for the night. During the long session of the Twenty-Ninth Congress, members repeatedly left for long stretches of the day and in the evenings, causing one local paper to chide the people's representatives. By August 8, after a long, hot summer session in the House, when congressional business no longer seemed so pressing, some members simply did not want to return to the House chamber after a relaxing meal.[23]

The leadership in the House and Senate did have some recourse if members were missing and the body could not get a quorum, particularly if there was a full gallery of men and women waiting to see the proceedings. As Horace Mann described to his wife in early 1850, someone would begin the process by making a motion for the "roll" to be called. Once the clerk of the House completed the roll, he went back to the list of absentees to see if any had come in while he was going through the names. If members were still unsatisfied with the number of men missing from the House, they would "order the door to be closed & send the Sergeant-at-Arms to bring in the absentees. He goes & [drags] them in like school boys & they have to make an apology or excuse for their absence." At this point, Mann continued, "if the House see fit to excuse them for some good cause, there is an end of it," but "if they have no excuse, then they are *generally* let off on paying the fees of the Sergeant-at-Arms, perhaps $3 or $4."[24]

Such recourse was rarely taken, however, particularly at the end of a long session, when galleries tended to be emptier. Moreover, members could avoid being corralled by the sergeant at arms by remaining somewhere in the Capitol building itself. There were excellent hiding places in the building to escape unpleasant debate, the least of which were the other chamber or the Supreme Court rooms. David Outlaw was disgusted by the practice of remaining close by but failing to stay for the debates. He wrote home that "the fear manifested by some members, that it shall be seen by the yeas and nays, that they were absent, I utterly despise. Many of these men, run into the House to vote, and are out again as soon as their names are called."[25]

Although Outlaw might have been critical of some of his colleagues for leaving the House chamber, he was guilty of this practice on more than one occasion. The North Carolina representative frequently spent time in the Senate while the House was meeting and even missed one of freshman congressman Abraham Lincoln's early speeches on the Mexican War. The Supreme Court was a common hiding place for members with an interest in

Figure 4. Floor plan of the ground story of the original Capitol. The Halls of the House of Representatives and Senate were located one floor above. As the picture illustrates, congressmen had many places they could go inside the Capitol to escape debate or to hold a confidential meeting with friends. Benjamin Latrobe Architectural Drawings, Prints and Photographs Division, Library of Congress.

the judicial proceedings or who had business there. John Berrien spent much of the Twenty-Ninth Congress arguing cases in front of the Supreme Court chamber rather than listening to speeches in the Senate. Others, like Massachusetts representative Charles Francis Adams became annoyed with House proceedings and went to watch the Court for a break. New York representative Solomon Haven explained to a friend, "I sit in the reporters seat in the court room . . . I do not go up stairs with the House—I have not been there since Saturday last. I am entirely disgusted with all their doings up there and much prefer the quiet sober & conservative atmosphere of this room."[26]

One of the more common places to find delinquent senators or representatives was the so-called Hole in the Wall. A small room near the old Senate Post Office in the basement of the Capitol, the Hole in the Wall was a restaurant that Sergeant at Arms Robert Beale was rumored to have started in the late 1840s. Although the restaurant served some food and also offered cigars, Beale's primary purpose was to provide a place for senators to drink alcohol while taking a break from congressional work. As Isaac Bassett, an old Senate page, remembered, "When ever they [called] the y[e]as and nays I nue [knew] whar [where] to find serten [certain] Senators, in fact they [told] me" they would be at the Hole in the Wall. Initially, the restaurant catered only to senators, but eventually representatives found their way to the Senate side.[27]

By the 1850s, the Hole in the Wall was not the only drinking space in the Capitol; both houses had congressional drinking rooms, and some members stored personal stashes of alcohol in adjacent cloakrooms or even in their desks. Upon leaving the Senate in 1852, North Carolinian Willie Mangum was eager to have a friend remove "treasonable things" from his desk drawer. A notorious drinker, Mangum undoubtedly left a bottle or two of alcohol at his seat. Sometimes an eager Speaker of the House or Senate vice president would impose restrictions on the drinking rooms. John Breckinridge ordered the private Senate drinking room shut down during late night sessions in 1858. Speaker Robert C. Winthrop similarly closed the bar under the House wing, which "gave rise to much private grumbling, including not a few letters of remonstrance from members of both parties."[28]

The upshot of these drinking rooms was that even if members were present in the House or Senate, some were in no condition to participate in congressional debate. Not that being drunk prevented them from trying. Ohioan Salmon Chase described one such scene in August 1852 in which senators were maneuvering over an amendment to an important bill: "A tipsy Senator gets up & opposes it. Wine makes him merry and he makes Senators merry. . . . So we go." As Chase intimated, some congressmen were ambivalent about the extent to which fellow members got drunk. Charles Francis Adams described his House as "partly comical, partly humiliating. Here was a body which ought to be the most imposing and dignified popular assemblage in the world, reduced to a handful of members amusing themselves with the extravagances of two or three tipsy persons among their number."[29]

Others were mortified by the behavior of their colleagues. Tennessee teetotaler Robert Hatton frequently recorded his "disgust" with open drunkenness in the House chamber in his diary. On one such occasion, he noted that "a large number" of the representatives "were *drunk* and acting the fool completely." Hatton was particularly appalled by Virginian William Smith, "who consumed the day in a long speech, drank three tumblers of egg-nog, while speaking, taking from the hands of the page, and drinking it in presence of the House!" Unfortunately for Hatton, drinking during debate was not uncommon in either house of Congress. A few senators were notorious for keeping glasses of wine on their desks while speaking. And pages could occasionally be relied upon to procure bottles of liquor for thirsty congressmen.[30]

Certain members became known for their drunken exploits. South Carolinian Andrew Pickens Butler was among the more congenial drunks, while others seemed to thrive during debate while liquored up. Robert Winthrop thought Kentucky representative Tom Marshall a "really eloquent & able man" even though "his dress, breath, whole air & aspect would indicate his tendencies, even should he chance to be sober at the moment." According to Ohio representative Samuel S. Cox, Texan Louis Wigfall was similarly "a master drinker" with "rare gifts of oratory." A constant presence in the Hole in the Wall, Wigfall gained such a reputation that Cox thought an appropriate tombstone for the Texas congressman might read: "Here lies a man, than whom no one could hold a greater quantity of liquor!"[31]

Not every member could be as self-possessed while under the influence of alcohol, however. While visiting the Senate one afternoon, Ohio representative Joshua Giddings saw "several members of that body greatly intoxicated,—too much to appear in public." Jacob Collamer was mortified to find that his Vermont colleague, James Meacham, was a "private tippler." Collamer was particularly frustrated to find that Meacham had become the object of derogatory remarks in the House for his drunken behavior. Indiana representative John L. Pettit was also a less-than-effective drunk and even broke his leg after falling down while intoxicated. Tennessean William Polk was often so drunk he could "hardly manage his vocal organs" while attempting to make a speech in the House.[32]

A few intoxicated members could certainly be a nuisance during debate. But the impact of liquor in the Capitol became much worse in the last few days of a session. Forced to sit until very late hours to finish congressional business, including some of the most important and expensive bills of the congressional term, members frequently imbibed more than usual. Anyone who visited the House or Senate at the end of the session could see the members sitting up all night, having a "noisy, tipsy time of it."[33]

Such celebratory drinking was frequently a subject of frustration and scorn among some of the more straightlaced members. Once a regular drinker himself, Texan Sam Houston returned to Congress in the late 1840s a committed teetotaler with total disdain for the behavior of his colleagues in these last few days. "At the close . . . of each session," Houston complained to his wife, "the members either from fatigue, or great thirst, are in the habit of using *something*, in their water, which has a tendency, to increase their loquacity. The effect is to keep, members who wish to attend to business, in a very unpleasant state of mind" listening to "the most prosy, and impertinent speeches." Houston and some of his more temperate colleagues did occasionally lose patience with drunken congressmen. After witnessing two days of drinking and carousing in March 1849, Houston finally lit into his fellow senators on the last day of the session for their silly drunken behavior. He announced, "I have felt the most painful and intense emotions upon witnessing [the] spectacle exhibited here. . . . I have felt deeply that . . . we should cover our heads with shame."[34]

In terms of late session drunken revelry, the evening of August 8, 1846, was no exception. On the evening that the House passed the fateful Wilmot Proviso, certain senators and representatives had gotten themselves liquored up to withstand the late hours of business. President Polk heard the reports of congressional misbehavior as he was turning in for the night. "Great confusion, I learned, prevailed in both Houses during this night's Session," the president noted in his diary, "and what is deeply to be regretted several members as I was informed were much excited by drink. . . . From all I learned it was a most disreputable scene." Yet even Polk knew that while the presence of drunken congressmen in the Capitol at the end of the session may have been disreputable, it was far from unique.[35]

Although the body that met on August 8, 1846, had its share of drunken miscreants, a majority of members came to the Capitol with most, if not all, of their faculties. But even those who were present and sober were not necessarily attentive. Mid-nineteenth-century congressmen operated without the frills of modern offices and staffs. The burden of corresponding with constituents could be heavy, not to mention writing home to loved ones and friends. As a result, members spent much of the time during daily debate catching up on their correspondence.

A poor or dull speech was as good a reason as any to stop paying attention. And dull speeches were apparently plentiful. Georgia representative Alexander Stephens remarked to his brother, "I have more time here . . . while long uninteresting speeches are being *bored* upon a listless House." The House might have had more members to make dull speeches, but the Senate, in terms of boredom, was no better. Upon walking over to that chamber to escape the House debate, one representative noticed that only half the Senate body was sitting and listening to the speaker. Some of the speeches were uninteresting (even if they were loud). According to Sam Houston, other orators simply "fail[ed] to command the attention of the Senate." Houston was known for multitasking while sitting in the Senate chamber. Draped in a Mexican blanket and a military headdress, Houston often lounged in one of the front rows of the Senate, whittling wood into hearts to present to female onlookers in the gallery.[36]

Even a particularly compelling speech from a prominent politician was not necessarily cause for an attentive House or Senate. John Fairfield, a long-time Maine senator, was a well-respected member of Congress. Yet his colleagues often did not take the time to listen to his point of view. As Fairfield explained to his wife after one such experience, his speech "created no extraordinary sensation at all. The Senators kept right along, some reading, some writing and some taking snuff, just as if nothing had happened!" Poor Fairfield was not alone. William Seward described a similar scene where Ohio senator George Pugh "entertained us three and a half hours with an argument on a private claim. Fatigue, heat, and depression had made us all languid. Except the Chairman, not one man listened, and yet we could not leave."[37]

Congressional inattentiveness could reach a fever pitch on "personal bills" days, where individual congressmen (rather than committees) introduced legislation. During these sessions few, if any, members could force themselves to listen to the speakers, instead choosing to write letters or gossip with desk mates. Some even slept at their desks or on the sofas that lined the walls of the House chamber. During a long session, the scene in the House or Senate could sometimes border on comical. According to David Outlaw, during the Thirtieth Congress, "Several of the Senators were considerably fuddled, and at times the Senat[or] on the floor, had the extreme felicity of hearing himself, no body else being on the floor, the members either being asleep on the sofas in the lobby, or in the outerooms, [or] off drinking."[38]

In addition to letter writing, congressmen used the space near their desks in the House and Senate as a sort of substitute office, a place to chat with fellow members and other men allowed on the floor of the two chambers. By rule, the only people allowed to enter the floor besides congressmen themselves were the president and other executive officers, diplomats, governors, Supreme Court justices, and people who previously held each of those positions, including ex-members. Although the regulation might have seemed restrictive to visitors, the number of persons milling around the floor could add up, particularly considering the prevalence of ex-congressmen who returned to Washington as lawyers and lobbyists.[39]

Cabinet members, especially those who had once been congressmen themselves, often spent time in the Capitol. For example, in 1851 recently appointed secretary of state Daniel Webster frequently visited his old stomping grounds in the Senate, finding an empty seat and talking with members sitting next to him. Other floor guests simply came to chat with old friends or new members. When Charles Francis Adams was elected to the House in the late 1850s, Supreme Court Justice John McLean paid him a special visit during a debate, not to talk about legislation currently before that body but rather to discuss aspects of the *Amistad* case that Adams's father (John Quincy Adams) had argued before the Supreme Court several years before.[40]

The result of all of this activity and conversation was that even those trying to listen to a speech could not always hear. The Senate was small enough that most of the members could catch the gist of debate even from the back rows of the chamber. In the House, however, the ability to hear was further complicated by the immense size of the chamber and its poor acoustics. Thus, sitting at a desk near the Speaker's chair was crucial. Unfortunately, congressmen had assigned seats, which meant that the most attentive or diligent members did not always get the best position to hear.

This was particularly true at the time of the Twenty-Ninth Congress. Until the mid-1840s, long-serving members were generally able to get the best seats. During those years, House desks were assigned in a somewhat casual way; at the end of one session, members would reserve their seats for the next term. By the beginning of the Twenty-Ninth Congress, however, newer members had become frustrated with the old system. In December 1845, they forced the House to adopt a method whereby the clerk randomly drew names, and congressman selected seats in the order they were called. As a consequence, some of the newer and lesser-known members obtained the best seats in the House. Robert Winthrop was one of the unluckier members, complaining to his friend that he was so far from the front that he was "almost beyond reach of taking part in common & casual deliberations." David Outlaw similarly told his wife, "Where I sit, there are but few persons whom I can hear, and the House is such a babel, that you hardly know what you are about." By the time Outlaw came to the House, congressmen were used to the lottery method of drawing for seats. Yet Congress passed the Wilmot Proviso at the tail end of its first session with the new seating arrangement. Undoubtedly, some members did not return to the House on the evening of August 8 because they were unlikely to hear the debates or any other business from their assigned seats.[41]

Certainly there were times when congressmen were quiet and focused on debate. The chaos of the House and Senate would occasionally subside for an important speaker or speech. The thrill of an address by one of the more well-regarded and famous members of the body could be cause for silent and attentive audiences. When Henry Clay returned to the Senate in 1850, packed galleries sat in complete silence while he delivered several speeches. Men like John C. Calhoun and Daniel Webster received similar respect from House and Senate members, who gathered together to hear the famous orators in their waning days.[42]

Congressmen were also more likely to pay attention to debate during the first few days after the election of the Speaker, or during a critical vote on an important measure like the Walker Tariff. In the waning hours of a debate when the House or Senate expected to pass pending legislation or just before a critical vote, members could become more respectful of congressional speeches. Such was the case during a protracted battle for the Speakership in December 1859, when Republicans wanted to ensure their success. Almost sixty members pleaded with Illinois representative John F. Farnsworth not to speak on the floor of the House for fear of ruining their chances at a successful election. Most signed a private petition asking him to remain silent.[43]

Still, more often than not, members in the House and Senate were less than attentive. Congressmen and observers alike called the House of Representatives "noisy," "rowdy," and "distracting." Charles Francis Adams described business in the House as "pandemonium." Horace Mann referred to the body as "a bee-hive much more in noise than in industry." Many would agree with Iowa representative Lincoln Clark that their place of business was "a perfect tower of Babel." The Senate could also reach a deafening pitch, creating problems for the reporters in the gallery assigned to describe each day's deliberations. Reporters were given seats at the back of the hall and did not have immediate access to the floor. As one newspaper editor explained, even "under the most favorable circumstances it is difficult for [reporters] to hear distinctly." On August 8, 1846, at the end of a long session, the House and Senate were so noisy and chaotic, the *Washington Daily Union* was unable to fully report what transpired during the debates.[44]

In fact, it was quite difficult for the newspapers to accurately report what was happening in Congress on most occasions. Aside from making an inordinate amount of noise and creating scenes of absolute mayhem in their chambers, congressmen operated within the complex rules of the House and Senate, rules that some reporters did not fully understand. Most important, congressmen had their own code of conduct for handling the day-to-day activities of their houses, a code that the American public was not privy to.[45]

One key aspect of the congressional code was to control the kind of information that the public received. As sort of an unspoken rule, congress-

Figure 5. Rendering of the new chamber of the House of Representatives in 1857. Members of the House, particularly those with seats in the back rows, often used the areas around their desks to hold conversations and conduct business unrelated to congressional matters. Printed in *Morrison's Stranger's Guide and Etiquette for Washington City and Its Vicinity* (Washington: W. H. & O. H. Morrison, 1860), Munger Research Center, Huntington Library, San Marino, Calif.

men allowed each other to edit, remove, or substantially add to speeches they had given in Congress when preparing them for publication in newspapers or pamphlets. Members understood that colleagues might want to alter their speeches after delivery and so gave each other time to do so. For example, Robert Hatton allowed his Tennessee rival John Wright time to adjust his initial comments before making a reply. Hatton noted in his diary: "Wright's [speech] did not appear in the *Globe*, this morning. He is remodeling, or, as I am informed, re-writing it—will be out to-morrow. He asked me not to reply to it 'til I see it revised. Will not, as he wants to alter it."[46]

Congressmen also negotiated with reporters to edit speeches they thought might be misunderstood. During the session in which the Wilmot Proviso passed, congressmen and senators were no strangers to revising their speeches. Willie Mangum was particularly concerned about the impact of his speech on the Walker Tariff, earlier in the summer of 1846, and accordingly sent a note to the editors of the *Congressional Globe*, asking to make some corrections before it went to press. A member could also become embarrassed by remarks in the House or Senate that turned out to contain falsehoods. Sometimes after making such a speech, a congressman would completely rewrite what he had said before it was published. Other congressmen might ask the reporters to remove a speech entirely, leaving no trace of it in the record for his constituents to see.[47]

Lawmakers also altered their speeches after the fact to prevent their fellow congressman from taking offense at something said during the course of debate. Sometimes such a misunderstanding was handled merely by making a "personal explanation" on the floor of the House or Senate. In these personal explanations, a congressman would "clarify" a previous speech in an attempt to erase any misapprehension that he had meant to cause offense. As historians have previously remarked, such personal explanations were extremely common in the mid-nineteenth century. Occasionally they were so common as to prevent any other business from getting done. One such circumstance in February 1858 prompted *Harper's Weekly* to remark: "Nearly half the working hours of Congress last week were taken up by personal explanations. . . . Congress will soon have been three months in session. What law has been passed during that period? What work done?"[48]

Rather than making a personal explanation, some congressmen simply chose to eliminate the offending sentences from the record book. For example, Senator James Buchanan was eager to erase any ill will between himself and Kentuckian John J. Crittenden during one of the Pennsylvanian's speeches. Accordingly, in an apologetic letter to Crittenden, Buchanan explained, "It is not too late yet to suppress all these remarks. . . . The debate will not be published in the *Globe* until to-morrow evening; and I am not only willing, but I am anxious, that it shall *never appear*." Buchanan suggested the two men pay a visit to *Globe* editor John C. Rives to arrange the matter.[49]

Members who got involved in a personal tiff were keenly aware of the impact such a disagreement could have on their constituents (for better or worse) and looked to find a way to change the course of debate in their favor. Congressmen could be particularly nervous about what reporters were publishing when it came to "affairs of honor." In one such case in June 1858, a Republican senator, Henry Wilson of Massachusetts, and California Democrat William Gwin got into a heated argument during debate in the Senate. Deeply offended by some insult in the course of the Northerner's remarks, Gwin eventually challenged Wilson to a duel. Yet neither man really wanted to fight. So Gwin authorized William Seward (a friend of both parties) to suppress the debate. Unfortunately, because word had already gotten out to Massachusetts that Wilson had been challenged, his Senate friends had trouble figuring out a way to erase what had happened in the *Globe* without upsetting Wilson's constituents. As Seward explained, there was seemingly no way around the conflict that allowed both men to save face, "Gwin having challenged and been denied that satisfaction, couldn't ask Wilson to explain or retreat. Wilson might explain, but couldn't offer to do so after a challenge had been received." The New Yorker tried to fix the problem by offering an explanation on Wilson's behalf, but the Massachusetts Republican's allies said it would ruin his reputation. So Seward consulted with his friend, Senator Jefferson Davis of Mississippi. Davis "suggested that Wilson should offer an explanation, the challenge being suspended." But again, Seward explained, Wilson's friends "insisted that would ruin him. They would rather see him hacked to pieces." In the end, Seward, Davis, and John Crittenden arbitrated the dispute over dinner at Seward's house on F Street, and the group decided that certain remarks would be stricken from the record.[50]

Wilson and Gwin were not the first members to worry about their reputations, nor would they be the last. Congressmen instinctively tried to promote themselves to their constituents, sometimes worrying less about how they appeared to their colleagues in the Senate or House itself. A speech that came off as "rambling" could be edited to appear stately and influential in the columns of the *Daily National Intelligencer*. Similarly, the chaos of the House chamber could prevent even the loudest member from being heard, but his speech was often reported as "eloquent" and "well-received," by a partisan press or even reporters eager for a bribe. Such bribes were common according to North Carolina congressman Kenneth Rayner.[51]

A bribe might also compel a newspaper reporter to publish a speech that had not even been delivered. Freshman member Bernhard Henn, of Iowa, was able to convince a reporter to publish remarks he had written up on a railroad bill in 1852. The rub was that Henn had never obtained the opportunity to get on the floor and make the speech in the first place. This maneuver infuriated fellow Iowan Lincoln Clark, who had been trying to speak on that very subject without success. As Clark explained to his wife, "It is probable my constituents think it strange that my *colleague* should be out in an elaborate speech upon an important subject while I am mum." Yet Clark could not stop a practice that was actually fairly common. Some congressmen even had a habit of going to the floor and announcing that they would spare the House any waste of their time and would merely write up their comments and have them published.[52]

Clark touched on another aspect of the unwritten congressional code of conduct in his frustration with Henn. Generally, as a newer member, it was better to be seen and not heard in your first few sessions in Washington. Few elder statesmen had the patience to listen to a new member whom they did not know or recognize. Michigan representative Kinsley Bingham explained the problem to his wife: "About half of the house are old members . . . they understand the manner of conducting business—The rules of the house are perfectly familiar to them—and they will not tolerate a young member's talking." Bingham saw firsthand that "nothing makes a young man so unpopular, or so soon destroys his influence as talking—when a new member gets on the floor to speak—they will whisper about who's that? who's that? Is that a member?" As a result of this unwritten congressional code, several young members put off their maiden address on the floor of the House until late in their first session. For example, David Outlaw began his term in Congress in December 1847 but did not make a regular speech until the following August. Younger members were also discouraged from obtaining the floor too frequently. One speech was enough to introduce oneself to the rest of the members. Those who proceeded less cautiously got "the reputation of being officious, and [would] not be listened to." The Twenty-Ninth Congress had more than a hundred new members in the 1845–46 session, including David Wilmot. While older congressmen had undoubtedly familiarized themselves with most of their colleagues by August 1846, longer-serving members were still less likely to yield the floor to freshmen speakers. Wilmot himself had been mostly quiet during the first session, generally toeing the party line on issues like the Walker Tariff.[53]

Because of the unwritten rule that newer members were expected to defer to the more experienced congressmen, those newer members sometimes struggled to satisfy their constituents. Yet motivating one's constituents to come out and vote was generally the ultimate goal and was crucial to a final aspect of the unwritten congressional code of conduct: because members were keenly focused on satisfying constituents, they often performed business in the House and Senate as though it was a theatrical stage. As Outlaw explained, "there is no such thing as parliamentary debate in either House of Congress. Both are the theaters for harangues and addressed not to the bodies themselves, but to the passions and prejudices of the people."[54]

Senators and representatives made a show out of every aspect of congressional debate from speeches to physical barbs. The dispute between William Gwin and Henry Wilson illustrates that disagreements between members in either house could have a different public and private meaning. Just be-

cause two congressmen were hostile in public did not mean they were un-
civil outside of congressional debate. During the long 1850 summer, Robert
Winthrop frequently found himself the subject of nasty attacks on the floor
of the House, but many of the members would later apologize for incivility.
In one such case, Winthrop remarked that Jefferson Davis "abused me like
a pickpocket, though, after the debate was over, he came to me & expressed
his regret at having made use of the expression 'degraded himself.'" Hamilton Fish similarly sent a private apology to Davis after making an insulting
comment in his direction in the Senate.[55]

Some "opponents" even became close friends in the social settings of
Washington daily life. Hothead Henry S. Foote of Mississippi was known
for repeatedly insulting William Seward during debate. One politician's wife
caught one of these violent speeches early in January 1850 while sitting in the
gallery. Foote "rose for just about an hour and with the most violent ges-
tures and manner, abused and ridiculed Gov. Seward. . . . I expected every
moment he would be called to order, and yet one could not help laughing—
some of his hits were so good." Even so, Foote and Seward were actually
remarkably friendly in private. Typically, no one mentioned these private relationships on the floor, but South Carolina senator John C. Calhoun found
Foote's relationship with Seward to be grotesque. Just before his death in
1850, Calhoun publicly criticized Foote on the floor of the Senate for his
friendly association with the New York Whig. Still, Calhoun was an exception. While the South Carolinian refused to associate with any Northerners
outside of Congress, most of his Southern colleagues were not so discrimi-
nating. Seward was a particular favorite among his brethren from the other
section, and the New York Whig maintained close relationships with many
of the fiery Southerners who publicly repudiated him.[56]

Although many were friendly outside of the Capitol, there were some
politicians who publicly and privately despised one another, even if they
came from the same party or held many of the same political positions.
Henry Foote and Missourian Thomas Hart Benton had one of the nastier
rivalries in the Senate. One morning in April 1850, their distaste for one
another finally reached a breaking point during debate on Henry Clay's
resolutions for compromise. Benton, who had been carrying on for some
time against Southern members who seemed immovable on the California
issue, made a negative allusion to the recently deceased John C. Calhoun.
Although Foote and Benton actually agreed on many of the finer points of
the compromise provisions, their personal rivalry, both public and private,
prevented Foote from allowing any such slight to the great South Carolin-

Figure 6. The Foote-Benton dispute caused momentary chaos in the U.S. Senate. Cartoon rendering, Prints and Photographs Division, Library of Congress.

ian to pass unnoticed on the Senate floor (regardless of Calhoun's critical comments of Foote earlier that session). He rose and began to defend Calhoun's honor.[57]

Benton, whose disdain for Foote was particularly elevated because of the latter's recent efforts to undermine his authority in Missouri, got up from his chair and began to move toward his rival. The Mississippian, who occupied a seat on the outer circle by the vice president's chair, began to retreat from Benton, backing down the aisle as Benton advanced. Foote then pulled out a Colt pistol and pointed it at the Missourian. This enraged Benton even more, who reportedly pulled open his shirt and announced to the Senate, "I have no pistols. Let him fire!" Chaos quickly ensued in the chamber as members rushed to break up the clash without violence. Eventually both men were subdued, and Foote turned his gun over to New Yorker Daniel S. Dickinson. Benton would demand that Foote be expelled, but a committee to investigate the dispute ultimately would absolve the Mississippian.[58]

Although Foote and Benton clearly disliked each other, it was more than just animosity that caused such a scene in the Senate in April 1850. After all, Old Bullion did not really believe Foote was out to kill him. Otherwise he would not have let Robert Winthrop seat him next to the Mississippian at a dinner six weeks later. In fact, regardless of the fact that both men preferred a sectional compromise, Foote had been trying to goad Benton into a public argument for several months. As early as January, Foote had so insulted Benton on the floor that the latter took his hat and coat and walked out of the Senate.[59]

In the context of an unwritten congressional code of conduct, the point of this disagreement was an exhilarating example of political theater, made not for Foote's fellow congressmen but for his constituents back home. As historian Michael Holt points out, by supporting a compromise in the 1850 session, Foote had effectively dismissed Mississippi Democratic orthodoxy in favor of sectional conciliation. Angry at Foote for his betrayal, the Democrat-controlled legislature in Mississippi eventually would censure him in November for his votes on the compromise. Foote was well aware that by working with the likes of Clay and Webster he was not ingratiating himself to his Democratic constituents. But a fight with Old Bullion on the floor of the Senate, particularly in defense of Calhoun, would be worth its weight in political gold.[60]

Other senators and congressmen were well aware of the theatrical impulse behind the Foote-Benton dispute. As the findings of the select committee to investigate the scene demonstrate, few were particularly concerned about guns and mischief on the floor of the Senate, other than its public ramifications. If nothing else, the rivalry created amusement. As the long session progressed slowly over the next few weeks, David Outlaw even joked, "Unless we can get Foote and Benton or some other public spirited individuals to get up a scene, we shall die of ennui."[61]

Public displays of insult and injury were critical for bolstering support back home. This was true in combative disputes but also in speeches during the regular course of debate. Congressmen had a name for such speeches: buncombe (sometimes spelled "bunkum" or "bunkomb"). Buncombe speeches were basically the equivalent of stumping for yourself in the House or Senate by making an inconsequential speech solely to please your constituents. As one former congressmen explained them, buncombe speeches "bear no relation to the subject nominally before the house—but upon politics—not politics in the best sense of the word—not even party politics, but [personal politics] among particular candidates for office or relating to the state, or districts to which the members belong." Few people in the House or Senate listened to these speeches, and yet one could be guaranteed to find members who delivered them busily preparing their buncombe speeches for the press the following day, hoping to have an influence back home.[62]

Such stump speaking in the Capitol did frustrate some members, particularly when a congressman used the time to insult his colleagues. Robert Hatton disliked the practice as he thought it tended to degrade the House. As he explained, buncombe speeches could be "of a most disgraceful character, full of low and vulgar personalities, resulting in the utter confusion of the House." Speaking for buncombe could also seem like an incredible waste of time. During the long session of 1858, for example, congressmen spent several weeks discussing the arrest of General William Walker during an expedition in Nicaragua as a way of demonstrating to their constituents a grave sincerity either in favor of or opposed to filibustering south of the United States. With other important business, such as the Lecompton Constitution, on the table, buncombe speeches on filibustering expeditions did not move legislative action along.[63]

Regardless of how much time it wasted or how unpleasant some found the practice, speaking for buncombe was both common and expected. Everyone did it. On one occasion in September 1850, Sam Houston criticized his fellow senators for "moving on, as usual pow wowing & speaking for Buncombe, and not attending to business, as we should do." Yet Houston himself would sometimes make buncombe speeches. In the midst of an 1851 debate on the finality of the Compromise of 1850, he spent a considerable amount of time discussing "the mysteries of the Wilmot Proviso—the History of Texas, and other topics intended for Bunkomb." Some congressmen even concocted entire bills or resolutions aimed at energizing their constituents and nothing more. Edward Everett accused John Slidell of such behavior after Slidell introduced a bill during a debate over neutrality laws during the Thirty-Third Congress. Even those like Missouri senator David R. Atchison, who preferred not to participate in the "*puffing* and *swelling*" of buncombe speechmaking, were encouraged to "conform in some degree even to the vicious habits of the age in which we live" in the interest of motivating his constituents.[64]

The noisy and disorganized theater of Congress, and the prevalence of buncombe speeches in particular, provided a critical context in which the Wilmot Proviso was able to pass in August 1846. In fact, the proviso seemed to fit the very definition of buncombe agitation. Upon learning of the Wilmot amendment the following day, President Polk noted his feelings about the provision in his diary. Polk had served in the House of Representatives for many years and, as a former Speaker, was intimately acquainted with how members conducted business in that body. "I learned that after an exciting debate in the House" on the $2 million provision, "a bill passed that body, but with a mischievous & foolish amendment. What connection slavery had with making peace with Mexico is difficult to conceive," the frustrated president noted. "This amendment was voted on to the bill by the opponents of the measure. . . . Had there been time, there is but little doubt the Senate would have struck out the slavery proviso & that the House would have concurred." As his diary entry indicates, Polk noted the intense debate over the $2 million bill itself, but considered the Wilmot Proviso a sort of silly add-on by a few hotheaded members who were unhappy with his administration. Clearly, for Polk, the initial sectional vote meant little aside from playing political games and, in all likelihood, agitating for buncombe.[65]

Senators, representatives, and even Washington newspapermen also paid little attention to a slavery provision, introduced in the waning hours of the session, with a questionable motive behind it. The two leading Washington newspapers did not concern themselves at all with the sectional vote. As previously noted, the *Daily Union* merely regretted that the bill had not passed. The editors of the Whig newspaper, the *National Intelligencer* (Washington) similarly disregarded most of the debate. The paper registered Wilmot's attempt to undermine the bill but attributed it to angry House members trying to flex their legislative muscle to demonstrate the reduced influence of a president who passed unsatisfying legislation like the tariff.[66]

To the free-soil congressmen who crafted the Wilmot Proviso, the amendment was more than just stump speaking and agitation. Many of these men returned to their home states invigorated by the sectional vote. Some antislavery Northern Whigs also celebrated the triumph. New Yorker Washington Hunt wrote excitedly to New York political boss Thurlow Weed about the proviso, that the Northern bloc vote was "pregnant of great things. It required much good management to unite the whole northern representation. It was my good fortune to bear a humble part in concerting our plans. It is one of those incidents which one always remembers with pride." Hunt and others would continue to push for the Wilmot restriction both at home and in Washington.[67]

Furthermore, the Wilmot Proviso eventually *became* more than just a single buncombe proposition to which few in the House even paid attention. Early in January 1847, Preston King, a fiery antislavery New Yorker, reintroduced the slavery restriction, this time to the president's request for $3 million to fund negotiations with Mexico. In mid-February the House passed the amendment on a 115 to 106 vote, with all Northern Whigs voting in favor and only 19 of the 76 Northern Democrats voting against. Here was a second House vote in favor of the bill. And here Washingtonians began to pay closer attention to the sectional votes on a slavery amendment. John C. Calhoun took the lead in repudiating the measure, and other Southerners followed suit. Anger reached a fever pitch by the middle of the session, and for the next three years the Wilmot Proviso played a constant role in congressional debate.[68]

Still, through the summer of 1850, and even after the passage of the compromise that year, speeches on the Wilmot Proviso in both the House and Senate tended to lean toward political theater. Yes, Southerners were angry, but insulting Northerners and threatening disunion was a terrific political tool, as everyone in Congress was keenly aware. Take, for example, a speech by Robert Toombs, delivered in December 1849. Toombs railed against the Wilmot Proviso, explaining that "I do not hesitate to avow before this House and the country . . . that if by your legislation you [permanently exclude slavery from the territories] *I am for disunion*; and . . . I will devote all I am and all I have on earth to its consummation."[69]

Historians have often cited this speech and others as evidence of the sectionalizing impact of the Wilmot Proviso on Congress. Yet, antislavery Ohioan Salmon Chase was in the chamber when Toombs spoke and found the performance merely an example of political theater. "Toombs spoke breathing vengeance against all supporters of the proviso, and dissolution in the event of its adoption," he explained to a friend. "The whole scene was dramatic & entertaining. One or two were frightened by the stage thunder; but most understood the manufacture, and disregarded it." Chase recognized that Toombs himself favored a compromise when the session formally began and believed that the slavery crisis could be properly settled in a way to preserve the Union. A few of the more inexperienced congressmen might have misunderstood Toombs as really threatening the breakup of the country, but Chase knew what the speech was actually about.[70]

Ultimately, the theatrical element in Toombs's Wilmot Proviso speech and in congressional debates throughout the 1840s and 1850s illustrates the extent to which historians have overvalued the recordings in the *Congressional Globe*.[71] This is not to suggest that the *Globe* debates are useless or should be ignored entirely; but they should be read with a critical eye. For, amid all of this theater, not to mention the chaos and disorganization, it was incredibly difficult for members to organize voting blocs or discuss possible legislation on the floor of the House or Senate. As a result, political discussions and negotiations, particularly over a heated topic like the Wilmot Proviso, tended to happen elsewhere. Ultimately, many Washington politicians explained, politics often took place "*beneath the surface*," in private conversations.[72]

Few were privy to private negotiations, and congressmen worked to keep them from the public. Washingtonians were careful not to say too much in their letters home, for fear that an unfriendly post office agent might let the correspondence slip into the wrong hands. If a Washington politician knew his letter would pass through a sympathetic postal agent, he might be more forthcoming, with instructions to burn the letter after reading. But most correspondents insisted that they must wait to say things in person. As Solomon Haven explained to his wife "Great events frequently turn on very small pivots. The whys & wherefores of various things that are occurring here, I will explain to you when we meet."[73]

Typically, when congressmen finally were able to discuss the "whys & wherefores" of political business, they did so outside the halls of the House and Senate. As Charles Francis Adams remarked, "The House was obviously a very unsuitable place for a confidential interview." Instead, these conversations happened in areas throughout Washington: in political and social clubs, at dinner parties, in chats among desk mates and in Capitol antechambers. They happened in boardinghouses and hotels, in drinking rooms and gambling dens, and even in the rooms of the Supreme Court. Political decision making, in other words, often happened outside the legislative halls of the nation's capital.[74]

CHAPTER TWO

Odd Fellows, Teetotalers, and Young Indians

Washington Associations and the Election of 1848

A little over one year after David Wilmot introduced his famous amendment, a young lawyer and former state legislator from Illinois made his first appearance in Washington as a new member of the Thirtieth Congress. Abraham Lincoln arrived in the capital city with his wife and two children on December 2, 1847, and four days later joined his colleagues in the House of Representatives to begin the new session.

The Thirtieth Congress promised to be work-intensive, as Whigs and Democrats continued to battle over the progress of the war with Mexico. Unlike in the Twenty-Ninth Congress, Whigs had gained a majority in the House (115-107) and would play an important role in the session. In the preceding months, the party had finally developed a policy that Whigs thought could bridge any division between North and South and neutralize the increasingly divisive Wilmot Proviso; they argued the United States should claim "no territory" from the war. To Whigs, the "no territory" stance ensured that Congress would not become embroiled in a cross-sectional fight that could destroy their party. Furthermore, it placed Democrats in a tight position. Whigs consistently questioned President James K. Polk's claims that a Mexican assault had started the war. They also expressed concerns that the president's real intentions were to acquire vast new lands in the West rather than simply protecting American honor. By stressing "no territory," Whigs would ask voters in the upcoming 1848 elections to judge both the causes and the consequences of the war.[1]

In the meantime, Polk was trying to bring the conflict to a close in a way that pleased fellow Democrats. On the second day of the new session, the president submitted his annual message to Congress asking for funds to end the war and claiming the expansive territories of New Mexico and California as partial compensation from the Mexican government. The president triumphantly asserted that he was about to conclude a war that Mexico had initiated when it "invad[ed] the territory of the State of Texas, striking the first blow, and shedding the blood of our citizens on our own soil." Polk's message ensured that ending the war with Mexico would become a high priority for the Thirtieth Congress.[2]

The 1848 presidential election also weighed heavily on the minds of all who entered the Capitol on that December morning. Experienced congressmen knew that the session before a presidential election would inevitably focus on candidates and nominations. As North Carolina Whig David Outlaw lamented, "This whole session will be devoted to President making, and to this end, the public good will be subordinate." To make matters worse, several of the potential presidential candidates were senators, cabinet members, and even Supreme Court justices; all would be courting nominations throughout the winter. As Senator Thomas Rusk (D-Tex.) remarked, "The all engrossing subject . . . at Washington is the next Presidency. The Whigs as well as our party are bad off for the right kind of material out of which to make one and I fear whichever party may succeed we shall have a jack ass in the Chair." Ultimately, the two most important issues of the session—the war with Mexico and the next president—would become intertwined over the course of the next eleven months.[3]

When Lincoln took his seat in the Hall of the House, he hoped to contribute substantially to both issues. The Illinois representative was no political neophyte; he had served four terms in the Illinois legislature and had been intimately involved in state politics for years. He also had the advantage of being the only Whig representative from his home state; Whig leadership in Washington would have to rely on him to evaluate the pulse of Illinois voters. Most important, Lincoln was ambitious. Not only was he prepared for his congressional experience; Lincoln also had plans to work hard to obtain a leadership position in the Whig Party in Washington. Overall, Lincoln was optimistic that he could make a name for himself in the upcoming session.[4]

The Illinois Whig found his first opportunity to address the House on the issue of the Mexican War a mere two weeks after the session began. In response to Polk's annual message, Lincoln presented what would later be known as the "Spot Resolutions," a speech railing against what he thought was an unconstitutional and needless war. He asked the president to prove that Mexico had started the conflict, referring directly to Polk's assertion that Mexican armies had spilled blood on American territory. Was it really U.S. territory? Lincoln demanded that Polk demonstrate to Congress whether "the particular spot of soil on which the blood of our *citizens* was so shed, was, or was not, *our own soil.*" Shortly after Lincoln's Spot Resolutions, Massachusetts Whig George Ashmun submitted an amendment declaring the war had been "unnecessarily and unconstitutionally begun by the President"; it was adopted by the votes of eighty-five Whigs, including Lincoln. Yet the Illinois representative was not satisfied with a mere vote. A week later, Lincoln spoke again on the war, demanding that the president respond to his resolutions. Bitterly, he told the House that if Polk failed to address Whig concerns, the president would show that "he is deeply conscious of being in the wrong."[5]

Although Lincoln was proud of his efforts in the House of Representatives, few newspapers outside of Illinois reported on Lincoln's speeches. His fellow congressmen were similarly unimpressed; the House did not take up his resolutions, and his colleagues offered little or no reaction to his strong words. Furthermore, as David Donald has pointed out, President Polk paid no attention to Lincoln's accusations in the Spot Resolutions; he did not mention the Illinois Whig in his long-winded diaries.[6]

Given the way Congress operated in the mid-nineteenth century, Lincoln's failure to inspire his colleagues is unsurprising. Many of his fellow congressmen missed Lincoln's speech entirely. Others saw no reason to pay attention to a new member they had never seen before; they preferred to talk with desk mates or write letters home. Clearly, Lincoln had not yet learned the unwritten rules of the House of Representatives, which discouraged new members from being too visible in their first few months in Washington.[7]

As a smart and experienced politician, however, Lincoln quickly became aware of his inability to influence his fellow representatives. After his first month of congressional speaking, the Illinois Whig began to defer to older and more experienced colleagues. Although he faithfully attended to his duties in the House, Lincoln no longer believed he could make an impact by delivering well-crafted party-line speeches. Yet he remained an ambitious politician, and rather than abandoning his pursuit of political fame, Lincoln sought a new path to Whig leadership. He would make his mark upon joining a small Whig faction in Washington known as the "Young Indian Club."

The Young Indian Club began as a cross-sectional group of Whig congressmen dedicated to discussing some of the more pressing issues in national politics. Organized in December 1847, the Young Indian Club quickly became committed to promoting Mexican War hero Zachary Taylor as the Whig nominee for president in the 1848 election.[8] Membership was small—five Southerners and two Northerners—and oddly included a range of political experience, with four congressional freshmen alongside three seasoned Washington veterans.[9]

The seven members came together both for their interest in nominating Taylor and because of the peculiarities of living together in Washington. Each man had strong personal and political reasons for wanting Taylor as the nominee. All five Southerners were interested in Old Zach in part because he was a slaveholder. Since early 1847, South Carolinian John C. Calhoun had called for Southern unity against the Wilmot Proviso, and Southerners would need a strong proslavery candidate in order to neutralize the Calhoun threat. Taylor was a perfect choice, considering that he owned more than 100 slaves.[10] But there were other, more specific reasons for supporting the war hero. Georgia representatives Alexander Stephens and Robert Toombs preferred Taylor to longtime Whig leader Henry Clay in an effort to obtain more sway in state races. The Georgians were less concerned about the national race—Georgia frequently went Whig—and more interested in diluting the influence of older Georgia Whigs like John Berrien. By contrast, freshmen representatives from Virginia Thomas Flournoy, John C. Pendleton, and William Ballard Preston, believed Taylor would help reshape the Whig Party to make it more palatable to their home state. Although he was more of an old-line Whig on economic issues than the Virginians, Lincoln similarly believed Taylor could win Illinois, a state that typically voted Democratic. Finally, Connecticut representative Truman Smith, who had long served as a de facto Whig national party chairman, believed that Taylor offered Whigs the best chance to win the presidency in 1848.[11]

There were others besides the seven Young Indians who preferred Taylor, so how did this eclectic group come together? Robert Toombs's connection to the three Virginians provides the first clue. When Toombs arrived in Washington in December 1847, he selected Mrs. Selden's boardinghouse for his temporary residence in the city. Coincidentally, Flournoy, Pendleton, and Preston chose the same house for the first session of the Thirtieth Congress. Toombs counted fellow Georgian Alexander Stephens as his closest friend in Washington, and the latter repeatedly visited Mrs. Selden's that winter. Both Georgia representatives had known Truman Smith since their first session in Washington. As an active campaigner and one of the most prominent Whig leaders in Washington in the mid-1840s, Smith was a critical ally in any push for the presidency. Stephens or Toombs (or both) likely recruited him.[12]

Lincoln also left no official record of how he initially became involved with the Young Indians, but a congressional seating chart may offer another clue to the group's curious membership. When the Illinois representative entered the House in December 1847, he was among the last to pick a seat. Only three options remained on the Whig side, but Lincoln was so little known that the congressional reporters did not immediately record his choice. It is possible that he selected the open seat situated directly behind Pendleton and Flournoy, giving Lincoln the opportunity to become intimate with them in the House itself.[13] According to one representative, this area of the House was called the "Cherokee Strip," perhaps a veiled reference to the Young Indian Club.[14] Regardless of how he joined the group, Lincoln quickly became an active member. And by early 1848, the Young Indian Club had begun meeting regularly at Mrs. Selden's boardinghouse, debating issues like state sovereignty and Whig politics. Meetings were lively—the men were known for "raising the War Whoop"—and the members did not always agree. But they enjoyed each other's company nonetheless.[15]

Historians have generally overlooked the importance of Lincoln's membership in the Young Indian Club, and some biographers fail to mention the group entirely.[16] This oversight likely stems in part from scholars who have overestimated Lincoln's individual influence in Congress. As explained in chapter 1, however, the culture of Congress gave Lincoln little opportunity to make a name for himself on an individual level.[17]

More important, scholars have discounted the larger context in which the Young Indians operated: the club was just one of the many Washington associations that politicians participated in during the antebellum period. Social and cultural historians have long stressed the importance of the "associational spirit" of the mid-nineteenth century, particularly in the form of reform movements such as temperance and abolitionism. Through the prism of these organizations, scholars have ably demonstrated the extent to which women, African Americans, and other marginalized groups found a voice in nineteenth-century politics.[18] Yet these associations were not limited to the powerless or disfranchised; Washington politicians, like their compatriots throughout the country, were members of numerous benevolent associations, fraternal organizations, political clubs, and religious groups.[19]

Back home, congressmen were more than just politicians; they had other occupations, intellectual interests, alma maters, and social lives. Upon arriving in the capital city, these men did not abandon their backgrounds. Washington itself was home to chapters of several national organizations, such as the Freemasons, temperance societies, and literary clubs. Some, like the American Colonization Society, had headquarters in the District. Congressmen who arrived in the capital city could join churches representing their home denominations and attend meetings at the local Odd Fellows lodge. Others joined Washington-specific associations in the district, such as the board of regents of the Smithsonian Institution, or created clubs like the Young Indians in order to advocate for a particular agenda.[20]

In one important sense, however, D.C. associations would be different from those in politicians' home states: Washington was a cross-sectional city, which meant that lawmakers would generally attend clubs and organizations with members from many different parts of the country. Federal politicians quickly adjusted to this uniquely cross-sectional atmosphere. For, amid the chaotic and often unfriendly culture of Congress, newer and less experienced politicians could find Washington associations a welcoming and intimate place to voice one's views or, in some organizations, to escape political discussion entirely.

Ultimately, these associations had three critical consequences for the men of the antebellum period. First, some associations gave Washington politicians a welcome respite from the rigors of congressional debate. While congressmen spent their afternoons discussing tense issues like the Wilmot Proviso and the end of the Mexican War, they could spend an evening or a weekend with like-minded friends, discussing other stimulating but often less-pressing topics, such as agriculture, education, the evils of modern society, or the challenges of immigration. Occasionally these conversations could iron out the details of pending legislation.

Second, local associations provided many Washington politicians with the unique experience of a diverse and predominantly cross-sectional social life. Lawmakers who were active in one of the many organizations, religious centers, clubs, or political factions generally were guaranteed to work with men from other regions of the country, and sometimes even other political parties. In other words, associational life in the capital city allowed Washington politicians from one part of the country to make strong friendships and alliances with men from the other section. For example, during the winter of 1848–49, Lincoln and his fellow Young Indians quickly came to admire one another's political abilities. In February 1848, Lincoln told his friend William Herndon that Stephens gave "the very best speech of an hour's length, I ever heard. My old, withered, dry eyes are full of tears yet." Stephens similarly enjoyed Lincoln's company, and later remarked that the "kind-hearted" Illinois representative was his closest associate in Congress excepting Robert Toombs.[21]

Finally, Washington associations often gave individual congressmen—and particularly those who were newer to the political scene—a louder voice in pursuing their agenda. Lincoln would have little influence in nominating Taylor on his own, regardless of whether he was well liked among his colleagues. By working with the Young Indian Club, the Illinois Whig could exert more influence on other members of the Whig Party in choosing the next president. Certainly not every congressman who came to Washington participated in club life, but, as Lincoln discovered, those who did often found the city and the Capitol an easier place to navigate. Overall, Lincoln's experience in Washington was part of a larger story of associational culture in the capital city.

■ The men who came to the capital city in the 1840s and 1850s were not typically career politicians in the modern sense. Some of them had little experience in politics. Others had been long-serving state and local representatives but, like the young and energetic Abraham Lincoln, had no real national reputation. Before coming to Washington, these men had served in various jobs in their home states, from doctors and merchants to ministers and newspaper editors. The most common occupation, however, was the one Lincoln called his own: the legal profession. The lawyer-turned-politician track to Washington was so common that of the 309 men who served in the Thirtieth Congress, 239 of them had been practicing attorneys.

What made antebellum politicians different from modern legislators, however, is that most kept their jobs as lawyers, doctors, editors, or planters while serving in Congress and other political positions. Pay was notoriously low, and most congressmen could not afford to live in Washington for part of the year while simultaneously maintaining their property and families back home. Moreover, some Washington politicians had lucrative law practices or agricultural investments and therefore had no interest in abandoning their large sources of income.[22]

As a result, Washington politicians often found themselves balancing their political careers with other professional interests. During a congressional session, lawyers might leave town temporarily to try a case back home or go missing from the halls of the Senate or House of Representatives to argue a case before the Supreme Court. Looking after hometown legal cases

Table 1. Primary Professions of Members of the Thirtieth Congress

Farmers, planters, or engaged in other agricultural pursuits	13
Skilled and unskilled laborers	
(blacksmith, mason, saddler, tailor, miner)	10
Bankers and merchants	20
Medical professionals	13
Lawyers or judges[a]	239
Military officers	1
Ministers	3
Newspaper editors	3
Unknown/career politicians	7

Source: *Biographical Directory of the American Congress, 1774–1996.*

[a]In this group, 21 of the 239 lawyers also engaged in agricultural pursuits, such as planting and farming. Many congressmen, including lawyers, had secondary professions in one (or more) of the other categories.

while living in the capital could be time-consuming for congressional members; Lincoln's correspondence is littered with letters pertaining to his cases in Illinois. Similarly, Washington politicians had to monitor their plantations and investments even while conducting congressional business.[23]

A critical way for lawmakers to keep up with their hometown jobs was to organize or join a local association that advocated for their professional interests. Congressmen with medical training, for example, might work with other doctors in the area at the Medical Society of the District of Columbia, a local chapter of the American Medical Association. There they could interact with well-regarded physicians like Frederick May and Samuel Busey, who coincidentally lived at the same boardinghouse as Abraham Lincoln in 1848.[24]

Washington politicians who owned farms or simply had an interest in agricultural development were active in the United States Agricultural Society. Organized in 1852 with the help of a few sitting congressmen, the society held an annual convention at the Smithsonian Institution as well as regular board meetings. Vice presidents were elected from every participating state, and the group passed yearly resolutions aimed at affecting legislation in Congress. Like Lincoln's Young Indian Club, membership in the U.S. Agricultural Society among Washington politicians was relatively small but also cross-sectional. Some of the society's members in the 1850s included Senators Stephen A. Douglas (D-Ill.), John P. Hale (R-N.H.), and Thomas J. Rusk (D-Tex.), as well as Representatives James Doty (D-Wisc.), Meredith P. Gentry (W-Tenn.), and William F. Hunter (W-Ohio).[25] Although these men found themselves at different points on the political and geographic spectrum, members of the U.S. Agricultural Society tended to agree about promoting new agricultural techniques such as improving farm implements and using purebred livestock.[26]

Joining the U.S. Agricultural Society allowed members to collectively advocate for their vision of progressive agriculture. Several of the men had previously been involved in one of the many smaller agricultural groups throughout the United States in the 1840s and early 1850s. Yet organizations like the Massachusetts Agricultural Society had not been able to dramatically influence farm legislation in Congress. By gathering in Washington, politicians could coordinate a more unified effort. For example, in January 1857 the U.S. Agricultural Society, which boasted its largest attendance to date, passed a resolution calling for the creation of agricultural colleges throughout the United States. The idea was not new—the Illinois Agricultural Society had passed a similar resolution as early as 1852—but Congress had not acted on the suggestion.[27]

One of the members of the Agricultural Society that year was Republican Justin Morrill, a Vermont representative in Congress. Morrill took the first step toward putting the U.S. Agricultural Society resolutions into action in December 1857 by introducing legislation that would provide federal land grants for agricultural colleges throughout the union.[28] Although President James Buchanan would eventually veto the land-grant college bill, the House and the Senate passed Morrill's legislation in 1858 and 1859, respectively. Support for the bill came mostly from Republicans, but the Agricultural Society was fortunate to have the presence of several of its vice presidents and delegates in Congress during both houses' votes. In the Senate, four Southerners—three of whom had been delegates to the Agricultural Society meeting in 1857—helped pass the bill 25 to 22. Four Democrats who were society delegates skipped the vote entirely, in all likelihood in order to let the bill go through.[29]

The Agricultural Society was not the only organization in Washington for politicians with outside professions and interests. For educators, one of the greatest benefits of coming to Washington was the close proximity to the District's famous Smithsonian Institution. Established by Congress in 1846, the Smithsonian became the American center for philosophical, scientific,

Figure 7. Sketch of the Smithsonian Institution. Photograph Collection, Historical Society of Washington, D.C.

and religious research and education in the mid-nineteenth century. Professor Joseph Henry, its first secretary, organized weekly lectures on subjects as varied as European journalism, coal, and "Potential Physics."[30]

For Massachusetts Whig Horace Mann, regularly attending the Smithsonian's events was one of the more attractive aspects of living in Washington. As a distinguished educator, Mann frequently was invited to give lectures and workshops for teachers. On one such occasion in March 1850, Mann left his place in the House of Representatives to speak in the afternoon to several invited guests. Mann's colleague Edward Everett had a similar association with the Smithsonian Institution, lecturing there several times while temporarily retired from Congress in the late 1840s. In 1849 Everett's friend Robert Winthrop hoped to entice the former Harvard University president into running for Congress again by appealing to his interest in the Smithsonian. Winthrop explained that if he came to Washington, Everett would not have to waste too much time in the House or Senate. Rather, he told his friend, "You might spend a considerable portion of your time in advancing the interests of the Smithsonian & National Institutes."[31]

Some who wanted a bigger role in the operations of the Smithsonian could campaign for a nomination to its board of regents. The board, which consisted of three members of the House, three members of the Senate, the vice president, the chief justice of the Supreme Court, the mayor of Washington, and six citizens at large always included men from states both north and south of the Mason-Dixon line. For example in 1856 and 1857, Senators Stephen A. Douglas (D-Ill.), James M. Mason (D-Va.), and James Pearce (Opp-Md.) served as regents along with Representatives William English (D-Ind.), Benjamin Stanton (R-Ohio), and Hiram Warner (D-Ga.). Such service was more than just an empty honor; regents attended board meetings every January and cooperated on committees throughout the year to promote the interests of the institution. In the early years of the Smithsonian, regents had responsibilities like deciding on building plans and budgeting. Politicians who became involved with the institution were generally proud of their role and, as Joseph Henry described "jealous of their prerogatives" of serving on the board.[32]

Not all Washington lawmakers were interested in intellectual organizations like the Smithsonian or even the Young Indian Club. For some, the most important associations they joined in Washington were religious in nature.[33] The politicians who came to Washington in the 1840s and 1850s belonged to a variety of Christian denominations and had differing levels of interest in practicing while in the capital. Upon arriving in Washington, however, they soon discovered that churches in the capital would be somewhat different from their churches back home.

By 1846, most of the Christian denominations in the United States had split along the Mason-Dixon line. Northern and Southern Presbyterians, Baptists, and Methodists had developed competing conceptions of Christian republican values.[34] But in Washington, the ecclesiastical divide was more complicated. The capital city did have a number of options for worship. For example, in 1855 Washington boasted as many as three Baptist, six Episcopalian, one Lutheran, nine Methodist, six Presbyterian, and four Catholic churches. Yet not all these meetinghouses were friendly to temporary residents, or convenient to lawmakers' boardinghouses or hotels. Most Washington politicians, therefore, chose one of nine or ten options, with usually no more than two choices per denomination. Typically, men from both sections attended each church.[35]

Observant politicians often found church a place of comfort, a way to escape—albeit temporarily—the rigors of lawmaking. As a result, an odd combination of politicians from different geographic sections and political viewpoints often ended up at the same chapel. Michigan representative Alpheus Felch described one such amusing scene at the First Presbyterian Church on 5th Street in May 1848, where he saw President Polk and his wife. As he explained, the Polks "sat on one side of the pulpit and on the other sat

Gen [Lewis] Cass [D-Mich.], the most prominent candidate for his place at the White House." If this was not coincidence enough, "In the rear of the President, next pew, sat Col [Thomas Hart] Benton [D-Mo.], whose claims to the same distinguished position might, but for some indiscretions, be as strong as any man in the nation." Other occasional attendees at the 5th Street chapel included Virginians Thomas Ritchie, a well-known newspaper editor, and Democratic representative Roger Pryor. Supreme Court Justice John Catron of Tennessee and his wife also frequently visited the First Presbyterian Church.[36]

St. John's Episcopal Church at the top of Lafayette Square was another popular option. Open since 1815, St. John's was the prayer house of choice for many of Washington's fashionable residents, such as wealthy banker William W. Corcoran and fellow socialite Benjamin Ogle Tayloe. But several prominent politicians also became regulars during their years in the capital city. Parishioners included such diverse men as Democratic president James Buchanan; Speaker of the House James L. Orr (D-S.C.); Senators George Badger (W-N.C.), Hamilton Fish (W-N.Y.), and William Seward (W-N.Y.); and the King brothers, James and John, of New Jersey and New York. At St. John's, like the First Presbyterian Church, men were members not because of their section or party but rather because of their allegiance to that particular denomination.[37]

Because of the cross-sectional makeup of these churches, most pastors went out of their way to avoid sectionally divisive sermons. Antislavery men acknowledged that ministers who insisted on preaching about slavery were likely to have "a very thin crowd" and probably could not succeed in getting a permanent church in Washington. Even by the late 1850s amid increasing religious polarization throughout the country, Washington congregations tried to avoid the subject of slavery. Preachers who broke this code were often criticized. As Washington resident Benjamin French reported, in one such case, a Reverend Conway made an "imprudent" sermon about slavery during a Unitarian service in December 1857. Congregants were furious but longtime D.C. minister Orville Dewey smoothed over the controversy "and healed the troubles in a great measure."[38]

Unfortunately, attending church in the city was not a luxury that all politicians could afford, particularly poorly compensated members of the Senate and House of Representatives. Depending upon the church, a pew could be pricey: North Carolina senator David Settle Reid paid eighteen dollars for pew 26 at the First Baptist Church on 10th street in 1858 and twenty-one dollars for the same pew in 1859. Most federal politicians already paid

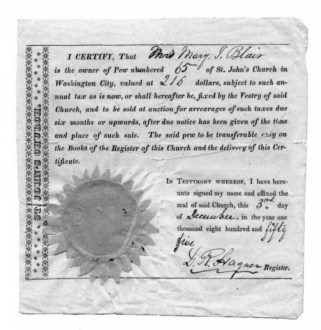

I CERTIFY, That Mrs Mary J. Blair is the owner of Pew numbered 65 of St. John's Church in Washington City, valued at 216 dollars, subject to such annual tax as is now, or shall hereafter be, fixed by the Vestry of said Church, and to be sold at auction for arrearages of such taxes due six months or upwards, after due notice has been given of the time and place of such sale. The said pew to be transferable only on the Books of the Register of this Church and the delivery of this Certificate.

IN TESTIMONY WHEREOF, I have hereunto signed my name and affixed the seal of said Church, this 3rd day of December, in the year one thousand eight hundred and fifty five

J. R. Hagner Register.

Figure 8. Church pew receipt from St. John's Church in Lafayette Square. Blair-Janin Family Papers, Historical Society of Washington, D.C.

for pews in their hometown churches and for many, securing an additional pew in Washington for the few months they were in town was an extravagant expense. Furthermore, many politicians were uncomfortable going to churches where they did not have pews. As David Outlaw remarked to his wife, "I should like to go to Church, but I do not fancy going into one and gazing about like a fool for a seat. All churches ought to be free. This appropriation of pews is all wrong."[39]

A few got around the expense by repeatedly receiving invitations from local Washingtonians to sit in their pews. Edward Everett frequently joined Whig newspaper editor William W. Seaton at the Unitarian Church, while Missourian Edward Bates visited the Old School Presbyterian Church on F Street with his friend Joseph C. G. Kennedy. But some politicians remained uncomfortable visiting the local meetinghouses. Lincoln Clark explained to his wife that it was hard for him to attend one of the local churches because "I feel not so much anxiety to attend these meetings among strangers."[40]

For men like Clark who disliked feeling out of place, the best option was often worshiping at the Capitol itself. At the beginning of each session, congressmen selected a chaplain for each House to say daily prayers during the term. The two chaplains also split duties preaching in the Hall of the House on Sundays. As Michigan representative Kinsley Bingham explained in January 1848, "The chaplains of the two houses preach alternately—the senate's chaplain is a Methodist and preached to day—Members of Congress and strangers in the city [g]o there—the seats of the members are graced with many beautiful women." Capitol services were meant to be a substitute for a formal church, but were typically less organized. One snooty outsider described the service as "very little like church, & nothing but the Novelty carried us, we sat in the seats of the hall of Representatives—it was full, but rather common looking people." Regardless of their informality, services at the Capitol were frequently packed, sometimes leaving late arrivers without a seat.[41]

Several members of Congress regularly attended preaching at the Capitol, among them Senators Jacob Collamer (W-Vt.), Alpheus Felch (D-Mich.), and Robert M. T. Hunter (D-Va.) as well as Representatives Robert Hatton (Opp-Tenn.) and David Outlaw (W-N.C.). Some, like Collamer and Felch, were less picky about who was preaching. In 1851 Felch went to services no matter whose turn it was, as he thought Methodist preacher Henry Slicer, the chaplain of the Senate, was "a good & honest man, though not a great man," while Congregationalist Reverend R. R. Gurley, the chaplain of the House, was "a most excellent man . . . modest, yet a very good preacher—though not a very eminent man." Others were more discerning. Outlaw often skipped services on Sunday when Slicer—"a fat, greasy Methodist"—was preaching, while Hatton disliked Gurley, whom he thought was too "prosy."[42]

If a congressman regularly attended services in the Hall of the House, he often had to be a bit more open-minded about the services. Guest preachers routinely graced the halls of the Capitol, spanning the ecclesiastical spectrum from Catholic priests to Quaker leaders, and even the occasional Jewish rabbi.[43] On the second Sunday of Lincoln's arrival in Washington, Archbishop John Hughes of New York led the Capitol service. A bipartisan and cross-sectional group of fifty-three representatives, including Lincoln's friends William Ballard Preston and John Pendleton, had invited Bishop Hughes to come down for the service a few days earlier. Attendance at the Capitol during Hughes's sermon was large, particularly among members of Congress, although some left the meeting disappointed with the archbishop. Massachusetts representative Artemas Hale noted in his diary: "He was a good speaker, but his discourse was not so able as I expected from a man so distinguished."[44]

Although attending service either at the Capitol or in a formal church setting could provide an escape from the typical legislative activities of congressmen in Washington, religion and politics in the city could occasionally clash. One crucial way in which the two mixed was in electing the chaplains to the Senate or House of Representatives. Local ministers, particularly those who had previously served in the post, occasionally electioneered for the honor. For example, William Hodges, the minister of Christ Church, an Episcopal chapel located at the Navy Yard in D.C., was particularly anxious to be chaplain in 1853. He appealed to Virginia representative Charles Faulkner, who was an active member of Hodges's church when in Washington, to help him win the chaplaincy in 1853. Hodges explained that the House had not had an Episcopal representative in many years. He appealed not only to Faulkner's religious tendencies but also to his sectional allegiances: "The chaplaincy of the 'House' has been so long in the hands of other denominations of Christians & generally northern men, it seems to me time to give an Episcopalian & Southerner (Virginian) a chance." Methodist minister Henry Slicer, who had frequently served as chaplain in the 1840s, also repeatedly campaigned for the position, asking for help from both Northerner Alpheus Felch and Southerner David Settle Reid. Some chaplain candidates even recruited congressmen to help with their election. Indiana Democrat Jesse Bright asked his Senate colleague Robert M. T. Hunter to help elect a Baptist minister to the position in 1865. Referring to Hunter's housemates Andrew Pickens Butler (D-S.C.) and James M. Mason (D-Va.), Bright told his friend: "I must tax you so far as to ask you to remind Judge Butler & Mr. Mason that we have never had a Baptist Preacher for a Senate Chaplain and Mr Hill is [in] every way worthy."[45]

Occasionally votes for chaplain could become sectionally motivated. Tennessee representative Robert Hatton complained bitterly in March 1860 about certain Southern senators who tried to influence the vote. "The scene during the progress of the balloting was disgraceful," wrote Hatton in his diary, "I have great contempt for all such foolery." Yet the course of debate in voting for chaplain was not typically contentious. The diversity of religious beliefs in the House of Representatives meant that congressmen from the same section and party could have different preferences for prayer leaders. Even during the supposedly sectional March 1860 chaplain election that Hatton described, sixteen congressmen nominated chaplains, including five Republicans, two Northern Democrats, five Southern Democrats, and four Opposition party members. Friends Horace Maynard and Emerson Etheridge, both Opposition men from Tennessee, nominated two different preachers; so did Elihu Washburne and William Kellogg, both Republicans from Illinois.[46]

Amid these conditions, lawmakers had varying levels of interest in church.

Members of the Young Indians provide a sampling of involvement. Lincoln left no record of which chapel he preferred in 1848 and 1849 (if he went to church at all), but other Young Indians were more active churchgoers. Toombs regularly attended the 8th Street Methodist Episcopal Church during the 1840s and 1850s, particularly when his wife was in Washington with him. Stephens also went to church most weekends, but he moved around; occasionally he went with Toombs to the 8th Street church, but other times he liked services at the Capitol or the Presbyterian Church on 4½ Street where the famed Reverend B. Sunderland was the pastor.[47]

Although some of the Young Indians were religious, none was particularly active in religious organizations outside of church. While Lincoln, Stephens, and Toombs spent evenings debating the Constitution, other fellow federal politicians became intimately involved in religious and benevolent causes in the city. Some of the more devout Washington politicians actively participated in groups such as the D.C. chapter of the American Bible Society. A national organization with headquarters in New York City, the Bible Society's sole mission was "to encourage a wider circulation of the Holy Scriptures, without note or comment." The society boasted several prominent federal politicians as members, including Supreme Court Justice John McLean of Ohio and Georgia senator John M. Berrien.[48]

Upon arriving in Washington, men like John Thompson (R-N.Y.) and James McDowell (D-Va.), who were members of hometown branches of the Bible Society, energetically joined the efforts of Washington's chapter. In May 1848, McDowell and two of his House colleagues, James G. Chapman (W-Md.) and Richard W. Thompson (W-Ind.), provided keynote speeches at a Washington Bible Society meeting. Local organizers also repeatedly asked McDowell to represent the society at events in the North. Like membership in the Agricultural Society or Smithsonian Institution, or even the Young Indians, participants in the Bible Society were guaranteed to have close interactions with men from both sections. And, like these other Washington associations, members worked on issues outside of controversies over slavery.[49]

While many benevolent associations in Washington, like the Bible Society, had nothing to do with the "peculiar institution," one popular group specifically focused on the problem of slavery, the American Colonization Society (ACS). Founded in 1817, the society's mission was to send free and freed black men and women back to Africa as a means of alleviating the slavery and race problem in the United States.[50] Prominent politicians such as James Madison and Henry Clay were among the first supporters of the

ACS, and the society remained popular with a number of Southern politicians in the 1820s and 1830s. Many of these Southerners saw slavery as a "necessary evil" and hoped that through colonization, slavery could someday be eradicated. Yet by the late 1840s, some Southerners had begun to believe slavery was a "positive good," and increasingly defended the institution against the efforts of abolitionists and other antislavery groups. Under these circumstances, the American Colonization Society increasingly came under attack by men from the Deep South.[51]

Regardless of its controversial place in the South, however, the ACS remained popular among many of the politicians who came to Washington in the antebellum period. The ACS purposely held most of its meetings in December and January in order to overlap with the congressional session and allow congressmen to attend. Several Washington politicians even served as delegates to the national meetings from their home state societies, including such diverse representatives as John Moore (W-La.), Jeremiah Morton (W-Va.), O. S. Seymour (D-Conn.), Frederick P. Stanton, (D-Tenn.), Benjamin Thompson (W-Mass.), and Lincoln's fellow Young Indian, Truman Smith.[52]

The Colonization Society was prominent enough that many of its meetings and lectures took place in the Hall of the House of Representatives. The ACS board repeatedly asked its congressional members to reserve the Hall for big events. During Lincoln's first January in Washington, a large crowd gathered at the Capitol to hear Society president Henry Clay and Senator Thomas Corwin (W-Ohio) give lectures on the benefits of sending freed slaves to Africa. The meeting was so popular among local Washingtonians that David Outlaw remarked: "There was an immense crowd, some going there an hour before sunset."[53]

Although the Colonization Society did not typically meet during work hours, sometimes Washington lawmakers put their interest in colonization ahead of their political duties. Burdened already with his responsibilities as a Bible Society member, churchgoer, and Smithsonian participant, Edward Everett had to skip work as secretary of state in order to fulfill his duties as an ACS vice president. Everett noted in his diary, "Staid at home today to prepare my speech for the Colonization Society. This I regretted but it seemed unavoidable. With the utmost exertion to do so, I have not been able to find time to do it in the week."[54]

Like Everett, who had commitments to a variety of other groups in the city, several members of the ACS were also active in a second benevolent association in Washington: the American Temperance Union. Although federal politicians were often known for drunken revelry, some lawmakers were adamant abstainers. Horace Mann was an active participant in the Washington temperance organizations and often spoke at national meetings in New York during the congressional session. Mann even tried to convince his Massachusetts colleague Charles Sumner to stop drinking and join a temperance group (Sumner politely demurred). For interested politicians, there were opportunities to meet other temperance advocates in the capital city. Washington boasted ten divisions of the American Temperance Society, as well as a chapter each of the Independent Brothers of Temperance, the Sons of Temperance, and the Cadets of Temperance. Temperance groups met weekly and were generally welcoming of enthusiastic lawmakers.[55]

For Southern temperance promoters, in particular, Washington was a place to find kindred spirits in what was a drink-heavy society. As Ian Tyrrell has shown, temperance advocates disproportionately lived in New England states and were typically scarce in the South.[56] Yet some Southern politicians who came to Washington in the antebellum period were strong temperance advocates. Reformed Senator Sam Houston, for example, was active in both the Sons of Temperance and the American Temperance Union at home in Texas. While in Washington, Houston was able to attend regular temperance organization meetings and travel within the Chesapeake region to give lectures and speeches on the benefits of abstinence. As he explained to his wife, "I have become more pleased, with temperance than I have ever been previously."[57]

In the antebellum period, temperance societies in Washington—and throughout the United States—were more than just groups of benevolent activists. One appealing aspect of groups like the Sons of Temperance for Washington politicians was that the groups had begun to take on the role of fraternal organizations, adopting secret rituals and symbols.[58] In fact, several traditional fraternal groups still existed in Washington, including both the Freemasons and the Odd Fellows. Fraternal organizations had come under attack by an increasingly strong anti-Masonic movement in the late 1820s and 1830s, but by the time Lincoln arrived in Washington in 1847, they had made a substantial comeback in American society, albeit with less elaborate ceremonies attached to them. The *Daily National Intelligencer* boldly proclaimed that "it will be gratifying, no doubt, to many friends of the order to learn that masonry is in a prosperous condition" in the city.[59]

The Masonic fraternity included membership of numerous Washington politicians, with as different political and geographic backgrounds as James Buchanan (D-Pa.), Lewis Cass (D-Mich.), John Crittenden (W-Ky.), Charles

Faulkner (D-Va.), Edwin Stanton (R-Ohio), and Lincoln's fellow Young Indian Robert Toombs. In part, the fraternity was able to attract such a diverse group because discussion of slavery or other politically charged issues was strictly banned. After long debates over slavery in the territories, many politicians were often eager to escape further discussion of the peculiar institution. At meetings with fellow masons throughout the city, members focused instead on "brotherly love and self improvement," uniting white men from around the country.[60]

Masons and Odd Fellows both met routinely in the District—typically every other week—and also participated in a variety of local ceremonies, such as laying the cornerstone at the Washington Monument or marching in funeral processions of fallen members. Masons from other states were particularly involved with local chapters during initiations of new members or leaders. Washington resident Benjamin French, who became the District grand master in December 1849, described the scene of his initiation. According to French, the Grand Lodge of Freemasons met at the Masonic Hall at four o'clock in the afternoon, and at five o'clock they walked to the nearby Unitarian church. Once there, "a very eloquent and appropriate address was delivered by Hon. Joseph R. Chandler [W-Pa.], P. G. Master of Pennsylvania." At that point French was "installed as Grand Master of the District" by William C. Dawson (W-Ga.), who was, at that time, the grand master of the state of Georgia. The attendance of men from both sections was not unusual: as long as federal politicians were in good standing with their hometown Masonic organizations, they were repeatedly invited both by newspaper advertisements and by word-of-mouth to join in local meetings.[61]

By the time Lincoln arrived in Washington in 1847, secret rituals and ceremonies were not limited to fraternal organizations. Nativist societies (anti-immigrant, anti-Catholic groups) had begun sprouting up in cities throughout the North. Starting in the 1830s, Irish and German Catholics moved to the United States en masse. Nativists blamed these new Irish and German residents for what they perceived as America's social, political, and economic deterioration. Most important, they feared a papal plot by Catholic immigrants to subvert America's republican institutions. By the early 1850s, nativists were called "Know-Nothings," and had organized a large political movement with more than a million members throughout the country. Politicians even began running as Know-Nothing candidates under the "American" Party label.[62]

As a budding political group, the Know-Nothings became attractive to anti-immigrant residents in Washington, and in 1853 members in the District formed a formal council. Congressmen who ran on the American Party ticket typically belonged to chapters in their home state, but some, like Tennessee Know-Nothing Emerson Etheridge, also applied for membership in the District of Columbia council. If a congressman's nativist credentials checked out, the Washington Know-Nothings enthusiastically accepted him. The number of Know-Nothing politicians who preferred membership in the District council to their home state organizations became so large that the national organization finally passed a rule "forbidding the councils of this district, from receiving the members of Congress into the order" so as to preserve the standing of hometown councils. Still, like the masons, Washington Know-Nothings invited their brethren from other chapters to join in their meetings, advertising their activities in their local newspaper, the *American Organ*.[63]

Know-Nothings were not the only political group to attract followers in Washington, D.C. Lincoln's Illinois rival Stephen Douglas was intimately involved with a branch of the Democratic Party known as "Young America," which championed territorial expansion, market growth, and societal reform. De facto campaign committee organizations like the National Democratic Association and its Whig counterpart also invited a small group of party members into their ranks. Leaders in these associations met to analyze reports that regularly came in about state races from congressmen and other politicians.[64]

Although groups like the National Democratic Association had a long-standing place in the Washington community, not all organizations in the city were permanent. Building on the associational spirit of the mid-nineteenth century, Washington politicians found it easy and useful to organize temporary political groups to advocate for or against a party's presidential candidate or a particular issue. Democrats who were anxious to elect Franklin Pierce in 1852 could join the Washington "Pierce Club." Similarly, a group of Northern Whigs who opposed the Kansas-Nebraska Act in 1854 recruited congressmen and other Washington citizens to a "Union Emigration Society," dedicated to fighting the act. The society attracted men such as Missourian Francis P. Blair, New York antislavery advocate Preston King, and Lincoln's Young Indian colleague Truman Smith.[65]

Smith, like many Washington lawmakers, bounced in and out of Washington political associations as they organized or died out. The Young Indian Club, however, was one of his more rewarding memberships; the group was overwhelmingly successful in promoting its nominee. By the end of March 1848, Lincoln boasted that between forty and forty-five Whig representatives had committed themselves to Taylor. The Young Indian Club was responsible for many of these supporters, and Lincoln had done his fair share of recruiting. One of his likely converts was Ohioan Joshua Giddings. That Giddings, a committed antislavery man, could support the same candidate as such a strong proslavery Southerner as Robert Toombs, may be surprising. But Lincoln probably used his powers of persuasion at the dinner table at Ann Sprigg's boardinghouse, where the two were messmates.[66]

The pro-Taylor group also had some help from events on the ground out West. In late February, President Polk sent the Treaty of Guadalupe Hidalgo to the Senate. The agreement would end the war with Mexico, but it would also create problems for Whigs: the document ceded approximately 500,000 square miles of territory in return for a payment of $15 million to Mexico. Although the party had adopted a "no territory" policy in 1846 and 1847, many Whig leaders understood that opposing peace (even if it meant acquiring vast amounts of territory) undermined their initial antiwar stance. In essence, the treaty made their 1848 presidential campaign strategy of "no territory" moot. Thus, with no real issue guiding the Whig Party in the upcoming election, the treaty helped propel Taylor ahead of Clay as the favorite to win the nomination.[67]

Still, the outcome remained undecided, and the Young Indians worked hard to rally support for Taylor all the way up to the Whig Convention in June. Three of the club members would be delegates to the meeting—Smith, Flournoy, and Preston—but many other supporters, including Lincoln himself, came to the Philadelphia assemblage to help with their efforts. By the end of the convention, Lincoln and his club mates had succeeded in their cause: Zachary Taylor would become the next Whig nominee for president. In November 1848, the Hero of Buena Vista defeated Lewis Cass to become the second (and last) Whig to win the office.

In the months following the election, the Young Indians stayed in touch and collectively hoped to reap the rewards of their efforts to nominate Taylor. Individually, some were successful. The president tapped William Ballard Preston to serve in his cabinet as secretary of the navy. Both Toombs and Stephens were reelected to Congress and expected to take active leadership roles in the next session. Stephens even had a chance to become the Speaker of the House.

Other club members were not so lucky. John Pendleton lost his reelection bid in Virginia and scrambled unsuccessfully for an appointment from the new president. Toombs tried to help out the Virginian and wrote to Preston asking if he could find a way to convince the president to find him a diplomatic post. "I know your embarrassments upon the foreign appointments in Va. . . . [and I have] a most painfull aversion to extending myself . . . at any time, in reference to office," Toombs told Preston. "But . . . you know his appointment would be very agreeable to me, is there any prospect of it?"[68]

Lincoln was similarly unsuccessful. Although serving in Congress did not initially enamor him, Lincoln found himself regretting a promise he had made not to run for reelection. He eventually decided to seek a patronage position as commissioner of the Land Office to continue his political career. The Illinois Whig also solicited Preston's help with the position, reminding him: "No member of the cabinet knows so well as yourself, the great anxiety I felt for Gen: Taylor's election, and consequently none could so well appreciate my anxiety for the success of his administration." Preston tried to help his friends in the Young Indians, but he had only so much power in a cabinet that had substantial numbers of supporters to placate.[69]

Still, Lincoln could leave Washington with the comfort that he had made his mark on the Thirtieth Congress. Joining the Young Indians allowed Lincoln to make close relationships with other legislators and to advocate for his party agenda. And the Young Indians were successful in large part because of their strong organization. As a small but tight-knit group, they became a powerful force in the first session of the Thirtieth Congress. Most important, the relationships that the Young Indians made would have an impact on future events. In 1860, when Lincoln was elected president on the anti-South platform of the Republican Party, his old Southern colleagues remembered the Illinois representative as a moderate. Similarly, Lincoln's experiences with the Southern Young Indians in 1848 gave him a skewed impression of Southern secession in 1860; his memories of working with Stephens and others suggested to Lincoln that conciliation was possible.[70]

In the meantime, newly elected President Taylor would arrive in Washington in the spring of 1849 with a mess on his hands. With the end of the war, and the acquisition of a vast swath of territory, congressmen and other Washington lawmakers would struggle to bridge a widening conflict between Northerners and Southerners over the fate of slavery in the West. Moreover, conflict over the Wilmot Proviso still loomed large as Northern legislatures repeatedly instructed their senators to vote for the provision. Ultimately, congressmen would turn to the Compromise of 1850 to settle the controversy. But not without a prolonged debate and a little help from Washington's social butterflies.

CHAPTER THREE

Behind the Curtain
Where Great Men Relax

Capital Social Life and the Compromise of 1850

On February 5, 1850, Kentucky Whig Henry Clay calmly sat at his desk in the Senate looking over a stack of papers. The nearly seventy-three-year-old Clay, who had devoted almost his entire life to public service, was preparing to deliver an important speech to the body; he would clarify the series of resolutions he had proposed a few days earlier aimed at resolving the deepening conflict over territory acquired in the Mexican War. An expectant crowd had gathered in the galleries before breakfast, and late arrivers found standing room or took seats on the floor of the chamber. Many of the women who came to watch the "Great Compromiser" whispered about the other senators in the hall, pointing out men like Texas Democrat Sam Houston and Ohio Whig Thomas Corwin. Because of Clay's age and stature, most members of both houses had come into the Senate to hear the speech, an exception from their typical indifference. Finally, Clay placed the papers he had been fiddling with in his desk and gracefully rose from his seat to thundering applause. Over the next two hours the Kentuckian delivered an inspired speech, in his famously mesmerizing voice, asking his fellow congressmen to come together and save the nation from sectional discord.[1]

Clay's speech was a welcome break from the anger that had roiled the Capitol over the previous two months, stemming in large part from disputes over the Mexican Cession. Dealing with the new territory proved tricky for a number of reasons.

First, since David Wilmot introduced his initial proviso in 1846, the proposal had continued to frustrate congressional efforts to effectively organize the territories. Wilmot's amendment had become even more problematic by the opening of the Thirty-First Congress, however. In the summer of 1849, state legislatures throughout the North had instructed their senators to vote to attach the proviso to any legislation organizing the Mexican Cession. House members received similar requests to guard Northern interests and prevent slavery from entering the new territories. By the time Congress assembled, fourteen out of fifteen Northern states had called for passage of the Wilmot Proviso. Meanwhile, more and more Southerners threatened secession should the proviso become law.

A second issue concerned Texas. Any congressional settlement over the Mexican Cession would have to include a defined boundary line between the Lone Star State and the new territory known as New Mexico. Yet, leaders from Texas and the New Mexico territory disagreed about where this line should be. Disagreement among residents in the area regarding the boundary threatened to become violent, and Washington legislators were concerned about keeping hostility to a minimum. In addition, congressmen disagreed over whether to appease the Texans, who wanted the United States to help pay for the enormous debt Texas had racked up as an independent republic. The debt concerned Easterners as well; it existed primarily in the shape of bonds that the Republic of Texas had issued between 1836 and 1845, which were owned by businessmen in New York and Boston. Overall, the Thirty-First Congress faced a series of hurdles in peacefully organizing new territories.[2]

Sectional disagreements over the Mexican Cession quickly leaked into congressional business. When the session began in early December, House members struggled to elect a Speaker, as Whigs held a slight majority. Six Southern Whigs stubbornly withheld their vote from the previous Whig Speaker, Robert Winthrop of Massachusetts, primarily because of continuing tensions over the Wilmot Proviso. Eventually, after sixty-three ballots, Democrats were able to elect Georgia Democrat Howell Cobb to the Speakership on December 22.[3]

To make matters worse, President Zachary Taylor appeared to be unconcerned with the position of Southerners on the Mexican Cession. A Southerner and a slaveholder himself, Taylor was even related by marriage to future Confederate president Jefferson Davis. But Southern Whigs soon discovered that he could not be trusted; as Georgia senator John M. Berrien explained, the president seemed to have an "*indifference* to the extension of slavery in the territories." Taylor confirmed Southern fears about his position on the Wilmot Proviso upon finally submitting his annual message to Congress on Christmas Eve.[4] The message explained that, as the executive, Taylor did not have the authority to dictate measures to the legislative branch and could veto a bill "only in extraordinary cases," hinting that he would not veto the proviso. The president did not help matters when, in a special message to the House and Senate at the end of January, he clarified his own proposal for the Mexican Cession. Taylor recommended that Congress immediately admit California and New Mexico as states in the Union and suggested that Mexican law—which barred slavery—remain in force until statehood. Additionally, he showed no interest in catering to Texas's interests, infuriating Southern Democrats but also some members of his own party; men like Alexander Stephens and Robert Toombs, who had worked so hard to nominate Taylor, found themselves at odds with the Whig president.[5]

Following Taylor's message, many Southerners began to dig in their heels on the slavery issue. In October 1849, Mississippi legislators had called for a Southern convention in Nashville the following summer. By the beginning of February 1850, five Southern states had committed to sending delegates, while others adopted resolutions expressing their approval of the convention. Thus, when Clay delivered his resolutions, Congress had been in session for two months with no solution in sight. The men and women who gathered in the Senate chamber that February morning hoped that Clay, who had played a critical role in assuaging sectional discord during the Missouri Compromise and the nullification crisis of 1833, would provide the answer they had been looking for.

Clay was aware of how Taylor had alienated Southern allies and therefore tried to make his proposal more balanced than the president's. He offered eight provisions, including several that appealed to Southerners, such as resolutions proposing a more stringent fugitive slave law, asserting that Congress had no right to interfere with the slave trade in the South, and denying the expediency of abolishing slavery in the District of Columbia. To appease Northerners, he included provisions such as admitting California as a free state and specifying that Mexican law regarding slavery still applied to the governments for New Mexico and Deseret (modern-day Utah). His boundary proposal favored New Mexico over Texas, and although he suggested the federal government should assume the Texas debt, he purposely left the payment amount unspecified. In May 1850, Clay formally submitted most of his proposals in a single bill, called the "omnibus," along with separate provisions for the Fugitive Slave Law and limiting the slave trade in the District. He urged the Senate to act quickly on his solution.[6]

By trying to please everyone, however, Clay wound up satisfying almost no one. Even his olive branches to both sections caused frustration; for example, his use of the word "inexpedient" angered Southern Democrats, and the proposition to admit New Mexico and Deseret without strictly banning slavery infuriated Northern Whigs. As a result, while many of his colleagues desperately wanted sectional compromise, the Kentuckian's plan simply did not gain enough support. Congress would negotiate over Clay's proposals for months before the omnibus eventually disintegrated in July. While some sections of the final Compromise of 1850 resembled Clay's initial proposals, Clay himself would play a minimal role in both the provisions and negotiations of the final settlement.[7] Instead, younger members like Stephen A. Douglas (D-Ill.) and Thomas Bayly (D-Va.) pushed through a substantially altered set of bills in September. Douglas also wisely split up the provisions into individual bills, so that Northerners could vote for the provisions they preferred, and Southerners could do the same.[8]

It took the entire summer of 1850 and the longest congressional session since the adoption of the Constitution to negotiate a settlement. How did these congressmen eventually find a compromise? What factors contributed to its success? Why did so many Northern congressmen reject their states' instructions to attach the Wilmot Proviso to the Mexican Cession? Historians have offered a variety of reasons for why the compromise was finally able to pass. Part of the impetus for a settlement clearly came from a commitment to the Union and an American tradition of compromise. As Peter Knupfer has argued, sectional disputes were as old as the Constitution itself, but so were the compromises that settled these controversies. The American people had come to rely on compromise as an important tool in maintaining the Union.[9]

The political system also played a critical role. When the final votes were taken in the House and Senate in September, supporters of individual parts of the compromise were overwhelmingly Northern Democrats and Southern Whigs. As Michael Holt explains, on a national level, this breakdown can be attributed to nineteenth-century party mechanics and the need for interparty conflict. In each section of the country, the Whig and Democratic parties offered alternative ways of adjusting the territorial issue to voters. Northern Democrats and Southern Whigs supported the same solution in opposition to the other party in their section.[10]

Perhaps even more important than ideology and party mechanics, however, was good old-fashioned greed. As Holman Hamilton has argued, key supporters of the compromise bill were aligned with the Texas bond lobby. Washington banker William W. Corcoran and several of his colleagues held a large portion of the bonds that made up the Texas debt. If a compromise bill provided for paying off the debt, these bankers stood to make a considerable amount of money. Thus, during congressional debates, bank lobbyists could be found milling about the floor of the House and Senate pressuring members to support the compromise.[11]

Hamilton's work on Corcoran and the Texas bondholders was an important discovery in documenting how the Compromise of 1850 finally passed. Yet, Corcoran's position was motivated by more than just greed. Corcoran and his colleagues who lived in Washington on a permanent basis had a vested interest in maintaining cross-sectional comity for both pecuniary and personal reasons. Were the Union to falter, Washington would likely lose its place of prominence in the country, leaving D.C. residents with little prestige and saddled with the burden of choosing sides between Southern and Northern friends. "The interests of Washington are all conservative," read an 1858 article in *De Bow's Review*. "Sectional misrule and oppression would speedily dissolve the Union, and the dissolution of the Union would be the death-knell of its metropolis." Thus, the city's "great power" must be implemented "to heal dissension, to prevent sectional oppression, and to restore amity between opposing, hostile, and contending sections." Another wealthy Washington resident emphasized this point; Benjamin Ogle Tayloe, later wrote to Corcoran, "To be *sure* of preserving for a while longer, our glorious Union . . . in which, pecuniarily, you have ten times more interest than myself, though I am as much devoted to the hallowed compact as you can be; we must avoid sectional controversy and sectional candidates."[12]

The easiest way for Corcoran, Tayloe, and other wealthy residents to help maintain the Union was to facilitate cross-sectional interaction in the social circles of the city. Many of these men lived in a fancy neighborhood called "Lafayette Square," situated across from the White House. Hosting parties, dinners, balls, and other social events at their houses, Washington residents helped provide an atmosphere of intersectional sociability. Moreover, they built upon and perpetuated the precedent of mixing politics and social life in the capital city. Intersectional sociability could also have the opposite effect; members from the North and South who *opposed* compromise were also likely to discuss strategies at parties, balls, dinners, and other events. Their efforts ultimately failed but they, too, used Washington social life to their advantage.

Overall, by the antebellum period, politics and social life were critically linked in Washington in a variety of ways. To begin with, participating in Washington society often made a political statement. Appearing in the president's drawing room or at a cabinet member's reception showed support for the administration, while, conversely, missing such an event could be evidence of disapproval. Moreover, men who were more visible at parties and dinners were more likely to play a powerful role in congressional business. A congressman who attended more social events was often better able to work with his colleagues on an intimate level. This was true to a large degree because political discussion and decision making frequently happened during social events. Politicians who participated in the city's social life could guarantee a voice in political negotiations that happened outside the halls of the Capitol building.

The intermixing of Washington's social and political life had several implications for federal politics in general, and the Compromise of 1850 in particular. As with the District's clubs and organizations, social events provided numerous instances of cross-sectional interaction. These gatherings created a group of political insiders who worked within the bubble of Washington society. Most important, they gave politicians opportunities to negotiate with men from other states, regions, sections, and parties. During the long first session of the Thirty-First Congress, the subject of compromise graced the lips of nearly every politician in every social situation of the city. "The topics incident to the points in dispute between North and South," according to a Washington correspondent from the *Boston Daily Atlas*, were "the absorbing, all-engrossing staple of discussion in Congress, and of conversation at the dinner table, at the levee, even at balls, at parties, and soirees,—and the subject of jokes and bon-mots at the card table."[13]

In the end, political conversations in social situations helped lead the country toward compromise. And importantly, they led to some congressmen voting directly in opposition to the expressed wishes of their home-state legislatures on slavery issues.

■ Lasting from December 1849 until the end of September 1850, the first session of the Thirty-First Congress kept legislators in the capital city much longer than usual. As a result, Washington residents experienced one of the liveliest winters they had seen in many years. The city was always more vibrant when Congress was in session; the population swelled and prominent men and women were expected to give regular parties. As D.C. resident Henry Wise explained, the city, before the session begins, "is as dull as possible, and seems only waiting the organization of Congress to start into life." When congressmen finally arrived in Washington, they were "omnipotent and omnipresent," New York senator William Seward told his wife. "Senators, Representatives, Speakers, Sergeants, Pages, and Messengers swarm in the streets and hotels. They meet you at table, on [Pennsylvania] avenue, crowd the lobbies and fill the drawing-rooms."[14]

While Congress was in session, Washington residents could enter into a variety of levels of social engagement. For a member who preferred to remain aloof from the social extravagances of the city, a base level of participation involved exchanging cards and "making calls." Custom dictated the number and types of calls one had to make, and Washington etiquette books outlined these requirements for those who were new to the city. According to one such guide, there was a necessary pecking order beginning with the president and the vice president. These men had the privilege "not to be aware of the return of any individual, however distinguished, to the metropolis, until he shall have received a visit from him in person." Next in line were the justices of the Supreme Court who were "entitled to the first visit from Senators and Representatives" and after that came senators, who were "entitled to the first visit from the member of the House of Representatives." Not surprisingly, "the same order of priority is applied to visits between the ladies of the above-named officials." In other words, calling was a necessary act in order to maintain good relationships with fellow politicians. One did not want to offend friends or acquaintances. As New York Democrat William Marcy explained, "I have many visits I ought to make to members of congress which I cannot omit without drawing on me the charge of incivility."[15]

For the politicians themselves, "calling" did not necessarily have to involve visits. Members of Congress could simply send their cards to the appropriate dignitaries. Michigan representative Kinsley S. Bingham explained the process to his wife, Mary: "I took 100 cards to the post master of the House. He did them up in neat envelopes and sent them to all the foreign Ministers the President and the heads of departments and all the Senators — this is etiquette." The card system was efficient, according to North Carolina representative David Outlaw, since "if a man were required to make all his visits in person, he would have time for no other business."[16]

Although only a portion of politicians brought their wives with them to the city, these women were also expected to engage in proper etiquette. And, in contrast with their husbands, they were expected to make all of their calls in person. As a result, women spent much of their time going from house to house making visits. While wives of representatives were expected to call first, senators' wives then had to return those calls, which could amount to 400 visits or more. Furthermore, Judith Rives, wife of Virginia senator William Cabell Rives, could complain that "it is a matter of some consequence to take the rounds once, for all that are neglected, are irreconcilably offended." When Mary Bingham joined her husband in Washington, she quickly learned how exhausting visiting could be. "Being a Senators wife I am not obliged to call, only on those who have called on me, but that is a task indeed," she grumbled. "Last week Mrs Senator [Hannibal] Hamlin and myself hired a hack and pretty much payed all visits . . . but when we got home we found about fifteen Ladies had been to see us in our absence." Ohio senator Thomas Ewing's wife, Maria, reported to her sister that "you may judge I had a terrible day on Tuesday when I tell you there were 48 calls." Because of all these social niceties, New York representative Lorenzo Burrows's wife remarked that "the Ladies all say, that this is the most remarkable place for spending time, and accomplishing nothing." Still, most wives relished the opportunity to socialize, agreeing with First Lady Julia Tyler that "not to have all the company and in the very way that I do would disappoint me very much." And while others may have found the ritual tedious, women who came to Washington were often able to form relationships with other political families as a result.[17]

Men may have gotten off easy on calling during most days of the calendar, but once a year personal visits were necessary for both men and women to exhibit proper etiquette. Every New Year's Day, the highest dignitaries of the city, including the president, vice president, cabinet, and several other Washington socialites, like former first lady Dolley Madison, opened their doors for visitors. New Year's Day was "a day of hilarity and social enjoyment" in the capital city, according to Georgia representative Howell Cobb. "Christmas and New Years are great days in Washington," explained Michigan senator Alpheus Felch. "The custom is to call every where—and most of the gentlemen living here when I meet say 'we shall see you of course on New Years.' . . . It is almost *necessary* to call on the President and heads of Department on that day."[18]

Congressmen and other Washington politicians typically set out in pairs or small groups on the morning of the first, walking among the open houses and visiting friends and neighbors. In most private homes, various libations and cakes were laid out on tables for guests to enjoy while chatting with their hosts. Such visits were not limited to residents from the same section or party; rather, Washington politicians made calls to men and women of every state and political bearing. For example, during one wintry January morning, Representative Solomon Haven (W-N.Y.) made New Year's calls to everyone from Senators Thomas Corwin (W-Ohio) and William Gwin (D-Calif.) to Secretary of War Charles Conrad (W-La.) and the president. Similarly, Senator Jacob Collamer (W-Vt.) spent one New Year's Day visiting Lewis Cass (D-Mich.), Howell Cobb (D-Ga.), and John Bell (W-Tenn.). New Year's visits were rituals that politicians rarely passed up, regardless of ongoing political disagreements in Congress or even the weather. The snow and temperatures of only six degrees above zero could not prevent the members of the Thirty-First Congress from setting out into the streets of the city on January 1, 1850. As the newly elected Speaker of the House reported, "All the world and his wife are out today in their best bib and tucker, taking the grand rounds from the President's mansion to the humblest entertainer of New Year friends."[19]

While New Year's visits were limited to one day a year, many Washington politicians and their wives preferred to have a more active social life. A second level of social engagement was to see and be seen in the fashionable spaces of the capital city. Women, in particular, enjoyed walking up and down the promenade of Pennsylvania Avenue, from the western end of the Capitol building up to Fifteenth Street. "When the weather was not inclement, the sidewalk on the north side was thronged with well-dressed ladies and gentlemen belonging to the best classes of society," remembered one resident. These fashionables went "to and fro in pairs or groups, engaged in merry chat or profound discussion, according to their tastes and inclinations."[20]

The beautiful Library of Congress proved to be another common space for socializing. Visitors to the library included both lawmakers and Washington residents, male and female. The library was "a great resort for the fashionable," according to one congressman. "All along on each side are little recesses where the books are on shelves and people can go in and read and chat and do what they please." Because of its proximity to the halls of Congress, much of the chatter in the library was political. Congressmen who were bored with debate or were skulking to avoid a controversial vote used the room as a temporary escape from their hall. As a result, those who were not allowed on the floor of either congressional chamber sometimes stationed themselves in the library to try to press their political causes on members. Dorothea Dix, for example, who was a tireless advocate for prisoners and the mentally ill, spent much of her time in Washington at the library soliciting help from congressmen. During one such trip to the capital city in the summer of 1850, she could be found in the library almost daily.[21]

Attending grand balls, levees, and parties was another popular way to engage in the social life of the city. Washington had a specific time frame for many of these social events; the period from January to March was called the "gay season," when government officials and their wives hosted parties and balls throughout the city. During these months, not even sectional divisiveness could thwart the train of parties and balls. As Virginia Whig Alexander H. H. Stuart reported to his wife in late 1850, "The impression is we shall have a stormy session of congress but a gay winter in a social point of view." One standard of city social life during the gay season was the "Washington Assemblies." These parties, which had existed in Washington for many years, were originally "very ceremonious and exclusive," according to a local newspaperman. There was less exclusivity during the antebellum period, when Washington typically held three or four such gatherings per season, and they attracted much larger numbers of attendees.[22]

In order to promote the events, regular subscribers to the assemblies elected a group of society types and federal officeholders to serve as "managers." These managers encouraged Washington residents to buy season tickets, payment of a one-time fee for the privilege of attending all of the assemblies that season. The group of managers typically included men who were active in Washington social life and hailed from across parties and sections. For example, in 1848 the subscribers elected Senators Daniel Webster (W-Mass.) and Stephen Douglas (D-Ill.) and Representatives Edward C. Cabell (W-Fla.), Henry Bedinger (D-Va.), and Thomas Butler King (W-Ga.), along with local newspapermen Thomas Ritchie (D) and William W. Seaton (W) as managers.[23]

Another city event that attracted throngs of socialites during the gay season was the Birthnight Ball in February, an annual tribute to George Washington on his birthday. Diplomats and federal politicians of all stripes graced the party each year, and two or three nominated congressmen escorted the president to the event. Many looked forward to the ball, particularly certain members of the Supreme Court. Some of the more social justices like New Yorker Samuel Nelson and Georgian James M. Wayne proposed that the justices ought to arrive as a group. Only the curmudgeonly Peter V. Daniel objected, snidely remarking that once there, "we ought to have a *judicial jig* of course, and should perform it in our gowns, with broomsticks in our hands, like the witches in Macbeth." Apparently not everyone got the joke;

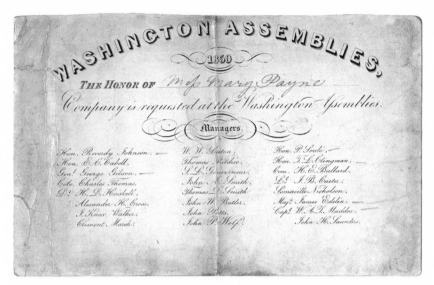

Figure 9. Invitation to the Washington Assemblies for 1850.
Hunton Family Papers, Virginia Historical Society, Richmond.

as he told his daughter, the excitement among the justices for the party was so great that "some of my brethren I verily believe would readily have given into this disgusting mockery."[24]

The few wives who came to Washington also played an important role in organizing large social activities during the gay season. Women could be scarce in the city, and such parties could enliven the spirits of men who missed their loved ones back home. Parties could be as simple as a gathering in one of the many hotels or as lavish as a masked ball. In later years, Virginia Clay, the wife of Senator Clement Clay (D-Ala.), remembered fondly her time in Washington in the 1850s, when "hospitality . . . of the capital was synonymous with an unceasing, an augmenting round of dinners and dances, receptions and balls. A hundred hostesses renowned for their beauty and wit and vivacity vied with each other in evolving novel social relaxations."[25]

Although women organized many of these grand parties, such gatherings were not free from political import and banter. In fact, parties provided the perfect opportunity for some women to press their political viewpoints or lobby for a family member to receive a political position. One editorial in *Harper's Weekly* noted, "There is not a soirée, or hop, or social gathering that our fair lobbyists do not improve the opportunity to present some private claim in the most attractive light." In fact, "you may believe that a pouting lip and a languishing eye is more potent with members than the most art-ful scheming of the male bipeds." In effect, even in a strictly social setting, women were unafraid to use the opportunity to talk with men for political purposes.[26]

Official engagements like presidential levees and receptions were another place where politicians could socialize in the city. Most Washingtonians felt both a curiosity and an obligation to visit these fashionable parties. As a re-sult, Iowa representative Lincoln Clark explained that "it is at these gather-ings that you will see almost literally all the world." Attendees gathered in various corners of the White House, chatting about books, music, or poli-tics. Such parties could also be the scene of high fashion and not-so-subtle courting. Observant attendees might see men like the notoriously flirtatious Louisiana senator Pierre Soulé leaving the party with pretty belles on their arms. "What fashion, what display," remarked one newcomer to the levees. "What coquetting, what diplomatic speeches, what a squeeze."[27]

If one was less inclined to go to a "jam" at the president's, he could choose instead to visit the White House during the reception evenings, when the crowds were a bit smaller. Receptions usually took place twice a week, de-pending on the presiding president, and included somewhere between 50 and 100 guests an evening. Similarly, politicians could show support for the administration by attending many of the levees and receptions put on by members of the president's cabinet. Parties were extravagant; according to one etiquette book, "It is the custom for each of the members of the Cabi-net, once or twice during the season . . . to give a grand fête, rather cele-brated for the number of guests than any thing else." Receptions were less elaborate but no less important. Each cabinet member (or his wife) selected one day during the week to hold receptions, serving "light refreshments" to various political guests in the city. In January 1850 members of Taylor's cabinet each chose a day, with Secretary of the Treasury William Meredith selecting Mondays.[28]

Members of Congress, in particular, took seriously the responsibility of visiting the president and his cabinet during either the levees or the recep-tions. During James Polk's administration, for example, Texas Democrat Sam Houston was careful to visit the White House on reception nights "often enough to let it be known, how I stand with the administration. Straws show, how wind blows." Maine senator John Fairfield agreed, com-plaining to his wife on the eve of one presidential levee, "I had rather be whipped than go, but circumstances render it unavoidable." Congressmen were similarly responsible for paying their respects to the various cabinet members, even if they were not well liked. Vermonter Jacob Collamer complained in 1856 that "it is my duty to go to the reception of each of the Secretaries [at least] once." Collamer was well versed in this rule of Washington etiquette, having served in Taylor's cabinet as postmaster general.[29]

A critical aspect of these official levees and receptions was the standard that each administration set for social interaction. Houston and Fairfield felt an obligation to attend Polk's receptions in large part because Polk set the expectation that loyal partisans should support the administration politically *and* socially. Zachary Taylor, on the other hand, had not cultivated a strong social relationship with other Washington politicians, and this would become a significant problem during the Thirty-First Congress, when he and Clay battled over provisions for compromise.

Contrary to the Polk administration, Taylor and several members of his cabinet had done little to ingratiate themselves to the Whig leadership in Congress. Taylor himself was a political outsider, never having served as a Washington lawmaker. He seemed unsure of his duties as host at such events. "The truth is I do not see how President Taylor can command the respects of any body," Alpheus Felch joked, "The old General is found *bobbing* about the room in the midst of the visitors scarcely distinguishable from any of the comers and goers." David Outlaw complained, "Old Zach whatever else he may have, is certainly not very remarkable for the [social] graces." Supreme Court Justice Peter V. Daniel agreed, telling his daughter that President Taylor "seems to be without topics for conversation, suggests nothing, & makes the most common place replies. His aid[e] Col Bliss (master of ceremonies) tho' said to be an intelligent man, appears to be very unskilled in the power of entertaining."[30]

A socially weak president was bad enough, but the cabinet did little to help matters for the Taylor administration. Several members of the Whig Party already considered the cabinet to be "wholly impolitic." Many of the elder Whig statesmen, such as Henry Clay and Daniel Webster, were appalled by the cabinet's unwillingness to court them socially. Secretary of War George W. Crawford was perhaps the worst offender. The Georgia Whig refused to hold reception days and made no attempt to socialize with fellow Whig politicians. "He is wholly unfit for his present place," complained a frustrated Alexander Stephens. "He takes no interest in public affairs . . . he has formed no acquaintances with the members of Congress . . . [he] is rigid green and austere in his intercourse." Overall, Crawford was "a cipher except in the discharge of the clinical duties of his office. . . He has none of the elements of a states man about him."[31]

Like Stephens, many of the men who helped put Taylor in office became concerned about the cabinet's inability to court Whig support in social situations. John J. Crittenden, who was a leader in the original movement to elect Taylor but had returned to Kentucky to serve as governor by 1850, heard the news of the ineffective cabinet from a variety of Washington correspondents. Many echoed the tenor of Kentucky representative Humphrey Marshall's remarks on the cabinet's day-to-day interaction: "The Departments have taken no pains whatever to put themselves in connexion with the legislators of the country." With such complaints arriving nearly daily, Crittenden offered a word of advice to his friend, Secretary of State John M. Clayton: "I am some times apprehensive of your want of care & caution in *little* things—It seems to me to be the penalty—the curse of high station, that a man must be always on his *guard*—always prudent, even in respect to the *little things* of his office." Yet Clayton, too, could not escape a bad social reputation in Washington; he was considered obsequious and prone to lying, even earning himself the nickname "Sir John Falstaff." In sum, when it came to social engagements, Taylor's administration was "weak and inefficient," according to one observer. Taylor was "known to be illiterate, & his Cabinet feeble," claimed another.[32]

The Taylor administration's social ineptitude turned out to be a significant problem. Taylor was already on thin ice with many Whig congressmen for his approach to the Mexican Cession, and the president's social demeanor did him no favors in promoting his plan for compromise. The president had also disappointed several of his supporters by failing to remove Democrats and appoint Whigs to important patronage positions around the country. For some, the administration's unwillingness to court Washington politicians at social engagements was the last straw. And as a result of these social failings, fewer politicians felt an obligation to present themselves at the White House and at cabinet events. By the opening of the Thirty-First Congress, relations were cool between the executive branch and the rest of Washington's politicians. One local observer remarked that at Taylor's first levee of the 1850 season "there were not so many people as usually."[33]

Taylor was a bit more successful in courting politicians through another ritual of Washington's social life: White House dinners. During the mid-nineteenth century, presidents hosted such dinners weekly, usually following Friday receptions. Diners included both men and women, and when guests arrived at the White House, they were escorted into gendered anterooms where they could adjust their hair and prepare for dinner. Servants

Figure 10. Presidential reception at the White House, 1858. *Harper's Weekly*, March 13, 1858. Prints and Photographs Division, Library of Congress.

then distributed little slips of paper indicating which lady each man was supposed to take into dinner. This way, couples were mixed up in order to facilitate better conversation. Meals were long—frequently lasting from five o'clock to nine o'clock or later—and elegant, often with courses of fish, meats, and pies. Following the dinner, guests retired to the reception room, where the men could smoke cigars and chat among themselves.[34]

These dinners were not just about social niceties, however. They served a political purpose in two ways. First, an invitation to dine at the White House was an acknowledgment of a congressman's position of influence or an attempt to smooth over some disagreement. For example, in 1858 Texas congressman Guy Bryan became frustrated with President James Buchanan over a patronage appointment in Huntsville. As Bryan understood, the president had invited him to dine in "an effort to please me." After dinner, Bryan explained to his wife, when the party retired to the reception room, the president "took a seat where I was standing & opened a pleasant conversation," alluding to the Huntsville matter and hoping to clear the air between them.[35]

Second, as Bryan's experience suggests, guests at presidential dinners frequently found themselves discussing political issues. Congressmen talked of bills before the House or upcoming elections. President Polk and his vice president, George M. Dallas, discussed patronage during one such dinner in March 1846. Similarly, John C. Calhoun explained his position on the Mexican War to the president after an extravagant dinner that December. Diners also sometimes found themselves on opposing sides of an argument. At one such event in February 1848, President Polk and John Gayle (W-Ala.) exchanged friendly barbs. When the group retired to the reception room, Gayle remarked that he had made an effort to speak in Congress earlier that day. According to one guest, Gayle joked: "Mr President if I had succeeded I rather think I should not have broken bread with you to day'—intimating that he would have abused his excellency so severely, he would not have invited him to dinner, or if he had, he could not have accepted the invitation."[36]

At no time was the presence of politics at presidential dinners more evident than during the early months of the Thirty-First Congress, when lawmakers were burdened with increasing sectional tension. By the end of February, several solutions to the territorial crisis were floating around Washington, including the separate plans by the president and Henry Clay. Both proposals left Southerners cold, and Taylor, in particular, continued to lose the support of Southern Whigs who saw his plan as a threat to slavery. Finally, Tennessee senator John Bell introduced a third plan on March 1, which was more appealing to his brethren from the South. Bell's proposal divided California by the Missouri Compromise line and subdivided Texas into more slave states. Still, with so many suggested solutions and no real consensus, Congress found itself in significant chaos. By the beginning of March, a solution seemed unlikely.[37]

As a result, the topic of the Mexican Cession could scarcely be kept out of conversation, even during a formal White House dinner. On the evening of Bell's proposal, the president invited a group of antislavery men to dine. Guests included Senator William Seward (W-N.Y.), who had become a confidant of several members of the cabinet, as well as Representatives James Doty (D-Wisc.), Horace Mann (W-Mass.), Joseph Root (FS-Ohio), Amos Tuck (FS-N.H.), and James Wilson (W-N.H.). Mann found himself seated very close to the president and, as he explained, the subject quickly turned to the sectional disagreement: "The President entered into conversation about the Union—said it was impossible to destroy it, 'I have taken an oath to support it,' said he, '& do they think I am going to commit perjury[?]'"[38]

In one respect, however, this presidential dinner was an exception to typical Washington gatherings. Taylor invited all Northern antislavery men to his March 1 gathering, but presidential dinners tended to be diverse and cross-sectional. Usually, antislavery men found themselves seated next to slaveholders, cabinet members mingled with Supreme Court justices and congressmen, Whigs and Democrats shared a glass of wine. And, for the most part, all got on pleasantly. For example, at one presidential dinner during the Thirty-First Congress, Representative James G. King (W-N.J.) was seated in between two Democratic senators, Lewis Cass and Sam Houston. The trio "got along very well," and the next day King even made Houston a present of some grapes they had been discussing over dinner.[39]

The president certainly was not the only one to host social dinners in the city. Congressmen with means, cabinet members, diplomats, and other local politicians gave frequent dinner parties. In fact, a politician who was so inclined could become endlessly occupied by social events. As Virginia congressman Muscoe Garnett explained to his mother, dinners and "parties come every night next week, to most of which I have an invitation." William Seward agreed, telling his wife: "There is no time here to think even of home. Society, with interested cares, intrudes and exacts help every hour, night and day." Ohio Whig Benjamin Wade similarly became irritated by the constant socializing: "In about an hour I have got to part for a party where I expect to be untill one or two oclock at night," Wade wrote his wife Caroline. "And what is still worse, I am engaged in the same manner and contemptible business for every night this week." According to the newspapers, even prominent visitors could become swept up in the busy social life of the city, "din[ing] one day with a Foreign Minister, the next with a Southern Senator, the third with a Northern Representative, and the fourth with a metropolitan resident." Particularly during the 1850 session, one congressman explained, "Almost every evening, there is a party given by some of the magnates."[40]

So many dinner parties occurred nightly that a politician could occasionally find himself in the awkward position of mixing up the days of his engagements or showing up at the wrong house. Alexander Stephens made one such blunder, which he described in a short story to his brother, Linton. Having never been invited to Edward Everett's before, the protagonist (Mr. Stephens) asked a hack driver to take him to the Massachusetts orator's house. Upon entering the parlor, he waited some time, watching guests go in and out: "Time rolls on—more company arrives—Mr. Stephens not having seen any thing of Mr. Everett and beginning to think everything looked strange he came subject of a suspicion that all was not right." His story continued, "Whereupon he steps up to [James] Abercrombie [W-Ala.]—and says—'Look here where did you come to—what place is this—?' 'It is [French minister Count de] *Sartiges'* [house], I came to Sartiges to dinner!' replied Abercrombie 'where did you come to?' 'I came to Everett's' said Mr S."[41]

The regular round of dinners could be so exhausting that the carousing took its toll. Tennessee representative Meredith Gentry accidentally missed one of William A. Graham's dinner parties because of late visitors the night before. He explained what happened in an apology letter to Graham: "Feeling somewhat drowsy, I laid myself down upon a Sofa, and fell into a deep sleep, from which I did not awake until 8 o'clock, quite too late to keep my engagement. I was provoked with myself beyond expression." Gentry was quick to apologize and hoped his mistake would not influence his social relationship with Graham. As he wrote, "I fear such an apology can scarcely excuse me for so great a breach of Etiquette; but I throw myself upon your kindness, and pray your pardon."[42]

Not all congressmen came to Washington hoping to engage in an active social life. Some, like Tennessee representative Robert Hatton, chose to keep out of the spotlight. Joining in the extravagances of the city could also be exhausting. As one aide complained, "I am getting fatigued with overwork, feasting, and gayety. The incessant calls on me during the day allow no time for rest, and the numerous feasts and parties absorb my evenings and keep me out late." Soon after congressmen arrived, however, Washington's social butterflies came to know their audience. As Hatton explained, "It is soon found out here who are fond of company and parties, by their acceptance or non-acceptance of invitations. Those that take the start, are kept in the whirl; those, who, at first, keep out, are afterwards overlooked."[43]

In contrast to Robert Hatton, many enjoyed the social experiences of Washington. While work in the House or Senate could be dull, Solomon Haven told a friend that "there are many things for which I like Washington and my relations with people here in & out of public life have been very pleasant." Muscoe Garnett agreed. "I have been a good deal in society," he told his mother, "[and] find my time pleasant in that respect." Some even enjoyed it a little more than they should. Texan Guy Bryan eventually decided to leave Washington because his wife begged him to. It was not that she disliked living in the capital city. Rather, she told him, "I love the life too much; if you should return here for two years more, the life would unfit me to be a good wife and mother."[44]

Furthermore, if a congressman hoped to have influence with his fellow politicians, an active and cross-sectional social life, particularly involving regular dinners, was a must. As one observer explained, "Dining in Washington is a great element in politics. The lobby man dines the Representative; the Representative dines the Senator; the Senator dines the charming widow, and the charming widow dines her coming man." By staying out of society, lawmakers also risked their reputations and ability to influence political events. Even men like Justice Peter V. Daniel, who preferred to remain aloof from social engagements, knew they paid a price. "I have found that those who neglect this [social] duty are generally punished for it, by the prevalence of dissatisfaction" among other politicians, Daniel explained. "I feel myself the great disadvantage of having withdrawn myself so much as I have."[45]

At their first dinner parties, freshmen congressmen quickly discovered the political importance of social engagements. Lincoln Clark was invited to one such gathering at the house of Senator William R. King (D-Ala.). "I was never behind the curtain where great men relaxed before," Clark wrote to his wife that evening. The group, consisting exclusively of men, discussed many of the political topics of the day. "There was a great flow of wit, some disclosure of information, and some smut." Incoming congressmen asked experienced politicians to show them the ropes in Washington social circles. New to Washington in 1852, Congressman Sherrard Clemens asked his Virginia colleague to "adopt me as your protégé during the session."[46]

As they gained experience, lawmakers began to recognize the importance of dining for accomplishing political objects. For example, upon arriving in the capital city in the late 1850s, Massachusetts representative Charles Francis Adams got his bearings and then set out into Washington society. Although shy by nature, Adams knew that his "next labour must be to draw in persons from other states so as to supply some point for the concentration of a social influence here." Over the next few months, Adams would accept invitations to dinners almost nightly.[47]

Overall, like presidential affairs, dinners thrown by diplomats, wives, and politicians themselves had two important features to them. First, they were frequently cross-sectional. Even the most intimate family dinner tended to include men and women from both North and South. Second, they tended to have political relevance. Some dinner parties required attendance for a show of political support. But most important, social affairs included an enormous amount of political discussion. Whether at a fancy diplomatic dinner or a quiet family gathering, politics permeated every aspect of Washington social life.

The city's many diplomats threw some of the most exquisite dinner parties with international delicacies and spirits. Foreign ministers were anxious to wine and dine Washington's fashionable and powerful (typically the same set). When ministers hosted elegant dinner parties for their American friends, politics was a common topic of conversation. Sometimes diplomats invited politicians over for the nineteenth-century equivalent of modern-day business dinners. During the Taylor administration, Secretary of State John Clayton occasionally spent a "quiet dinner" with the English minister, John Crampton, where the two discussed foreign relations. Other parties were designed for pleasure, with politics simply mixed in. At a pleasant gathering at the Russian minister's in 1856, that included among others, Senators Thomas Bayard (D-Del.) Jesse Bright (D-Ind.), Judah Benjamin (D-La.), and Thomas Pratt (W-Md.), conversation quickly turned to the topic of the pending Army Bill.[48]

As the Russian minister's party suggests, many of the dinners that diplomats hosted were cross-sectional. Yet ministers were by no means interested in creating an unpleasant social engagement. They were sensitive to Washington social standards, and were careful to invite men and women who would enjoy each other's company. Ministers typically followed the advice of Washington's etiquette books, which outlined proper invitation guidelines: "Great circumspection is necessary in inviting guests to a dinner; for as they are necessarily introduced to each other, no one should be invited who would not be perfectly agreeable to the others." In other words, diplomats typically tried to stay out of any American political controversies in the capital city, while simultaneously entertaining a broad swath of Washington's social elite.[49]

Still, ministers could also occasionally use social engagements to emphasize their political opinions. While they did not typically get caught up in bills on the floor of Congress, diplomats did have an interest in politics that affected American foreign policy. The ability to talk freely in negotiations and trust the other party could be critical to diplomatic success in Washington. For example, American politicians worked well with Lord Francis Napier, the British minister from 1857 to 1859, but greatly mistrusted his replacement Lord Richard Lyons. Napier was a favorite of Washington socialites, particularly New York senator William Seward, who even organized a farewell ball in the Englishman's honor at Willard's Hotel. By contrast, as one historian explains, "Lyons was an eccentric character." He disliked what he thought of as female emotionalism, which made him hesitant to interact with women, and he was uncomfortable with direct eye contact. Moreover he did not drink or smoke cigars, making him an outlier among many Washington politicians. After such good relations with Napier, President James

Buchanan was skeptical of his new British minister's unwillingness to engage in the overlapping realms of politics and social life in the capital city.[50]

Perhaps the most vivid example of these foreign dignitaries mixing politics and social life is when Lajos Kossuth visited Washington in 1852. Kossuth was a political reformer who led Hungary's struggle for independence from Austria in 1848. Although his revolution failed, Kossuth's fame prompted something akin to hero worship by many American politicians. By the early 1850s, Kossuth had also become something of a political football among Whigs and Democrats. The American public's interest in the Magyar forced both political parties to consider his cause in the presidential election of 1852.[51]

Kossuth's arrival in Washington was marked with much fanfare, particularly among the Democrats. But not all were pleased by his presence, including the city's many diplomats. Led by the Austrian minister, Chevalier J. G. Hülsemann, the foreign corps exercised its social status to protest the Hungarian's presence. When the subscribers of the Washington Assemblies offered to waive Kossuth's entrance fee, this was simply too much for Hülsemann. He sent the Assemblies' managers a three-page letter detailing the ministers' objections, which included a variety of issues but dwelt particularly on the Hungarian's free admission. In the letter, Hülsemann "respectfully suggests that the illustrious Magyar should pay his five dollars, like any other mortal." Otherwise, "he, M. Hülseman [*sic*], and all the gentlemen of the foreign Legations, will feel themselves obliged to withdraw their names from the subscription list!" In fact, all of the ministers refused to attend the first assembly because of Kossuth.[52]

Washington lawmakers, on the other hand, had to weigh the complaints of the foreign ministers with the social statement of visiting with Kossuth. When supportive congressmen held a dinner for the Hungarian on January 7, 1852, politicians had to make a choice: go and alienate the foreign corps, or not go and make a problematic political statement. Lawmakers who chose the former were making a point of showing their support for Kossuth. As one observer asked John Crittenden, "Is Kossuth a candidate for the Presidency?" Certainly the politicians were treating him that way! "All the candidates were there, and acted as if they thought themselves second fiddlers to the *great leader* of the orchestra in that *humbug theatre*."[53]

Most of the Supreme Court justices decided to skip the dinner, but Justice James M. Wayne accepted the invitation. His fellow justice Peter V. Daniel speculated that Wayne went because he "is thought by some to be seeking high political promotion, even the Presidency." Several teetotaler congressmen skipped the dinner as well, since tickets cost $8 for dinner and $3 for wine. But those who declined the invitation to dine with Kossuth were sure to attend a party in the Hungarian's honor the following night. As Lincoln Clark explained to his wife, "I concluded to go, lest I might be *noticed*."[54]

For many lawmakers, one of the most pleasant aspects of diplomatic parties was that they tended to include both women and men. Ministers were anxious for their wives to enter Washington society, and a mixed-gender dinner was a good way to facilitate that process. In fact, because only a fraction of congressmen brought their wives with them to Washington, politicians were pleased to attend almost any dinner party with a gendered mix.

Although wives may have made the dinner more pleasant, the meals were no less political. If the men preferred to keep political talk to a minimum in front of the ladies, they had plenty of opportunities to discuss such issues once the women had left the table. While visiting Washington on legal business in 1854, Edwin M. Stanton explained to his wife the typical pattern at these dinners: "While ladies are present the conversation is usually upon general or interesting topics but after their departure wine and segars, drinking, eating, and political or personal topics neither elevating or refining in their tendency ensue." Not surprisingly, it was hard to keep men from discussing the events of the day when they got together. After all, most of these men spoke openly with their wives about their own political opinions, even if some women were uninterested in such topics. So, at dinner parties, men continued to use little discretion. William Seward described one such dinner at Mr. and Mrs. Hamilton Fish's house in December 1853. The guest list included many senators such as David R. Atchison (D-Mo.), John Bell (W-Tenn.), Robert M. T. Hunter (D-Va.), and Truman Smith (W-Conn.). "A dull time it must have been for Mrs. Fish," Seward thought. "The conversation turned, of course, on senatorial things, election of printers, etc."[55]

The Fish house was not the only place where men and women, North and South, met over dinner. Massachusetts senator William Appleton, for example, counted North Carolina senator George Badger among his closest friends. The two families dined together frequently and even had Christmas together in 1854. Similarly, Peter V. Daniel enjoyed a "pleasant" party at Maryland Whig Reverdy Johnson's house in 1849 that included Howell Cobb (D-Ga.), several foreign ministers, and Daniel Webster. In 1857, Varina Davis, the wife of Jefferson Davis (D-Miss.), found herself seated near two antislavery political giants, William Seward and Solomon Foot (R-V.), at one of Mrs. William Gwin's (D-Calif.) dinners. While Varina had become friendly with Seward by this time, she might have felt some initial trepidation in sitting so near to Foot. Yet she found "they were pleasant." Such cross-sectional, cross-gender dinners were no more unusual in 1850; Varina herself remembered an enjoyable party from January 1850 that included Lewis Cass (D-Mich.), Howell Cobb, Mrs. Stephen Douglas (D-Ill.), Mrs. Robert Walker (D-Miss.), and Robert Winthrop (W-Mass.).[56]

There were exceptions, however. One notable cross-gender Northern dinner group met weekly at Dr. Gamaliel Bailey's house on C Street. Bailey was the editor of the *National Era*, an abolitionist newspaper in Washington, and was a chief organizer in the antislavery cause. Beginning in 1851, Bailey entertained a variety of antislavery men and women on Saturday evenings. Among his regular guests were Kinsley Bingham, Ohio Free-Soiler Salmon Chase, and Horace Mann, as well as any of their female relatives who happened to be in town. Horace Mann's wife, Mary, enjoyed her time at Dr. Bailey's, calling it "the pleasantest place we go to" in Washington. Still, talk at these parties tended to be overwhelmingly political. Mary noted that "guests are invited into the dining room after they have talked politics till they are tired."[57]

Ultimately, at dinner parties across the city, men and women engaged in conversations about the action of Congress, rulings in the Supreme Court, or patronage. While Bailey's parties included section-specific guests, they were no less political. Such gatherings gave antislavery congressmen the opportunity to discuss pressing issues with like-minded men and women specifically from the North.

Yet, because of the paucity of women in the city, dinner parties in Washington frequently included only men. Men's parties tended to be more informal and often included a fair share of crude stories and drunken jibes. A stuffy congressman could even find himself the butt of an unpleasant joke or two. At one raucous party at Louisiana Whig Charles Conrad's house, John Berrien became the unfortunate target of such gags. The dinner party was so large—including more than twenty people from both Northern and Southern states—that men on one side of the table could scarcely hear anything going on among the guests on the other side. Alexander Stephens, who was sitting close to Berrien, explained, "At our end of the table we had some few but no loud laughter while down at the lower end the *roar* at one time became boisterous." His colleague Howell Cobb (D-Ga.) later told him the joke. As Stephens explained to his brother, Senator John Clarke (W-R.I.)

"is a great wag and sometimes a wit," and that evening he was joking about Berrien's "cold precise style of speaking in the Senate." Clarke mused that it "reminded him of an old quaker in his town who one night said to his good lady in bed, 'Sarah my dear I think thee better get up and go to the cubbourd [*sic*] that sits in the corner of the kitchen and get the candle that thee will find on the left hand corner of the third shelf from the bottom and light it and bring it here for I think our son Dicky has beshit himself.'" Poor Berrien had no clue what had been said.[58]

Telling tall tales over drinks at a men-only party was a pleasant pastime for many Washington politicians. But more times than not, political talk came up over the course of a cross-sectional dinner. For example, Massachusetts Free-Soiler Charles Sumner found himself discussing the state of America's political parties at a long banquet hosted by a few members of the Supreme Court. Sumner sat next to Senator Albert Gallatin Brown (D-Miss.), "who thinks slavery divine," and near Supreme Court Justice Benjamin Curtis. Similarly, Daniel Webster and South Carolinian James Petigru discussed disunion movements in the South at an intimate men's dinner in 1851. At a party at Charles Conrad's in 1852, members from all sections found themselves discussing the Mexican indemnity. Washington lawmakers also casually talked politics at cross-sectional dinners during the critical first session of the Thirty-First Congress. In May 1850, William Seward hosted the two Illinois senators, Stephen A. Douglas (D-Ill.) and James Shields (D-Ill.), as well as Jackson Morton (W-Fla.), and the four discussed the prospects for passing Clay's compromise bill.[59]

When it came to mixed-gender parties or dinners for men only, guest lists were overwhelmingly cross-sectional, and sometimes even cross-party. The experience of New York senator Hamilton Fish in Washington in the mid-1850s does much to illustrate this point. Members of the Fish family were among the most prolific entertainers in the city, and Hamilton Fish kept meticulous notes of who was invited to each of his dinner parties. For example, while serving in the Thirty-Second Congress, Hamilton Fish and his wife threw six cross-gender dinner parties, and guests included men and women from both sections at all six. Fish also threw nineteen dinner parties for men only, inviting men from both sections to all but one. During the Thirty-Third Congress, Fish's wife convinced him to host a few more cross-gender parties—nine—and all were cross-sectional. Out of eleven men's parties, all but two were cross-sectional. While not all members entertained as thoroughly as the Fishes (or made as many notations), the New Yorker's guest lists offer an important perspective on Washington society. All the men and women who dined with the Fishes themselves were exposed to counterparts from the other section and sometimes the other political party.[60]

Not only did Fish throw his own parties, but he was invited to many dinners around the city hosted by other socialites. Fish was so popular he would sometimes be invited to four or five dinners in a single night. Take for example, his experience in the Thirty-Second Congress. From December 18, 1851, to February 28, 1853, Fish was invited to seventy-seven different dinners. He went to many of them, including those hosted by William Aiken (D-S.C.), William Appleton (W-Mass.), Charles Conrad (W-La.), Thomas Corwin (W-Ohio), Edward Everett (W-Mass.), President Millard Fillmore (W-N.Y.), William Graham (W-N.C.), William Gwin (D-Calif.), Samuel Hubbard (W-Conn.), John P. Kennedy (W-Md.), William R. King (D-Ala.), William Seward (W-N.Y.) and Alexander H. H. Stuart (W-Va.).[61]

Other entries on Fish's dining list included invitations to parties given by some of Washington's wealthier residents. Many congressmen, including Fish, considered local residents' dinners some of the most pleasant during their time in Washington. Men like Washington banker Elisha Riggs, Benjamin Ogle Tayloe, and particularly William W. Corcoran spared no expense in wining and dining congressmen, cabinet members, and other politicians. Corcoran, for example, "lives in great splendor," Peter V. Daniel explained after his first dinner with the banker. He "serves his guests on silver gold & the finest glass & porcelain." The food at these parties typically was considered "the best I have ever seen any where in Washn," in the words of one member. Virginia Clay remembered, "The hospitality of Mr. Corcoran's home . . . was a synonym for 'good cheer' of the most generous and epicurean sort." Virginia noted that she was not the only one who thought so. One evening she and her husband ran into Georgia Democrat Howell Cobb on the street: "Been to Corcoran's," he told them. "I wish the Treasury were as full as I!" More times than not, politicians often left these men's houses echoing the words of George Dallas, "a more brilliant and exquisite entertainment, in every respect, I never enjoyed."[62]

In part because of the entertainments but also as a result of the company, local Washingtonians' dinners tended to be great fun for lawmakers. Dallas had "enjoyed" the dinner at William Corcoran's with Caleb Cushing (W-Mass.), James M. Mason (D-Va.), and Isaac Holmes (D-S.C.), among others. Edward Everett similarly remarked after spending an evening at Riggs's with Thomas Bayly (D-Va.), Judah Benjamin (W-La.), and Jesse Bright, "friendly & unrestrained intercourse with neighbors & associates contributes materially to soften the asperities of life."[63]

Such dinners also dripped with political discussion. For example, in 1856 Riggs hosted a meal for "eight and twenty gentlemen," all from different sections and including "all the best brag and poker players of the Senate," as well as a variety of House members and diplomats. Over a lavish series of courses, the group discussed foreign policy and other pressing political issues. Similarly, a small party at local newspaperman Charles Eames's house prompted Charles Francis Adams to remark, "Much gossip on politics." William Seward joined Congressman George W. Jones (D-Tenn.) and Senator Archibald Dixon (W-Ky.) for dinner one night and found himself deep in the middle of a conversation about slavery. Seward explained to his wife, the two men tried "to convince me how wrong I am and how I persist in ruining great prospects." Still, he insisted, "they were very kind." Overall, Seward's experience with these Southern congressmen illustrates a critical point about this political discussion: even congressmen who fundamentally disagreed about subjects like slavery or the role of government saw such talk as a normal part of Washington social life.[64]

William Corcoran's social circle deserves particular attention in understanding the relationship between politics and social life during the 1850 session. In addition to owning a reputation as a lavish entertainer, Corcoran had been a financial powerhouse in Washington since Andrew Jackson's presidency. In the late 1830s, he had worked with Elisha Riggs, to form Corcoran & Riggs bank, attracting the business of numerous Washington politicians and subsequently that of the Independent Treasury and other federal agencies. Although Corcoran and Riggs eventually dissolved their partnership (amicably), both men remained important players in the Washington financial scene. Corcoran, in particular, repeatedly loaned money to various congressmen and was among the most active in pressing private claims against the government for a sizable fee of 10 percent.[65]

By 1850, Corcoran also had tremendous sway with federal politicians, and not just because they owed him money. Over the years, he had cultivated relationships with many of the city's most prominent political players. In the early 1830s, he counted Mississippi senator Robert J. Walker as one of his closest confidants, and he also considered Jesse Bright (D-Ind.) and James Buchanan (D-Pa.) good friends. Buchanan, in particular, had become "greatly attached" to Corcoran, and the banker would become a critical ally during the former's presidential term later in the decade.[66]

Although Corcoran himself had grown up a Democrat, he knew that to better his business interests he should eschew (the appearance of) partisanship. Many of his friends were of the "Loco Foco" persuasion, but

Figure 11. William W. Corcoran, 1798–1888, was one of the greatest entertainers in Washington in the mid-nineteenth century. Prints and Photographs Division, Library of Congress.

the banker also included Whigs in his inner circle. Corcoran bought his Lafayette Square mansion from Daniel Webster during the Tyler administration, and the two remained close until Webster's death. Later in the decade, he became friendly with Edward Everett, repeatedly inviting the Massachusetts Whig to stay with him while in Washington. Indeed, Everett told Corcoran, "I feel that you have allowed me to find a second home in your house" in the capital city.[67]

Politicians who spent any time in Washington quickly came to understand Corcoran's influence on political affairs, regardless of which party was in power. Senators, Supreme Court justices, and cabinet members competed to pay first respects to the banker by asking him to dinner or accepting one of his invitations. Others received friendly advice to quickly cultivate a relationship with Corcoran. James Watson Webb, a prominent newspaper publisher and New York politician, offered one such suggestion to William Seward. When Seward left for his first term in the Senate in November 1849, Webb instructed him to get to know the banker, to "cultivate him as a *friend* who will always be faithful to whatever he professes. I have found him so; and I know there is no man in Washington who can so well serve you in a thousand ways as Corcoran."[68]

Thus, by February 1850, when Clay delivered his speech on the compromise resolutions, Corcoran was one of the biggest players in Washington life. His investment in the capital city—financially, politically, and socially—

had few rivals. At no time were these investments more important than in negotiations over the compromise. To begin with, a compromise would bring a resolution to the Texas debt issue, and Corcoran stood to benefit significantly from a favorable settlement. Corcoran had loaned money to a variety of lobbyists and a few politicians in Washington to help purchase Texas bonds; some of his agents included former Indiana Congressman John W. Davis, the influential newspaperman Francis Grund of Pennsylvania, and, most important, James A. Hamilton, a former congressman from South Carolina. Other investors hired Hamilton to serve as a lobbyist for the Texas bondholders, giving him a double interest in forging a deal. In addition, Corcoran understood that his political influence was directly tied to his financial capabilities. Adjusting the Texas bond problem would keep him politically connected.[69]

Finally, Corcoran could only lose socially from continued disagreement over the Mexican Cession. Arguments over the territory had produced considerable talk of disunion, and the banker was even friendly with a few politicians who were interested in attending the Southern Convention in Nashville. Corcoran knew that disunion meant two things for himself socially. First, if the nation divided, he would have to choose sides. This was no easy task since Corcoran counted men from both sections, like James Buchanan and Robert J. Walker, as his closest friends. Corcoran wanted to avoid picking one side or the other so that eventually, during the secession crisis of 1861, he fled to Europe rather than face the choice. Second, disunion likely meant an end to Washington's prominence. In the capital city, Corcoran was a social king, but outside the city he was less well known and had fewer friendly connections.[70]

So, what could Corcoran do to produce compromise? As a longtime resident of Washington and political confidant to many congressmen, Corcoran understood that most of the maneuvering over a sectional compromise would not happen in the halls of the Capitol. He could not have been surprised by an article in the *North American Review*, which complained in July 1850, that "over three hundred distinct essays upon the subject of slavery in the Territories have been spoken in the House over the past six months" but "not one of them have any effect upon the proceedings of the House, except to delay its action."[71]

Corcoran's power lay in combining his financial interests with his political and social skills. Importantly, some of his biggest loans went to men who, as former members and newspaper editors, had access to the floor of the House. Davis, Grund, and Hamilton could be found in the Capitol during critical votes and particularly when the bills finally passed. As Grund wrote to a friend, "I have worked for the Compromise & the Texas Boundary, and continue to use all my energies to bring about peace." Most congressmen were perfectly aware of the role of the Texas bond lobby's operations in Washington. Horace Mann explained to his wife that "should the bill pass, the [Texas] stock will be worth a premium. Now when so many persons [have] interest, will they not influence members? . . . Should the bill eventually pass, there are members who will not escape imputation & suspicion."[72]

Similarly, Corcoran could use his wealth to reward members who promoted a congressional compromise that included adjusting the Texas debt. The most glaring example of such "generosity" included a gift to Daniel Webster. When Clay gave his speech on February 5, several of the Senate's prominent leaders had not yet expressed their opinions, including Webster and South Carolina senator John C. Calhoun. Struggling with illness, Calhoun asked James Mason (D-Va.) to read what would be his last speech to the Senate on March 4. Unsurprisingly, Calhoun railed against the antislavery sentiment of the North and held that section responsible for saving the Union. Finally, on March 7, the last of the great triumvirate responded to Calhoun. Webster delivered a thundering address, calling for moderation and a commitment to the Union. "There are natural causes that would keep and tie us together," he argued in front of packed galleries. Perhaps drawing on personal experience he remarked that "there are social and domestic relations which we could not break, if we would and which we should not, if we could." Corcoran was delighted by the speech, and that evening sent the Massachusetts senator a thank you in the form of $1,000 and a cancellation of Webster's debts, which included more than $5,000. Responded Webster, "If there be a man in the Country who either doubts your liberality, or envies your prosperity, be assured I am not that man."[73]

Other important players in the compromise also cooperated with the banker. Corcoran likely helped to smooth over old animosities between Clay and Thomas Ritchie, the fiery newspaperman from Virginia. For years Ritchie and the Kentucky senator were sworn enemies, after the Virginian continually harped on Clay's supposed "corrupt bargain" with John Quincy Adams to become secretary of state in 1825. But the two worked together during the 1850 compromise negotiations in favor of a settlement. At least one contemporary was convinced that Ritchie had received a bribe to support the compromise. Could this money have come from Ritchie's good friend and neighbor William Corcoran? More concrete evidence exists that

Corcoran worked financially with Stephen A. Douglas (D-Ill.), the man who was ultimately responsible for pushing through the compromise in August. After the compromise passed, Corcoran helped the Illinois senator purchase bonds for the recently developed Illinois Central Railroad, in Douglas's words, "according to the understanding between us."[74]

Yet Corcoran advocated for compromise in another important way: through various social events over the course of the summer. From February to May, he hosted eleven dinner parties at his mansion in Lafayette Square. Guests included numerous senators who could provide critical votes for the omnibus. Nine of these eleven dinners included men only. Corcoran was clearly aware of the possibility for discussion of the compromise since he repeatedly stacked the invitation deck with pro-compromise members, lobbyists, and a few members who might need convincing. For example, on February 16, he hosted a dinner that included among others, Alabama Democrat William R. King, who was a moderate but was not entirely convinced that compromise was possible, along with Thomas Ritchie, Jesse Bright, and Speaker of the House Howell Cobb. James Buchanan, an old friend of King's who had been in town the past few days, also joined the group. On March 9, only two days after Webster's speech, Corcoran invited Francis Granger and James Hamilton to join him at a dinner with Georgia Whigs John Berrien and William Dawson, Lewis Cass (D-Mich.), Thomas Hart Benton (D-Mo.), and Robert M. T. Hunter (D-Va.). With the two lobbyists at the table, one suspects the group could not help but discuss the compromise efforts. And perhaps the two Georgians needed further convincing: Dawson dined at Corcoran's again with John Davis on April 6, while Berrien joined Henry Clay at the table on May 22, exactly two weeks after Clay had presented the so-called "Omnibus" compromise bill to the Senate.[75]

We will never know exactly what was said at Corcoran's table in those summer months. None of his guests left a record of the conversations, and even Corcoran, who kept almost obsessive records of his incoming and outgoing letters, left a suspicious gap in his correspondence during the summer of 1850. Yet, given the overwhelmingly political nature of dinner parties in the 1850s, we can guess at some of the possible conversation. And, importantly, such political discussion happened at diverse, cross-sectional tables. Corcoran did not host a single party in the spring and summer of 1850 that catered to one section only. The men, and sometimes women, who came to Corcoran's knew they would be seated next to guests from other regions of the country.[76]

Unfortunately, Corcoran's hopes for the bill hit a snag in July during negotiations over the Omnibus bill. Clay's Committee of Thirteen reported the bill on May 8 and throughout the next two and a half months, senators made twenty-eight attempts to amend the bill, six of which passed. William Dawson introduced one such amendment on July 30, effectively giving Texas control over New Mexico's civil government east of the Rio Grande. Several senators disliked the amendment, particularly James A. Pearce (W-Md.). So the following day, Pearce moved to strike out the New Mexico section from the Omnibus, with the purpose of replacing it with the unamended version. But Pearce, who supported cross-sectional compromise, did not foresee what came next. After Pearce's move passed, opponents of the compromise took the opportunity to effectively strike out every provision in the bill other than the section organizing Utah as a territory. The Senate then passed the stripped-down bill.[77]

Because of Pearce's amendment mistake, we will never know how a vote on the original omnibus would have broken down. Yet Clay's original bill was unlikely to pass. By combining all of his resolutions into one omnibus, Clay had alienated many of his supporters from the North and South. In order for a real settlement, sharper (and younger) minds in the Senate understood that the individual provisions of the compromise needed to be voted on separately. This is what happened after Clay skulked out of Washington in disgust a few days later. Stephen Douglas, working with a contrite Pearce, managed to reframe the various provisions into individual bills. Importantly, the new settlement called for a $5 million payment to Texas bondholders.

Although Douglas proved a better manager than Clay in Senate negotiations, he needed some help from Washington society in order to push the bill through. Corcoran had already helped to build a base of support for the compromise over the previous few months. But Taylor's death on July 9 would also play a significant role in the compromise negotiations. When Vice President Millard Fillmore (W-N.Y.) took over the reins of the White House in mid-July, he initially supported the omnibus. Once it fell apart, however, he began to play a much bigger part in promoting a new settlement.

Fillmore was a career politician, having served in the House of Representatives in the late 1830s and early 1840s before his election on the Taylor ticket. As vice president, he had spent the previous year as the presiding official of the Senate. According to one newspaperman, Fillmore had managed the Hall in an "impartial manner" that "had given satisfaction to the Senators." Most congressmen were also satisfied with Fillmore's choices to fill the cabinet. New secretary of the interior Alexander H. H. Stuart of Virginia bragged to his wife about "the kind feeling displayed towards me by members of both houses." Many were particularly delighted by the addition of John Crittenden as attorney general and Daniel Webster as secretary of state, considering that both men had served in Congress for many years and each counted several members as close friends.[78]

Yet President Fillmore also had another considerable advantage over President Taylor; he and the members of his cabinet were significantly more adept at the important social niceties of the capital city. As one observer explained of the new president, "He is very much liked, entertains a great deal, & keeps the house in better order than most of his predecessors." Another Washington socialite agreed, remembering that "during Mr. Fillmore's administration society in Washington was especially brilliant and delightful." The president and the cabinet "shone conspicuously in the society of the time." Ultimately, with his political and social savvy, Fillmore was able to improve relations between the two ends of Pennsylvania Avenue, at least for a portion of Whig members.[79]

Together, the social graces of William Corcoran and the Fillmore administration had an important hand in promoting compromise. Take Corcoran's dinner guests lists as one example. Senators passed six different bills that made up the compromise between July 31 and September 16—one each for Utah, Texas (August 9), California (August 13), New Mexico (August 15), the Fugitive Slave Law (August 23), and abolition of the slave trade in the District of Columbia (September 16). Four senators supported all six bills. In addition, seven other senators voted "yea" on five of the six bills but abstained on the sixth. These included Jesse Bright (D-Ind.), Lewis Cass (D-Mich.), Stephen A. Douglas (D-Ill.), Alpheus Felch (D-Mich.), Moses Norris (D-N.H.), James Shields (D-Ill.), and Presley Spruance (W-Del.). Of these men, all but Norris and Spruance spent at least one evening dining at the Corcoran household between February and June. If we discount the vote on the District of Columbia, which did not happen until September 16, Corcoran entertained fifteen of the twenty-five senators who voted for or abstained from at least four of the provisions. One of his guests was John Clarke (W-R.I.), who surprised a number of people by dodging the vote on the Fugitive Slave Law as well as the Texas boundary.[80]

Overall, the possibility for compromise graced the lips of nearly every person who inhabited the city during that long summer. While the political and cross-sectional nature of Washington social life was not the only factor in passing the Compromise of 1850, settlement was likely impossible without it. Furthermore, the role of Washington social life in negotiations over the Compromise of 1850 mirrored the normative experience of federal politicians who came to the city in the mid-nineteenth century.

Over the next few years, congressmen who took part in the compromise negotiations continued to meet in the numerous social spaces of the city. And even after President Fillmore officially signed the compromise bills in the late summer of 1850, proponents found themselves repeatedly defending their decisions against critics, North and South. Finally much of the anger began to die down with the election of New Hampshire Democrat Franklin Pierce as president in 1852 until a new polarizing issue—the "Nebraska Territory"—reopened sectional debates in January 1854.

CHAPTER FOUR

An F Street Mess

Federal Living Arrangements and the
Kansas-Nebraska Act of 1854

Stephen A. Douglas was not the most attractive man in Congress. One newspaper correspondent described him as "very short in stature, but of such physical proportions, aside from this lack, as instantly to attract the attention of a stranger." The Illinois Democrat had "a very large head, connected with broad and powerfully-built shoulders by a short, full neck; a chest sufficiently roomy to contain the lungs of a giant, and a pair of short, dumpy legs." Yet Douglas's leadership and sociability in Washington helped solidify him as the "Little Giant," a nickname used to describe his "marvelous ability" in contrast with his physical stature. After Douglas successfully ushered through the various provisions making up the Compromise of 1850, his political career took off. He quickly became one of the leaders of his party in the Senate and was soon considered by many of his colleagues as the frontrunner for the 1852 presidential nomination.[1]

Although he lost that nomination to Franklin Pierce of New Hampshire, Douglas anticipated that the first session of the Thirty-Third Congress would be both productive and personally satisfying. With an overwhelming Democratic majority in both houses of Congress and a Democratic president in the White House, party members expected to easily implement their legislative agenda.[2] The Illinois senator knew he was destined to play a critical part in that work; in the winter of 1853–54, Douglas remained the powerful chair of the

Senate's Committee on the Territories. The position was advantageous for the Illinois Democrat, who had a substantial financial and political interest in the future of the western territories. Since his first term in the House of Representatives, Douglas had hoped to organize the lands west of Iowa and Missouri in order to facilitate construction of a transcontinental railroad. The northern route would begin in Chicago, Douglas's home base. But most congressmen considered the region's vast lands to be Indian territory.[3]

Douglas got some help in his Nebraska mission from residents on the ground. By the early 1850s, men from neighboring states had begun to call for an organization of the new lands. Spurred by this growing interest, Douglas introduced legislation in March 1853 to create the "Nebraska Territory." Although Congress failed to act before the short session was over, Douglas believed that he could easily push through the legislation when the members reassembled in December.[4]

When federal politicians descended on Washington that fall, many were similarly hopeful. Since the passage of the Compromise of 1850, Congress had generally moved beyond the trying territorial questions of the late 1840s. Relations between North and South had softened and the remaining years of the Fillmore administration were relatively stable, at least on the surface. Some Southerners, like Mississippi Democrat Jefferson Davis, still objected to the compromise and its implementation of territorial sovereignty in New Mexico and Utah. Popular sovereignty, complained Davis, threatened Southern rights by giving settlers—or "squatters" as he called them—the opportunity to make a final decision on slavery. Yet, Davis's complaints largely fell on deaf ears; a majority of the Democratic Party endorsed Douglas's efforts, and the new president considered the territorial conflict settled.[5]

The session commenced on December 5, 1853, and on December 14, Iowa Democrat Augustus Dodge introduced a bill to organize the Nebraska Territory, which strongly resembled Douglas's March effort. The Senate quickly referred Dodge's legislation to the Committee on the Territories, and the chairman spent the next few weeks working with members to reshape and prepare the bill for debate. On Wednesday, January 4, 1854, the Senate Committee finally published its report on the Nebraska Territory, organizing the area between the Canadian border and the Missouri Compromise line. The legislation contained twenty provisions and adopted the language of the Utah and New Mexico laws that when residents applied for statehood, these states "could be admitted with or without slavery as their constitutions prescribed."[6]

By referring to the Utah and New Mexico laws, Douglas had performed a crafty trick. The Illinois Democrat had long been a proponent of popular sovereignty and sought to apply the principles of self-determination in Nebraska as well. In using the language of the Compromise of 1850, Douglas believed he could simultaneously avoid controversy over the Missouri Compromise of 1820, which barred slavery north of the 36°30′ latitude, and which many Northerners considered sacred. By leaving the bill vague, by saying nothing about the status of slavery in Nebraska, Douglas hoped to garner support from both sections of the country.[7]

Still, some Southerners remained unsatisfied. Men like Missouri Democrat David Rice Atchison had long considered the 1820 compromise a threat to slavery and a violation of the Constitution. Atchison wanted to organize Nebraska but simultaneously refused to vote for any bill that did not repeal the Missouri Compromise restriction in the new territory.[8] As president pro tempore of the Senate and acting vice president, Atchison held some political sway. He and others pressured Douglas to clarify his intentions regarding slavery in the bill, and on Tuesday, January 10, the Illinois senator arranged for newspapers to release a twenty-first provision, supposedly omitted by "clerical error." This new section specified, "all questions pertaining to slavery in the Territories, and in the new states to be formed therefrom are to be left to the people residing therein, through their appropriate representatives." In essence, Douglas made disruption of the Missouri Compromise restriction more explicit, though the bill did not specifically repeal the line.[9]

Douglas was again confident that he had sufficiently tackled the slavery issue in Nebraska when he encountered a new setback. On Monday, January 16, less than one week after Douglas released the missing provision, Kentucky Whig Archibald Dixon rose in the Senate and announced that when it was in order, he intended to introduce an amendment directly repealing the Missouri Compromise line. Dixon's announcement would force Southern Democrats to take a more forceful position against the Compromise line, and had the potential to unite Whigs against the measure. Partially because of this potential, New York Whig William Henry Seward later claimed that he was the one who prompted Dixon to make such a move. While the Kentucky senator had political reasons of his own for promoting the repeal of the Missouri line, the two men had probably discussed the issue over dinner a few weeks before.[10]

Whether Seward was ultimately responsible for Dixon's declaration or not, the move irritated Douglas, who had proceeded cautiously on the Missouri Compromise issue. More important, it was embarrassing for Southern Democrats, who understood that the Whig-sponsored amendment threatened to outflank them on the slavery issue at home. Overall, Dixon set off a panicked reaction among Democrats, who spent the next week trying to regain the upper hand.[11]

Key to calming the storm was Representative Philip Phillips. Even before Dixon's announcement, the language in Douglas's bill had concerned the Alabama Democrat. As a moderate, Phillips supported the idea of popular sovereignty; but he believed Douglas's bill did not legally implement that policy. As he explained, the declaration of popular sovereignty in the Nebraska bill was "a *delusion*, 'holding the word of promise to the ear, and breaking it to the hope.'" Because the Missouri Compromise barred slaveholders from coming to the new territory with their slaves, only non-slaveholders would be able to vote to decide if the new constitution would include slavery. As everyone knew, men who hailed from the North were not likely to promote the peculiar institution. Because he was a member of the House of Representatives, however, Phillips would not be able to participate in Senate discussion. So, he decided to talk the matter over with some of his associates in the other chamber.[12]

Phillips lived in a small, red, brick house on F Street, a few doors east of Seventh. Following Dixon's announcement, the Alabama Democrat walked the little more than two blocks down to Atchison's house on F between Ninth and Tenth Streets, behind the Patent Office. Atchison shared his living space with three other powerful Southern Democrats: Virginia senators Robert M. T. Hunter and James M. Mason held the chairmanship of the Finance and Foreign Relations Committees respectively, while Andrew Pickens Butler, of South Carolina, was chair of the Judiciary Committee. The four men had long been messmates in Washington.[13]

After discussing the matter with Phillips, Atchison invited Douglas to be part of the conversation. The three men met in the Missouri Democrat's room and discussed the specifics of Phillips's argument. Douglas apparently left satisfied of its merit; a few days later he asked Phillips to formally write out a repeal of the Missouri Compromise. The Alabama representative did as he was asked but wanted to confer with his colleagues in the F Street Mess before formally submitting the repeal draft. Atchison, Butler, Hunter, and Mason discussed the bill with Phillips at the end of the week and on Saturday, January 21 Douglas got word of their approval.[14]

The next step was to convince the president that repealing the Missouri Compromise line was a good idea for the Democratic Party. Although

Pierce typically refused to meet on the Sabbath, Secretary of War Jefferson Davis convinced the president to talk with Douglas and his colleagues. So, at nine o'clock on Sunday morning, Phillips, Douglas, and another moderate Democrat, Kentucky senator John C. Breckinridge, gathered at the F Street Mess. Douglas, who had spearheaded the meeting with Pierce, arrived in a carriage (also called a "hack") from his private residence on I Street and New Jersey Avenue, near the Capitol, while Breckinridge walked over from his room in Mrs. Murray's boardinghouse. Douglas invited Atchison to join him in his hack ride to the White House, while the other five men followed on foot. During the nearly two-hour meeting with the president, Douglas and the Southern congressmen were able to convince Pierce that a new Nebraska bill repealing the Missouri restriction was essential for keeping the party together. By the end of the conference, Douglas was ready go forward with the repeal, convinced of full support from the president and other key Democrats.[15]

On Monday, January 23, Douglas surprised many of his colleagues, who had not been privy to the preceding week's negotiations, by presenting a substantially altered bill. The revised legislation created two new territories—Kansas and Nebraska—and declared that the Missouri Compromise line was "inoperative and void," having been "superseded by the principles" of the Compromise of 1850. Once Douglas made his announcement, the Pierce administration gave the new bill legs, spreading the word that support for Douglas's Kansas-Nebraska measure would become a test of party orthodoxy.[16]

Although David Atchison and his F Street messmates played a critical role in reshaping the Kansas-Nebraska Act, historians disagree about their motives and those of the other key players, Douglas and Pierce. Douglas's biographer, Robert Johannsen, has long argued that the Little Giant had always intended to repeal the Missouri Compromise; the F Street Mess merely provided the appropriate wording. Others insist that Douglas was forced to change his bill by the F Street junto. Angry over the president's willingness to give Free-Soil Democrats key patronage positions, Atchison and his messmates threatened to withhold Southern votes from the Nebraska bill if Douglas did not include a repeal.[17]

Without new evidence, we are unlikely to know the extent of each man's motives. Yet one thing is certain: whether Douglas had always approved of the repeal or not, the F Street Mess became intimately involved in reshaping the Nebraska bill. Given this role, perhaps the more important question is, How did a group of men who "messed" together in an old house on F Street become so instrumental both in formulating the Kansas-Nebraska bill and in historical accounts of this legislation?

The answer lies in the living arrangements of Washington politicians in the mid-nineteenth century. Scholars have long acknowledged the importance of congressional messes in the lives of antebellum politicians. As William W. Freehling has argued, during this period "boarding houses were congressmen's homes away from home." Yet few have investigated what really transpired in these residences. Such a gap in the historiography is surprising given that Washington living arrangements were the most intimate setting in which politicians could interact.[18] And interact they did. Whether in a boardinghouse or hotel, messmates spent hours together chatting in communal or individual parlors, visiting each other's rooms, and sharing the dinner table. While not all of the discussion was political, congressmen who roomed in the same house got to know each other on both a personal and professional level. Many made or strengthened long-lasting friendships in their houses. Like the members of the F Street Mess, messmates frequently returned to the same living space year after year, hoping to meet old friends and associates. For those members who could afford to live in private housing, neighborhoods such as the fashionable areas of Lafayette Square or Union Row were similarly important. Politicians who lived in these small communities made frequent visits to each other's houses for dinners (both formal and informal), worked together on neighborhood landscaping and water projects, and formed important friendships and alliances.

While it serves as an example of messmate friendships, in one way the F Street Mess was different from most congressional housing arrangements in the mid-nineteenth century: it was composed of men who hailed exclusively from the South. Although there were some other sectional boardinghouses, most congressmen who chose to live in a house or hotel with other members became messmates with at least one man from another section of the country. While the interaction between Northerners and Southerners who lived in private housing is more difficult to measure, there were no exclusively sectional neighborhoods in Washington; many Southerners lived right next door to men from the North.

Ultimately, the experience of the men who messed together in that F Street house is part of a larger story of Washington living arrangements in the mid-nineteenth century and their impact on political behavior. While the F Street Mess was atypical in its sectional makeup, the political discussion that flowed among its members was not. In order to fully understand how Atchison, Butler, Hunter, and Mason could have such an important influence on congressional negotiation, we must have a better understanding of the way that Washington politicians interacted with one another in the houses and hotels of the capital city.

■ In December 1853, the congressional reporter took down the housing information of 292 federal politicians, including congressmen, Supreme Court justices, and cabinet members. Although a few lawmakers had not yet reached Washington for the long session, the reporter submitted his notes to J. and G. S. Gideon, Printers, who put together a *Congressional Directory* available to both politicians and the public. The *Directory* helped the men and women of Washington find the private residences, boardinghouses, or hotels of the various political figures just in time for paying respects during the New Year's Day festivities. For example, many were sure to visit re-elected Speaker of the House Linn Boyd (D-Ky.) at the United States Hotel on Pennsylvania Avenue or elder statesman Thomas Hart Benton (D-Mo.), who lived in a private house on C Street between 3rd and 4½.[19]

Like their forbearers, a large number of congressmen and other federal politicians who arrived in Washington that December had chosen to share a house or a hotel with one or more of their colleagues. Only 68 of the 292 members recorded by the congressional reporter lived alone or messed at a boardinghouse without other politicians. The remaining 224 members shared their living space. As table 2 demonstrates, a majority of these politicians—66 percent—lived in cross-sectional housing:

The 148 congressmen and other politicians who chose to live in cross-sectional houses in 1854 were not unique. Throughout the 1840s and 1850s, Washington lawmakers overwhelmingly chose to live in such housing. In 1847, for example, 62 percent of congressmen who chose to live in a boardinghouse or hotel with other members became messmates with a man from another section of the country. By 1855, that number was still 67 percent. Even in 1861, after South Carolina had seceded and the country faced the prospect of increased divisiveness, 65 percent of congressmen who lived with other members chose cross-sectional housing.[20]

Moreover, not all of the city's sectional housing occurred by choice. While some congressmen—like those in the F Street Mess—did choose their residence on the basis of sectional or regional composition, others ended up in a sectional house by accident. For example, Simon Cameron (D-Pa.) had intended to live with North Carolina Whigs Willie P. Mangum and David Outlaw in 1848 and even told the congressional reporter that he was taking residence there but eventually was unable to join the house. Outlaw was

Table 2. Housing Choices for Members of the Thirty-Third Congress in the First Session

	Cross-Sectional Housing	Sectional Housing
Northerners	88	49
Southerners	60	27
Total	148	76

Source: Boardinghouse, hotel, and private residence information can be found in the *Congressional Directory for 1854*.

especially disappointed. In addition to preferring a larger mess, he enjoyed living with members from different states. He explained to his wife that he did not mind if his messmates were "abolitionists." In fact, "all the Northern, North Western and Eastern people of all political parties are opposed to slavery. But I do not believe that a large majority of them desire to interfere with it, as it exists in the Southern States." In regard to "opposition to slavery in the abstract," he continued, "we have a great many abolitionists at home." Many of Outlaw's colleagues must have agreed as they continued to live in cross-sectional houses and hotels throughout the 1850s.[21]

The politicians who arrived in Washington in December 1853 had their choice of three types of residences—boardinghouses, hotels, and private residences—but boardinghouses were overwhelmingly the living arrangement of choice for Washington politicians in the 1840s and 1850s. From 1846 to 1849 between 70 and 80 percent of members elected to board in a house rather than stay in a hotel. These numbers would dip some by the 1850s, in part because the number of hotels in Washington had grown, giving members a greater opportunity to bargain for a more suitable room price. Yet politicians continued to live in boardinghouses in great numbers. Such was the case in the first session of the Thirty-Third Congress, when 85 politicians lived in one of the city's hotels and 26 chose to rent or buy a private house, in comparison with 181 men who called a boardinghouse their temporary home.[22]

One reason why boardinghouses were popular was their proximity to the workplace. For those who preferred a shorter walk, houses were primarily situated on Capitol Hill or near the various departments where politicians might have business. By contrast, most of the hotels were located on Pennsylvania Avenue close to the White House and nearly a mile from the halls of Congress. Boardinghouses lined the streets surrounding the Capitol building, including the popular "Carroll Row" on the east side of 1st

Street between A and East Capitol (where the Library of Congress's Jefferson Building now stands), where Illinois Congressman Abraham Lincoln boarded while in Washington. Business-savvy locals who lived near the halls of Congress could make good money by renting their extra rooms to various congressmen. For example, Wilson Fairfax, a draftsman at the U.S. Coast Survey, and his wife rented their two extra rooms on A Street to Willard P. Hall (D-Mo.) and Charles Murphey (Unionist-Ga.) in 1851.[23]

Another critical reason for living in a boardinghouse rather than a hotel was cost. Members of Congress did not receive stipends for housing arrangements, and boarding was generally less expensive than the alternative. In 1845 vice president–elect George Mifflin Dallas (D-Pa.) paid eighty-three dollars to stay at a hotel for one week, but spent only forty dollars per month at Mrs. Levi Williams's house in the same neighborhood in 1848. Similarly, David Outlaw paid fourteen dollars per week for a single room at Mrs. Carter's boardinghouse in 1847 and, much to his chagrin, forty dollars per week at Gadsby's Hotel the following year. Outlaw traveled alone to Washington, but others who brought their wives needed at least two rooms—including a parlor or a room for servants. Although women were often happier amid the social gaieties of the hotels, cost could be prohibitive. Two rooms and board at Mr. Chipman's boardinghouse on Pennsylvania Avenue and 6th Street cost thirty-four dollars per week in 1859, while Willard's Hotel charged fifty-five to sixty dollars. In terms of hotel living "the prices here are *awful*," Representative Edwin Morgan (W-N.Y.) wrote his brothers. Georgia representative Robert Toombs told his wife, the hotels simply charged "exorbitant rates."[24]

Unfortunately, with cheap rent also came cheap amenities. Boardinghouse apartments tended to be badly furnished and occasionally odorous. The rooms were primarily a place for members to "store their documents and demijohns"; they were not fancy suites suitable for entertaining. As Dallas explained, his lodgings at Mr. Henry Riell's were "comfortable" but far from being "splendid" or "magnificent." The rooms had a "true republican" character to them.[25]

Meals at boardinghouses tended to be sparse or repetitive. At a pricier house, members might be treated to meats, berries, and pies, but most had fewer options. One Ohio congressman was served mackerel every morning during his time in Washington. Upon leaving his landlady at the end of the season, he reportedly marched over to the breakfast table, picked up a mackerel by the tail and jokingly declared, "Good-bye old fellow; I'm sorry to leave you, you've been such a good friend to me; for almost a year we've met daily, and though you used to stink occasionally, you behaved pretty well on average." Sometimes mackerel was better than the alternative, however. Virginia congressman Muscoe Garnett heard from fellow members in 1857 that "the boardinghouses are so bad" that the "ladies say that they can get nothing to eat & have been for some days going to restaurants to breakfast & dinner."[26]

In spite of these deficiencies, many congressmen chose to live in boardinghouses for reasons other than cost or proximity. As Clement Clay (D-Ala.) remarked, "there is much more real comfort, quiet & privacy in a smaller boardinghouse" where only a few members were present. Within this quiet and private living arrangement, boardinghouses offered the opportunity for messmates to make close friendships. Outlaw explained such reasoning to his wife. "By being in a mess," he told her, "you form a more familiar acquaintance with those composing it." Messmates spent considerable time together. They sat together at meals, the most significant being dinner, which typically took place between three and six o'clock. They congregated in each other's rooms and in the parlor after Congress had adjourned for the day, playing piano or whist, a popular card game. They even traveled together to the Capitol, the Library of Congress, and White House balls and to make social calls.[27]

According to their correspondence, messmates tended to enjoy each other's company. As Michigan Democrat Kinsley Bingham's wife, Mary, explained, "You would think where there are so many together that some of them [her messmates] might not be very agreeable but it is not so, we are all very friendly none of them put on airs and we feel quite at our ease." Massachusetts Whig Horace Mann similarly enjoyed the company of the other boarders at Mr. Charles Gordon's on Capitol Hill. Although he was an antislavery man himself, Mann particularly liked Delaware senator John Clayton, whom he called "the most interesting man you ever saw—Full of sense, information & knowledge of the world; & as playful as a boy . . . round in honorable feeling & moral principle." Years later, when the two no longer messed together, Mann still looked upon Clayton as a friend. Besides, if a politician did not like his messmates, it was easy enough to move somewhere else. Boarders did not make contracts with their landlords and felt free to leave if they were unsatisfied with the amenities or the company. As Outlaw explained, "a man can change his boardinghouse as often as he pleases, and I shall unquestionably exercise this high prerogative if things do not go to suit me."[28]

The relationships that politicians made while rooming together in Washington for one session were by no means superficial. Congressmen repeatedly returned to their lodgings from previous sessions having enjoyed the company of their former messmates. Georgian Alexander Stephens stayed at Mrs. Carter's boardinghouse on Capitol Hill for at least four sessions with many of the same members, including Supreme Court Justice John McLean of Ohio and Rhode Island representative Henry Cranston. Similarly, future president James Buchanan of Pennsylvania and Alabama senator William R. King roomed together in Washington for several years.[29]

During congressional recesses, some members coordinated to be sure they took rooms at the same mess the following session. Georgian Thomas Butler King made fast friends with fellow Whig Robert Schenck of Ohio at Mr. Stettinius's boardinghouse on Louisiana and Sixth during the first session of the Twenty-Ninth Congress. The two corresponded about living together again the following session. Schenck wrote to King, "I will hope to meet you [in Washington], my dear fellow, returned to our old quarters, with health entirely reestablished, as well as in bounding spirits." Indiana Whig Caleb Blood Smith and North Carolina Whig Robert Treat Paine, a future congressman who came to Washington as a member of the Mexican Claims Commission, also arranged to board their families together during the Thirtieth Congress. As Paine told Smith in a letter: "Nothing will give us greater satisfaction than to live under the same roof with you & I hope that you will when you engage rooms for yourself engage another close by for me." Simon Cameron (D-Pa.) and Edward Hannegan (D-Ind.) reserved a room at Boyd's for their good friend Willie P. Mangum (W-N.C.) in January 1849, so that it would be vacant when the latter finally arrived in Washington. Similarly John M. Berrien (W-Ga.) promised to include Abraham Schermerhorn (W-N.Y.) in any boardinghouse arrangement he procured during the summer of 1850.[30]

Messmates could even become like family. Upon learning that his messmate, Senator Alexander Barrow (W-La.), had died, William Archer (W-Va.) was beside himself; as a friend remarked, Barrow "was a great favourite of the Archers." Georgia Whig Alexander Stephens had roomed with Supreme Court Justice Joseph Story of Massachusetts during the winter of 1844–45 at Mrs. Carter's and was devastated when the judge died over the summer. During the first session of the Twenty-Eighth Congress, Stephens and Story had become friendly, and Stephens was "much pleased with him." When the Georgia congressman returned to his house in November 1845, he told his brother that "it was all I could do to refrain from tears."[31]

Earlier in his congressional career Stephen Douglas had actually joined one of his messmates' families. While serving in the Twenty-Ninth Congress, Douglas and North Carolinian David Settle Reid became close while messing at Mrs. Wimsatt's. Douglas occasionally made trips to North Carolina with his friend, particularly after Reid introduced him to his young cousin, Martha Martin. With Reid's blessing, Douglas and Martha became romantically involved, and the two were married on April 7, 1847. Unfortunately for Douglas, young Martha died while giving birth to their third child in January 1853. Reid, who was then serving as governor of North Carolina, wrote Douglas to console him for his "indescribable" pain and "irreparable" loss.[32]

In addition to creating friendships, boardinghouse arrangements allowed politicians to discuss each other's views on a variety of topics from slavery to religion. Perhaps because work was never far from their minds, boardinghouse members frequently discussed political issues, just as they did at dinner parties and other social occasions. Conversations were frequently casual. Sarah B. Seddon, the wife of Virginia Democrat James A. Seddon, talked politics with two of her messmates—a clerk of the House and Josiah Anderson (W-Tenn.)—over the morning newspapers. Alexander Stephens walked in on a pleasant conversation among messmates about the Congress of Mexico at Mrs. Selden's boardinghouse in 1848. During negotiations over the Compromise of 1850, Kentucky congressman Linn Boyd often discussed the progress of Clay's bill with his messmate, Senator Henry S. Foote (D-Miss.). As Massachusetts Whig Robert Winthrop remembered, "Of mess dinners there was a continual interchange. Not confined to one particular party, they were as a rule very informal."[33]

Other conversations could become more serious. While Abraham Lincoln was serving in Congress, the Wilmot Proviso was a frequent topic of conversation at Ann Sprigg's boardinghouse on Carroll Row. Lincoln lived with men who held a variety of views on slavery and the proviso, including fiery Free-Soiler Joshua Giddings of Ohio and Mississippi congressman Patrick Tompkins. According to a fellow boarder, if a conversation about slavery or the proviso became too heated, Lincoln "would interrupt it by interposing some anecdote, thus diverting it into a hearty and general laugh, and so completely disarrange the tenor of the discussion that the parties engaged would either separate in good humor or continue the conversation free from discord."[34]

The prevalence of political discussion among messmates could also create some surprising coalitions. Another diner at the Sprigg mess during Lincoln's time was proslavery Missouri journalist and entrepreneur, Duff Green, who owned a house down the street. Although he had been a longtime friend and confidant of South Carolinian John C. Calhoun, Green maintained a good relationship with his fellow diners at Mrs. Sprigg's, regardless of their political viewpoints. In January 1848, he even intervened when local proslavery activists arranged to sell Henry Wilson, a black waiter who worked at Mrs. Sprigg's, to Williams's Slave Pen. Wilson was a favorite of Giddings, who was known to have free blacks in his room on occasion. Angry and in search of a solution, Giddings turned to Green, who helped arrange for Wilson's release on the condition of full payment to his original owner. Although one historian has argued that bad press for the proslavery cause motivated Green, the Missourian's close relationship with the Sprigg mess and the cross-sectional sociability of Washington likely influenced his behavior.[35]

While men who messed together often talked politics, those who lived alone could feel temporarily excluded. When Stephens arrived at Mr. Crutchett's in November 1855, no other members had yet joined his house. As a result, Stephens "hear[d] no news in the political world." Horace Mann found the same difficulties upon moving to an empty boardinghouse with his family. Although Mary Mann thought it was nice to be in a place with "no smoking, no drinking, no carousing," she admitted that it "cuts my husband off from society a great deal." Mann himself could occasionally be frustrated by the situation, telling a friend, "I see less of men, in consequence of this mode of living, than I should be glad to."[36]

Overall, while Southern members of the F Street Mess were discussing the possibility of repealing the Missouri Compromise line, men who lived in cross-sectional boardinghouses across the city were conducting similar conversations with messmates. And boardinghouses were not the only place where such political conversation was common. Men who lived in one of the city's hotels similarly found themselves discussing political issues with cross-sectional messmates as well.

Hotels differed from boardinghouses primarily in regard to size and amenities. Washington's hotels held anywhere from 100 to 500 people, and up to 50 members could find themselves in the dining quarters of Brown's Hotel or Willard's in the 1850s. Hotels were also large enough to accommodate the throngs of visitors to the capital, whether in town for lobbying or sightseeing. As result, the feeling of a hotel was usually less intimate than a boardinghouse, and members often found that they had little time to themselves. While staying at Brown's Hotel in 1847, Texas senator Sam Houston complained to his wife that "my room is crowded whenever I am in it. Indeed, I have so much company, from all parts of the U[nited] States, that

I am compelled to sit up every night." Kentucky Whig Henry Clay had a similar experience when stopping at the U.S. Hotel in 1848 and eventually decided to stay at a friend's private house rather than face the throngs of visitors.[37]

Although Clay and Houston preferred a quieter setting, social interaction was a positive feature for many members looking to live a more public lifestyle. Unlike boardinghouses, hotels provided ballrooms and barrooms in which members and other city residents could gather. As Texas congressman Guy M. Bryan explained to his wife, "There is one advantage in being at a Hotel you are more per force & per inclination in company."[38]

Partially because of this social atmosphere, the few congressmen who brought their wives to Washington were more likely to choose residence in a hotel for the session. Hotels lined the sidewalks of Pennsylvania Avenue, giving women easy access to this fashionable promenade, including the neighborhood's many shops and markets. Women like Henrietta Reid, wife of David S. Reid, who planned to visit Washington for a week or two during the session, often pleaded with their husbands to stay at a hotel rather than a boardinghouse. Others who spent the season in Washington, such as Virginia Clay, wife of Senator Clement Clay (D-Ala.), took joy in creating a homey atmosphere in the hotels and maintaining close social relations among their messmates. At Brown's, Mrs. Clay spent considerable time with the families of James L. Orr (D-S.C.), Miles Taylor (D-La.), and George Pugh (D-Ohio). "It was distinguished company," Virginia remembered.[39]

Hotels were also better equipped to provide more pleasant accommodations and amenities for their boarders. Many of them, like the National and the Willard, were refurbished in the late 1840s and early 1850s and contained large, airy rooms. By 1854, a politician who was willing to pay for nicer accommodations could acquire a parlor facing the avenue with a bedroom in the back. Even the men who chose to live in boardinghouses understood that members "live better at the hotels, and really in this place of abominations one hardly knows when he is at a respectable boarding house." In addition to providing pleasant rooms and meals, hotel managers often went the extra mile to please their customers. During a long day of work, a hotel like Willard's might send a meal up to the Capitol for its residents, while boardinghouse men went hungry.[40]

Some hotels were popular for their ability to provide certain Southerners with a place to temporarily house their slaves in the city. For example, the owner of the St. Charles Hotel, on Third Street and Pennsylvania Avenue, kept "roomy underground cells" equipped with heavy iron doors. "In case of escape," the proprietor advertised, "full value of the negro will be paid by the proprietor of the Hotel." Such assurances were important, as the presence of a strong group of abolitionists in Washington meant that slaves were sometimes induced to escape. For example, in July 1850 slaves belonging to Georgia Whigs Robert Toombs and Alexander Stephens conspired with white antislavery activists to run away from the city. Although the escaped men were eventually captured and brought back to Washington, Toombs and Stephens lived in boardinghouses and therefore had no assurance of recovering their slaves' financial value.[41]

Although the St. Charles was known for its slave quarters, it was by no means a "Southern" hotel. In 1854, amid the controversy of the Kansas-Nebraska Act, the St. Charles housed five Northern congressmen and two Southern representatives. Similarly, the hotel provided rooms for Tennessee Democrat Andrew Johnson in 1859, but also antislavery senator Hannibal Hamlin of Maine and Michigan representative Charles E. Stuart. In fact, no matter which hotel a member chose for his residence, he was sure to find it home to men from both sections. Between 1845 and 1860, not a single hotel in the city was reserved exclusively for Northerners or Southerners. Because of the fluid nature of hotel residency, a proprietor might occasionally end up with clients exclusively from the North for a session or part of it. But, the following year, a cross-sectional clientele was restored.[42]

Just as in boardinghouses, these cross-sectional hotel residents tended to enjoy each other's company. Federal politicians repeatedly tried to keep their hotel messes together from session to session. Henry Clay was known for having a "coterie" of friends at his hotel, including "Jack" Taylor of Ohio and John Minor Botts of Virginia. The practice continued into the antebellum era. When New York Whig Lorenzo Burrows arrived in Washington in December 1850, he and his wife settled into their old rooms. "We are at the National," Burrows' wife, Lizzie, explained to her children, "but are undecided whether we shall remain. Many of your Pa's friends are very anxious that he should." Michigan senator Alpheus Felch reported that the boarders at the St. Charles enjoyed the hotel so much that they returned almost every session. The group had the reputation of being so pleasant that the rooms always filled up and the landlords constantly had to turn away congressmen who were eager to join the mess.[43]

For some, a hotel mess came to symbolize a circle of friends, particularly among the women of the group. Virginia Clay, who lived for many years at Brown's Hotel with the same families, described Stephen Douglas's second wife, Addie Cutts, as a "firm friend" even though she "never, strictly speaking, [was] a member of our 'mess.'" Others simply enjoyed the company of men from other sections of the country. Newly appointed Supreme Court Justice Benjamin R. Curtis of Massachusetts arrived in Washington in December 1851 and took a room in Brown's Hotel where he was delighted to find "some pleasant people in the house." Iowa representative Samuel Curtis enjoyed his hotel so much that he recommended "any of our friends coming this way will find it every way agreeable to stop here."[44]

Because of the number of properties in the city, politicians were also able to select a hotel that contained only friendly residents. For example, Georgia senator John M. Berrien took a room in Brown's Hotel in 1851 in order to "avoid some associates not altogether agreeable to me." Rivals from the same state also tended to choose different hotels. In 1849 Berrien stayed at the Exchange Hotel, while his adversary, Robert Toombs, took up residence at the National. Newspaper editors and other politicos also followed Berrien's and Toombs's example. In December 1855, Albany editor Thurlow Weed chose Willard's Hotel while visiting the city, while rival editor (and former New York congressman) Horace Greeley stayed at the National.[45]

Just as they did in boardinghouses, federal politicians felt comfortable discussing politics and other personal issues with their fellow messmates in hotels, particularly at the dinner table. Several of Alpheus Felch's colleagues at the St. Charles Hotel discussed the possibilities for Pierce's cabinet in the fall of 1852, even suggesting Felch himself as a candidate. Ohio Free-Soiler Salmon Chase frequently discussed political topics at mealtime at the National Hotel. Every night during dinner, he sat at a table with Berrien, Henry Clay (W-Ky.), Charles Conrad (W-La.), John P. Hale (FS-N.H.), and Jonas Phoenix (W-N.Y.). Chase's place at the table was right next to Berrien, and although, he told his wife, "you may imagine that I could easily prefer another place . . . being there I keep on never minding the Judge's peculiarities, and endeavor to bring into action only his more estimable qualities." Overall, a friend of New York Democrat William L. Marcy noted, men and women "freely express themselves to each other at our public Hotels."[46]

Conversations about political topics whirled through the hotels in 1854. Willard's Hotel was the site of many political discussions over the dinner table among prominent residents like Senators George E. Badger (W-N.C.), Lewis Cass (D-Mich.), and Sam Houston (D-Tex.), as well as Congressmen Preston Brooks (D-S.C.), Solomon Haven (W-N.Y.), and newcomer William Marcy Tweed (D-N.Y.). For example, Cass and Haven, who had long been messmates at Willard's, chatted about the possibility the Nebraska bill would pass, as well as Cass's perspective on the Clayton-Bulwer Treaty, an increasingly problematic 1850 agreement between the United States and England that harmonized their interests in Central America.[47]

Several prominent Democrats who messed at Brown's Hotel speculated about their party's cohesiveness on Kansas and the Pierce administration's course in patronage among other issues. Connecticut congressman Colin M. Ingersoll discussed such topics with other Democratic residents like Representatives George Houston of Alabama, John Letcher of Virginia, and William A. Richardson of Illinois. Ingersoll reported, "The general feeling among the members seems to me to be this: They have come on here determined to give the Adm[inistration] an honest support so long as it is true to democratic measures." Overall, in 1854, hotel residents felt as comfortable as their colleagues in the F Street Mess when it came to conversing about important political subjects.[48]

While they might miss out on the hustle and bustle of the hotel experience, men with means could afford to procure a third type of Washington living arrangement: a private house. Although their circumstances differed from their friends in hotels and boardinghouses, congressmen who chose to live in private residences still developed key relationships and engaged in political discussion on account of their living arrangements. Rather than isolating politicians from each other, the lifestyle of private living could provide numerous opportunities for congressmen to make friends with their neighbors. These men often congregated at each other's houses for dinner or a game of cards. During the spring months, William Seward told his wife, residents of his F Street neighborhood might be found sitting on the stoops of their houses smoking cigars and chatting with one another.[49]

Only those with cabinet or diplomatic appointments or private wealth could afford such lavish living conditions in the city. Private homes tended to be large and expensive. In 1850 Secretary of the Navy William Graham (W-N.C.) bought a house on H Street that cost him $8,000 and contained about 3,000 square feet. New York senator Hamilton Fish considered obtaining a house in the West End for $10,000 before eventually settling in the Lafayette Square neighborhood.[50] Others preferred to commission new homes from local builders. For example, in 1857 Vice President John Breckinridge and Minnesota Democrat Henry M. Rice employed locals to construct houses next to each other on First Street, near New Jersey Avenue, each forty-eight feet wide by fifty feet deep.

If they expected to spend only a short while in Washington, politicians could save a little cash by renting rather than purchasing a family home. Prices varied: Pennsylvania Democrat J. Glancy Jones found a residence that cost $3,000 per annum in 1857, while California senator William Gwin paid $1,500 that year. Supreme Court Justice James M. Wayne rented a small cottage in the Lafayette Square neighborhood for only $750 in 1852; a similarly small house on I and Twentieth Streets cost $800 in 1857.[51] Most houses, whether for purchase or for rent, did not include furnishings. This was no small issue, as Alexander H. H. Stuart admitted to his wife. Stuart sheepishly told her: "We shall have to incur a good deal of expense" for furniture. Several Washington houses included up to six rooms, and needed furnishings for bedrooms, parlors, and dining rooms. Occasionally, those who lived in private houses paid a little bit extra to rent furnishings or brought their finer belongings from home. But furnished or not, the cost was substantial.[52]

Another large expense for private living was the staff required. Homeowners or renters had to pay for employees like a cook and a coachman, which would have been supplied by a hotel or boardinghouse. Frequently this included renting slaves from owners in the District of Columbia. Certain Washington slaves and servants developed a reputation for sophisticated attention to the city's elite. As one clerk in the Navy Department told his boss, "There are a number of experienced male and female servants here, of undoubted character, who eagerly seek after places in the families of the Secretaries, taking great pride in the position." Yet, such high-class service could be expensive. William Graham paid a monthly rate of eight dollars for a cook, as well as twelve dollars for a manservant belonging to Robert E. Lee. Another Washington homeowner got a better deal, hiring a slave girl for five dollars per month to keep her rooms, set the table, and help her dress.[53]

Others thought they could save a little money by bringing slaves or servants from home. The wife of Virginia Democrat Roger A. Pryor remembered filling their house on New Jersey Avenue with "good Virginia servants." Yet Washington's city laws could sometimes make this action tricky. Supreme Court chief justice Roger Taney brought a free black servant with him from Maryland, only to see him arrested after a few days in the city. According to District laws, free blacks were prohibited from settling in Washington with the intent to seek employment. Only after some considerable discussion with and help from a prominent lawyer, James Carlisle, was Taney permitted to keep his servant with him in Washington.[54]

Once federal politicians were willing to pay all the expenses associated with private living, they could select a house in one of the many neighborhoods of Washington. Some chose a residence on Capitol Hill or "Gay

Street" in Georgetown, which was often more affordable. Politicians who wanted to immerse themselves in Washington's fashionable society, however, tended to choose between two of the most popular neighborhoods: Union Row (Chinatown in modern-day Washington, D.C.) and Lafayette Square, in front of the White House.

The Union Row neighborhood stretched from Sixth to Ninth Streets, east to west, and from E to G Streets, north to south, effectively a three- by two-block square. Congressmen of all political backgrounds lived on Union Row, including Representative Robert Schenck (W-Ohio) and Senators Robert Toombs (D-Ga.) and David Yulee (D-Fla.). During the 1854 session, the area was home to several political leaders in Congress, including key players in the framing of the Kansas-Nebraska Act. The occupants of three red-brick houses that lined the north side of F Street between Sixth and Seventh Streets included Philip Phillips and New York antislavery leader William H. Seward, along with Supreme Court Justice Peter V. Daniel of Virginia. Senator Charles Faulkner (D-Va.) lived practically next door, on Sixth between E and F. Just three blocks down, Representative Thomas Cumming (D-N.Y.) and Senator Jackson Morton (W-Fla.) shared a house on the south side of E Street, between Eighth and Ninth. And Cumming and Morton were themselves only a block and a half from the now-famous F Street Mess.[55]

A second popular housing spot, the Lafayette Square neighborhood, stretched from Fourteenth to Eighteenth Street, east to west, and Pennsylvania Avenue up to H street south to north, with the center in the middle of President's Square, facing the White House. The neighborhood was home to many of the most prominent politicians who repeatedly graced the halls of Congress or the departments. Residents over the years included the likes of Lewis Cass (D-Mich.), Thomas Ewing (W-Ohio), William L. Marcy (D-N.Y.), James L. Orr (D-S.C.), John Slidell (D-La.), and Daniel Webster (W-Mass.).[56]

While politicians typically stayed in the square for a session or two, there were also more permanent residents in the neighborhood. Dolley Madison remained in Washington long after her husband, former president James Madison, passed away. She entertained in a lavish house on the corner of H Street and Madison Place (see House 29 in figure 12). The wealthy family of Benjamin Ogle Tayloe lived only a few doors down on Madison Place (see House 32), in an odd-shaped building often referred to as the "Octagon." William W. Corcoran's mansion graced a corner at the top of the Square where H Street, Connecticut, and Jackson Place intersected (see House 11).

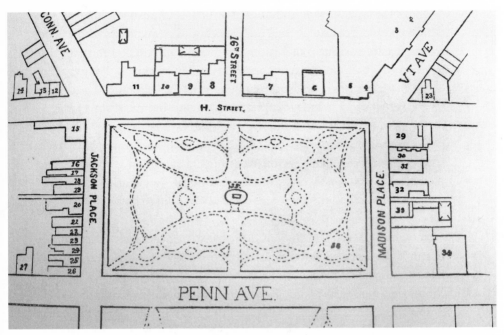

Figure 12. Sketch map of the center of the Lafayette Square neighborhood
and its houses from the mid-1870s. Wilhelmus Bryan Collection, Prints and
Photographs Division, Library of Congress.

Corcoran made his house into one of the brightest attractions in the city,
which in turn made Lafayette Square the center of Washington's social activities.[57]

During the first session of the Thirty-Third Congress, when Douglas
pushed through the Kansas-Nebraska Act, Lafayette Square was home to
several prominent politicians in Washington. William Appleton (W-Mass.)
rented the Decatur House—considered "one of the best houses in Washington"—on the southwest corner of H and Jackson Place, diagonally across
from Corcoran. Thomas Ritchie, the fiery newspaperman from Virginia,
lived in a small house next door to Corcoran. Just to the west of Jackson
Place, on Seventeenth Street and H, lived both New York senator Hamilton Fish and Attorney General Caleb Cushing. Senator Edward Everett
(W-Mass.) bought a house one block down on G Street and South Carolina
representative William Aiken lived around the corner. On the other side
of the park, Supreme Court Justice John Archibald Campbell of Alabama
and Maine representative Moses Macdonald lived in houses on Fifteenth
and G.[58]

One of the biggest responsibilities of owning a house in Washington was its upkeep, and because of their neighborhoods' reputations, those who lived in Lafayette Square or Union Row were concerned with maintaining clean streets, running water, and other urban amenities. For example, during the late 1850s, owners of the houses on the west side of Lafayette Square, on H Street, rallied together to try to improve their surroundings. They contracted surveyors to tackle neighborhood flooding by installing more sewers and fixing water mains and to "grad[e] and gravel" the street. All of this work required petitions and cooperation among the neighbors. In essence, the men and women of Lafayette Square frequently had to communicate with one another if for no other reason than to navigate Washington's city ordinances.[59]

Homeowners also had to consider what to do with their houses upon retirement or loss of political office. Particularly as the cabinet turned over, politicians frequently swapped houses with their replacements. Yet the men who owned houses in Washington seemed to pay little attention to their prospective tenants' political or state affiliations, regardless of the fact that they would have to communicate regularly. In March 1857, when James Buchanan was sworn in as the new president, one resident joked, "Such an excitement in the house renting never has [been] known . . . Lord Napier [The English Minister] has finally taken the Fish house & . . . The Gwins [family of California Democrat William Gwin] took Gov Aiken's house at a rent of $1500 a year; & the Dixon's have [North Carolina Democrat] Mr [James C.] Dobbin's house." The Republican Blair family of Maryland also agreed to rent a house to South Carolina Democrat James Henry Hammond, while former Whig leader John Crittenden of Kentucky rented his house to Senator William Bigler, a Pennsylvania Democrat.[60]

If a politician who owned a house in one of the fashionable neighborhoods retired from office, he might also rely on his neighbors to help find a buyer or renter. For example, in early 1854, Edward Everett became so sickly that he decided to quit his position in the Senate and return to Massachusetts. Yet he could not simply abandon the house he purchased on G Street. So he enlisted his son-in-law, Henry Wise (nephew of the Virginia Democratic governor of the same name), who was living in Washington, to help him find a suitable renter. William Corcoran also agreed to help out. After some negotiations, Jefferson Davis decided to take the house in December. While the Mississippi Democrat could occasionally be a demanding tenant, Davis and Everett maintained a friendly correspondence. More important, the Wises, who spent much of the 1850s living in Washington, joined the Davis family's small social circle.[61]

As their friendship with Henry Wise and his wife, Charlie, indicates, the Davises' social circle grew while they lived in Everett's house to include other members of the neighborhood. In fact, in Lafayette Square, politicians could frequently be found at one another's houses for dinner or drinks. In 1850 brothers John A. King (W-N.Y.) and James G. King (D-N.J.), who lived in Decatur House, frequently visited other square residents, including Secretary of the Treasury William Meredith (W-Pa.), Secretary of the Navy William Ballard Preston (W-Va.), and Thomas Ritchie of Virginia. A few months later, upon renting a house in the neighborhood, Alexander H. H. Stuart began visiting with the families next door, exchanging pleasantries and furnishing tips. While in Washington, Everett repeatedly spent hours at William Corcoran's house, where he met other current and former residents such as Jesse Bright (D-Ind.), James Buchanan (D-Pa.), and John Slidell (D-La.).[62]

House proximity also created friendships in Union Row. Upon moving to F Street in December 1855, Virginia Clay was delighted to find her neighborhood populated with prominent and pleasant politicians. Virginia clearly intended to socialize with her neighbors; she bragged to her father that Senators John Bell (Opp-Tenn.), John Thomson (D-N.J.), and John B. Weller (D-Calif.) all lived nearby. William Seward's immediate neighbor, Philip Phillips, was one of his closest confidants, and the two frequently discussed political issues. Although Seward was an ardent opponent of slavery, the New Yorker had never let political differences over the peculiar institution keep him from cultivating friendships. He developed a long-standing relationship with Southern-born Democrat William Gwin, senator from California, and during the Taylor administration, had become intimate with Jefferson Davis, visiting the Mississippi native frequently at his home in Washington.[63]

By 1854, the New Yorker had become a regular visitor to the Phillips' abode, and was particularly friendly with Mrs. Phillips. The two disagreed strongly with one another about slavery and other political matters, and their conversations could occasionally "clash in sparks and fire," according to the Phillips' daughter, Caroline. Still, she added, the two families "ever met with renewed civility" following these disagreements, and remained close throughout the rest of the decade. With such strong opinions about the Nebraska Territory and its effect on political parties, no doubt Seward and Phillips discussed events surrounding Douglas's legislation. Perhaps Phillips became active in negotiations at the F Street Mess because Seward had alerted him to Dixon's intentions to push for repealing the Missouri Compromise line.[64]

If Seward and Phillips helped spur the repeal of the Missouri Compromise line, political conversations in houses and hotels throughout the city did not stop after Douglas proposed his new bill on January 23. Among the first to discuss the issue were Lafayette Square residents Edward Everett, Attorney General Caleb Cushing, and Charles Eames, the Democratic editor of *The Union*. Eames hosted the two men at his house on G Street in early 1854, and the Nebraska bill quickly came up. According to Everett, Cushing explained that the Pierce administration supported the repeal of the Missouri Compromise line "to occupy the mind of Congress, and divert them from the strain between the Northern and Southern wing of the [D]emocratic party."[65]

Perhaps more important, the few remaining Free-Soilers in the city, who had been discussing the repeal of the Missouri line since Dixon's announcement, finally arranged for newspapers to publish "The Appeal of the Independent Democrats in Congress" less than twenty-four hours after Douglas reported the new Kansas-Nebraska bill. Signed by two senators and four representatives, the protest insisted that Douglas's measure was a "bold scheme against American liberty," part of "an atrocious plot" to spread American slavery. The "Appeal" shocked many congressmen, particularly Southern Whigs who risked being grouped with abolitionists if they opposed the bill.[66]

Over the next month and a half, both Whigs and Democrats struggled to keep their parties unified in debates over Douglas's bill. And while leaders argued over the issue on the floor of the Senate, Washington's politicians discussed, argued about, and negotiated their positions in boardinghouses, hotels, and private residences around the city. As Hamilton Fish told a friend in mid-February, "Although there is no probability of a final vote on the Nebraska bill for some days . . . there is much being done, in private conversations."[67]

Finally, after sitting all night, the Senate passed Douglas's Kansas-Nebraska Act at five o'clock on the morning of March 4, with nine Southern Whigs supporting the bill. After a longer struggle in the House, the bill passed on May 22, by a vote of 113-110. The president signed the Kansas-Nebraska Act into law on May 30. Douglas was truly pleased, and considered the drafting and passage of the bill as one of his greatest accomplishments. The Kansas-Nebraska Act, he told a friend, would "impart peace to the country & stability to the Union."[68]

Yet, the bill would do anything but provide stability. Reaction to the Kansas-Nebraska Act throughout the North was overwhelmingly negative. In Washington, frustration over the bill took hold almost immediately. The morning that the act passed the House, a group of Northern congressmen who opposed the repeal of the Missouri Compromise met at Crutchett's boardinghouse on Sixth Street, where Massachusetts Whigs Edward Dickinson and Thomas Eliot had rooms. According to one of the attendees, the men gathered at the house "discussed the necessity of forming a new party from anti-slavery extension Whigs and Democrats, and the name of Republican was suggested." Angry Northern politicians would spend the next few years organizing a new party specifically opposed to the spread of slavery.[69]

In the meantime, Douglas himself faced scrutiny from his constituents back in Illinois, many of whom were outraged by the repeal of the sacred Missouri Compromise line. The Little Giant began to receive threatening letters in Washington. On his way home at the close of the session, the anger was palpable; "I could travel from Boston to Chicago by the light of my own effigy," he reported. Over the next two years, American debates over slavery became more heated, reaching a fever pitch in May 1856, when a South Carolina representative would viciously attack a Massachusetts anti-slavery leader in his seat in the Senate. The caning of Charles Sumner would shock many in cities across the North, causing them to decry their brethren to the south as the "Slave Power." But in Washington, the reaction was more complicated.[70]

CHAPTER FIVE

The Most Immoral and Corrupt Place in the Union

Vice, Violence, and the Caning of Charles Sumner

In the early afternoon on Thursday, May 22, 1856, Congressman Preston Brooks sat at the back of the Senate chamber, clutching his gutta-percha walking cane and waiting. To anyone who noticed him, the handsome thirty-six-year-old from South Carolina must have appeared uncomfortable, exhausted from lack of sleep, and very likely tipsy from drink. Most important, Brooks's tired face likely revealed a deeper emotion: anger.[1]

Brooks believed he had good reason to be angry. At the beginning of the week, Massachusetts senator Charles Sumner had gravely insulted Brooks's cousin, South Carolina senator Andrew P. Butler, while delivering a two-day philippic entitled "The Crime against Kansas" in front of packed Senate galleries. The speech chronicled events in Kansas since passage of the Kansas-Nebraska Act two years earlier, from the perspective of the antislavery senator. Since then, Northerners and Southerners had come to blows over the fate of slavery in Kansas itself. Much of the trouble began in March 1855, when former senator David R. Atchison led a group of Missourians over the border to try to influence the vote over slavery. These "border ruffians" helped create a government in Lecompton that basically stripped antislavery men of constitutional rights. When Northern settlers created a rival government in Topeka, friction among the territory's residents ensued. Finally, on May 21, the day before Brooks sat waiting in the Senate chamber, the Lecompton government sent officials to arrest free-state leaders in the town of Lawrence. In the course of doing so, the Lecompton mob proceeded to burn several buildings and destroy two printing presses. While no one was actually killed in the fracas, Republicans quickly labeled the event "Bleeding Kansas."[2]

Debate in Congress mirrored much of the tension in Kansas itself; Sumner was one of many antislavery congressmen to voice disapproval. But Sumner's speech stuck out primarily for his shocking choice of language; the Massachusetts senator invoked imagery of rape and prostitution to describe the spread of slavery into Kansas. Sumner also accused several prominent Democrats of crimes against the territory, including the architect of the Kansas-Nebraska Act, Illinois senator Stephen A. Douglas, President Franklin Pierce, and Brooks's cousin, Andrew P. Butler. Elderly and sick, Butler had returned home to South Carolina for a few days and was not in the chamber during the speech. Nonetheless, in Sumner's closing remarks, the Massachusetts senator questioned Butler's honesty—"he cannot open his mouth but out there flies a blunder"—and he ridiculed South Carolina's prominence in the history of the United States.[3]

Though a member of the House of Representatives, Brooks was not present for Sumner's speech, but he verified rumors of its combative tone in a newspaper summary of the remarks the following morning, Wednesday, May 21. With Butler out of town, Brooks could not let the Massachusetts knave get away with insulting his family and his home state. The South Carolinian determined to meet Sumner on his way to the Capitol and punish him unless the Massachusetts senator made an adequate apology. Brooks took his friend, Virginia representative Henry Edmundson, along to serve as a witness. The two men waited for Sumner on Pennsylvania Avenue near the entrance to the Capitol but Sumner unknowingly spoiled the plan by arriving in a carriage, avoiding the spot where Brooks and Edmundson were lying in wait.[4]

The next morning, Thursday, May 22, after an evening of plotting and drinking with his colleague Laurence Keitt (D-S.C.), Brooks again tried to intercept Sumner on his way to the Capitol, this time accounting for the possibility of a carriage. At eleven o'clock, the South Carolinian settled himself at the entrance to the grounds where he had a good view of the street and the Capitol steps. If Sumner arrived by carriage, Brooks would still be able to reach him by running across the grounds and up the steps to the place where the carriages stopped. Soon after the South Carolinian got settled, however, Edmundson passed him on his way to the Capitol and put a wrench in Brooks's plan. As Edmundson explained, Brooks would have to exert a lot of energy to reach Sumner if he came by carriage, which would likely "render him unable to contend with Mr. Sumner, should a personal conflict take place." This was a critical concern, as the forty-five-year-old Sumner was physically stronger and larger, weighing at least thirty pounds more than the six-foot, 170-pound Brooks. Brooks took Edmundson's advice and decided instead to approach the Massachusetts senator in the Capitol itself.[5]

By noon on Thursday afternoon, as Brooks sat in the adjourned Senate waiting for Sumner at the back of the hall, his anger was boiling over; after almost two days of anticipation, the South Carolinian could hardly contain himself as he sat in the adjourned Senate waiting for Sumner. Keitt, who was in on the plan, joined Brooks at the back of the Hall. They kept their eyes on the Massachusetts senator who was sitting obliviously at his Senate desk four rows up, franking copies of his Kansas speech. Finally, when all of the ladies left the chamber, Brooks rose and walked over to Sumner's desk with Keitt in tow. "Mr. Sumner," Brooks began, "I have read your speech twice over carefully. It is a libel on South Carolina and Mr. Butler, who is a relative of mine."[6]

As the words left his mouth, Brooks raised his cane and used it to strike Sumner repeatedly over the head. The shocked senator tried to get up but could not dislodge his chair. As Sumner finally wrenched the desk from its moorings and stumbled into the aisle, Brooks continued to beat him, even as the cane shattered. Brooks got off approximately thirty lashings over the course of one minute before the other senators in the room realized what was happening. Kentuckian John J. Crittenden spotted the scene and rushed toward the men, calling out "Don't kill him," but was intercepted by Keitt. Determined to let Brooks continue, Keitt raised his own cane and called out "Let them alone, God damn you." Crittenden's colleague, Georgia senator Robert Toombs, rushed to save the Kentuckian from his own beating as Sumner finally fell to the floor, unconscious. In an attempt to prevent any further violence, a few congressional bystanders helped move a bloodied Sumner to a sofa in the Senate lobby.[7]

The caning of Charles Sumner had both short-term and long-term consequences. In the immediate aftermath, Brooks was arrested and awaited trial by a Washington court. Members of Congress also felt a duty to respond. Within twenty-four hours, the Speaker of the House of Representatives, Nathaniel Banks (R-Mass.) appointed a small committee to investigate the assault, including three moderate Northerners and two Southern Democrats. The following Monday, the committee began interviewing witnesses, as well as Sumner himself. The Senate also created a committee to look into an official congressional response. Like the House version, the investigating committee membership was overwhelmingly moderate.[8]

Because Brooks was not a member of their body, the Senate Committee ultimately decided that it had no authority to discipline a representative, leaving the House in charge of punishment. On June 2, the House Investigating Committee in the Case of the Assault on Mr. Sumner published the testimony it had gathered, as well as formal majority and minority reports. The majority report declared that the House "has the power and ought to punish the said Preston S. Brooks for the said assault, not only as a breach of the privileges of the Senator assailed . . . but as an act of disorderly behavior." The committee also recommended that Brooks's accomplices—Edmundson and Keitt—be censured. The majority voted to expel 121-95, but proponents did not gather the necessary two-thirds vote. Brooks decided to resign anyway and returned to South Carolina determined to win reelection (which he did).[9]

Sumner's sympathizers also had little success with the city trial. After his arrest, Brooks immediately went free upon payment of $500 bail. When the trial finally commenced, Sumner decided not to testify while recovering from his injuries. Partially for this reason, Brooks was excused with a $300 fine on July 8. And while Brooks escaped substantial punishment, Sumner struggled to regain his health, unable to resume his duties in the Senate for almost three years.[10]

While the Sumner-Brooks debacle was handled with a degree of moderation in Washington itself, outside the Capitol it became a topic of discussion and agitation, North and South. Throughout the slave states, Southerners hailed Brooks as a hero, and many sent him letters of support and new canes to replace the one shattered in the beating. Northerners were appalled by this Southern reaction, using it as further evidence of a Slave Power conspiracy. Antislavery leaders argued that "Bleeding Kansas" and "Bleeding Sumner" were just two examples of Southerners trying to take away Northern freedom. The reaction to the caning helped draw new supporters to the Republican Party.[11]

Ultimately, as many historians have argued, the caning of Charles Sumner had a critical impact on American sectionalism.[12] But within Washington, where politicians had witnessed the ordeal unfold firsthand, reaction was different. While some extremists from both sides of the Mason-Dixon line threatened further violence, the overwhelming response of Washington politicians was to move on from the event. Moreover, although tensions between some members from the two sections rose in the weeks following the beating, congressional relations quickly returned to normal. According to New York senator William Seward, by the middle of June "the anger of both parties in Congress" had "cooled." Another Washington resident agreed, writing on June 5, "the Sumner affair has flamed out." Even Sumner's Republican colleagues continued to pursue cordial relationships with men from the South, much to the Massachusetts senator's dismay. As Sumner wrote angrily to a friend, "On my visits to Washington" since the attack, "I observe that the [R]epublicans fraternize most amiably with men who sustain every enormity, even with those who were accomplices *after* if not before the act under which I am suffering."[13]

Understandably devastated by his injuries, Sumner must have forgotten what living in Washington was really like. Day-to-day life in the capital city was replete with less than respectable behavior, including not only drinking, gambling, and womanizing but, most important, violence. Unlike today, when media outlets quickly report our politicians' smallest moral indiscretions, such behavior was generally kept quiet, or at least contained, within the city's political fraternity. In all likelihood, Washington lawmakers refrained from sharing such stories because immorality cut across both sectional and party lines. Politicians gathered together at taverns, brothels, and gambling houses. In fact, no one was immune from at least witnessing episodes of profligacy, licentiousness, and violence in hotels and barrooms, on the street and even in the halls of the Capitol itself. As New York congressman Solomon Haven explained to his wife, "I concur in your wonder that men should [do] so very foolish a thing as Mr Brooks has done but it is a very natural [consequence] of the violence of the day."[14]

As Haven suggested, Brooks's outburst on May 22, 1856, was not the first violent attack in Washington, nor would it be the last. Violence was simply a part of the city's daily operation and was often a by-product of morally lenient behavior, including the consumption of alcohol, gambling, womanizing, and other misdeeds. As a result, while people outside of the city railed for or against the caning of Senator Sumner, federal politicians went on with their lives. To understand why Washington lawmakers reacted as they did, why the caning had less of an impact on federal politicians in the capital city than it did on the American public at large, we must explore the event in the context of the capital community.

■ By the time of Brooks's infamous attack in May 1856, Washington had garnered a reputation for violence and vice. Newspapermen, common citizens throughout the United States, and retired politicians spoke of the city's "moral iniquity." Many echoed the sentiments of an 1848 *New York Herald* article that remarked that Washington had "engendered" a "moral and political degeneracy . . . during the period of nearly a half-century." Washington was "a bad place to raise a man's family . . . and a still worse place to leave his family in when he dies," agreed an observer. The city could better be described as "a mob," explained another, "three fourths of which was characterized by utter destitution of good breeding." Even former politicians were relieved to have "escaped from the corrupt and corrupting atmosphere of Washington."[15]

City residents and politicians themselves were no less aware of the city's many drawbacks. During their sermons, Washington's ministers frequently considered topics of violence, licentiousness, and lack of virtue among the city's populace. On the weekend following the Sumner caning, several clergymen preached about "the downward tendencies of civilization in Washington." But 1856 was not necessarily rock bottom. Indiana Free-Soiler George W. Julian believed "political morality" in Washington "was at a very low ebb during the period covered by the Thirty-First Congress," in 1850 and 1851. Others considered the latter part of the decade to have even greater moral corruption. "I really believe," wrote a newly elected Zebulon Vance (D-N.C.) to his cousin in 1859, "in point of wickedness and vice, that cities at the bottom of the Dead Sea were holy places compared to this."[16]

Worse, it was hard for politicians to avoid being swept up in the immorality. As Horace Greeley wrote to a friend in February 1856 about his experiences in the "infernal hole" of Washington: "Did you ever stay in a place where you didn't dare look in the glass when you got up in the morning for fear of seeing a scoundrel?" Although specifics rarely made it into national newspapers, congressmen's indiscretions quickly became fodder for the Washington rumor mill, and there was no shortage of stories. After living in the capital city for only three months, one shocked politician wrote his wife, "I believe this to be the most immoral and corrupt place in the Union, if one half I have heard be true."[17]

Perhaps the most innocuous form of bad behavior in the antebellum capital was the seemingly endless consumption of alcohol among federal politicians. As one congressman remembered, "the vice of intemperance was . . . fearfully prevalent" in the antebellum period. Upon arriving in Congress in 1859, Tennessee Opposition member Robert Hatton lamented to his wife, "I am the only one, so far as I know, the only Member of Congress . . . that does not drink." While Hatton may have exaggerated the prevalence of alcohol consumption, congressmen celebrated any number of occasions—such as electing a Speaker, the Christmas or New Year holidays, the visit of an international celebrity, an important vote, or even a day off—with a round of drinks. Even locals knew that on any given day, there could be a "great deal of drunkenness in the City."[18]

Regular drunken behavior was not limited to congressmen. Supreme Court justices, cabinet members, and even the president himself indulged enough to receive notice. Justice Joseph Story, for example, was known to have a bottle of brandy every night at dinner. While serving as secretary of state under Milliard Fillmore, Daniel Webster (W-Mass.) was considered a "Triumphant Drunk." Rumors swirled throughout Franklin Pierce's presidential term that he was a "drunkard of bad moral character."[19]

Some of these rumors, like those about Webster and Pierce, were partially born out of political animosities. In a variety of newspapers and magazines, hometown politicians accused their opponents of drinking too much in an effort to discredit them. For example, Republican papers often targeted Illinois Democrat Stephen A. Douglas as being intemperate. Not to be outdone by their adversaries, the Democratic-leaning *Weekly Wisconsin Patriot* struck back. "We do not pretend that Mr. Douglas is a strict temperance man," the editors explained, but "we can name not less than ten Republican Senators who drink more than he, and among that ten one William H. Seward, who is held up to us as a model of temperance."[20]

Although periodicals and political leaders outside of Washington criticized the drinking habits of their opponents, those in the city itself understood the prevalence of alcohol consumption among its residents. While teetotaling congressmen may have disapproved of the prevalence of Washington drinking, they knew it crossed both party and section. As a Senate page later explained, "I have been ask[ed] by male and femails over time [whether] I ever saw Mr Webster under the influence of *Lickir*. I have frankly, but who have I not seen under the influence of Lickir[?] Most all of the [great] men of that day drank." How else could one explain that a bar in one of the fashionable hotels took in approximately $21,000 for drinks over the course of a little more than a year?[21]

The prevalence of alcohol consumption in the city had two important consequences for how Washington operated in the mid-nineteenth century. First, because politicians hailing from all states and parties tended to indulge in alcohol, Washington's drinkers often made or strengthened cross-sectional relationships. After dinner or the adjournment of Congress for the day, many politicians—particularly those whose wives did not come to Washington—would break into small groups and make a trip to one of the city's many taverns or a friend's home. A number of federal lawmakers kept their houses stocked with wines, rums, and other spirits, ready to ply on interested visitors. Some even cooperated in making large alcohol purchases together to make sure they were prepared for a season of entertaining. During the second session of the Thirty-Third Congress, New York senator Hamilton Fish worked out a deal with Supreme Court Justice James M. Wayne of Georgia in which both men secured sixteen dozen bottles of Madeira wine. And buying wine could be expensive. Sellers typically urged patrons to buy twenty-two-bottle lots at the price of $15.50 per bottle, which, at five bottles per gallon, meant that buyers paid approximately $75.50 per gallon.[22]

Such extravagant purchases of wine and spirits meant plenty of opportunities for drinking at parties and other gatherings. Brothers James and John King, of New Jersey and New York respectively, often spent evenings drinking at the house of their Lafayette Square neighbor, newspaperman Thomas Ritchie. They occasionally brought along William Meredith (W-Pa.) and William B. Preston (W-Va.), as in one evening when the group imbibed "some of Uncle John's punch," which was home-brewed by a year-round resident in the city. William Graham (W-N.C.), Fillmore's navy secretary, also hosted terrific drinking parties. At one such gathering, Senator Benjamin Wade (W-Ohio) remarked that "the quantity of the wine furnished [was] as important a topic as anything." The group went through numerous bottles amid constant laughter. "No ladies were present," Wade continued, "so we got pretty silly." Moses Grinnell (W-N.Y.), Ogden Hoffman (W-N.Y.), and Samuel Southard (W-N.J.) were known for hosting raucous drinking parties at their boardinghouse. On one occasion the three held a "contest" between members from the North and South as to who could produce the best bottle of wine. Fourteen bottles later, South Carolinian Isaac Holmes was declared the winner. At the close of the night, all members present agreed that they should all compete again soon.[23]

While many of Washington's politicians enjoyed the occasional drinking party, others distinguished themselves for being regular drunks. Few could surpass the drinking acumen of Felix McConnell of Alabama, who "was [not] himself unless intoxicated" or Missourian John Jameson who was "never sober." One of the city's most notorious drinkers was Senator Willie P. Mangum (W-N.C.), who counted several congressmen as his drinking buddies, including Simon Cameron (D-Pa.), Edward Hannegan

(D-Ind.), William T. Haskell (W-Tenn.), and James T. Morehead (W-Ky.). The North Carolinian even made plans to live with some combination of these friends during several sessions in Washington.[24]

Hannegan also spent time drinking with members from his own political party, including Henry A. Wise (D-Va.) and Franklin Pierce (D-N.H.), who had all served in Congress together in the early 1840s. In the run-up to Pierce's nomination for the presidency in 1852, Hannegan and Wise were careful to keep the secret of their old behavior from the public. Even so, Wise fondly remembered at least one "frolic" from their days in Congress together. Similarly, Thomas Corwin (W-Ohio) used to share a few drinks with John Crittenden (W-Ky.) and James A. Pearce (W-Md.) when the three men served in Congress together in the mid-1840s. After temporarily retiring from Washington in 1853, Corwin must have missed these outings. "Does Crittenden drink as hard as ever?" he jokingly asked Pearce in a letter in May 1856.[25]

While Corwin and Wise had pleasant memories of their drunken exploits in Washington, others came to see their pasts as problematic. While serving as the commissioner of Indian affairs in Washington in 1849, Kentucky Whig Orlando Brown employed a young man named A. S. Loughery at the bureau. Little did Brown know that Loughery had become a common drunk after losing all of his money. As Loughery later explained to his old employer, "Dissatisfied with myself, I made the matter worse by drinking too much; In this I found but too many *friends*." One such friend was Senator James D. Westcott, Jr. (D-Fla.), a fairly notorious drinker himself. While out on one of their many exploits, the two men discussed Indian policy in Florida, during which Westcott confessed he preferred war to the peace that Brown was pursuing because he wanted "to see Seminole blood running."[26]

The story of Loughery and Westcott helps to illustrate a second important consequence of drunken behavior in the capital city. Because of the inherently political nature of Washington, residents could not help but discuss politics at taverns or late-night drinking parties. This could be problematic, as tipsy leaders were sometimes loose-lipped. For example, while serving as a senator in 1856, John M. Clayton (Opp-Del.) insulted English minister John Crampton by using offensive language while discussing the Clayton-Bulwer treaty. In response, Crampton asked a number of senators, including William Seward (R-N.Y.), to defend him. As one observer explained, alcohol was clearly to blame for the disagreement: "The fact seems to be, that Mr Clayton is not infrequently boozy, & when in that condition wanders in his talk."[27]

At the end of the decade, Republicans faced a similar problem from their newly elected Speaker of the House, William Pennington (R-N.J.). Massachusetts representative Charles Francis Adams explained the issue this way: "It is impossible to regard Mr Pennington with indignation, for he means no offence—and yet it is equally out of the question, to feel respect for a man who has no bridle on his tongue after a couple of glasses of wine stimulate his absurdities." Perhaps the worst political mistake of all was letting alcohol influence one's behavior in and out of Congress. Drinking both the evening before and the morning of the caning no doubt influenced Brooks's actions in May 1856. If Brooks had been sober, might he have struck Sumner only once or twice rather than thirty times?[28]

Beyond producing erratic behavior, drunkenness among Washington's politicians could have an important impact on what happened in everyday lawmaking. Some imbibers could not be counted on to show up for important votes. Georgia Democrat Alexander Stephens became frustrated by the inability of the House to pass the army bill only a few months after the Sumner caning, in large part because of tippling. "We lost the last question *twice*," Stephens told his brother, because "two of our men here [missed] their votes by being out of their seats—to get a drink of liquor." Similarly, during the tense election for Speaker of the Thirty-Sixth Congress, certain Democrats, such as James Stallworth, who was "still drunk and absent in Alabama," could not be counted on for votes. Texas representative Timothy Pilsbury could not even be relied upon to show up at the House regularly. During the Thirtieth Congress, Pilsbury "divided his time between drinking and getting married," complained his Senate colleague Thomas Rusk.[29]

Overall, the free flow of alcohol in Washington and even the Capitol itself left congressmen susceptible to poor choices or costly political mistakes. Worse, it gave lobbyists and office seekers the opportunity to take advantage of inebriated politicians. Fred Butler's saloon on Fourteenth Street was often used as a place where men jockeyed for office and favors. As one newspaper correspondent explained, when an office seeker hoped to have an impact, Butler himself was typically in on the ruse: "If the party 'treating' be an office-seeker, and the party treated a man of influence, Butler asks the office-seeker—'Do you want all you ax [*sic*] for?'" explained the reporter. "If the wink is in the affirmative, Butler gives the man of influence a 'stunner,' which is sure to secure to the office-seeker a very full hearing." Although the newspaperman admitted "This is an odd way of doing things," he explained that "it is within the range of diplomacy" in Washington. Providing alcohol did not always have to come at a tavern, however. The dinner table was also a good place to ask for favors, and an abundance of wine and food could sometimes help along negotiations. "We have introduced here, a regular system of lobby influence," North Carolina congressman David Outlaw complained to his wife during the Twenty-Ninth Congress. "New York has sent on heaven knows how many of her . . . Aldermen, at the expense of the City, to procure a Branch Mint in that place. They have been plying the members with dinners, &c and will [I] expect succeed."[30]

Alcohol and food were not always necessary for lobbyists or office seekers to influence Washington's politicians. The biggest problem for most lawmakers in the mid-nineteenth century was a lack of money, which could, in turn, leave them susceptible to outside influence. Almost everyone in the capital city complained bitterly about their salaries, from congressmen to cabinet members, Supreme Court justices to clerks. "The members of the Executive & Legislative branches of the government are generally speaking not men of wealth," explained Massachusetts Whig Edward Everett, although he was an exception to this rule. "They live here at great cost—few have a dollar to spare." In 1856, when Brooks attacked Sumner, congressmen were paid eight dollars per day, while cabinet members had an annual salary of $8,000 and clerks made somewhere between $800 and $1,600 depending on their experience. Compared with the cost of living in the city and of supporting a family back home, the pay was simply inadequate. "I am every day anxious about money affairs," explained Congressman Samuel Ryan Curtis (R-Iowa), upon taking his place in Washington. Similarly, second-generation Alabama senator Clement Clay told his mother, "I am not surprised now, at Father's indebtness [sic] on leaving Washington, for with only two of us to support, I find it impossible to save anything of my per diem and mileage."[31]

In addition to working other jobs while serving in Congress,[32] members tried to remedy their salary woes in other ways. Some simply borrowed money from friends who were better off. Although he made some extra money working as legal counsel in Supreme Court cases, Maryland Whig Reverdy Johnson received loans from friends all over the city, with promises to pay back in a few weeks or months. Willie Mangum, who needed extra cash to help support his drinking habits, made many of his friends angry by not paying them back in a timely fashion. Indiana senator Jesse Bright had to borrow from one political friend back in Indiana to help pay back another political friend in Washington. Bright also borrowed money from William Preston (W-Ky.) and asked his friend for an extension on the loan.[33]

Others gave in to payoffs and other forms of corruption. While it is difficult to tell how widespread bribery really was in Washington, the perception among lawmakers was that it was everywhere. In addition to simple claims that politicians frequently saw "downright corruption" in the capital city, there were several tangible instances of buying votes and of fraud. In 1857 North Carolina representative Robert Treat Paine accused another member of trying to bribe him with $1,500 cash for a vote in favor of the Minnesota Railroad bill. A few weeks later, the House Corruption Committee found four members guilty of offering money for votes. Congressmen also faced corruption among the Capitol staffs. In 1845 the clerk of the House was found stealing from the House contingent fund, and in 1850 the Democratic candidate for doorkeeper was found forging pensions. If members needed some extra cash, bribery seemed to be one option.[34]

To avoid loans and pay-offs, some congressmen simply pushed for a raise. On a variety of occasions throughout the nineteenth century, members tried to pass legislation increasing their salaries. After several unsuccessful attempts earlier in the decade, the Thirty-Fourth Congress passed a pay raise only a few months after the Sumner caning. The law made congressional pay annual, at a rate of $3,000, and backdated the law to the beginning of the session, December 1855. By backdating their pay, congressmen did cause something of a commotion: "You will hear a great *fuss* about members *raising* their pay, & going back with the law to last Session," Texas senator Sam Houston explained to his wife. Yet, even when the pay change went through, Washington's politicians still struggled to meet their living expenses. As the *New York Herald* complained the following session in February 1857, "The Members of Congress are generally poor, and between oyster salons, gambling dens, and other nocturnal drawbacks in the federal city, a considerable number of our national law makers are always 'hard up.'"[35]

The *Herald* made a fair assessment of behavior in Washington; in fact, gambling and other "nocturnal drawbacks" such as womanizing were perhaps the greatest vices in the capital city. Although some lawmakers disapproved, this behavior was simply part of Washington culture. And just as in the pervasive drinking that took place throughout the city, the politicians who engaged in this behavior came from a variety of states and parties throughout the country. As a result, evening vices could have a significant impact on Washington politics.

Whether in a formal or informal setting, card playing and betting were widespread in the city. Those who preferred an informal venue often created weekly games involving a few friends. Among nineteenth-century Washingtonians, the most popular pastime was "whist," an English card game similar to bridge, which involved partners and trick taking. Many politicians played whist with their boardinghouse mates or other close friends after dinner or on the weekends. Both Mississippi Democrat Jefferson Davis and his wife, for example, were avid whist players and could be found in a game with George E. Badger (W-N.C.) and Samuel Vinton (W-Ohio). Local doctor Samuel Busey had a regular game with John M. Clayton (W-Del.), as well as two other city residents who hailed from the North. Virginia Democrat John Y. Mason, who was secretary of the navy under James K. Polk, was always looking for a fourth for his game with Sidney Breese (D-Ill.) and William L. Marcy (D-N.Y.). On one evening in December 1848, they invited Vice President George M. Dallas to join them, and after betting until almost eleven o'clock at night, Dallas was out $1.50.[36]

The best-known whist lover in the city was Marcy himself, who could always be relied upon for a game of cards. His playing partner, John Mason, could easily entice him to leave his duties for a few hours to enjoy whist with mutual friends, including the Democratic newspaperman, Thomas Ritchie of Virginia. "Mr. Ritchie has purchased a large lot of cards, and appropriated a very cozy room to the purposes of whist," Mason wrote Marcy while the latter was out of town. "Won't this bring you and won't this carry you there[?]" According to one newspaperman, Marcy loved to play but hated to lose. In fact, he disliked losing so much that his card-playing colleagues could occasionally use this weakness to achieve political ends. Secretary of the British Legation Henry Labouchere explained that, while serving in Washington in the late 1850s, he had at least one such experience with Marcy. As Labouchere reported to the newspaperman, he went with the British minister "to a pleasant watering-place in Virginia," where they met Marcy, who was then serving as secretary of state. The topic for discussion was a reciprocity treaty between Canada and the United States, but "Mr. Marcy, the most genial of men, was as cross as a bear. He would agree to nothing." Puzzled, Labouchere asked Marcy's secretary "What on earth is the matter with your chief?" Replied the secretary, "He does not have his rubber of whist." The two British men quickly found a solution to Marcy's temper by playing whist every night with the secretary of state and his aide, and purposely losing. As Labouchere explained, "The stakes were very trifling, but Mr. Marcy felt flattered by beating the Britishers. . . . His good humor returned, and every morning when the details of the treaty were being discussed we had our revenge, and scored a few points for Canada." Labouchere may have overstated his influence, but the comfort of playing a friendly game of whist clearly had some impact on the secretary.[37]

Those who were more serious about gambling were likely to play brag poker or faro at one of the city's formal gambling dens. Such establishments lined Pennsylvania Avenue in the mid-nineteenth century, stretching from the White House, past the National Hotel and toward the Capitol. Just a few steps from the National, politicians could find at least three famed gaming establishments: Pringle's, Pendleton's, and the "Corner House," which stood opposite the Hotel. Far from being run-down buildings, most of these gambling saloons included "the most gorgeous entertainment spread for the gratification of the appetite, the most expensive wines, and the most abounding hospitality."[38]

Pendleton's was the most elaborate and well respected of the gambling houses in Washington, in part because of the reputation of its owner. Edward Pendleton was an upstanding member of Washington society, who belonged to one of the first families of Virginia. His wife was also well known in social circles as the daughter of Robert Mills, the architect of the Treasury. Pendleton kept a beautiful house on Pennsylvania Avenue with a variety of rooms for relaxing, eating, drinking, and, most of all, card playing. Frequent visitors alternatively called it "The Palace of Fortune," or the "Hall of the Bleeding Hearts," depending upon where their luck lay.[39]

When Pendleton died suddenly in 1858, many of the country's newspapermen gained access to the mansion for the first time, as the furniture and house itself went up for auction. Editors flooded Washington trying to catch a glimpse of the famous gambling den, and many described it in great detail in their papers. According to a correspondent for the *Boston Post*, gamblers entered the building and immediately went up a flight of stairs. Upon knocking on the door at the top, an African American man looked through a small aperture and determined whether you could enter. If you passed his test, he led you into an anteroom that contained several columned decanters of alcohol and waiters with trays of whiskey sours and other spirits, which the host welcomed you to drink. Just past the anteroom was the "Sporting hall," where the games took place. This game room was beautifully decorated so as to give its visitors a taste of luxury, including carpeting "from the Orient," expensive paintings, embroidered lace curtains, and "mirrors of mammoth size reflecting your form and features from a score of gleaming embrasures." Men sat at rosewood-polished circular tables around the room, but as a visitor "they heed you not—their eyes having another and stronger attraction." Many of these men, as the editors explained, had been prominent members of Congress, cabinet members, and other politicians. Years later, one well-connected newspaperman remembered that, particularly in the outer parlors one could see "leading members of Congress, quietly discussing the day's proceedings, the prospects of parties, and the character of public men."[40]

Two of the more frequent visitors to Pendleton's and other gambling houses in the city were Humphrey Marshall (W-Ky.) and Thomas Pratt (W-Md.). Marshall served as a representative in the Thirty-First and Thirty-Second Congresses and, upon arriving in Washington, situated himself at the National Hotel, which had a close proximity to Pendleton's. He was universally known for his gambling proclivities; one paper remarked that he "spent much more of his time" in the "gambling hells [*sic*] of Washington than in his seat on the floor of the House of Representatives, or in attending to his duties." Perhaps because he was a hard drinker, Marshall rarely won any money at these establishments. On being appointed minister to China in 1852, the Kentuckian was rumored to have gambled away six months pay and was forced to accept a loan from Pendleton in order to reach his diplomatic post. While he left no official record of gambling, such behavior could explain why he frequently complained of being "infernally poor."[41]

Pratt, on the other hand, was a fairly successful gambler. A Whig senator from Maryland, he was known as "the King of Poker" because of his fondness for and skill at the game. Pratt had the honor of winning the largest sum ever taken from Pendleton's gambling house a few years after the Sumner attack—a cool $15,000. Because of the unspoken agreement among politicians not to publicize their misdeeds, however, the story was falsely reported in papers around the country. These newspapers claimed Pratt's Maryland colleague, Senator James A. Pearce was the winner, and exaggerated the payout to $180,000. Frustrated, Pearce fiercely denied any such behavior, claiming he had never set foot in a gambling house before, let alone won any money. The real story—Pratt's winnings—never came out publicly. Senator William Pitt Fessenden (R-Maine) explained the circumstances to ex-senator Hamilton Fish (W-N.Y.): "The story annoyed Pearce as you may suppose—particularly as he did not love Pratt well enough to be a willing father to his sins. We all applied to Pearce for a loan, of course." As Fessenden suggested, even though he and the Marylanders were from two different parties and sections, none of them intended to give up the truth, except privately, to a member of the congressional fraternity.[42]

In addition to forming personal connections, gambling houses also provided ample room for corruption and shady lobbying deals. Men who lost their money at the faro table had to find a way to pay back the dealers or risk being ruined. Rather than face the consequences of his gambling debts, Mississippian Colonel Lewis Taylor, a clerk in the office of the first comptroller of the treasury of Washington, forged $15,000 in treasury notes. Another government employee committed suicide after losing his money to gambling. As clerks, these men probably did not have the respectability or power to borrow money or receive a bribe.[43]

Congressmen, on the other hand, had plenty of respectability and power, and therefore could become susceptible to under-the-table proposals from lobbyists. While most congressmen did not leave records of their dealings with men seeking political favors, a majority of Washingtonians believed that gambling houses were the sites of many such crooked coalitions. Men seeking favors learned quickly how to take advantage of one of the many politicians who frequented these houses. "A strong lobbyist will permit himself to lose heavily at the poker-table, under the assumption that the great Congressman who wins the stake will look leniently upon the little appropriation he means to ask for," one observer explained. "As the appropriation is sure to be twenty-fold the loss at cards, it is plain that the loser really plays the best game at poker." Such behavior among lobbyists was so common that one paper insisted Pendleton's and other halls "have done more to demoralize legislation than all the other debasing and corrupting influences which have been brought to bear upon weak, venal, or needy members of Congress."[44]

Gambling halls were not the only places that lobbyists and other office seekers used their influence. Because Washington was known as "a city of profligate men and abandoned women," those in search of jobs or votes could also use the sexual promiscuity of the nation's capital to their advantage. Willie Mangum described one such example of using sex for office at a dinner party in late 1847. According to David Outlaw, who was one of the guests at the party, Mangum explained that his experience occurred when the Senate was considering John C. Spencer's nomination to the Supreme Court in 1844, and "it was pretty well known that he would be rejected unless some of the Whig Senators would vote for him." Spencer told a young friend of his that if he could secure a Whig vote for him in the Senate, the young man could have a clerkship in the Court. Apparently this young man had a pretty sister because "M[angum] was sent for, introduced into this girl's bed room, she dressed in dishabille, and told if he would vote to confirm the nomination she could deny him nothing." According to Mangum, the young man used his sister to try the same stunt with Georgia senator John M. Berrien.[45]

It was all in good fun for Mangum to share this story over drinks with a few friends. But as in their approach to their gambling colleagues, politicians typically did not discuss infidelity and other sexual behavior with newspapermen or those outside the political fraternity who might publicize the acts. Outlaw was no exception to this general rule. While he reported cases of sexual immorality to his wife, he never let these stories slip to newspapermen. And, from Outlaw's perspective, there was much to report since, outside of lobbyist influence, there was already a significant amount of womanizing, infidelity, and general female immorality taking place, even by nineteenth-century standards. Outlaw himself noted a number of stories of congressmen going home with married ladies, women sending married men valentines, and even a senator producing a child out of wedlock with a boardinghouse owner.[46]

Isaac Bassett, a senate employee for more than half a century, left similarly detailed private accounts of sexual misdeeds, including those of the most prominent members of Congress. According to Bassett, lawmakers whispered around the Capitol in the 1830s that Daniel Webster, the famed Massachusetts orator, had a black son with a waitress who worked at Gadsby's Hotel. Bassett also claimed to have firsthand experience of South Carolina senator John C. Calhoun's profligate ways. When Bassett was appointed as a Senate messenger, one of his jobs was to deliver mail to the members. Calhoun, who had known Bassett for some years, told the messenger to do more than just bring the mail to his house; he left instructions for Bassett to enter his boardinghouse room and leave his letters on a designated table. One evening, just as it was getting dark, Bassett claims he entered Calhoun's room only to hear some rustling in one of the corners. The messenger turned around "and saw a very fine looking *ladie* on the sofa with Mr Calhoun. She seamed to be very much excited. She said 'let me go he will expose me.' 'O No,' [said Calhoun] 'it is only the messenger with my *mail*, I *dont* mind him.'" The next day, Bassett learned that the woman was the wife of a navy officer who boarded at the same house.[47]

Word of this sort of behavior did reach the public on occasion, particularly when violence of some sort was involved. This can be illustrated by two examples, both of which took place in Lafayette Square. The first was a whirlwind romance and near elopement between the wealthy banker William W. Corcoran's daughter, Louly, and the secretary of the Spanish legation, a Mr. Muruaga, in May 1858. Louly was the heiress to her father's great fortune—rumored to be somewhere around $5 million—and the banker was not willing to let a Spanish secretary steal his daughter. Upon learning of their flirtation, Corcoran banned Muruaga from his home and forbade Louly to see the Spaniard. But the secretary ignored the order, arranging to meet the young lady at the Corcoran house one afternoon while her father was visiting with his friend, Senator Jesse Bright (D-Ind.). When Muruaga came to the front door and the young heiress led the secretary into the gallery, a servant spotted them and hurried to Bright's house to inform on the couple. Corcoran and Bright stormed back to the house and a row ensued; after being ejected from the house, Muruaga threw his glove in the banker's face by way of a challenge, and Corcoran drew his pistol. Fortunately, the exchange was broken up before anyone was hurt.[48]

Because the collision between Muruaga and Corcoran happened outside the banker's home on Lafayette Square, in full view of bystanders, it became news in papers throughout the country. As *Harper's Weekly* noted, the story "caused great excitement in fashionable circles, though every effort [was] made to prevent and suppress it." The public nature of the tryst also had another, considerably more political, consequence. For years, Corcoran had considered President James Buchanan one of his closest friends. Following the incident with Muruaga, the banker asked Buchanan to demand that the Spanish government bring the secretary back to Spain. Yet the demand would certainly cause a disagreement with the Spanish government, and thus the president refused. Furious, Corcoran broke off his friendship with Buchanan, and the two did not reconcile for several months, until Louly became engaged to George Eustis, a representative in Congress from Louisiana.[49]

A second, even more public example, which took place in February 1859, was the exposure of a tryst between Teresa Sickles, the wife of Senator Daniel E. Sickles (D-N.Y.), and Philip Barton Key, the U.S. Attorney for the District of Columbia—the same U.S. Attorney who prosecuted the civil case against Brooks in 1856. Key, who was known to his friends as "Barton," had lost his wife nearly six years before and had since become "renowned as a lady's man," enjoying the company of several fashionable women in the city. In 1858 Barton quickly became enamored with Teresa after meeting her at one of Mr. Sickles's weekly parties at his home on the west side of Lafayette Square. In good time, according to one newspaper, "at balls, at parties, in the street, at receptions, at theatres, every where, Mrs. Sickles was invariably accompanied by Phil Barton Key." Washington's residents may have been discreet with reporters, but they still passed rumors among one another. By January 1859, whispers about a budding romance between

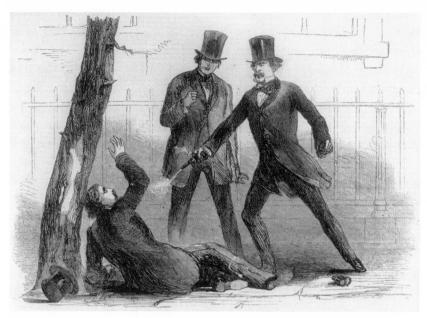

Figure 13. "Homicide of P. Barton Key by Hon. Daniel E. Sickles, at Washington, on Sunday, February 27, 1859." *Harper's Weekly*, March 12, 1859. Prints and Photographs Division, Library of Congress.

Barton and Teresa were rampant. Sickles got word of his wife's infidelity after a party at his house one evening, when he received an anonymous tip that the couple often met secretly in a house leased by one of the city's free African Americans.

Filled with rage, Sickles forced his wife to confess and demanded that she explain to him how the two arranged their meetings. Tearfully, Teresa admitted Barton would wave a handkerchief from a window in the Club House, which stood across Lafayette Square directly opposite Sickles's mansion. A few days later, Sickles saw the signal from the Club House. Without hesitation, he marched out to the square and waited for the U.S. Attorney to arrive. When Barton came out of the Club House, the New Yorker pointed his gun and called out, "Key, you scoundrel, you have dishonored my house, you must die." Barton retreated backward toward 16th Street, begging the senator, "Don't shoot me." But Sickles stood over Barton, aimed his pistol and repeated his words, "You villain, you have dishonored my house, and you must die!" And with that, he shot Philip Barton Key dead. Satisfied, Sickles walked a few blocks to Attorney General Jeremiah Black's house and surrendered himself to the authorities.[50]

The Sickles trial, which took place in April, was a fiasco. The New Yorker's lawyers, including future attorney general and secretary of war Edwin M. Stanton (D-Ohio), argued that Sickles had gone temporarily insane. After deliberating for seventy minutes, the jury agreed with the defense and acquitted the New Yorker. The verdict met with a mixed public reaction, and Sickles briefly retired from private life before returning as a general in the Civil War.[51]

Although Sickles's case was the most famous example of violence stemming from romantic engagements, his was by no means the only one. Violent arguments between various Washingtonians were quite common in the mid-nineteenth century, and they frequently involved the use of weapons. As the wife of one former congressman from Massachusetts mused, "What is Washington? Why Washington . . . seems to be a kind of city where people stab each other & knock each other down when ever they feel like it, so that the news from it is generally quite playful and enlivening." For example, a man named Colonel Lee, who served on the Washington city counsel and worked as a clerk in the pension office, accused an Alexandria native, David Hume, of picking his pocket at one of the president's levees. The two met a few days later at Lee's office, and Hume demanded an apology. Lee refused, prompting Hume to strike Lee with his cane. Lee then drew a revolver and shot him, killing him instantly. In another broken up tryst, a man shot his wife's lover four times in September 1850.[52]

This sort of violence was commonplace among Washington's politicians. Congressmen, cabinet members, and others engaged in a variety of different violent altercations throughout the antebellum period, from drunken fights at hotel bars and in gambling houses to formal duels between enemies, arranged with friends to serve as seconds. All of this violence was not limited to disputes between Northerners and Southerners. Intrasectional violence was common, particularly when alcohol and insults mixed in one of the many taverns or hotel bars. In one example, former congressman Jeremiah Clemens (D-Ala.) was enjoying himself at a drinking house with his friend, Congressman Presley Ewing (W-Ky.), when another man named Harris entered the bar. Ewing offered to introduce Harris to Clemens, and when Harris refused, Clemens struck him over the head with a heavy pistol. Similarly, Representative James B. Clay (D-Ky.), son of the famed Kentucky Whig Henry Clay, got into a violent argument with General Cullom of Kentucky while the two were drinking at a Washington barroom. Cullom became irritated by some of Clay's remarks and called him "the degenerate son of an illustrious sire," whereupon Clay called him a "d—d liar," and

Cullom struck him. Eventually the two worked out their differences with the help of Senator Albert G. Brown (D-Miss.) and Joseph R. Underwood (W-Ky.).[53]

Northerners had their share of intrasectional disputes as well. What started as a friendly meeting on Eighteenth Street between Representatives William English (D-Ind.) and William Montgomery (D-Pa.) quickly turned violent when Montgomery refused to speak to English or shake his hand. "I speak to no puppy, sir!" called out the 200-pound Pennsylvanian. According to one report, the significantly lighter, 150-pound English "immediately struck [Montgomery] with a heavy lignum-vitæ sword-cane across the head, knocking him partially down and into the gutter, and breaking the stick." Rattled, Montgomery grabbed a brick from the street and threw it at English who quickly dodged behind a post. Their disagreement was resolved only when a mutual friend persuaded English to apologize.[54]

Friendly card games could turn ugly after nothing more than an insulting remark. In August 1856, two Democratic congressmen got into a quarrel in the midst of a card game; William Richardson of Illinois challenged Edson B. Olds of Indiana to a duel. Daniel Sickles managed to get himself into a nasty fight with a fellow New Yorker named J. McLeod Murphy only a few years before he shot Barton Key. The two men argued in the lobby of Willard's Hotel when Murphy accused Sickles of "assailing his private character." Unsatisfied with Sickles's response, Murphy challenged the congressman to a duel, which he refused. A few days later, Murphy gained access to Sickles's hotel room, and finding the congressman in bed, "attempted to cowhide him."[55]

One of the most memorable examples of a congressman becoming involved in reckless violence occurred only a couple of weeks before Brooks attacked Sumner. On May 8, 1856, around eleven o'clock in the morning, Representative Philemon T. Herbert (D-Calif.) arrived at Willard's Hotel, where he regularly took his meals, and asked a boy from the dining room for his breakfast. Because of the late hour, the boy told Herbert he would have to get permission from the kitchen, at which point the Californian flew into a rage. Herbert screamed "clear out, you Irish son of a bitch" at the boy and then at the headwaiter, Thomas Keating, who was standing next to him. Herbert must have been unsatisfied with Keating's verbal response because he proceeded to punch the headwaiter in the neck with his pistol. Keating then threw a plate at the Californian. The fight escalated until Herbert shot Keating through the lungs with a revolver.[56]

Herbert's behavior made national news. When Northerners learned that

Herbert originally hailed from Alabama, some of them added the Keating shooting to the list of crimes against their section by reckless Southerners. As one historian explains, "the Republicans' case against Brooks's bullying attack on Sumner was already in place before that incident occurred; they were already making it against Herbert." Yet, for most Washingtonians, including both politicians and locals, the random violence was simply par for the course. "It appears to be a common practice to carry revolvers to the breakfast table," joked Washingtonian Henry Wise to his father-in-law following the shooting. The local paper, the *Daily National Intelligencer*, reported the shooting but did not editorialize on the matter and, after a second city trial in July, a jury acquitted the Californian. Herbert returned to his post in the House.[57]

Although Herbert's attack on Thomas Keating was impromptu, other congressmen engaged in more formal violence by issuing a challenge for a duel. These duels included some cross-sectional quarrels but also a number of intrasectional pairs. Many of these "affairs of honor" had their origins in some sort of disagreement in the House or Senate. Representatives Thomas L. Clingman (W-N.C.) and William L. Yancey (D-Ala.), for instance, arranged a duel in 1845 after trading barbs in the House. The following year, Thomas Bayly (D-Va.) and Garrett Davis (W-Ky.) similarly exchange heated remarks that led to an official standoff. One of the most famous duels in the late 1850s was between Representatives Galusha Grow (R-Pa.) and Laurence Keitt (D-S.C.), Brooks's old accomplice in the Sumner attack.[58]

Although duels were one way to settle congressional differences, sometimes disagreements did not make it outside the Capitol. Grow and Keitt, for example, had it out on the floor of the House before agreeing to a formal encounter. The congressmen were drowsy after a long night of work and at two o'clock, Grow went over to the Democratic side of the House to complain about a motion by John Quitman (D-Miss.). Keitt got in Grow's way, and the two exchanged angry words before the South Carolinian grabbed the Pennsylvanian by the neck and began to choke him. Suddenly, about thirty congressmen were involved in the row. Alexander Stephens, who watched the melee from his seat, got some fun out of the situation when he saw William Barksdale (D-Miss.) and Elihu Washburne (R-Ill.) approach each other. Washburne aimed a blow at Barksdale's forehead, but as Stephens described, "the blow struck a little too high and only sent Barksdale's wig a flying." According to the Georgian, "this enraged [Barksdale] more than if he had been felled sprawling on the floor—Few persons knew he wore a wig—He quit the fight and went searching for his *scalp* which was gone and being trampled." Amid roars of laughter at Barksdale losing his hair, the uproar died down, and the congressmen returned to their seats.[59]

Long-serving members of the House had other ridiculous stories of fisticuffs in the Capitol building. Hugh Haralson (D-Ga.) and George W. Jones (W-Tenn.) got into a "regular boxing match" on the floor of the House in 1848 when Jones accused Haralson of improper voting. The two men struck each other and knocked over a desk before they were separated, at which point Haralson and Jones shook hands and apologized to the House. A couple of members suggested that a committee be appointed to investigate the matter, but instead the House passed a vote accepting the apologies and moved on. John Sherman (R-Ohio) and John V. Wright (D-Tenn.) got into a similarly ridiculous tiff that prompted Sherman to throw "a quantity of wafers into Wright's face." Wright then attempted to strike Sherman, but was stopped by James Morrison Harris (AM-Md.), who sat near the Ohioan. As in the previous case, House members simply ignored the disagreement between the two men.[60]

As these stories illustrate, violence was common in mid-nineteenth-century Washington, even in the Capitol itself. The culture of a knockdown society allowed politicians to settle their differences and occasionally even apologize. Furthermore, a congressman did not have to be unpleasant or disliked to be involved in vice and violence. Mangum and Marcy were both well regarded personally by many of their colleagues. Haralson was typically considered a harmless drunk, and Sherman and Wright both had their share of friends.[61]

Perhaps the best example of a well-liked congressman who became embroiled in Washington's immoral and violent culture was Brooks himself. As Virginia Clay remembered, Brooks "was one of the most magnetic and widely admired men in the capital" before his attack on Charles Sumner. Local socialite Benjamin French wrote in his diary in February 1857 that he met the South Carolinian several years earlier at a dinner at the National Hotel and that Brooks, "made the most favorable impression on me then and from that time onward till his attack on Mr. Sumner. I regarded him as a most amiable & worthy gentleman."[62]

Most important, these instances of violence did not cause Northerners to blindly group Southerners together as oppressors, or vice versa. Throughout the North (and within the Republican Party in particular), local politicians excoriated the Southern "Slave Power"; and in the South, Democratic newspapers and party leaders railed against abolitionists. But in Washington, politicians continued to hold a more nuanced view of men from the other section. Perhaps the best example of this approach was an exchange between two Massachusetts men—abolitionist Theodore Parker and Republican senator Henry Wilson—two years after the Sumner attack. In May 1858, Parker got word that Wilson had attended the funeral of South Carolina senator Josiah Evans and made several complimentary remarks about the deceased. Surprised and even angry, Parker wrote Wilson asking the Massachusetts senator how he could praise one of Sumner's attackers. Wilson replied that Evans, "was a slaveholder but in all other matters noble and just and on this question very moderate for his section." The South Carolinian, he continued, "was loved by all of us here. . . . You know my hatred of slavery and that I believe it a crime to hold men in bondage, but I know also that a man may be a kind and generous man and be a slave holder. Evans was such a man and I do not believe he had an enemy here." As for Sumner, he had defended the Massachusetts senator "at some risk" to his own reputation. Moreover, he insisted, "when the case demands it I will risk my life to vindicate him, but he can not ask me to differ from every man who has differed from him." In other words, Evans may have been a Southerner, but he was still a friend; and Sumner, of all people, should have known better.[63]

Ultimately, the caning of Charles Sumner did have an important impact on American sectionalism and perhaps even the coming of the Civil War. But this influence did not necessarily extend to politicians in Washington, D.C. Living in the rough and rowdy capital city where violence and vice reigned on street corners, in hotels, and even in the Capitol itself, most politicians saw events like the caning in context. Such a view helps to explain why Nathaniel Banks, the Speaker of the House, appointed a moderate committee to evaluate the event, and why the attack was rarely discussed in Washington circles in the coming years. Rather than rehashing the Sumner attack, Washington politicians were infinitely more concerned with the future of Kansas. Over the next two years the fate of that territory, and particularly its constitution, became a central discussion point in the capital city. And amid that discussion, two men from two different parties struck up a friendship that would have critical consequences for the rest of the decade.

CHAPTER SIX

We Know No Lecompton Here

Cross-Partisan Relationships and the Fight over Kansas

By the mid-1850s, John Jordan Crittenden was part of a dying breed. The seventy-year old senator from Kentucky had been one of the earliest supporters of the Whig Party from its inception in the mid-1830s. Many of his old Whig colleagues, such as Henry Clay and Daniel Webster, had passed away. Others had left the party to join the fledgling Republican organization in the North, or switched over to the Democrats in South. The Whig Party was so depleted that Crittenden himself would have to find a new political organization.[1]

Unlike some Southern Whigs, the Kentucky senator had no intention of switching allegiances to the Democrats. Crittenden had long opposed that party's ideological tenets, and recent events had strengthened his disapproval. In 1854, when Stephen A. Douglas and other members of his party passed the Kansas-Nebraska Act, the Kentuckian was deeply troubled. Temporarily retired from Washington politics during that year, Crittenden wrote to a colleague of his strong opposition. Not only did he dislike the idea of popular sovereignty, but he believed that repealing the Missouri Compromise was a mistake that would produce increased sectional agitation.[2]

Crittenden was devastated to see those fears realized. The Kansas-Nebraska Act had done nothing but create violence and discord in the territory, resulting most recently in "Bleeding Kansas" out west and "Bleeding Sumner" in Washington. Crittenden believed that Democratic policies were much to blame for these events. Thus, retaining his opposition to Democrats' policies, the Kentucky senator turned instead to the American Party, the political arm of the nativist Know-Nothing group. American party membership among Washington politicians was small—in December 1857 they counted only five senators and fourteen representatives—but several of them had come over from the old Whig Party. And many of these men, including Crittenden, retained an ideological bond with their former Whig friends.[3]

During the first session of the Thirty-Fifth Congress, Crittenden and his fellow Americans would have to face the consequences of popular sovereignty and other Democratic mistakes head on. In February 1858, President James Buchanan submitted to Congress the frame for a state government in Kansas—the Lecompton Constitution. The Lecompton document was, by all accounts, a violation of the principle of popular sovereignty. The final document allowed slavery in the state even though antislavery men outnumbered their rivals 17,000 to 7,000. The free-state men had boycotted the election of delegates to a convention tasked with drawing up the constitution and had similarly refused to participate in a final referendum. Ignoring these concerns, Buchanan and his cabinet lieutenants pressed for its approval.[4]

Crittenden was troubled by the administration's attempts to pass so dubious a document. He became one of the loudest opponents of the sham constitution in the Senate. In late March, he tried to replace the bill with a new one providing for a resubmission of the Lecompton Constitution to the people of Kansas in a carefully controlled vote. Yet, Democrats had a 41-25 majority in the Senate over Americans and Republicans. Even with a handful of defections, the Democratic majority easily passed the Lecompton Constitution by the end of the month.[5]

Luckily for Crittenden, opposition was stronger in the lower house. On April 1, the fourteen American Party members joined with Republicans and some Northern Democrats in substituting Crittenden's version for the Lecompton Bill, 120-112. Following this vote, members of a Senate-House conference committee met and negotiated a compromise, agreeing on a substitute called the English bill. Under this legislation, Congress would resubmit the constitution to the entire Kansas population, and if they rejected the Lecompton document, Kansans would not be able to apply for statehood again until the population reached 90,000. The Buchanan administration decided to support the English bill to save political face, and both houses passed it in April 1858. In June, the elderly Crittenden left Washington and returned to his home in Frankfort, Kentucky, to spend a month or two relaxing away from his political duties.[6]

Not long after Crittenden arrived home, he received a letter from an old Whig associate in Illinois, Abraham Lincoln. Crittenden and Lincoln had been friendly since at least 1848 when they served in Congress together. During that first session of the Thirtieth Congress, Crittenden boarded at Mrs. Selden's, where four of the seven Young Indians also had rooms. The Kentucky senator was sympathetic with the Young Indian cause; like Lincoln, he had long supported his Kentucky colleague, Henry Clay, for the Whig nomination but thought Zachary Taylor had a better chance to win in 1848. Crittenden may have even sat in on a few of the Young Indian meetings. In addition, Lincoln's wife, Mary Todd, hailed from Kentucky and knew Crittenden through her father. Overall, the two men had much in common, and Lincoln admired Crittenden.[7]

That summer, Lincoln, who had joined the fledgling Republican movement, was in the midst of a heated political battle against Illinois Democrat Stephen A. Douglas for a U.S. Senate seat. Lincoln believed he had a good chance to win, in large part because many in Illinois and throughout the North opposed Douglas's Kansas-Nebraska Act and its increasingly negative impact on the territories. But as the summer dragged on, Lincoln began to hear rumors that Crittenden was supporting Douglas in the election. Puzzled, he sent the Kentucky senator a letter on July 7 asking for clarification. There is "a story being whispered about here that you are anxious for the re-election of Mr. Douglas to the United States Senate," he wrote. "I do not believe the story, but still it gives me some uneasiness. . . . You have no warmer friends than here in Illinois, and I assure you nine-tenths . . . of them would be mortified exceedingly by anything of the sort from you."[8]

The response was not what the Illinois Republican hoped. "Mr. Douglas and myself have always belonged to different parties, opposed in politics to each other," Crittenden admitted. Nonetheless, the Kentuckian *had* made several positive remarks about Douglas and had allowed them to be published in newspapers in Illinois and Washington. Crittenden was sorry that his feelings about Douglas's reelection had upset his old Whig colleague but, he told Lincoln, "I must confess that I still entertain them, and whatever I do must correspond with them."[9]

Why would Crittenden, who strongly opposed the Kansas-Nebraska Act and its effects and who was a longtime colleague and acquaintance of Abraham Lincoln, throw his support behind Douglas? Part of the answer comes from the Lecompton battle that Crittenden had just fought in Washington. As the Kentuckian explained to Lincoln, Douglas had surprised much of Congress when he decided to break with the Buchanan administration over the fraudulent constitution. "Mr. Douglas's opposition was highly gratifying to me," Crittenden told Lincoln. But the Illinois Democrat's position was not gratifying to Buchanan. Over the next few months, Buchanan and his friends actively campaigned against Douglas in Illinois, willing to sacrifice a Democratic seat to be rid of the Little Giant. Crittenden thought Douglas was being unfairly punished for his principled opposition. "I could not but wish for his success and triumph over such persecution," he wrote.[10]

Yet the Buchanan administration's "persecution" of Douglas could not have been enough for Crittenden to support the man who authored the dreadful Kansas-Nebraska Act and who had spearheaded the distasteful policies of the Democratic Party for at least a generation. No, there was more to it. The two men had actually formed a bond—a friendship even—over the course of the last session. To begin with, Douglas had not just opposed the Lecompton Constitution, he had supported Crittenden's calls for a new vote. He even wrote the Kentuckian a note in March praising his "great and patriotic speech" against Lecompton. Crittenden and Douglas each felt a sense of fraternity toward the other man as a result of working through the Kansas debacle.[11]

The two men had also strengthened this bond in the social circles of the capital city. Before this first session of the Thirty-Fifth Congress, Crittenden and Douglas had served in Washington simultaneously for some years, but had never been close or run in the same social circles. They had their political differences, certainly, but for a long time they were also divided by age and experience; Douglas joined the Senate in 1847, at the age of thirty-four, when Crittenden was sixty and had first served in Washington thirty years before. From the perspective of an elder statesman like Crittenden, the Illinois firebrand was young and inexperienced. But by 1858, Douglas was not only a veteran of Congress, he also had a new wife who could help him better navigate social life in Washington. In November 1856, he had married Adele Cutts, a stunning and popular young woman who came from a fashionable family of the capital. Together, Douglas and Adele began to take a more prominent role in Washington society.[12]

As Adele was a major player in Washington social life, so too was Crittenden's wife, Elizabeth Ashley. Crittenden had taken the Missouri widow as his third wife in 1853, and since then Elizabeth had become popular among all the ladies of Washington. As one senator's wife remembered, "One met dear old Mrs. Crittenden everywhere. She was of the most social disposition." Mr. and Mrs. Crittenden were friendly with Buchanan, but spent little time in the president's social group. After the very public dispute between

Buchanan and Douglas, the Little Giant and his wife also spent less time with his Democratic rival. Amid Washington's small social sphere, John and Elizabeth Crittenden generally ran in the same circles as Stephen and Adele Douglas. For example, Adele and Elizabeth could be found in the Senate galleries together during the early debates over the Lecompton Constitution, and the Crittendens were among the Douglases' guests at an elegant party at the end of January 1858.[13]

Crittenden and Douglas were not simply united by common outrage against the Buchanan administration; the two men had developed a cross-partisan friendship in 1858 in part because of the experience of living in Washington. In fact, the capital city promoted not only cross-sectional sociability but also individual relationships across party. The word *individual* is critical to understanding these relationships. Washington lawmakers felt strongly about their political allegiances. Whigs, Democrats, Republicans, and other partisans did not abandon their political organizations upon arriving in the capital city. But in the course of negotiating a bill or socializing in the city, two men with very different party backgrounds could become friends. Many of these relationships grew out of the shared experience of working in the House, the Senate, the cabinet, the Supreme Court, or even as president of the United States. Serving in one of these roles in the federal government was an exceptional experience; few Americans would have the opportunity to know what it was like, and as a result, these Washington bodies or offices could produce a sense of fraternity among men from different parties.

This fraternal instinct manifested itself in three ways. First, most federal lawmakers tried to remain on good terms with colleagues in their specific political body. Even if they disagreed on party (or sectional) issues, and stated those feelings strongly in speeches and publications, most politicians were still comfortable interacting in pleasant ways with their fellow lawmakers. There was often a difference between public excoriation of the other political faction and private sociability across party lines. Second, the shared Washington political experience, particularly of serving in a high-profile job like president or Speaker of the House, could produce mutual appreciation and understanding across party lines. Men who served as secretary of state or attorney general were quick to help each other make a smooth transition from one administration to the next or provide critical updates on the progress on each other's projects while serving in the cabinet.

Finally, out of this fraternity and sociability grew a number of cross-partisan friendships among the men who lived in the capital city. These friendships could be both long lasting and influential. As in the case of

Crittenden and Douglas, they often crossed partisan *and* sectional boundaries. Therefore, in order to fully understand why Crittenden would come to support Douglas in the 1858 Illinois Senate election, we must look at their experience in the context of Washington's cross-partisanship.

■ At the beginning of each new Congress, politicians with a variety of experience descended on Washington. Several freshmen lawmakers arrived in the capital for the first time and knew only a few members from their home state or, in some cases, their college; they may have met a few others during party caucuses just before Congress opened. Others had been absent from Washington temporarily because of lost elections or short-term retirement and would recognize several old, friendly faces. A few had been serving in Congress for so long they knew almost everyone in the body. Yet, regardless of their experience, all who arrived in Washington made their way to the Capitol and entered the House or Senate for the first day of the new session. Before each body was called to order, there was a general shaking of hands, introductions and funny reminiscences, and new members became part of the House or Senate fraternity. After a few weeks in their political body, many echoed the words of Michigan Democrat Alpheus Felch, a new senator in 1847, "I have been introduced to most of the Senators—and a more pleasant and gentlemanly set of men I have never met."[14]

Particularly at the beginning of a long session, politicians faced the prospect of many hours with their colleagues in the Capitol, and they knew that their time would be more pleasantly spent if they got along well. Work in the Capitol certainly was not always harmonious; angry exchanges in the form of duels and other violence were a critical part of the Washington lifestyle. Yet the prevalence of congressional fighting and the general sociability of the chambers were not mutually exclusive. Despite personal disagreements and occasional violence, lawmakers strove to make their workplace tolerable by maintaining amiable relations among most of the members.[15]

Senators, in particular, were proud of the cordial interaction between themselves and their colleagues from both parties. For example, Texas Democrat Sam Houston was delighted to report to his wife, "I am on amicable terms with the members of the senate generally." Fellow Texan Thomas J. Rusk similarly boasted to a friend, "I have had the good fortune here to acquire the friendship of many of those whose good opinion is most desirable as well amongst Whigs as Democrats." Even in August 1856, only a few months after Preston Brooks's attack on Charles Sumner, New York Republican William Seward told his wife, "It gives me pleasure to say that as the session draws to a close, it is likely to end in more pleasant relations between other members of the Senate and myself than have ever before existed." Specifically, Seward felt that "the Democrats are generally respectful and kind."[16]

Because the House of Representatives was a larger body than the Senate, politicians there generally found it harder to get to know all of their fellow members. Yet, many representatives felt an equally strong impetus to get along with their colleagues. After a few months in Washington, Guy M. Bryan (D-Tex.) was happy to inform his wife, "I have laid now a foundation with my colleagues. . . . I have the[ir] respect." David Settle Reid (D-N.C.) served in the House for two terms in the 1840s and after a stint as governor of North Carolina, was then elected to the Senate. Upon arriving in the upper chamber in 1854 he was pleased to find that "a considerable number" of his former House colleagues "are now in the Senate, and it was a subject of remark among us when we met to-day." If a representative decided to make a trip to Washington after retiring from his congressional duties, he was met with equally pleasant remembrances. Visiting the capital city after leaving to become the governor of Georgia, Howell Cobb (D-Ga.) was "much gratified with the reception I have met, from my old friends, it could not have possibly been more cordial." Similarly, Lincoln Clark (D-Iowa) returned to the Capitol for the first time in several years and told his wife, "Saw several old acquaintances—they seemed glad to see me."[17]

Many Washington lawmakers could maintain such pleasant relationships with members across party lines because they were able to separate colleagues' political positions from their personalities. Perhaps this is best illustrated by politicians' feelings when a popular member of the House or Senate passed away. During the course of the next few days, men who knew the deceased well—including politicians from both sections and parties—read thoughtful eulogies and reflected on the deceased. Following the death of John C. Calhoun (D-S.C.) in 1850, Daniel Webster (W-Mass.) told a friend "seldom agreeing with him for the last 20 yrs, I yet feel touched, at the prospect of his death. . . . Personally, good feelings have always subsisted between us, & I shall most sincerely lament his death." When Alexander Barrow (W-La.) died in 1846, a new member who did not know Barrow personally was moved by the emotions of nearly every man in the chamber on both sides of the aisle during the eulogies. As Artemas Hale wrote in his diary, "It seems[Barrow] was a man universally respected, esteemed and loved—it was no formal unmeaning ceremony but the spontaneous outpourings of sincere heartfelt grief."[18]

Even those who clashed over political issues could feel a deep sense of loss in the passing of a friendly colleague. During the Thirty-First Congress, William Seward (W-N.Y.) and Thomas Rusk (D-Tex.) had their differences; in fact, Seward tried to goad Rusk into a backroom agreement in the Senate, but later backed out, much to the irritation of the Texan. Yet the two eventually repaired their broken relationship and even worked together on a telegraph bill in 1857. Thus, Seward was heartbroken when Rusk committed suicide later that year, and the New Yorker insisted upon delivering a eulogy in the Senate. "It is true, that I was not his kinsman, nor his neighbor, nor even his political associate. I was, nevertheless, attached to him by bonds strong as the charity that consecrates even those relations," Seward told his fellow senators. "I was his captive; an adversary overpowered . . . by his generosity, in my first encounter with him here in this field of sectional strife, released on parol [sic], a prisoner at large, but devoted to him by gratitude for the period of my whole life."[19]

Mourning surpassed partisanship during the more ceremonial aspects of congressional funerals as well. If the funeral took place in Washington, men of all political stripes tended to participate in the ceremony. For example, when John Quincy Adams (W-Mass.) died while serving in the House in 1848, pallbearers included Thomas Hart Benton (D-Mo.), Linn Boyd (D-Ky.), and John C. Calhoun (D-S.C.), in addition to Joseph R. Ingersoll (W-Pa.) and Truman Smith (W-Conn.). A few months after Adams's death, Representative James A. Black (D-S.C.) passed away. Black's funeral also included a cross-partisan group of pallbearers; among them were Henry Cranston (W-R.I.), William Cocke (W-Tenn.), John Harmanson (D-La.), Washington Hunt (W-N.Y.), Thomas Ligon (D-Md.), John McClernand (D-Ill.), and Julius Rockwell (W-Mass.).[20]

Such friendly feelings were not limited to the deceased; lawmakers also got along pleasantly with political foes who were still living. Congressmen did differ substantially on subjects such as tariffs, internal improvements, the legacy of Andrew Jackson, and especially slavery. Members voiced these opinions in debate, and were careful to state their positions strongly, particularly when speaking for buncombe. But politicians often felt differently about one another in private. Maine Republican William Pitt Fessenden, for example, despised the opinions of South Carolina Democrat James Henry Hammond on Lecompton, but, at the same time he thought Hammond was "socially a good fellow." Although Georgia Unionist Alexander Stephens disagreed with Henry Fuller (Opp-Pa.) on the Kansas-Nebraska Act, he explained that Fuller "individually or personally is a very good fellow—I like him well." Massachusetts Whig Robert Winthrop strongly opposed Alabama Democrat William L. Yancey's position regarding Texas annexation and other issues, but at the same time there were few Democrats for whom he felt "more interest or more friendly regard."[21]

The dichotomy between public and private relationships in Washington was often manifested in the Capitol itself when congressmen were operating "off the record." Winthrop took notice of this difference during debates over the Compromise of 1850. On the record, harsh words were exchanged on the Senate floor between the parties, and the Massachusetts senator faced much public criticism from Democrats Andrew P. Butler, Jefferson Davis, Henry S. Foote, and Pierre Soulé. But off the record, Winthrop told his friend John P. Kennedy (W-Md.), "I parted on good terms with them all." Massachusetts Free-Soiler Charles Sumner had a similar experience in 1852. After delivering a nearly four-hour speech in opposition to the fugitive slave law, Sumner received public excoriation from both Democrats and Whigs. Yet, as he told a friend, privately many of his colleagues complimented him, including Jesse Bright (D-Ind.), Lewis Cass (D-Mich.), James Shields (D-Ill.), Pierre Soulé (D-La.), and John Weller (D-Calif.). Sumner boasted, "Shields said 'it was the ablest speech ever made in the Senate on Slavery.'. . . Bright used even stronger language. Cass has complimented me warmly. Soulé has expressed himself in the strongest terms. Weller [used] strong terms of praise." Sumner knew these men could not state their opinions publicly, but was pleased by their kind words in private.[22]

Sumner's excitement about the praise from his Democratic colleagues may seem odd given his reaction to his 1856 attack and the behavior of his Republican colleagues in the years following. Yet, before the caning, Sumner generally got on well with his Democratic Senate colleagues, particularly outside the Capitol. Winthrop, who also hailed from Massachusetts but was not one of Sumner's biggest fans, joked about this private tendency to John P. Kennedy. Sumner was "a perfect lickspittle in private of those whom he reviles in his speeches," he explained. The Massachusetts Free-Soiler was friendly with men like Georgians Alexander Stephens and Robert Toombs, who had been Whigs until 1850, and one of Sumner's favorites from the Democratic side of the aisle was Pierre Soulé. Sumner and Soulé truly enjoyed each other's company and often made plans to visit each other socially even while disagreeing politically. Soulé "is of a generous nature; but sees things from a point of view very different from ours," Sumner told his friend Charles Francis Adams. "Personally, he awakens in me a warm friendship."[23]

As Sumner's experiences suggest, social interaction outside the Capitol of men from different parties was a key element in maintaining cordial relationships among colleagues. Partisans met at club gatherings, dinner parties, boardinghouses, and barrooms. Washington banker William Corcoran's dinner guest lists illustrate just how common such interaction was at his home; gatherings not only were cross-sectional but also crossed party boundaries. Sam Houston frequently commented on this sociability in his personal relationships outside the Capitol. After the Senate disbanded for the day, the Texas senator typically returned to the rooms in his hotel where "Whigs and Democrats alike visit me, and seem to eschew all political differences, in their associations with me."[24]

Another senator who frequently entertained men from both parties at his home was Stephen Douglas. During negotiations over the Lecompton Constitution, Republican members were occasionally spotted going into Douglas's house around dinner time or at other odd hours. Newspapers reported that several leading members of this party visited Douglas to discuss his position on Kansas, including Nathaniel P. Banks (R-Mass.), Anson Burlingame (R-Mass.), Schuyler Colfax (R-Ind.), Clark B. Cochrane (R-N.Y.), Benjamin Wade (R-Ohio), and former New York congressman Horace Greeley, fiery editor of the *New York Tribune*. Publicly accused of scheming with these Republicans for reelection, Douglas responded, "Men of all shades of political opinion have been in the habit of visiting my house for the ten years I have kept house in Washington."[25]

Although Douglas was trying to cover for his negotiations with Republicans—there was no doubt they had been discussing Kansas—his excuse was based in fact. Particularly by 1858, when Douglas and his wife Adele had become major players in Washington's fashionable society, men of all political stripes came to parties, dinners, and other gatherings at the Illinois Democrat's house. Even after abandoning the Southern Democrats during the Lecompton battle, Douglas continued to interact with a number of these men socially. In fact, by the following year, *Harper's Weekly* reported that Douglas was "never so popular with the . . . fashionable world" in Washington. One important example of this trend was Douglas's relationship with Guy M. Bryan (D-Tex.). Only a few days after the House defeated the Lecompton Constitution, Douglas had a small party at his home. Bryan was one of the guests, and Douglas invited the Texan to have a drink with him. A fellow Southern Democrat spotted them and looked surprised. As Bryan reported, his pro-Lecompton colleague "said, 'What! *You* drinking wine with Anti Lecompton'—I replied with my hand on the Senator's shoulder, '*We* know no Lecompton *here*!' '*You* are right Mr Bryan *we* know none *here*'!"[26]

While Douglas had relationships with Republicans, Democrats, and Americans from all around the city in 1858 and 1859, most of his closest friends came from the Senate. Because of the differing daily schedules required of men in either house of Congress, the Supreme Court, and the cabinet, it was often easier to make relationships in one's particular political body. Some lawmakers even felt their place in the Capitol was superior to others. This was particularly true among senators, who occasionally accused the House of Representatives of getting things accomplished only by "the sport of mere accident." By contrast, explained William Seward (R-N.Y.), the men of the Senate "act with unity of purpose." Senator Alpheus Felch (D-Mich.) agreed. "The Senate is a much more [quiet] and in every respect a more desirable place than the House," he told his wife.[27]

One body where cordial relations were critical to making daily interaction tolerable was the Supreme Court. Although Supreme Court justices were generally expected to rise above party differences, each member of the Court tended to retain political allegiances and ideologies. Furthermore, in the mid-nineteenth century, justices were known to operate as partisans, even running for president or other political office. As a result, members of the Supreme Court frequently formed close cross-partisan relationships while working and living in Washington. These men often boarded together and interacted socially in addition to working in their Capitol chamber.[28]

The importance of congenial relationships in the Supreme Court can be illustrated by the 1857 disagreement between Benjamin Curtis of Massachusetts, who was appointed to the bench in 1851 by Whig president Millard Fillmore, and Chief Justice Roger Taney of Maryland, a strict Democrat appointed during Andrew Jackson's presidency. In March 1857, the Supreme Court decided *Dred Scott v. Sandford*, a tension-fraught case regarding the citizenship of African Americans. Curtis and Taney strongly disagreed about what the Court should do—the chief justice issuing the majority opinion declaring that no black person could be a citizen of the United States and Curtis writing a dissenting opinion—but this was not where the difficulty lay. Taney and Curtis strongly disagreed on a number of issues but had kept their relations civil in and out of the courtroom. What set Curtis off was not so much a political issue as a procedural one. Curtis became angry when Taney refused to let the Supreme Court clerk distribute accounts of the *Dred Scott* majority opinion either for publication in the newspapers or for the private use of the other justices themselves. In the following months, the two men exchanged a series of nasty letters over the issue, and by the fall Curtis decided to resign from his position on the Supreme Court, having lost confidence in the process of the bench. Rather than creating a public uproar over the disagreement with Taney, however, Curtis blamed his resignation on the expense of living in Washington, a plausible excuse.[29]

Curtis's experience shows that the inability to get along could be so detrimental to the culture of the Supreme Court that one of the justices felt compelled to resign. This disagreement was particularly striking since most of the other Democratic appointees were sorry to see him leave the bench. In fact, they would miss Curtis *because of* his pleasant demeanor and sociability. Upon hearing of his resignation, two other Jacksonian justices, John Catron of Tennessee and James M. Wayne of Georgia, made these sentiments clear in letters to Curtis in September. "On personal grounds, I regret your resignation very much," wrote Catron. "I say in all sincerity, that in your case I never heard a word, nor saw an act calculated even to irritate. Your conduct afforded me pleasure in the consultation-room and your conversation delight over the social glass." Wayne agreed, telling the Massachusetts justice that he would miss him "privately as well as officially" and "shall ever cultivate for you and yours a very sincere friendship."[30]

Although the Senate and House were larger bodies, they were no less sociable than the Supreme Court. And the two easiest ways to forge cross-partisan relationships were through those houses' seating arrangements or while working together on an important bill. As in the modern Congress, both the Senate and House each had a center aisle that divided the chamber in half; one party typically sat on the left side of the aisle and the other party on the right. But these divisions were not uniform, particularly in the late 1850s when Congress included more than two parties and the groups were not equally divided. As a result, men from different parties could find themselves sitting next to one another in both chambers.

One example of this pattern can be seen in the seating arrangement of the Senate Chamber in the first session of the Thirty-Fifth Congress, when both houses would take up the Lecompton Constitution (see figure 14). Democrats had an overwhelming majority of thirty-six Senate seats. By contrast, Republicans held fifteen seats and a combination of men from the American Party, Opposition, and one Whig holdout made up the last nine members. Democrats occupied most of the seats on the right side of the chamber, with the exception of two American Party senators: Anthony Kennedy of Maryland and Sam Houston of Texas (who had been a Democrat until recently). But on the left side of the House, men with a variety of different political allegiances were thrown together; the eight Democrats who sat on the left were scattered among the Republicans, Americans, and Opposition men.

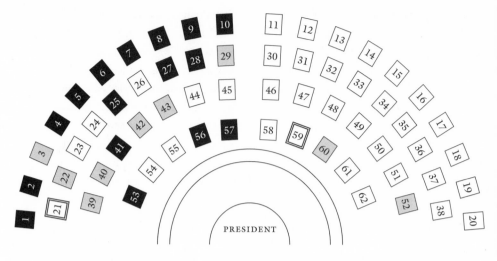

PRESIDENT

BACK ROW, LEFT
1. James R. Doolittle (R-Wisc.)
2. Lyman Trumbull (R-Ill.)
3. John J. Crittenden (AM-Ky.)
4. Zachariah Chandler (R-Mich.)
5. James Harlan (R-Iowa)
6. John P. Hale (R-N.H.)
7. William H. Seward (R-N.Y.)
8. Henry Wilson (R-Mass.)
9. Charles Sumner (R-Mass.)
10. Simon Cameron (R-Pa.)

THIRD ROW, LEFT
21. Empty
22. John Thompson (AM-Ky.)
23. James Pearce (D-Md.)
24. Robert Toombs (D-Ga.)
25. Benjamin F. Wade (R-Ohio)
26. Judah Benjamin (D-La.)
27. Solomon Foot (R-Vt.)
28. William P. Fessenden (R-Maine)
29. Jacob Collamer (Opp-Vt.)

SECOND ROW, LEFT
39. Charles Durkee (Opp-Wisc.)
40. James F. Simmons (W-R.I.)
41. James Dixon (R-Conn.)
42. Lafayette S. Foster (Opp-Conn.)
43. John Bell (AM-Tenn.)
44. George W. Jones (D-Iowa)
45. George Pugh (D-Ohio)

FRONT ROW, LEFT
53. Daniel Clark (R-N.H.)
54. Benjamin Fitzpatrick (D-Ala.)
55. Josiah Evans (D-S.C.)
56. Hannibal Hamlin (R-Maine)
57. Preston King (R-N.Y.)

BACK ROW, RIGHT
11. John M. Mason (D-Va.)
12. John W. Thomson (D-N.J.)
13. James Green (D-Mo.)
14. Albert G. Brown (D-Miss.)
15. Graham Fitch (D-Ind.)
16. Alfred Iverson (D-Ga.)
17. William Gwin (D-Calif.)
18. William Bigler (D-Pa.)
19. David C. Broderick (D-Calif.)
20. Trusten Polk (D-Mo.)

THIRD ROW, RIGHT
30. James Bayard (D-Del.)
31. Jesse Bright (D-Ind.)
32. Charles Stuart (D-Mich.)
33. Stephen A. Douglas (D-Ill.)
34. John Slidell (D-La.)
35. Jefferson Davis (D-Miss.)
36. W. K. Sebastian (D-Ark.)
37. Andrew Johnson (D-Tenn.)
38. James H. Hammond (D-S.C.)

SECOND ROW, RIGHT
46. Stephen R. Mallory (D-Fla.)
47. Philip Allen (D-R.I.)
48. David Yulee (D-Fla.)
49. Robert M. T. Hunter (D-Va.)
50. Clement C. Clay (D-Ala.)
51. David S. Reid (D-N.C.)
52. Sam Houston (AM-Tex.)

FRONT ROW, RIGHT
58. W. Wright (D-N.J.)
59. Empty
60. Anthony Kennedy (AM-Md.)
61. Asa Biggs (D-N.C.)
62. Robert W. Johnson (D-Ark.)

Opposition/Whig/
Americans

Republicans

Democrats

Empty

Figure 14. Plan of
the Senate Chamber
in the first session
of the Thirty-Fifth
Congress. Source:
*Congressional
Directory for 1858.*

These seating arrangements offer some clues to the friendships among men from different parties. For example, as shown in chapter 5, South Carolina Democrat Josiah Evans was well liked among Republicans. Perhaps the close proximity of his seat to those of Republicans Hannibal Hamlin and Preston King helps explain his friendliness. Surely it was easier to be pleasant rather than cold to one's neighbors. Furthermore, if a senator did not like the men around him, he could arrange to move. James Pearce (D-Md.) made a point of changing his seat in 1856 to seat 23, which he still occupied in 1858. Pearce wanted to get away from Henry Wilson (R-Mass.) whom he disliked personally. Again, this was not a partisan or sectional issue; Pearce was originally hoping to move next to William Seward (R-N.Y.) who occupied seat 7. But after some negotiation, the Maryland Democrat selected a seat closer to the front of the Senate.[31]

Seating arrangements in other sessions of Congress also had an impact on cross-partisan sociability. When Charles Sumner and Pierre Soulé became friendly in 1852, they sat only three seats away from one another. Starting in 1850, Sam Houston (then a Democrat) and Free-Soiler Salmon Chase repeatedly made arrangements to pair off together. It is probably not a coincidence that Chase sat next to Houston in the Senate during the first session of the Thirty-First Congress. John Bell and George W. Jones may have come from different parties but they repeatedly chose seats next to each other after they ended up at adjoining desks by lottery in December 1849.[32]

Sitting next to one another in Congress also created some friendships within parties. For example, Abraham Lincoln's relationships with the Young Indians may have begun because of the House seating arrangements in 1848. Alpheus Felch of Michigan also made friends with fellow Democrat Andrew Pickins Butler of South Carolina because the two shared a desk for several years. Felch and Butler bonded when the Senate adjourned for the day and the two men decided to walk home together. According to Felch, while walking up D Street, north of Pennsylvania Avenue, where Butler lived, "a gust of wind took the senator's straw hat off and started on its run." As Butler reached for the hat, a little dog grabbed "the truant hat," and dashed into "the open doorway of a private house." Butler quickly followed as the dog ran upstairs in the house and through the door of a bedroom. Two minutes later, Butler came rushing down the stairs; the senator had retrieved his hat but his face was "blushing scarlet" and "he was dreadfully agitated." Felch quickly learned from Butler what had happened. "'My God, Felch,' he whispered, 'she was taking a bath.' And he told me that the little dog had led him straight into a lady's bed chamber." According to Felch, the experience turned out to be beneficial to the Michigan senator. He explained that upon arriving at Butler's house, the South Carolinian remarked, "See here, Felch, if you will not tell this story on me, I'll vote for anything Michigan wants.'" More important, Felch claimed, "We both kept our word" until Butler's death in 1857.[33]

No doubt Felch exaggerated the extent to which Butler would defer to him in future negotiations. Yet such pleasant relationships among colleagues who worked together, particularly across the aisle, were possible in both the House and the Senate. In the lower house, a number of Republicans forged a relationship with Mississippi Democrat Reuben Davis after he helped newly elected Speaker William Pennington (R-N.J.) subdue a bout of congressional chaos in the chamber. In return, Pennington and James Buffinton (R-Mass.) arranged to let Davis retain two of the pages that he had appointed to the floor under the previous Speaker (who was a Democrat). As Davis explained, "I was always treated personally with great courtesy by the Republican members, although classed as ultra in my views."[34]

Another cross-partisan relationship grew out of negotiations over the Compromise of 1850. As explained in chapter 3, Northern Democrats and Southern Whigs, along with a few outliers from both parties were primarily responsible for coming together to pass the compromise. In the Senate, members of this cross-partisan group worked so closely together that they became friendly in later years. "Those who have acted together, in this great crisis," explained Massachusetts Whig Daniel Webster, "can never again feel sharp asperities towards one another." Webster's attitude toward New York Democrat Daniel S. Dickinson serves as one example of this newfound friendship. The two men had disagreed sharply in previous congressional sessions over various party issues. "In the earliest part of our acquaintance, my Dear sir, occurrences took place, which I remember with constantly increasing regret & pain," Webster acknowledged to Dickinson in a September 1850 letter, "because the more I have known you, the greater have been my esteem for your character, & and respect for your talent."[35]

As Webster suggested, forging a compromise like the one in 1850 was hard work. Men and women outside of Washington could not possibly understand the intense negotiation involved or the stresses of operating through an unbearably hot summer. A critical result of this experience was that lawmakers across the party spectrum had a mutual appreciation of the trials that went along with being a federal politician. This mutual appreciation created a sense of fraternity among men in each political body in the city, including the House, Senate, Supreme Court, and even the cabinet. Throughout the 1850s, the lawmakers who served in each of these bodies went out of their way to support colleagues from the other party both personally and politically.

Such support manifested itself in a number of ways. The men who served in the Supreme Court, for example, felt a willingness to help out their colleagues from different parties. Both Justices Catron and Wayne assured Curtis that although he was leaving the bench, the Massachusetts Whig could always rely on them for a favor. "If I can be of any service to you or yours, or to your friends, command me freely," wrote Catron. Among members of the House of Representatives, a kind parting word or a jab against a political enemy could be another way to express this fraternity. Massachusetts Whig George Ashmun heard the slights of other Democrats against his House colleague Howell Cobb (D-Ga.) in the months following passage of the Compromise of 1850. When Cobb temporarily retired from Washington to serve as Georgia's governor, Ashmun sent him a letter of congratulations and support. "I suppose that there are those who charge you with being no longer a Democrat," Ashmun wrote Cobb in October 1851, "but probably you and I should not agree any better about tariffs and annexation than ever. At any rate, I rejoice over the splendid triumph which you have achieved, for every reason except one—namely that it will keep you for a while out of Congress."[36]

Like their Supreme Court brethren, many House members also felt comfortable asking for political favors from their old colleagues, regardless of political affiliations. A few years after leaving Washington, North Carolina Whig Daniel Barringer asked a friend to share some political information with Stephen Douglas. The two men had met while serving in the House together, and Barringer considered Douglas his "personal friend." Similarly, Massachusetts Whig Robert Winthrop relied on Howell Cobb to keep him updated on news in the capital city once the Georgian returned to Washington in the Thirty-Fourth Congress. The two men not only came from different political parties but also had faced each other in the battle for Speaker of the House in 1849. After seeing reports in the newspapers of a similarly fiery battle over the speakership in December 1855, Winthrop wrote Cobb, "The long agony in the organization of the House carried me back to the day when you and I were *pitted* against each other for the Speaker's Chair." As former Speakers and political rivals for the position, Winthrop felt a sense of solidarity with the Georgia Democrat. He continued, "I rely on our old friendship surviving all personal and political competitions to secure my letter a *confidential*, as well as kind reception and I shall be very glad to hear from you at any time."[37]

Having served as a member of both the House and the Senate, Winthrop also relied on a number of his colleagues from other parties in the upper chamber to help him sort through political issues. After the election of his successor in 1851, the Massachusetts senator found himself unsure of when it was appropriate to resign from his position in the upper house. Unsatisfied with the answers from his state colleagues, he asked the advice of one of the oldest senators still in Washington, Alabama Democrat William R. King. King was happy to help Winthrop determine his obligations, and the two remained friendly until the former's death in 1853. Winthrop appreciated King's "high-toned regard for decorum and dignity."[38]

Other fellow senators asked for help in obtaining political positions for friends or letters of introduction. As a favor, Henry Clay provided a letter of recommendation for fellow senator George W. Jones (D-Iowa) to his friend Alexander H. H. Stuart (W-Va.). Clay wrote of Jones, "Although he is a Democrat, I have a great respect & regard for him and entertain great confidence in him." Massachusetts Whig Edward Everett found himself in a unique position to help some of his old Democratic colleagues when he left Congress in the 1840s to serve as the president of Harvard University. A number of Democrats (particularly those who hailed from the South) had children who were enrolled at Harvard during this time, and these men corresponded regularly with Everett. Everett exchanged letters with Robert Barnwell Rhett (D-S.C.) about the latter's son and nephew in 1847 and 1848. "They are both, I am most happy to say, most exemplary young men & excellent scholars," he told the South Carolinian.[39]

Everett himself sought the advice and guidance of old Democratic associates from the Senate when deciding whether to join the Constitutional Union ticket of 1860. Everett was unsure whether he should accept the nomination, particularly considering his place as vice president on the ticket, while John Bell of Tennessee was the presidential nominee. Having been out of the Senate for some time, Everett asked his son-in-law, Henry Wise, to consult with a number of his old political colleagues to gauge their opinions on the matter. Wise spoke with Jefferson Davis (D-Miss.), who had previously rented Everett's house in Washington, as well as Senate Democrats Judah Benjamin (D-La.), William Gwin (D-Calif.), and Stephen Mallory (D-Fla.). After consulting with these Democrats, Wise and his wife, Charlie

(Everett's daughter), reported that each man believed Everett deserved to be nominated for *president* rather than just V.P., but most encouraged him to accept. As Wise explained, these were "the opinions of Politicians, who tho' opposed to you in politics are yet your friends and admirers."[40]

Some of the more surprising instances of political bonding occurred between various cabinet members across party. Because of the partisan nature of presidential administrations, none of these men actually served together. Yet department secretaries from one administration often had to work with those in the next cabinet to make a smooth policy transition. These interactions tended to produce at least cordial relations between the outgoing and incoming secretaries and, in some cases, more than that. Take for example the relationship between James Buchanan, who served as secretary of state under James K. Polk, and his successor under Zachary Taylor, John M. Clayton (W-Del.). The two men had known each other for many years while serving in the Senate in the 1830s and 1840s, but they became particularly friendly after Clayton was appointed to the State Department. Just before coming to the capital city for the new administration in 1849, Clayton wrote Buchanan about the policy changes ahead. He closed his letter, "When I come to Washington . . . come to my house and stay with me. I am in your shoes now fully, and you can do yourself great credit by showing me how to wear them gracefully." Buchanan was certainly willing to help Clayton with the transition to the new administration. Yet, even though the two men were friendly, he was nervous about the *public* perception should he decide to stay with the Delaware Whig. As he wrote Clayton jokingly, "If I were to consult my personal predilection, although you are but little better than one of the wicked, I should rather stay at your house when I visit Washington, than any where else. But . . . your Wiggery might be suspected should I become your guest." Regardless, Buchanan promised to visit Clayton when he came to town.[41]

More than just offering friendly words, however, Clayton defended the policies Buchanan had pursued as secretary of state. As Buchanan wrote to Clayton in 1856, "I desire to repeat my thanks to you for the very able & kind manner in which you have sustained my diplomatic course." Two of the next secretaries of state, Edward Everett (W-Mass.), who served under Millard Fillmore, and William L. Marcy (D-N.Y.), who followed him in 1853, similarly enjoyed a friendly relationship during the transition to Franklin Pierce's administration. In a July 1853 letter, Everett assured Marcy he would be willing to help the New Yorker in any way he needed. "In fact," Everett assured him, the Massachusetts Whig was one of "the best supporters of your administration."[42]

If the limited number of cabinet members in the 1850s served to create a sense of community among colleagues from different administrations, the smallest political fraternity in the mid-nineteenth century was the office of the president of the United States. And even amid nasty campaigns and substantial political disagreements, presidents and their forebears tended to respect one another. Whig president Millard Fillmore, for example, was quick to defend Democratic rival James K. Polk against slander that he did not fulfill his presidential duties during the transition to Zachary Taylor's administration. One of Fillmore's correspondents commented that Polk was "heartless and cold" and even refused to dine with Taylor, when the latter arrived in Washington in 1848. Fillmore, who first served as Taylor's vice president was quick to snuff out this lie. "I know this to be untrue," Fillmore explained. "Genl. Taylor and myself were both invited to dine with him, and did dine with him before he left the White House, and I have no doubt all the civilities were extended by President Polk to General Taylor." Fillmore also remained on good terms with his own successor, Franklin Pierce (D-N.H.). The two men attended at least one Washington function together upon Pierce's arrival in Washington in February 1853, and when Fillmore's daughter Mary died in 1855, Pierce took time out of his busy presidential schedule to send the New York Whig a note of condolence. Fillmore was clearly touched. "That you should have remembered me in my sorrows amid the anxieties incident to the closing of a long session of Congress shews the deep sympathy of your breast," he wrote Pierce.[43]

Ultimately, the mutual respect that lawmakers felt for the other men in their political orbit helped create a pleasant (even if licentious and violent) workplace in Washington. Among lawmakers who spent long spurts of time in the capital city, moreover, this pleasant demeanor could create strong individual friendships across party. Some of these friendships would remain in the social realm, but others had an impact on Washington policy making. One example of such a relationship is that of John Rockwell (W-Conn.) and a Democratic clerk of the House Committee on Claims, Abel Rathbone Corbin. When Democrats controlled the House of Representatives in the mid-1840s, they quickly fired most Whig staff members and hired Democrats like Corbin in their stead. Rockwell was new to the House in 1845 and, after being placed on the Committee on Claims, quickly struck up a friendship with the Democratic clerk. When Whigs retook control of the House in 1847, Corbin's predecessor—James Young—begged the committee to rehire him and fire his Democratic nemesis. But Rockwell had become attached to the young Democratic clerk and helped Corbin keep his job.[44]

Unfortunately, Rockwell quickly lost his own position in the House, failing to be reelected for the Thirty-First Congress. Corbin was devastated and wrote Rockwell in early 1849, "I freely confess that I am mortified as well as sorry for the unpropitious result." The Democratic clerk also acknowledged the oddity of his feelings given the two men's different parties: "I have never before felt a deep and intense desire for a whig gentleman to prevail over one upon my own side for an office of such high dignity." But, he concluded, "without flattery I may now say to you that *no man* in your entire State can by any possibility achieve the position in the next House which everybody here know you would have taken from the very day of its organization."[45]

Even though Rockwell lost his seat in the House, the two men remained friendly. A few years, later, Rockwell returned to Washington to practice law in front of the newly organized Court of Claims. Unsurprisingly, he decided to go into business with Corbin both in lobbying Congress and in pursuing Court of Claims payments. Over the next few years, Washington's Whigs and Democrats hired Rockwell and Corbin for a modest fee. Some of the politicians who hired the two men included former Postmaster General Amos Kendall (D-Mass.), Senator George W. Jones (D-Iowa), and Abraham Lincoln. Although the two men did not abandon their party allegiances, they came to trust one another enough to do business together.[46]

A second, and more unlikely, cross-partisan friendship in the capital city in the 1850s blossomed between Senators Thomas J. Rusk (D-Tex.) and Truman Smith (W-Conn.). The two men had come to know one another during negotiations over the Compromise of 1850. Because that final bill provided for payment to Texas's bondholders in future years, several congressmen saw lucrative opportunities to invest in the state, including the two senators. In April 1853, Rusk and Smith drew up a contract with New York financiers Simeon Draper, O. B. Matteson, and John Stryker, investing approximately $15,000 in Texas lands. In May 1854, Smith decided to retire from the Senate and resumed the practice of law in New York. He kept an eye on the financiers—and particularly Draper, who frequently was slow to do as the investing Senators asked—and corresponded regularly with Rusk, who remained in Washington. Such cross-partisan business dealings could have greater implications for Washington policy making. Even though the compromise stipulated payment to Texas bondholders, Texas originally balked at paying the creditors. By 1853, when Rusk and Smith went into business together, investors in Texans bonds and lands prayed for a speedy settlement by Congress to maintain their profits. Now Washington investors could count on Smith to support their efforts in addition to the Texas Democrat.[47]

Like Rockwell and Corbin, in order to go into business together, Rusk and Smith clearly had to *trust* one another, and no doubt this trust came from working in the U.S. Senate in the early 1850s. One reason why this relationship has gone mostly unnoticed by historians is probably that the two men kept their relationship fairly quiet; newspapers did not print stories of their investment or interaction, and the two did not make public appearances together.[48]

Rusk and Smith were not the only ones to keep their cross-partisan relationship private. Others who feared public recriminations for working with the other party went out of their way to hide their private interaction from their constituents back home. John Clayton (W-Del.) and Thomas Hart Benton (D-Mo.) became friendly while living in Washington but were careful to protect their relationship from the public eye. The two men arranged secret meetings and staged chance run-ins to remain above suspicion. In June 1851, Benton wrote Clayton of a potential get-together: "At another time, and under other circumstances, I would certainly accept your kind invitation to meet you at your own house, but at present, and under existing circumstances I think it best that we should meet like other people do on the like occasions, *'accidentally.'*"[49]

Edward Everett (W-Mass.) was similarly hesitant to allow his friendship with Democratic newspaper editor Charles Eames to become public. The two men met frequently in Washington and kept up their correspondence when Everett retired from the capital city in 1854. While in Washington, Everett attended social functions at the Eames's house and had many private meetings, but tried to be discreet in pursuing their relationship, particularly while serving as secretary of state in the Fillmore administration. After sitting for an hour with Eames in December 1852, Everett mused, "rather a singular liaison this, the editor of the leading opposition journal daily abusing the administration of which I am a member."[50]

Although most politicians—including Eames, Everett, Benton, Clayton, Rusk, and Smith—made a serious effort to keep their cross-partisan relationships from the American public at large, Crittenden and Douglas were not so prudent. The circumstances *were* different in their case; Crittenden was more concerned with saving the Union and ending sectional discord than he was with his partisan image and, accordingly, he was willing to take the risk. Yet the consequences of his public support for Douglas were significant in three interrelated ways.

First, Abraham Lincoln never forgave Crittenden for supporting Douglas over him in the 1858 senatorial campaign. After two months of heated debates with the Little Giant throughout Illinois, Lincoln lost the Senate seat when Republicans failed to win control of the state legislature on November 2, 1858. Two days later, he sent Crittenden a letter that reflected his clear disappointment. "The emotions of defeat at the close of a struggle in which I felt more than a merely selfish interest, and to which defeat the use of your name contributed largely, are fresh upon me," he wrote. A year later, Lincoln gave a speech in Cincinnati where he publicly expressed his frustration that Crittenden and others had supported Douglas in 1858. Lincoln speculated that "Mr. Crittenden thought that his views would gain something," personally, by supporting Douglas. True, he described the Kentuckian as a man "whom I have always loved." Yet that probably came more from the speech venue's proximity to Crittenden's home state than anything else.[51]

Second, one can speculate that it was partially because of his frustration with Crittenden that, in the summer of 1859, Lincoln flatly spurned urgings that Republicans merge with anti-Democratic opposition parties from the Upper South. After his opposition to the Lecompton Constitution, Crittenden and several other moderate politicians, including men like Marylander Henry Winter Davis, and Pennsylvanian Nathan Sargent, tried to build on their success by creating a new political party dedicated to upholding the principles of the American Constitution and Union, appropriately called the Constitutional Union Party. In the summer and fall of 1859, Crittenden and others recruited men from around the country to join their fledging organization. The group hoped to find a cross-sectional presidential ticket and scheduled a nominating convention for the party to take place in May 1860.[52]

Two of the men at the top of their recruiting list were Lincoln and one of his Young Indian colleagues, Alexander Stephens of Georgia. In June 1859, Nathan Sargent, who had served as the sergeant at arms of the House during Lincoln's time in Congress, tried to recruit the Illinois Republican to their party. Similarly, Crittenden sent Stephens a letter inviting him to join the unionist group later that year. As Crittenden explained, "If such men as you would but espouse & lead in the movement, it could not but succeed—The feelings of the whole country favours it, & the whole country would be benefited by it." But neither Lincoln nor Stephens would join the new political organization. Lincoln told Sargent that "if the rotten democracy shall be beaten in 1860, it has to be done by the North." Thus, in the same month that the Constitutional Union Party chose its ticket, Lincoln would be nominated for president by the still almost exclusively Northern Republican Party.[53]

Finally, Lincoln's opinions about Crittenden did not soften after his 1860 presidential victory. In the weeks and months following his election, Lincoln did not seek out the advice of the old Kentucky Whig. Nor did he consider Crittenden for a position in his cabinet. And when the secession crisis came in December, Lincoln did not look to Crittenden for a solution.[54]

CHAPTER SEVEN

Like Taking a Last Leave of a Brother

The Washington Community Faces the Secession Crisis

The scene at Jefferson and Varina Davis's Washington residence on I Street on Sunday, January 20, 1861, was heartbreaking. Friends of the Mississippi couple, including both Northerners and Southerners, lingered in the house to bid their sad goodbyes to the senator and his wife. Less than two weeks earlier Alabama, Florida, Georgia, and Mississippi had all joined South Carolina in declaring secession from the United States. The Davises were in the midst of joining many of their Southern colleagues in leaving Washington. Even the most casual observer could tell that the senator and his wife were not at all prepared to go. Little of the packing had been done, and their three little children scampered around the house with the family's two pets—a parrot and a Newfoundland dog.[1]

Varina looked particularly forlorn. It had been a trying winter for the vibrant Washington socialite. After Republican Abraham Lincoln's election on November 6, 1860, she had heard countless rumors about the move toward secession. At first Varina discounted them; as she wrote her husband on November 15, "people talk so impudently of disunionism before me that I hunted up my old white satin flag: 'if any man call me a disunionist I will answer him in monosyllables. Jeff Davis.'" Both Davises had counseled patience and caution before going forward with something as serious as secession. True, Varina was unhappy with Lincoln's election and even declared that she would refuse to associate with Republicans from then on. But it was hard to follow through with that threat; one of Varina's closest friends was Elizabeth Blair Lee, the sister of Republicans Francis P. Blair Jr. and Montgomery Blair, who would be named to Lincoln's cabinet as post-master general. The two ladies maintained their relationship into December and January; Elizabeth even began to call her friend "Queen Varina," which the latter rather enjoyed. Now the Davises were departing the city for good, and Varina "was sad enough now that the time is come to leave all her friends."[2]

Jefferson Davis was also visibly "ill from distress of mind" that afternoon on I Street. The Mississippi senator, who had devoted nearly fifteen years to federal service, was planning to officially announce his departure from the United States government the following day. He would then travel to Mississippi with his family to join the Confederate cause. Before he left, however, Davis took the time necessary to write a note to his old friend and former chief, ex-president Franklin Pierce. In this emotional moment, Davis wanted to explain his decision. "Civil war has only horror for me," he wrote, "but whatever circumstances demand shall be met as a duty." Those circumstances had already been difficult. The week before Davis had said good-bye to his friend Caleb Cushing of Massachusetts, who had also served in Pierce's cabinet. "When we parted," he wrote Pierce, "it seemed like taking a last leave of a Brother." He felt a similar connection to the ex-president, remarking, "I trust . . . that you will not be ashamed of our former connection or cease to be my friend."[3]

For many, January 20 was only the latest date in a series of emotional goodbyes in the capital city that winter. When Louisiana representative George Eustis took his young bride, Louly Corcoran, back home in early January, both parties were "very sad about it," according to one friend, but he felt "obliged to go & she wished to accompany him." In early March, Louisiana senator John Slidell and his wife hurriedly packed up their house on H Street in preparation for heading south. As they put together their belongings, the Slidells said their goodbyes to friends who had dropped by. Two of their visitors were local Washingtonians William Corcoran (Louly's father) and Charlie Wise, the daughter of Massachusetts Unionist Edward Everett. All parties looked dejected, wondering if they would ever see each other again. Charlie herself was one of the more emotional friends at the Davis's farewell gathering on January 20. As a regular participant in Washington social life, she knew that Varina would be missed. "We lose a great deal, when she goes away," Charlie wrote her father.[4]

January 21 was a "delightful" wintry Monday. As Jefferson Davis made his way to the Senate, he saw the city's politicians and other residents leaving their boardinghouses, hotels, and private homes and heading for the Capitol. Crowds were gathering in both chambers as many had heard over the weekend that, in addition to Davis, Alabama's two senators, Clement C. Clay and Benjamin Fitzpatrick, had "settled their accounts" and "closed their affairs" in preparation for heading south. That morning, Washington's residents wanted to see for themselves the Southern congressmen relinquishing their duties in the Capitol to join the seceded states.[5]

The departure of Deep South Southerners was the latest nadir in a topsy-turvy winter full of speculation and fear for the union. Since Lincoln's election, Washington's residents had watched events in the capital city closely. Prospects for disunion looked serious in early December when the second session of the Thirty-Sixth Congress convened and South Carolina's senators were conspicuous by their absence. By midmonth, several Southern congressmen, including Davis, had declared reconciliation impossible. Less than one week later, South Carolina officially seceded from the Union. Prospects for a congressional compromise looked better near the end of December when both houses of Congress convened committees dedicated to reconciling the sectional divide. Among other proposals, the Senate Committee of Thirteen discussed a plan fashioned by Kentucky senator John Crittenden, which included reinstating the 36°30′ line that divided free from slave states. But these hopes were again dashed by New Year's Day, when the Senate committee failed to agree to a solution. Since then, a number of politicians had been working around the clock to try to prevent disunion.[6]

Despite these efforts, a caucus of Deep South men called for the creation of a Southern confederacy in early January. Once the states of Mississippi, Alabama, and Florida declared secession, it was only a matter of time before their federal officials would depart. And so, on January 21, politicians and their wives, city residents and visitors were gathered on the Senate floor and in the galleries waiting for the official announcement. Finally, at half past noon, Florida Democrat David Yulee rose and addressed his colleagues. Yulee, who had served in the Senate for almost two decades, declared that on account of his state's decision, he would withdraw from the body. Yulee's Florida colleague Stephen R. Mallory followed suit, as did Clay and Fitzpatrick, and finally Davis. Georgia Democrat Alfred Iverson had not yet received word of his state's action, and so he sat quietly through his colleagues' departures.[7]

Everyone in the Senate chamber that day understood the gravity of what was happening; the room was uncommonly quiet during the speeches. The completion of each man's statement provoked a new wave of emotion from the crowd. Senator Mallory wept openly as he pleaded for a peaceful separation. He felt full of "melancholy, sadness, regret, and depression." According to one newspaper, Mallory's speech "drew tears from the eyes of many Senators and spectators in the crowded galleries." The Alabama senators were similarly emotional and caused more weeping from the spectators. Jefferson Davis closed the announcements by explaining his reasons for leaving and offering to apologize to anyone whom he had offended while in Congress; he promised "all the reparation in his power for such offence."[8]

For a few moments after Davis's address, both the politicians and spectators sat in their seats, seemingly stunned. But soon enough senators from both sides of the aisle walked over to their departing colleagues and shook hands, bidding them goodbye and hoping for the best for everyone. Once all had said their farewells, Yulee, Mallory, Clay, Fitzpatrick, and Davis exited the chamber and left their colleagues to take up the question of Kansas's statehood. Two of the women in the gallery, the wife and daughter of former Alabama representative Philip Phillips, joined Jefferson Davis just outside the Capitol. As the three Southerners walked up Pennsylvania Avenue toward Davis's house on I Street, the Mississippian turned to the ladies. "Dear friends," he said with tears running down his cheeks, "this is the saddest day of my life."[9]

The scene at the Davises' house on January 20, the weeping and handshaking in the Senate on January 21, and the mournful goodbye letters throughout the winter and early spring all came with Southern politicians' decision to depart from the Union. How had this sorrowful situation happened? The well-known answer is that Congress did not devise an acceptable compromise that might have slowed or even reversed secession. As a number of historians have argued, the statesmen of 1861 "failed to prevent war in 1861." The question then becomes, why did Congress fail?[10]

One place not to look for an answer to that question is in any notable increase or escalation of sectional animosity between Northern and Southern members of Congress during that short session. Such an increase in animosity did not occur. During this tense time, in fact, residential patterns and social activities saw just as much intersectional cooperation and comity as had been the case since the mid-1840s. Even during the secession crisis, Washington continued to operate as a highly sociable cross-sectional and cross-partisan community.

More than anything else, the behavior of federal politicians during the secession winter helps to illustrate the important effect of the Washington community on federal politicians. This unique Washington living experience influenced the way that lawmakers handled the secession crisis in three critical ways. First, the bonds that politicians made across section and party while living in Washington gave them a distinctive understanding and approach to Lincoln's election. Those politicians who knew Lincoln when he served in 1848 did not fear him the way many Southerners did. Others were willing to give the president-elect the benefit of the doubt based on the testimony of mutual friends.

Second, the customs and etiquette of Washington's social community meant that politicians in the capital city dealt with the realities of their cross-sectional, cross-partisan city during the crisis itself. While men and women throughout the rest of the United States insulted, threatened, and belittled one another from afar, Washington's lawmakers did not have the comfort of distance. Politicians in the capital city still lived together, dined together, worked together, and saw each other on a regular basis. Yes, there were some who actively tried to avoid their colleagues from the other section. But this was often difficult when paying respects to neighbors on New Year's Day, attending dinner parties thrown by diplomats, or simply walking up the steps of the Capitol. And, as in years past, Washington's politicians could not help but talk about the political issues facing the nation during the winter of 1860–61.

Finally, Washington's lawmakers engaged with the secession crisis the way they were used to handling all political issues: by working together outside of the halls of Congress at dinners and parties, over drinks, and at the faro table. Some hosted small gatherings of congressmen and were sure to invite colleagues with critical votes on the compromise committees. In February, when a number of former federal politicians and other Border State men gathered in Washington at a "Peace Conference" to try to form a cross-sectional compromise, they all boarded at the same hotel—Willard's—to give themselves a greater opportunity to converse outside the formal proceedings. Politicians from different parties and sections who had worked together before, like Kentuckian John Crittenden and Illinois senator Stephen A. Douglas, were drawn to each other again during the winter crisis. Together they used all the political and social sway in their arsenals.[11]

Those trying to stave off secession were assisted by residents who were not federal politicians, like William Corcoran and Benjamin Ogle Tayloe, who had an important stake in the future of the Union. Many of these Washingtonians had investments in both the North and the South, not to mention friends and relatives in both places. Washington residents also feared for their own safety. History had shown them that their city would become the center of wartime drama: during the War of 1812 British soldiers had stormed the city, burning the White House to the ground. Others worried over the possibility of being swallowed up by the new Confederacy if both Maryland and Virginia were to secede. As a result, these city residents had a vested interest in keeping the Union together and preventing their own destruction.[12]

Ultimately, despite the efforts of Washington moderates and their local allies, Congress failed to pass a compromise acceptable to both sections. By April 15, when Lincoln called for 75,000 troops to recover American property in the South, the Civil War had arrived. Many of Washington's politicians would spend the next four years fighting some of the men they had formerly called colleagues. But their behavior during the second session of the Thirty-Sixth Congress sheds critical light on both the unique experience of living in Washington and the way that federal politicians understood the secession crisis.

■ Abraham Lincoln's election on November 6, 1860, sent a wave of panic through many parts of the South. Rumors spread that Lincoln and his party intended to emancipate all the slaves and create social equality among the races. Several state leaders counseled that Southerners should withdraw from the Union immediately, rather than wait for some overt act by the new president. Although his party did not control either house of Congress or the Supreme Court, Southerners believed that Lincoln would quickly be able to build up an extension of the Republican organization in their section through the power of federal patronage.[13]

Lincoln was not well known in the South. Most knew him only as the Black Republican candidate, a representative of the anti-South movement who was committed to eradicating their blessed institution of slavery. One Mississippi newspaper, for example, exclaimed that Lincoln wanted Southern men to "die like poisoned rats in their holes." After the election another editorial clamored for disunion, calling Lincoln a "bigoted, unscrupulous, and cold-blooded enem[y] of peace and equality of the slaveholding states." Many Southern papers simply equated Lincoln's views with those of anti-slavery senators Charles Sumner of Massachusetts or William H. Seward of New York, who had long been in the public eye and had long incurred the wrath of the slaveholding states.[14]

Among those who knew Lincoln personally, however, reaction was different. As a one-term congressman, Lincoln had made few lasting acquaintances from his time in Washington more than a decade earlier. Yet, several Southerners were among those who had developed relationships with the tall Illinois Republican, including a handful from the Young Indian Club. During the months before the 1860 election, three of the five Southern members of that group commented on Lincoln's moderation and his potential as president. At the end of October, only a few days before the election, Lincoln received a short letter from a man named W. T. Early, a resident of Pen Park, near Charlottesville, Virginia. Early had been talking with a couple of Lincoln's old Young Indian friends. "From a knowledge of your general character as a statesman I am satisfied that you are a real patriot & conservative," he told Lincoln. "My impression of your character has been recently strengthened by conversations with Hon T[homas] S Flournoy & W[illia]m B Preston of this State who served with you in the Congress of '47/9." Preston may have also discussed Lincoln's abilities with his cousin, former Kentucky Whig William Preston, who was at that moment serving the Buchanan administration as minister to Spain. The Kentuckian wrote to his sister in November, "I trust that Mr. Lincoln's Administration may receive the support of the Democratic party in every measure calculated to restore kind feeling and patriotic forbearance in the Country."[15]

And then there was Alexander Stephens. Although Stephens and Lincoln had not corresponded for some years, the Georgian still considered his old Young Indian associate a friend. In July 1860, Stephens received a letter from an associate, J. Henly Smith, asking if the South ought to secede if Lincoln and the Republicans won the November election. "No," Stephens responded, "*I would not* advocate disunion on that ground." But the Georgian went farther, explaining his reasoning: "I have no doubt Lincoln is just as good, safe and sound a man as Mr. Buchanan, and would administer the Government so far as he is individually concerned just as safely for the South and as honestly and faithfully *in every particular*." In fact, although Lincoln and Stephens had not seen each other in some years, the Georgian hastened to add about his old colleague, "I know the man well. He is not a bad man. He will make as good a President as Fillmore did and better too in my opinion. He has a great deal more practical common sense."[16]

Nor did Stephens change his mind once Lincoln won the election. On November 14, Stephens delivered a speech in the Georgia State Legislature with the purpose of calming the secessionist fervor. Should his state leave the Union because of Lincoln's election? No, he declared, "I tell you frankly, candidly, and earnestly, that I do not think they ought." Stephens's pro-Union speech set off a famed exchange between the Georgian and his former Young Indian colleague. The president-elect saw newspaper reports of Stephens's oration in the Georgia Legislature in late November, and wrote his old friend for a revised copy. Stephens responded that he never revised the speech and reports of its content in the papers were "substantially correct." He closed by reminding Lincoln, "the country is certainly in great peril and no man ever had heavier or greater responsibilities resting upon him than you have in the present momentous crisis."[17]

Perhaps emboldened by the Georgian's response, Lincoln kept the conversation going, promising Stephens on December 22 that his administration would do nothing to interfere with slavery either "*directly or indirectly.*" He explained, "I wish to assure you, as once a friend, and still, I hope, not an enemy, that there is no cause for such fears." Stephens responded in a long letter on December 30, offering a detailed perspective on the crisis and beseeching the president-elect to speak out and reassure Southerners that his intentions were good. Although he used strong language about the possibility of disunion, Stephens was careful to assure his old friend: "Personally, I am not your enemy, far from it; and however widely we may differ politically, yet I trust we both have an earnest desire to preserve and maintain the Union of the States."[18]

While prospects for the Union seemed dire when Jefferson Davis delivered his farewell address on January 21, those seeking a solution to the crisis felt a new wave of hope in early February. On Monday, February 4, delegates to the Washington "Peace Conference" began their deliberations at Willard's Hotel on Pennsylvania Avenue. Organized by pro-Union Virginians, the conference called on peace-loving states throughout the country to send representatives to Washington to help negotiate a settlement acceptable to all states. The delegates who came to the capital city included a number of former federal politicians, including some who had known Lincoln in the Thirtieth Congress. Still others came to Washington from Northern states to show solidarity with the peace efforts. For example, Robert Winthrop was part of a Massachusetts delegation that traveled to Washington to deliver a petition for conciliation. Winthrop had interacted with Lincoln while the former served as Speaker of the House during the Thirtieth Congress. The old Massachusetts Whig knew from personal experience that Lincoln meant no real harm against the South. Winthrop wrote his friend, John P. Kennedy of Maryland, in words that echoed Stephens's thoughts: "Lincoln is a very moderate man in every respect, & if Southern Senators &

Figure 15. Sketch of the meeting of the Peace Conference at Willard's Ball Room, 1861. *Frank Leslie's Illustrated Newspaper*, February 16, 1861. Photograph Collection, Historical Society of Washington, D.C.

Representatives will only keep their places, the Country will go along better than it has for some years past."[19]

After a few weeks in the capital city, Peace Conference delegates and other unionists were able to see for themselves what Lincoln's approach would be. On Saturday, February 23, the president-elect arrived in Washington after sneaking through Baltimore for fear of assassination. That afternoon, Lincoln proceeded to visit with a number of the delegates. Some of them, like North Carolinian Daniel Barringer and Reverdy Johnson of Maryland, knew the president-elect while serving in the Thirtieth Congress. Barringer wrote his wife of the interview the following evening, showing his respect for the new chief. The North Carolinian was appalled that Lincoln had to bypass visiting the people of Baltimore; "it is an imputation on their character that he could not pass through without being attacked by a mob," he complained. On the issue of Lincoln's intentions, Barringer wrote, "I think now [he] will be conciliatory & for peace." John Crisfield of Maryland was similarly complimentary, telling his son, "After all there may be some thing in him. I think him honest & well intentioned and capacity may be supplied him, if he call around him wise and prudent and upright advisers." After speaking with old acquaintances and new, Lincoln retired for the night. According to one newspaperman, all of the Southern delegates to the Peace Conference "freely expressed their gratification at his affability and easy manner."[20]

Although few men serving in Washington in 1860 and 1861 knew Lincoln personally, many knew his future secretary of state, William H. Seward. Outside Washington, Seward was perhaps the epitome of the Black Republican scoundrel. The New York senator had even received death threats from his detractors in the South during his years in Washington. "Allow me to say to you, that if we ever find you in Georgia, you will forfeit your odious neck, you scamp," read one from Savannah. Such strong language was not surprising; the New Yorker had been antagonizing Southerners for more than a decade with his denunciations of the "Slave Power." Seward had delivered one of his more infuriating speeches two years before on "the Irrepressible Conflict" between the North and South. In this address he explained a theory that slave and free states were on a collision course that would end in the destruction of the Democratic Party and the triumph of the Republicans. Worse, many believed that because of his prominence in the antislavery party, Seward would control the executive branch if Lincoln were elected.[21]

Among the people of Washington, however, Seward was actually well liked and even considered a moderate. Over the years, he had gained a reputation as one of the most pleasant politicians in the capital city. In the Senate, Seward was known for keeping his cool, never retaliating against a cruel accusation or a personal insult. He was delighted to help friends with political favors; even as the movement toward secession had begun to go forward, Southerners like former North Carolina senator Willie P. Mangum used their personal connections with Seward to advocate for patronage positions for their relatives. In a social setting, he got along well with nearly every politician in the capital city and counted a number of Southerners as his closest friends. On one occasion, he was invited by a former congressman to come down and visit a Southern plantation to see how it operated. Reportedly, "The frolic passed off very pleasantly indeed, and no one was more delighted than the New York Senator." Two of Seward's closest friends in the capital city were Jefferson and Varina Davis. The three had frequently talked about political issues, and according to Varina, Seward professed he often spoke for political effect rather than from conviction. As William Cooper has argued, Davis likely believed that a cross-sectional settlement was possible because of his relationship with Seward.[22]

The friendly relations between Seward and two other Southerners—North Carolina representative John Gilmer and Supreme Court Justice John Archibald Campbell of Alabama—similarly influenced their hope that a truce of some sort could be reached in early 1861. Because of an illness in his family, Gilmer had rushed home at the end of the congressional session but remained in contact with his Washington associates by mail. He implored Seward and other Northerners like Stephen A. Douglas to try to prevent a collision with the South. Campbell was also hopeful. After Lincoln's inauguration in March, Campbell wrote his mother that the new administration's "policy will be supremely pacific and not an opportunity will be given for collusion and bloodshed." Campbell trusted Seward, who had written him of such a policy the day before. In April, Seward repeatedly reassured Campbell that Fort Sumter would not be reinforced, an action that would probably lead to shooting between North and South. Like Gilmer, Campbell believed the New Yorker wanted conciliation. Both Southerners were disappointed when Seward proved wrong.[23]

A critical reason why Seward was able to work with Campbell in March and April 1861 was that the two were operating in the small city of Washington. In this capital city, politicians like Campbell and Seward negotiated within a community marked by a cross-sectional makeup in its day-to-day operations, even during the winter of 1860–61. Patterns of social life outside of Congress and the cabinet departments had become so ingrained by 1860 that even the secession crisis could not break them.

To begin with, politicians still lived in cross-sectional boardinghouses, hotels, and neighborhoods. While some lawmakers admitted that their housing options might be temporary, they nevertheless tried to find the best possible accommodations to suit their price range and proclivities. Despite any tension, 65 percent of congressmen boarded in a house or hotel with a man from the other section during the secession winter. In hotels, Southern politicians were guaranteed to see Northerners and vice versa, as not a single hotel catered to an exclusively sectional clientele. Neighborhoods remained diverse, particularly since most of these lawmakers either owned their homes or rented for both congressional sessions.[24]

For those who did not have private homes, the most popular place to live in Washington in the winter of 1861 was Willard's Hotel on Pennsylvania Avenue. Willard's had catered to a cross-sectional clientele for many years, but during the secession winter the hotel managed to attract its largest group of politicians yet. Fifty congressmen engaged rooms at Willard's in December 1860, including men with such varied political opinions as Simon

Cameron (R-Pa.), Jacob Collamer (R-Vt.), Emerson Etheridge (Opp-Tenn.), and John McRae (D-Miss.). In February, the hotel's profits grew to nearly $1,200 per day, when Willard's became the de facto living spot for delegates to the Washington Peace Conference. Henry Willard had managed this coup by providing the delegates with a grand meeting space to handle their negotiations; once the conference arrangements were announced, most of the men took rooms at his establishment. Daniel Barringer explained to his wife, "The Conference of the Commissioners is held in a large concert hall attached to this building and my room is within ten steps of it under the same roof, with a carpeted entrance all the way." In fact, the close proximity was part of the point. As pro-Union *Louisville Journal* editor George D. Prentice explained, "we seriously believe, that when the North and South meet each other face to face and eye to eye . . . they will be prepared to fraternize most cordially, and kick parties, politicians, platforms, and schemers" aside. The plan seemed to work: according to a correspondent for the *New York Herald*, "the Peace Commissioners, after adjournment," return to the hotel and "sit long at table, drink their wine with great gusto for men who came hither on such a solemn errand, and 'coerce' the best of Havanas in great profusion.[25]

Willard's also had the honor of hosting the president-elect when he arrived in Washington at the end of February. Although Lincoln had a number of offers to stay in private homes, the Illinois Republican believed that it would be good for the country for him to be more visible upon his arrival. When word got out that Lincoln was on his way, the hotel became "jammed full" with those who wanted to interact with him. With the president and the Peace Conference delegates all staying in the hotel, the rooms were drenched in political discussion.[26]

The National Hotel also catered to Washington's politicians during the secession winter. Twenty-nine congressmen and one Supreme Court justice, Samuel Nelson of New York, called the National home during the second session of the Thirty-Sixth Congress. Like Willard's, the hotel rented rooms to men of all parties and sections; that winter residents included the likes of Albert G. Brown (D-Miss.), John Crittenden (AM-Ky.), Graham N. Fitch (D-Ind.), and John Parker Hale (R-N.H.). Perhaps the group would have been larger had the hotel not carried a reputation for disease; back in March 1857 some thirty residents became ill while staying at the National, including James Buchanan, who temporarily took rooms there before his inauguration in 1857. As a result, when Lincoln was looking for a place to stay in 1861, his wife Mary Todd insisted they avoid the National. But the illness did not keep everyone away. Lincoln's attorney general, Edward Bates of Missouri, arrived in the capital city in late February and checked into the rooms a friend had engaged for him at the National. And at both the National and Willard's, the "condition of the country" was consistently "the absorbing topic of conversation."[27]

A number of long-serving politicians had more permanent living arrangements in Washington. A few, like Vice President John Breckinridge (D-Ky.) and Stephen A. Douglas (D-Ill.) owned homes in the city. In fact, these two candidates for president in 1860 lived right next door to one another. Others had multiyear rental agreements for houses in neighborhoods like Lafayette Square or Union Row. When men from the seceding states decided to withdraw from Washington, those who lived in private homes had to break a lease with their landlord. Such was the case with Secretary of the Interior Jacob Thompson (D-Miss.), who was renting Edward Everett's house on G and 18th Streets. Thompson planned to leave Washington in January and therefore asked Everett to break the lease a few months early. The Massachusetts Unionist had considered Thompson and his wife "very desirable tenants" and wanted to accommodate the Mississippian. As he wrote A. Hyde, the man in charge of his Washington business, Everett "had rather give up every thing than that Mr. Thompson shd think he was 'hardly dealt by.' I am quite willing to settle on any basis agreeable to Mr. Thompson," he continued. "I have been entirely satisfied with him as a tenant, & he shant go away dissatisfied with me as a landlord." In fact, the old Whig mournfully closed his letter, "Rather than have had him & his state secede, I would have let him live in my house rent free to the end of my days, though I had to go to the poor house for a shelter myself."[28]

After finding comfortable rooms in boardinghouses, hotels, and private homes during the second session of the Thirty-Sixth Congress, Washington lawmakers also settled into their daily lives in the capital city. Although many were nervous about the fate of the country, politicians still went to church, to club meetings, and to work in the Capitol building or departments. On Sundays during the secession winter, those who were regular churchgoers patronized the city's chapels, most of which catered to both Northerners and Southerners. Socialites like William Corcoran and Benjamin Ogle Tayloe continued to go to St. John's Church on Lafayette Square at the same time as William Seward and the Wise family. Seward even brought Abraham Lincoln to sit in his pew when the president-elect arrived in late February. Similarly, the first Presbyterian Church on Fifth Street catered to men from both sections in the winter of 1860–61. President Buchanan was still a regular attendant, as were Joseph C. G. Kennedy, superintendent of the Census Bureau and Representative Roger Pryor (D-Va.) and his wife. After accompanying Kennedy to services at the chapel on Fifth Street in early March, Edward Bates decided he would join the church.[29]

There were some changes to the religious makeup of the city during the secession winter, but these did not necessarily include the splintering of Northern and Southern parishioners. In fact, a new Presbyterian church opened up on 4½ Street in December, and the "capacious" sanctuary held nearly 1,200 worshipers the morning of its dedication, including several members of Congress from both sections. Similarly, while many Christian denominations were split sectionally across the country, the Methodist church in Washington had resolved its differences over the summer and now catered to men from all parts of the Union. As Tennessee congressman Robert Hatton explained to his wife, the "Congregation at our Church, greatly increased since last Winter — [is] decidedly more fashionable" as a result of the "accession from the Northern Methodist Church here, during the summer." Furthermore, the cross-sectional membership of the Methodist church included many who were willing to openly discuss the political turmoil of the time; following church on Sunday, December 23, Hatton had a long conversation with Supreme Court Justice John McLean of Ohio about the possibilities for war.[30]

Just as in years past, the Capitol remained a popular place for worship on the weekends among Washington's citizens and politicians alike. When President Buchanan called for a national day of prayer on January 4, 1861, "The Hall of Congress was crowded to excess," according to one observer. The masses had come to hear the Methodist chaplain of the House Thomas Stockton deliver one of his popular sermons. In front of a large cross-sectional audience, Stockton was not afraid to voice his love for the Union and prayer for peace. "O Lord Jesus, thou who hast promised to 'come quickly,' come now," the chaplain closed. "At least, in all the healing love and pity of thy Holy Spirit, come now . . . so shall all nations praise Thee, and, looking from afar exulting in our restored, confirmed, and perfect Union. . . . 'Behold! *How good and how pleasant it is for brethren to dwell together in unity!*"[31]

While cross-sectional churches were still in operation during the secession winter, so were the many clubs and organizations that existed throughout the city. Masonic groups like the B. B. French Lodge and Federal Lodge continued to meet biweekly, with a standing invitation to any Masons in Congress to attend. The Washington Sons of Temperance gathered at Trinity

Church on Fifth Street several times in January. And the Smithsonian Institution held almost daily lectures at its headquarters. A few politicians even had to spend time attending to other jobs and responsibilities. William Seward could be found in the Supreme Court arguing a case in early December while his colleagues met in the Senate. In early 1861, the board of regents for the Smithsonian was still made up of mostly Washington politicians. Three times in February 1861, when the committee met to discuss the coming year, participants included Stephen A. Douglas (D-Ill.), William English (D-Ind.), James M. Mason (D-Va.), former Whig James A. Pearce (D-Md.), and Benjamin Stanton (R-Ohio). These men may have disagreed about congressional compromises and the future of the Union, but they still had to work together in their capacity as board members.[32]

Federal politicians also tried to maintain a congenial workplace in the Capitol during the winter. When Massachusetts unionists Edward Everett and Robert Winthrop visited their old stomping grounds in the Senate Chamber in January, friends and acquaintances from all parties warmly greeted them. Even a visit by such a controversial figure as Lincoln himself did not disrupt the pleasant demeanor of the Capitol. Benjamin French, a city resident, was present in the House gallery and recorded his view of the visit in his diary that evening. "The members congregated around him at once & such a shaking of hands commenced as one seldom sees—cordial—even enthusiastic," he explained. "After being surrounded for say 10 minutes by his political friends, [Lincoln] passed over to the democratic side where he was quite cordially greeted by his political opponents."[33]

In addition to cross-sectional interaction in their workplaces, churches, clubs, and living arrangements, the politicians who came to Washington in the winter of 1860–61 also mingled at the many social events of the city. As one resident explained, "In spite of the troubles we are tolerably gay here and I am always going somewhere." Just as they did every New Year's Day, Washington's politicians came out in droves, going from house to house, visiting friends and neighbors. January 1, 1861, "was a beautiful day, and was as much enjoyed by our citizens as any previous holyday of the kind," reported the *National Intelligencer*. "Many citizens were 'at home' and received their friends with seasoned hospitality. At the Presidential Mansion . . . the attendance of citizens was considerable in point of numbers." Politicians made sure to pay respects at Stephen Douglas's house, which "had a large crowd" according to one visitor. And, as usual, Washington residents celebrated the day by eating holiday fare and drinking alcohol, occasionally to excess.[34]

President James Buchanan may have been nervous about what was happening in the Southern states in late December and January but that did not stop him from holding regular reception days at the White House and a variety of presidential levees. Hotels like Brown's held mixed-gender "hops," dancing parties known for being particularly raucous. Socialites also held evening parties open to a large number of Washington's lawmakers. Politicians who were so inclined could find parties and dinners to attend nearly every day of the week. For example, late January and early February were particularly lively in the city. Some events included:

January 29: Party at Judge John Archibald Campbell's
January 31: Reception at Judge John Archibald Campbell's
January 31: Gathering in Brown's Hotel Ladies Parlor
February 1: Party at former Maryland senator Reverdy Johnson's
February 4: Gathering at Delaware senator James A. Bayard Jr.'s
February 5: Reception at Speaker of the House William Pennington's
February 11: Party for peace commissioners at Ohio senator Thomas
    Corwin's
February 12: Party in honor of the Peace Conference at Stephen A.
    Douglas's
February 12: President Buchanan's last levee of the season
February 14: Musical soiree hosted by Stephen A. Douglas and wife
February 14: Party at Massachusetts representative Charles Francis
    Adams's

Although not all politicians went to every party, those who were prominent in Washington's social circles could often be found there. According to one newspaper, even Lincoln's first levee as president in March 1861 was a "jam," which attracted Washington's citizens and politicians alike.[35]

In addition to large social events, Washington's politicians also continued to interact in more private dinner parties. Throughout the late 1840s and 1850s, many of these dinners included men from both sections of the country and in the winter of 1860–61 this tradition continued. Henry Winter Davis (AM-Md.) and Speaker William Pennington (R-N.J.) both hosted cross-sectional dinner parties the week of Christmas, as did President Buchanan. In late January and early February, former Whig congressman Samuel Vinton and Illinois senator Stephen Douglas similarly invited cross-sectional groups to dine with them. Tennessee congressman Robert Hatton was one of twelve guests at one of Henry Winter Davis's parties in mid-February and enjoyed himself immensely: "The table was sumptuous—twelve courses!—

soup, fish, fowl and beast, etc. The wine flowed freely. . . . The dinner lasted two hours and a half" and the men who were interested (not Hatton, of course) got "high over wine and cigars."[36]

In a casual sense, the political situation was on everyone's lips during these events, even among those from different sections and parties. Former Massachusetts Whig William Appleton dined with President Buchanan in mid-December 1860, and the two "talked freely" about political affairs. As Appleton reported to his brother, Buchanan "fears the worst but not without hope that arrangements will take place, to avoid disunion & shedding of blood." Men also talked openly about their opinions in front of their families. On one afternoon in late December, Michigan senator Kinsley S. Bingham and his wife joined Illinois senator Lyman Trumbull's family for tea. Mary Bingham was pleased to have the "great treat" of hearing the men "discussing the politics of the day freely, and without reserve with one another."[37]

Just as in any mid-nineteenth-century dinner party, alcohol mixed with political talk could result in violence. In early January Robert Toombs (D-Ga.) and General Winfield Scott of Virginia had a "bout" at a dinner party at the house of John Thomson (D-N.J.). As one resident reported secondhand, "The first [Toombs] called the Old Hero a liar—whereupon the Genl rushed into him—but they were promptly parted." Yet this behavior was no more severe than other tense periods in Washington. Moreover, during the secession winter angry or violent outbursts appeared to be more the exception than the rule. Scott himself had been to several dinner parties that same week, including one at the Prussian minister's house, which included former senator Hamilton Fish of New York and William Corcoran and his son-in-law, George Eustis of Mississippi, who was preparing to leave town to secede with his state, as well as a few other guests. Aware of the bout with Toombs, Scott's aide remarked after the meal, "I witnessed no violent outbursts of sectionalism while at the table." Eustis did proclaim his attachment to the South, however.[38]

The fact that the Prussian minister invited men from both sections to dine with him illustrates the extent to which other city residents believed Northern and Southern guests could be comfortable with one another even during this tense time. In fact, some of the most prominent local Washingtonians used the cross-sectional social environment and their particular social sway to try to stave off disunion. These Washingtonians had a variety of motivations—financial, political, familial, and otherwise—for promoting Union and peace during the secession winter, just as they had during the Compromise of 1850. Washington residents knew that war could negatively influence their daily lives. Many were employed in government jobs or relied on throngs of visitors to the nation's capital to preserve their livelihood. As Assistant Postmaster Horatio King wrote James Buchanan on November 7, just after Lincoln's election: "My own [case] will illustrate the condition of thousands in this district. With us everything depends on the Union being preserved." A few weeks later, he added to New Yorker John Dix, "The existence of the Department depends on the stability of the Union." Federal politicians also noticed this intense Washington unionism. Henry Adams wrote to the *Boston Daily Advertiser* that "the citizens of Washington are in a most painful position, and the alarm is universal." North Carolinian John A. Gilmer agreed, telling his friend William Graham in December, "The anxiety [in Washington] from all quarters, (except the Southern *fire eaters*) to preserve the Union, is intense."[39]

Some of this anxiety was centered on the financial interests of Washington businessmen. Hotel owners were particularly concerned. Places like Willard's Hotel knew they would lose critical business, since nearly half of their political patrons were Southerners. Mrs. Smith, the owner of Brown's Hotel (which was also on Pennsylvania Avenue), had spent years cultivating a clientele that included some of the most prominent Southerners in the District. Men such as Alabama Democrats Clement Clay and Benjamin Fitzpatrick, as well as South Carolinian James L. Orr and Mississippian L. Q. C. Lamar returned year after year with their families to the same rooms at Brown's. Losing such regulars would certainly be bad for Mrs. Smith's business. Boardinghouse owners also had something to lose. Many of the families who owned such houses in the city were poor and relied on the goodwill of their patrons to keep them solvent. The Clement family, for example, ran a small boardinghouse on Capitol Hill that served as its primary source of income. When money was tight, the family would occasionally borrow from boarders.[40]

Perhaps the local Washingtonians most affected professionally by a civil war would be local bankers. Men like the Riggs' father-and-son banking team, as well as the wealthy financier William Corcoran, had substantial amounts of money invested in places as far reaching as New York, Illinois, Kansas, and especially Texas, where they were still collecting on Texas bonds settled in the Compromise of 1850. An unstable market was sure to create a financial dip for these men, and they would likely have to forfeit some of their loans. Corcoran, for example, had lent a considerable amount of money to members of Congress from both the North and South. Such financial concerns did not even include the friendships that men like Corcoran, Riggs, Benjamin Tayloe, and others had made.[41]

The social elite of Washington also feared the effects war and its possible devastation would have on their home city. Older Washingtonians had seen for themselves the damage wrought on the capital city by the war of 1812; during that conflict British soldiers occupied the city and set fire to numerous public buildings, including the White House itself. If they did not remember the War of 1812 personally, local and national newspapers certainly reminded them. Papers like the *Chicago Tribune* and the *New York Times* reported all sorts of rumors that the Southern states planned an attack on Washington before the war had even begun. Many, including the typically cautious *Daily National Intelligencer*, warned that the city would be in danger either during the official counting of electoral votes or during Lincoln's inauguration. Other D.C. residents wrote of the possible threat to the capital. One Washingtonian told New York newspaperman Thurlow Weed in December that he had "very serious apprehensions of what is very likely to transpire between this and the 4th of March . . . it is not at all improbable . . . that we may be under the necessity of fighting to ration possession of the Capitol and other public property."[42]

Would Washington even remain part of the United States? That was an important question that many city residents found themselves asking following the secession of South Carolina. After all, Washington had been ceded from Maryland, and there was talk throughout the Southern states that the District might be reclaimed into the Confederacy. Furthermore, if both Maryland and Virginia left the Union, Washington would likely have no choice but to join the Confederacy, losing its status as the nation's capital, not to mention its citizenship in the United States. If not, some fighting between the United States and the new Confederacy would likely take place on D.C. soil. As the *Daily National Intelligencer* argued in January, "We must maintain ourselves in this struggle or be utterly destroyed."[43]

As a result of these circumstances, a number of Washington socialites actively tried to prevent further conflict and disunion. Locals encouraged moderation in two ways. First, they tried to help federal politicians temper sectional animosities and find a solution to the crisis. Newspapers like the *Daily National Intelligencer* were instrumental in alerting Washington citizens (and the rest of their readership around the country) to various compromise options being discussed during the secession winter. Along with the *Intelligencer*'s political reportage, the paper's editor, William W. Seaton, preached moderation in numerous editorials and guest columns. At least twice a week from December into April, the paper pleaded with its readers to exercise moderation, to refrain from agitating in the District itself, to mind their neighbors. On January 21, the paper urged "the Representatives of the [North] . . . to avert [a conflict] that may ensue," not from any real differences between North and South, but rather from "a mutual misunderstanding between the people of the two sections."[44]

A second way that locals tried to prevent further disunion was to make their city the center of moderation and stability before the war. Although they could not reach average Southerners living in Athens, Georgia, or New Orleans, Louisiana, Washingtonians could have an impact on federal politicians still in the capital. Just as in negotiations over the Compromise of 1850, one tactic was to host dinners and parties during the session, welcoming men from both sections to their homes so that they could interact in a friendly environment. Although Corcoran had been ill for much of the winter of 1860–61, he invited a number of politicians to dine at his home during the second session of the Thirty-Sixth Congress. In mid-December, he hosted William Appleton of Massachusetts at the same dinner as Southerners John Slidell, Judah Benjamin, and Robert M. T. Hunter. On January 13, he again hosted John Slidell, along with former Whig George E. Badger of North Carolina, Winfield Scott, and four businessmen from the northeast. In February, Benjamin Ogle Tayloe similarly invited two North Carolinians then serving in the Peace Conference to dine with himself and at least one Northerner.[45]

Socialites were not the only men to use social events to press for political compromise. Politicians themselves used this approach throughout the winter. Stephen Douglas threw a large gala in mid-February and invited all the Peace Conference delegates, in addition to congressmen and other city residents. The throng included nearly 400 people, many of whom reconnected after not seeing one another for several years. At a dinner party at the home of Speaker Pennington, Kentuckian John Crittenden pressed Massachusetts representative Charles Francis Adams on the issue of compromise. In addition to Adams and Crittenden, Pennington's guests included Senators Zachariah Chandler of Michigan, James Dixon of Connecticut, and Lyman Trumbull of Illinois along with Representative Henry Winter Davis of Maryland, General Winfield Scott, and Scott's aid, Erasmus Keyes. As Adams described in his diary, "After we left the table, as I was turning to go out the door I heard [Crittenden] speaking earnestly to Colonel Keyes, and saying he could do no more," in regard to cross-sectional conciliation in the

Senate. Rather, "'The decision was in his hands.' I looked to see to whom he was alluding. He then touched me and said 'This is the man.'"[46]

Crittenden and Douglas were two of the most vocal proponents of compromise during secession winter. The relationship the two men had forged during negotiations over the Lecompton Constitution continued through the second session of the Thirty-Sixth Congress when they both pushed for peace and conciliation. In mid-December, they held a meeting at Douglas's house with four other pro-compromise Border State men, presenting for the first time Crittenden's plan for adjusting sectional difficulties. Following the meeting, the two men used their social and political sway to push for this congressional compromise and signed letters to former colleagues insisting that the Union could be saved.[47]

Other personal relationships played a role in trying to find a solution. Douglas's co-conspirator in the Kansas-Nebraska negotiations, former Alabama representative Philip Phillips, consulted the Little Giant on one of his plans for a cross-sectional compromise. President Buchanan made use of the old relationship between Abraham Lincoln and Kentuckian Duff Green from Mrs. Sprigg's boardinghouse in the Thirtieth Congress to try to gauge the president-elect's views on the secession crisis and the compromise negotiations then taking place in Washington. In late December, Buchanan entrusted Green with the task of traveling to Springfield to speak with Lincoln in person. The two men met for several hours, discussing the political situation in a friendly manner. Green later gave an interview for the *New York Herald* about the get-together, telling the reporter that he sought to "satisfy Mr. Lincoln that the movement in the South is not the result of any personal objection to him, nor of a desire or purpose to dissolve the Union" but rather for the South to receive some constitutional guarantees in regard to slavery. In return, he asked Lincoln for a public letter expressing his unwillingness to interfere with slavery in the states and requesting a constitutional amendment to that effect. Lincoln hesitated to speak publicly about the matter, instead addressing a letter to Green but sending it by way of Lyman Trumbull in Washington. Trumbull showed the letter to other Republican friends (at Lincoln's request) but did not allow it to become public. Still, Green must have retained some confidence in Lincoln; he told the *Herald*, he preferred peace to the "clamour for civil war."[48]

Green may have believed Lincoln's intentions were peaceful and conciliatory, but it was hard to convince other Southerners when the president-elect did not speak out. In fact, Lincoln refused to speak publicly about his views throughout the winter. In the three months following his election, he issued no public statements, made no formal addresses, and wrote no letters to widely read newspapers. He was silent. Letters from all over the Union streamed in, begging him to say something to assuage the South. In particular, Lincoln received letters from a large number of Washington politicians who, upon arriving in the capital in December, became greatly concerned with the possibility of secession. John Gilmer, who would work closely with Seward in March, repeatedly suggested that Lincoln speak out in order to mollify the South. After consulting with Gilmer in early December on the issue, Ohio Republican Thomas Corwin similarly suggested that Lincoln take some action. "I have never, in my life, seen my country in such a dangerous position," Corwin wrote to the president-elect on December 10. Other Washington insiders like Illinois representative Elihu Washburne and Indiana newspaperman John Defrees wrote Lincoln that the secession fervor was real and must be handled carefully.[49]

Even Stephens had suggested in one of his December communications to the president-elect that a timely word reassuring Southerners that he had no intention of interfering with slavery would do much to gratify his countrymen. But Lincoln said nothing. He maintained his public silence throughout the winter, breaking it only to help kill Crittenden's compromise plan in late December. Communicating from Springfield, Lincoln pressed the members of his party on the Senate Committee of Thirteen not to accept any plan that extended slavery; all five Republicans on the committee voted against the compromise.[50]

Why did Lincoln take this approach toward the sectional crisis during the winter of 1860–61? Lincoln tried to explain his silence to friends and supporters. He told them he greatly feared that the Southern press would twist anything he said to look aggressive and foolish. Lincoln had already spoken at great length about his love for the Union in previous speeches and had given numerous assurances that Republicans would not interfere with slavery where it already existed. As a number of historians have argued, Lincoln still believed that most Southerners were in favor of remaining within the Union, even if disunionist voices were ringing the loudest in the South at that particular moment.[51]

We now know that Lincoln deeply misread the secessionist impulse in the slaveholding states. But there were important reasons for this. As William Cooper has suggested, Lincoln did not have much knowledge of the South generally. What he did know came in large part from his wife's family in

Kentucky and the relationships he had formed with Southerners during the Thirtieth Congress. He disagreed with these men about slavery. But in conversations with men like Duff Green, Alexander Stephens, and others, he had found that they could oppose one another on one issue but come together on others. In essence, Lincoln believed that men from the North and South might disagree over slavery, but that this heated issue did not *define* relationships in the nation's capital. As he remarked to Stephens in his December 1860 letter, "You think slavery is *right* and ought to be extended; while we think it is *wrong* and ought to be restricted. That I suppose is the rub. It certainly is the only substantial difference between us." Lincoln was clear with all of his Republican lieutenants that he would not bend on the issue of slavery in the territories; he and many in his party believed that such a concession would destroy the Republican organization. But he *was* willing to compromise on slavery in other ways. In fact, he supported a proposed Thirteenth Amendment, which read: "No amendment shall be made to the Constitution which will authorize or give to Congress the power to abolish or interfere, within any State, with the domestic institutions thereof, including that of persons held to labor or service by the laws of said States."[52]

In the end, this constitutional amendment was all that congressmen in Washington could agree upon. The Thirty-Sixth Congress closed its second session on March 4, 1861. In the remaining hours of the term, nearly all compromise options were reviewed and discarded. Both houses had taken up the recommendations of the February Peace Conference but each had failed to pass them. A last-ditch effort to implement Crittenden's proposals did not get the required number of votes. With only the congressmen's proposed Thirteenth Amendment to show for themselves, most lawmakers knew they had not done enough to appease most Southerners. And so the session ended without a real political plan for conciliation. War was not inevitable, but the potential for conflict between Northerners and Southerners remained.[53]

The failure to create an acceptable compromise in Congress was a devastating blow for peace. But, to a large degree, events outside of Washington had prevented federal politicians from controlling the situation. From the confines of his home in Springfield, Lincoln misjudged the severity of Southerners' intentions. He, like other Republicans, remained skeptical of secession, believing Southern actions to be little more than idle threats. His attitude is somewhat understandable; after all, as historians David Potter, Elizabeth Varon, and others have shown, talk of disunion in both the North and South had existed for decades, but the Union remained intact. Even with the warnings from federal politicians, North and South, Lincoln and the radical Republicans would not bend.[54]

Events in the South were similarly instrumental in leading the country toward Civil War. As historians such as William Freehling, Michael Holt, and George Rable have shown, disunion was primarily a grass-roots movement; the act of secession was, in essence, an expression of Southerners' loss of confidence in the ability of their representatives to advocate for Southern interests. As Holt explains, "Whatever else secession represented, it was a rejection of the normal political process. It was a refusal not only to tolerate Republican possession of the executive branch but to trust the Democrats in Congress and the Supreme Court to protect Southern rights." The words of secession commissioners throughout the South echoed this theme. "The Federal Government has failed to protect the rights and property of the citizens of the South," wrote Alabama Secession Commissioner Stephen F. Hale, and the only way to retrieve those rights would be to leave the Union. Strongly repudiated across the South and handicapped by Republicans in the North, men like Gilmer, Campbell, Seward, Crittenden, and Douglas could do little to prevent disunion. In the end, external pressure trumped relationships and perceptions internal to Washington itself.[55]

Forced by this external pressure to abandon their beloved Union, Deep South men like Jefferson Davis quickly embraced the Confederate cause. Less than three weeks after his farewell to the United States Congress, the former Mississippi senator was selected as the provisional president of the Confederate States of America. His vice president, Alexander H. Stephens, one of Lincoln's old Young Indian friends, would deliver a spirited defense of slavery and his new nation in what came to be known as the "Cornerstone Speech," on March 21. Soon after, men like Clement Clay, Stephen Mallory, and John Slidell would become influential leaders of the Confederate cause, dedicated to fighting tooth and nail against their former country. These former Washington politicians had no doubt about the righteousness of their cause. They would not serve the Confederacy with any serious regret in 1861.[56]

Men from the Upper South like John Gilmer held out hope for the Union even after the departure of their Deep South colleagues. But soon, they too would join the Confederacy after Congress's peace efforts failed. In the immediate aftermath of their adjournment on March 3, a number of congressmen from both sections lingered in Washington to see Lincoln's inauguration the following day. After watching the inaugural parade march down Pennsylvania Avenue, politicians said their goodbyes to one another. Leaving the city brought out complex emotions for many. Some believed they would never again see their congressional colleagues. Tennessee representative John Vines Wright later reflected on his departure from Washington. As he explained, after the procession, he walked with three of his House colleagues—William T. Avery (D-Tenn.), Philip Fouke (D-Ill.), and John Logan (D-Ill.)—toward their hotels on Pennsylvania Avenue. On their way, the four men stopped in a local restaurant to share a round of drinks. "During the conversation it was suggested that when next we met it might be on the field of battle," Wright remembered. "This was probable, as each of us knew the sentiments and opinions of the others. It was also agreed that if either should be captured he was to be well treated."[57]

The Washington Brotherhood in War and Peace

On the morning of February 3, 1865, Union officials welcomed three Confederate peace commissioners aboard the *River Queen*, a steamer anchored near Hampton Roads, Virginia. Confederate president Jefferson Davis had sent these men— Vice President Alexander Stephens (Ga.), Assistant Secretary of State John Archibald Campbell (Ala.), and Senate President Robert M. T. Hunter (Va.)—to meet with Northern representatives and discuss possibilities for peace or at least a temporary truce. Stephens, Campbell, and Hunter settled in the steamer's saloon and waited. A short while later, Union president Abraham Lincoln and Secretary of State William Henry Seward entered the room.[1]

Before discussing any official business, the five men took the opportunity to exchange pleasantries and reminiscences. Stephens reminded the Union president of their time in Congress together in 1848 as part of the Young Indian Club. As the Georgian later described, Lincoln "responded in a cheerful and cordial manner, as if the remembrance of those times . . . had awakened in him a train of agreeable reflections, extending to others." The two men made mutual inquiries of their "intimate friends and active associates" from that time; Stephens asked after Truman Smith (Conn.) and Lincoln after Robert Toombs (Ga.), William Ballard Preston (Va.), and Thomas Flournoy (Va.). Seward and Hunter, who had served many years together in the U.S. Senate, traded similar reminiscences of times past.[2]

Finally the moment for business arrived. Seward assured all parties that the conference would be informal; no clerk or secretary was present to record what was said. In fact, the only outside party to enter the room during the meeting was an African American butler carrying drinks and cigars. Over the course of four hours, the five men talked openly about the possibilities for peace. The discussion concentrated on a suggestion that both sides suspend hostilities in order to unite against Napoleon III of France, who was trying to colonize Mexico. Napoleon's actions violated the Monroe Doctrine, a document that both Union and Confederate officials held dear. The idea was to postpone fighting between the Union and Confederacy until both sides could effectively expunge the French from the North American mainland. Union and Confederate officials each would divert their military resources to Mexico, thus uniting in a common cause that would, as Stephens explained, "almost inevitably lead to a peaceful and harmonious solution of their own difficulties."[3]

Although Stephens introduced the plan to invade Mexico, the idea was not his own. The strategy originated with Francis Preston Blair Sr., a political leader since the 1820s who, while loyal to the United States, had nonetheless maintained connections with both Northerners and Southerners during the conflict. Throughout the early years of the Civil War, Blair had cultivated a relationship with the Union president, offering advice and aid. So, in mid-January 1865, with Lincoln's permission and a passport, Blair went to Richmond with the hope of opening up communication between the warring parties. While in the Confederate capital, Blair interacted with many of his old associates from Washington and talked freely about prospects for peace. As Robert Hunter later explained, Blair's "representations were not without effect upon his old Confederates who for so long had been in the habit of taking counsel with him on public affairs."[4]

Blair's presence in Richmond also coincided with a growing peace movement among some members of the Confederate government. Foremost among these representatives was Henry S. Foote, a representative from Tennessee who had often clashed with Jefferson Davis while the two served together in Congress in the 1850s. In December 1864, Foote and others began calling for a peace convention in the Confederate Congress.[5] Perhaps with this movement in mind, on January 12, Blair met with Jefferson Davis for several hours, pressing the Confederate president on the issue of slavery. By the time Blair arrived in Richmond, the Confederates were seriously considering emancipating their slaves as a war measure. As a result, Blair told Davis, "the stumbling block of slavery" was now all but taken care of and could "scarcely be considered . . . an obstruction to pacification" between Union and Confederate officials.[6]

The January 12 meeting was the first of two conferences between Davis and Blair, which produced a short correspondence between the Confederate and Union presidents and a window for peacemaking. After Blair's second visit to Richmond, Davis decided to officially appoint peace commissioners for the purpose of negotiating with the Lincoln administration.[7] He called a private meeting with Stephens and Robert Hunter to discuss possible commissioners.[8] Stephens gave the president a number of suggestions for appointments, including Judge Campbell and Thomas Flournoy, whom Stephens believed was "a gentleman of distinguished ability" and, perhaps more important, was "well known personally to Mr. Lincoln." Stephens must not have been far off in this assumption, as Lincoln so kindly asked after Flournoy during the eventual meeting. Campbell was also a logical choice. In December 1864, the former Supreme Court justice had been making inquiries of friends in the Union as to whether some peace discussion was possible. As he explained to his former colleague, Justice Samuel Nelson, "I believe now that an honorable peace will relieve the country from evils, possibly more permanent and more aggravated than those which have been suffered." Campbell suggested other men he knew from Washington, including former Supreme Court Justice Benjamin Robbins Curtis, former Ohio senator Thomas Ewing, and the current secretary of war, Edwin Stanton.[9]

After taking Stephens's suggestions seriously, President Davis conducted a constructive meeting with his cabinet. In the evening, he formally announced that, along with Campbell, Hunter and Stephens himself would serve as peace commissioners. Davis left only minor clues as to why he chose these three men, but their senior positions in the administration were likely important; selecting them conveyed a sense of the mission's seriousness. Another reason, Davis later explained, was the "personal relations of personal friendship formerly existing between President Lincoln and Vice-President Stephens."[10]

On January 28, Davis met privately with Stephens, Hunter, and Campbell, and the group discussed the Monroe Doctrine proposal and their official instructions for the conference. According to Davis, he told them, "You are requested to proceed to Washington City for an informal conference" with President Lincoln "upon the issues involved in the existing war, and for the purpose of securing peace to the two countries." The following day the three commissioners departed Richmond and headed toward Petersburg, where the Union army was stationed under Lieutenant General Ulysses S. Grant. After arriving at Petersburg the evening of January 30, the three men sent word to the camp headquarters, presenting their hope to travel through Union lines to Washington where they would converse with President Lincoln. General Grant was temporarily absent from Petersburg, and so the ranking Major General, E. O. C. Ord, commander of the Army of the James, forwarded the request to Washington.[11]

Here the Confederate commissioners faced a problem over the language in their instructions. Early in his conferences with Blair, Davis had insisted that representatives of the Confederacy would negotiate on the basis of peace for "two countries." This was unacceptable to Lincoln, who had replied to Davis's letter by emphasizing a solution based on "securing peace to the people of our one common country." Blair had tried to minimize the discrepancy between the two positions while in conversation with Lincoln. Yet once the commissioners reached Petersburg with the hope of entering Union lines and eventually traveling to Washington, Lincoln could not accept any inconsistency. So Lincoln responded by sending instructions through T. T. Eckert, a War Department official. Eckert's job was to meet with the commissioners and see if they were willing to travel north on the basis of "one common country." If they did not agree, Eckert was supposed to deny the commissioners safe conduct through Union lines.[12]

Eckert did not get the opportunity to follow through on these instructions, however. Grant returned to Petersburg the morning of January 31 before Eckert even left Washington. The Union general was unaware of the correspondence between Lincoln and Ord and saw only a letter addressed to himself from the three commissioners asking to enter Union lines for the purposes of negotiating peace. Presuming the commissioners meant well, Grant sent a staff officer to welcome them into Union lines and await word from the president. At sunset, the staff officer reached the edge of the Petersburg lines and escorted the commissioners by train to Grant's headquarters. Grant then conducted the men to resting quarters on the steamer *Mary Martin*. The general later remembered, "I directed the captain to furnish them with the best the boat afforded, and to administer to their comfort in every way possible. No guard was placed over them and no restriction was put upon their movements." Campbell, Hunter, and Stephens made good use of their roaming capabilities, visiting both General Grant and General George Gordon Meade at their headquarters the morning of February 1. Although Grant had never met any of the commissioners, he knew them by reputation and, after conversing, found them "very agreeable gentlemen." Meade's wife was well acquainted with Campbell, however, and the judge asked after her family.[13]

Under the new circumstances allowed by General Grant, Lincoln had to alter his plan. The president was now willing to send an envoy to meet with the commissioners but did not have the intention of welcoming them to Washington under the "two countries" language. Thus, he dispatched Eckert to Petersburg to ask for a meeting based on "one common country" and simultaneously sent Seward to Hampton Roads to speak with the Southerners if they refused. On the afternoon of February 1, Eckert finally arrived at Union headquarters in Petersburg and presented Lincoln's instructions to the three Confederate commissioners. Again, the language proved problematic. Yet they told Eckert, "Our instructions contemplate a personal interview with President Lincoln at Washington, but with this explanation we are ready to meet any person or persons that President Lincoln may appoint at such place as he may designate." Perhaps most important, they insisted, "our earnest desire is that a just and honorable peace may be agreed upon." In the evening, the commissioners decided to appeal directly to General Grant, again asking to speak informally with Lincoln or some Union representative. Seeing the note, Eckert refused and telegraphed Lincoln that he would return to Washington the next day without the commissioners.[14]

Meanwhile, Grant was apparently moved by his conversations with the commissioners and their appeal to him. At half past ten that evening, he telegraphed Stanton, "I am convinced upon conversation . . . that their intentions are good and their desire sincere to restore peace and union." Aware that the men would now go to meet Seward at Fortress Monroe, he added, "I am sorry . . . that Mr. Lincoln cannot have an interview with [them]." Grant's thoughts on the commissioners' motives, in turn, had an effect on President Lincoln. Upon reading Grant's communication with Stanton, he made arrangements to join Seward at Fortress Monroe that evening. At half past nine the next morning, the commissioners departed Union headquarters and started the journey down to Hampton Roads.[15]

Once the conference began, it became clear that no real opportunity to create peace existed. Although he made the trip to Hampton Roads, Lincoln had no intention of agreeing to Blair's Mexico plan. The Union president would suspend military operations only coincident with Confederate surrender and the reestablishment of federal authority throughout the South. Nor did Lincoln mislead the Southern commissioners; he repeatedly

stated during the meeting that, in Stephens's words, "he could not entertain a proposition for an Armistice on any terms, while the great and vital
question of re-union was undisposed of." Similarly, the Confederate commissioners were unable to make full concessions. Campbell later wrote to
Hunter that "we were limited to making a *treaty* between the two countries." Under these circumstances, there was no real ground that either side
could give.[16]

Nonetheless, as later reports by all the parties indicate, the conversation
was pleasantly conducted, and no one left angry. Following the meeting,
Seward remarked that "the conversation, although earnest and free, was
calm, courteous, and kind on both sides." Moreover, at no time did the Confederates "either make categorical demands, or tender formal stipulations
or absolute refusals." The points at issue between the men "were distinctly
raised and discussed fully, intelligently, and in an amicable spirit." When the
parties adjourned, the men shook hands, and Stephens quietly urged the
president to reconsider his view on a possible armistice. Lincoln responded
kindly, "Well, Stephens, I will re-consider it, but I do not think my mind
will change, but I will re-consider." According to one account, the U.S. secretary of state even sent the Confederate delegation a bottle of champagne
to enjoy on the steamer ride back to Richmond. As a freedman carried the
champagne by rowboat to the Confederates, Seward called out to his Southern colleagues: "Keep the champagne, but return the negro."[17]

Ultimately, the meeting at Fortress Monroe highlights a number of critical points about federal politicians in the Civil War era. First, the fact that
the conference took place at all was a peculiar consequence of the Washington community in the mid-nineteenth century. All of the major players
had served in Washington in high federal offices for over a decade. In fact,
of the men involved, Lincoln had the least experience before assuming the
presidency in 1861. The meeting resulted from long-standing relationships
among Northern and Southern men, beginning with Jefferson Davis and
Francis Preston Blair Sr. and ending with Lincoln and Stephens. As these
relationships show, personal connections defined the boundaries in which
Civil War–era politicians operated.

The details of Blair's plan for peace also rested on these long-standing relationships. In many ways, Blair's idea to muster forces from both sides to
attack France in 1865 mirrored Seward's own proposal to prevent civil war
in 1861. On April 1, 1861, Seward had sent Lincoln a memorandum entitled
"Some Thoughts for the President's Consideration." Along with a number
of other policy suggestions, Seward argued that the United States could cre-

ate a foreign war with France or Spain, which had been meddling in Mexico and the Caribbean. From Seward's perspective, this would reunite the country against a common enemy. Although Lincoln did not take the suggestion seriously, the similarities between Seward's 1861 proposal and Blair's 1865 proposal are striking.[18] Blair and Seward were not friendly, in part because they came from different sides of the Republican Party—Blair had been a Democrat and Seward a Whig—so it is unlikely the two men discussed the foreign war plan. But Blair's son, Montgomery Blair, served in Lincoln's cabinet as postmaster general and may have learned of Seward's original plan from Lincoln or one of his secretaries at some point during the war. Thus, the contingencies of personal relationships influenced both the content and context of the discussion.[19]

Second, historians often talk about the Civil War as a brother's war, a war that split families. So too did the war split the Washington brotherhood. This separation was hard on many of the politicians who left Washington in the spring of 1861. And these men did not simply drop their associations during the war itself. Seward, in particular, tried to be helpful to former associates who had transferred allegiances to the Confederacy. Just before Blair went down to Richmond, the peace-seeking Henry Foote had tried to cross Union lines with his wife. The Confederate military captured Henry, but Mrs. Foote was able to make her way to Washington. Apparently Seward took special care of the ex-senator's wife while she was in the capital city. Lincoln was similarly kind to Alexander Stephens's nephew. While serving as a prisoner at Fort Warren after the war, Stephens recalled an incident at the end of the Hampton Roads meeting whereupon Lincoln asked if he could be of service to his former colleague in some other way. The Confederate vice president asked if Lincoln might be willing to help free his nephew, John A. Stephens, from prison on Johnson's Island. Upon returning to Washington after the conference, Lincoln telegraphed the prison to have John sent to him in the capital. The president gave John Stephens the "freedom of the city" while he was in Washington and then sent him safely to Confederate lines.[20]

Following the surrender at Appomattox, a number of Northern politicians also helped their former colleagues from the South escape prison sentences and acquire pardons. Seward, for example, was quick to forgive. His son, Frederick Seward, claimed that, to his father, "an enemy who had surrendered was an enemy no longer." Thus, when Robert M. T. Hunter arrived in Washington looking for a pardon, Seward invited him to dine at his house. According to Frederick Seward, "they sat at table talking of 'old times before the war,' and when Hunter raised his plate, he found his 'pardon' duly signed and sealed beneath it." Seward also tried to help the former Texas representative John Reagan who served as the Confederate postmaster general during the war. Reagan and Stephens were both sent to Fort Warren after the Confederacy surrendered. From there, Reagan wrote the secretary of state for aid, appealing to Seward's relationship with another former colleague, Texas senator Thomas Rusk. Reagan explained, "I was taught long ago by your associate in the Senate, General Rusk, who respected you much, and who was my friend, to believe that your heart and mind were large enough to enable you to deal justly and even liberally with an adversary."[21]

Perhaps the most surprising example of a Northerner reaching out to Southern captives was Massachusetts Republican Henry Wilson's efforts to help Stephens at Fort Warren. By the time he reached the Union prison, Stephens had become seriously ill and was suffering from the conditions and poor diet. Wilson, who had served in the Senate when Stephens was a representative from Georgia, visited his former colleague at Fort Warren and, seeing the poor conditions, went to Washington to complain. Stephens later explained, "however much I have differed with Mr. Wilson and do now differ with him, on many public questions . . . yet I believe he possesses many excellencies of both head and heart."[22]

Finally, the difficulties of facing off against one another during the war did not prevent many Washington politicians from reconnecting after Appomattox. In the late 1860s, Jeremiah S. Black of Pennsylvania and Georgian Howell Cobb, both of whom served in James Buchanan's cabinet in the 1850s, wrote each other often. "I never forget your interests for a moment," Black wrote to Cobb in April 1868. "My heart yearns to serve you." Buchanan himself remained on good terms with some of the most ardent former secessionists. After seeing an article about Buchanan's memoir in a local newspaper, South Carolinian Robert Barnwell Rhett felt compelled to write the ex-president: "The remembrance of the kindly relations which once existed between us forcibly came to mind," he told Buchanan. The Pennsylvanian was quick to respond to Rhett. "I believe there are portions of it you will not approve," he said. "but, if so, we shall agree to differ on political questions like friends, as we did in the ancient time."[23]

Buchanan's casual remark that friends could "differ on political questions" emphasizes the extent to which Washington politicians continued to value discussion and debate over conformity, just as they had in the antebellum years. In the 1850s, when the stakes were arguably higher, Northerners and Southerners could disagree on the subject of slavery without fearing an end to their friendship. Alexander Stephens similarly accepted debate and difference in the years following the war. One of his allies in the 1850s had been Pennsylvania representative J. Glancy Jones. By 1868, the two men had reestablished their former acquaintance, and Stephens looked to Jones for political news. In 1872, when the Democratic Party nominated Horace Greeley for president, Stephens discussed his displeasure with Jones, remarking "I saw very clearly that you and I who have so [often] and cordially agreed in the past were not likely to agree on the coming political canvass."[24]

Another person Stephens was anxious to see after the war was his remaining Northern friend from the Young Indian Club, Truman Smith. During the war years, Smith had faithfully served the Union as a judge of the court of arbitration under the 1862 treaty with England for the suppression of the slave trade. By the mid 1870s, he had retired from politics but was still corresponding with his old friend Stephens, who held no grudge against him for his service to the Union. Undoubtedly Smith enjoyed thinking about an earlier time in his life in Congress. When his young wife gave birth to twin sons in the early 1870s, Smith had named the boys Zachary Taylor and Abraham Lincoln. In December 1878, Stephens wrote Smith asking him to come down to Washington during the winter to spend some time with himself and their other Young Indian colleague, Robert Toombs. As he explained, "we three could talk over again the great battles of that memorable campaign of 1848, to say nothing of others."[25]

NOTES

Abbreviations

CAH   Center for American History, University of Texas, Austin
DU   Duke University, William R. Perkins Special Collections Library, Durham, N.C.
FIL   Filson Historical Society, Louisville, Ky.
HSP   Historical Society of Pennsylvania, Philadelphia
HUN   Huntington Library, Munger Research Center, San Marino, Calif.
LC   Library of Congress, Manuscript Division, Washington, D.C.
MHS   Massachusetts Historical Society, Boston
NARA   National Archives and Records Administration, Washington, D.C.
NYHS   New-York Historical Society, New York City
SCRC   Special Collections Research Center at the University of Chicago Library, Chicago, Ill.
SHC   Southern Historical Collection, University of North Carolina, Chapel Hill
UGA   University of Georgia, Hargrett Rare Book and Manuscript Library, Athens
UM-B   University of Michigan, Bentley Library, Ann Arbor
UM-C   University of Michigan, Clements Library, Ann Arbor
UVA   University of Virginia, Albert and Shirley Small Special Collections, Charlottesville
VHS   Virginia Historical Society, Richmond

Introduction

1. For a sample of historians who identify antebellum Washington as violent and divisive, see Nevins, *The Emergence of Lincoln*, 2:171–75; Potter, *Impending Crisis*, 199–224; Holt, *Political Crisis*, 194–96; Donald, Baker, and Holt, *The Civil War and Reconstruction*, 76–80. There are some exceptions, including Roy F. Nichols, who acknowledges significant cooperation and interaction across party lines. See Nichols, *Disruption of American Democracy*, 145, 150, 154.

2. Two critical developments in American historiography over the past few decades have made this type of analysis possible. First, scholars such as Steven Hahn, Stephanie McCurry, and many others expanded the boundaries and definitions of American politics. See Hahn, *A Nation under Our Feet*; McCurry, *Masters of Small Worlds*; Pasley, Robertson, and Waldstreicher, *Beyond the Founders*. Within these expanded boundaries, historians have shown that Americans connected with politics outside of the traditional structures of lawmaking, not just in the halls of Congress, state houses, and courts. Through the work of Catherine Allgor, Lori Ginzberg, and Elizabeth Varon, for example, we have learned more about how women practiced politics in ladies' parlors, at kitchen tables, and through benevolent associations. By applying social and cultural history to political problems, these historians have found new ways to understand political engagement. Allgor looks at the

Washington community to illustrate how the city environment influenced female political power in the Early Republic. Allgor, *Parlor Politics*, 2, 241; Ginzberg shows how kitchen table conversations in New York on women's rights led to political action. In essence, the shared experiences and convictions of a tightly knit community influenced these women's political behavior. Ginzberg, *Untidy Origins*, 12, 26. Varon argues that during the antebellum period women engaged with political activism through benevolent associations and thereby exerted their influence on political issues. Varon, *We Mean to Be Counted*, 1–6. Also see P. Baker, "The Domestication of Politics."

A second group of scholars has looked more directly at the male realm of politics. These studies have overwhelmingly dealt with the problem of "political culture"—what Daniel Walker Howe has called "an evolving system of beliefs, attitudes, and techniques for solving problems." These beliefs, attitudes, and techniques informed the behavior of lawmakers and other political actors. Since the 1980s, historians have used political culture to reexamine various aspects of American politics, including the role of newspapers, elections and campaigning, language, and particularly political parties. A few have even looked at the political culture of Washington, most strikingly, Joanne Freeman in her groundbreaking study of honor and politics in the Early Republic. Together, these trends in American historiography have helped frame my approach to antebellum Washington; I look at the underlying political culture of the capital city as well as the ways in which lawmakers engaged in politics outside the traditional political structures of Washington, most importantly outside the Capitol building. Howe, *Political Culture*, 2. On the development of political culture in American historiography, see Glendzel, "Political Culture." On the role of newspapers, see Pasley, *"The Tyranny of Printers."* On electioneering and campaigning, see Formisano, *The Transformation of American Political Culture*; Neely, *The Boundaries of American Political Culture*; Bensel, *The American Ballot Box*. On language, see Varon, *Disunion!*; Waldstreicher, *In the Midst of Perpetual Fetes*; and Robertson, *The Language of Democracy*. On parties, see J. Baker, *Affairs of Party*; Wiebe, *Self Rule*. On Washington's unofficial setting, see Freeman, *Affairs of Honor*.

3. This is not to suggest that these documents are unimportant. On the contrary, they are crucial to understanding partisan and sectional public debate throughout the antebellum era. But much like nineteenth-century newspapers, which were published by partisan presses, they must be read with a critical eye toward underlying motivations. Although scholars have long used the *Globe* to document congressional debate and negotiation, I argue in chapter 1 that public documents like the *Congressional Globe* have obscured our understanding of the way that Washington operated in the mid-nineteenth century. They give us an "official" record of political negotiation and decision making in Washington, but they offer few clues to the "unofficial" political arena, to what happened behind the scenes. The extent of speechmaking for constituents is neatly captured by contemporary journalists in the *North American Review* 71, no. 1 (1850): 229. Also see chapter 1. My thinking on this issue has been greatly influenced by Mark E. Neely's contention that nineteenth-century newspapers are "useless as barometers of public opinion" because of their overwhelming partisanship, while simultaneously serving as a critical tool in researching political history. See Neely, *The Union Divided*, x, and Neely, *The Boundaries of American Political Culture*, 29–30. Jonathan White expresses similar concerns about court records in the Civil War era. J. White, *Abraham Lincoln and Treason*, 8.

4. James Sterling Young famously documented this trend in *The Washington Community*, 250–53. Young argued that there was a key correlation between the way federal politicians lived in Washington—typically in boardinghouses containing members from the same region—and their voting behavior. These living arrangements, combined with what Young calls a "negative attitude toward power among the rulers themselves," undermined the ability of Jefferson-era politicians to effectively govern on national issues. Young's assertions have been questioned by a number of historians. See, for example, John, "Affairs of Office."

A few other historians took up Young's approach to congressional boarding arrangements in analyzing other aspects of Washington political life in the Jeffersonian and Jacksonian eras. See in particular Bogue and Marlaire, "Of Mess and Men," and G. White, *The Marshall Court and Cultural Change*. My work, while informed by Young, takes a different approach to the Washington community, including a number of other facets of social life in the capital city that Young does not consider.

5. Quigley, "Patchwork Nation"; Potter, "The Historian's Use of Nationalism." As Gary W. Gallagher has recently pointed out, the Union had a profound "historical, political and ideological meaning," to antebellum Americans. See Gallagher, *The Union War*, 46. Only a handful of historians have dealt specifically with the question of unionism. Rather, they often conflate it with the similarly nebulous concept of nationalism. These two ideas were intimately connected, and therefore unionism could also be seen as a commitment to American nationalism, particularly in the context of mid-nineteenth-century revolutions in Europe. See Onuf and Onuf, *Nations, Markets, and War*, 2–4; Fleche, *The Revolution of 1861*, 6, 37. Exceptions include Nagel, *One Nation Indivisible*, and Stampp, "The Concept of a Perpetual Union," 3–36.

6. Nearly every book on American nationalism in the antebellum era is connected specifically with the Civil War. For the Northern view of the nation, see Hess, *Liberty, Virtue, and Progress*, 5–17; Lawson, *Patriot Fires*, 12–13; Grant, *North over South*, 8–9. Grant argues that Northern nationalism developed as an expression of opposition against all things Southern. For a contrary view of how Northern nationalism developed, see Wongsrichanalai, "The Burden of Their Class," 9. For views of how the nation was synonymous with "southern values," see Quigley, "Patchwork Nation," 21; Carmichael, *The Last Generation*, 7, 180; Rubin, *A Shattered Nation*, 1–3; and Gallagher, *The Confederate War*, 72.

7. Anne C. Lynch, "A Sketch of Washington City," *Harper's New Monthly Magazine* 6, no. 31 (December 1852).

8. Furthermore, this personal bond did not mean a weaker attachment to slavery. As Edward Ayers and Andrew Torget have argued, many Southerners were hesitant to secede because they thought slavery was best protected inside the Union rather than in a new confederacy. Ayers, *In the Presence of Mine Enemies*, xix–xx; Torget, "Unions of Slavery," 9–34.

9. For the lack of preparation and hesitation, see Nichols, *Disruption of American Democracy*, 374–77; Alexander Stephens to J. Henly Smith, Crawfordville, Ga., December 31, 1860, in Phillips, "Correspondence," 526–27; Freehling, *Road to Disunion*, 2:405; Hitchcock, "Southern Moderates and Secession," 872–73; Barney, *The Secessionist Impulse*, 195–96. Barney argues that Jefferson Davis, in particular, "misread totally the political climate in Mississippi." Also see Potter, *Lincoln and His Party*, xxvii, 47; Varon, *Disunion!*, 14; and McClintock, *Lincoln and the Decision*, 9–10.

10. Randall, "The Blundering Generation." Randall and other revisionists of the 1930s and 1940s believed that slavery would have died of natural causes, had it been restricted to the southern United States. In particular, Charles W. Ramsdell argued that "those who wished [slavery] destroyed had only to wait a little while—perhaps a generation, probably less." Instead, "it was summarily destroyed at a frightful cost to the whole country." See Ramsdell, "The Natural Limits of Slavery Expansion," 151–71. In 1974 Robert Fogel and Stanley Engerman used the economic theory of cliometrics to disprove the "natural limits" thesis, arguing instead that slavery was adaptable and would have remained highly profitable for generations. See Fogel and Engerman, *Time on the Cross*, especially 58–106. In this work, Fogel and Engerman deemphasized the brutality of slavery, leading to a number of critical evaluations in the late 1970s and 1980s, particularly from historians such as Herbert Gutman and Peter Kolchin. See Gutman, *Slavery and the Numbers Game*; Kolchin, "Toward a Reinterpretation of Slavery." In 1989 Fogel revised the findings from *Time on the Cross* to account for many of these criticisms in *Without Consent or Contract*. Some historians remain unconvinced by Fogel's arguments about the capitalistic nature of slavery, but few question the logic that slavery was adaptable and may have lasted for generations. For a continued critique, see Kolchin, "More Time on the Cross?"

11. On the role of newspapers and print culture in general in facilitating sectionalism, see Pierce, "Networks of Disunion," 1–2, 9–24. On the grass-roots origins of secession, see Freehling, *Road to Disunion*, 2:349, 367; Holt, *Political Crisis*, 220–21; and Rable, *The Confederate Republic*, 21–23.

12. Freehling highlights political complexities and contingencies in the antebellum period that combined to provide the moment for secession to succeed. Egnal points to economic differences between the North and South in explaining why the war came. Freehling, *Road to Disunion*, 2:xiv–xv; Egnal, *Clash of Extremes*, 309–26.

13. Abraham Lincoln, "Second Inaugural Address," in Basler, *Collected Works*, 8:332–33. Both Varon and Ayers give detailed descriptions of the battles over Civil War causality. The modern fight is primarily between "fundamentalists" such as James M. McPherson, Eric Foner, John Ashworth, and Sean Wilentz and "revisionists" such as William Cooper, Michael Holt, William Gienapp, and William Freehling. Fundamentalists argue that the two sections had irreconcilable antagonisms, most importantly over slavery, that propelled the nation toward Civil War. Revisionists focus more specifically on intrasectional debates and contingencies that do not necessarily involve slavery, which help explain the timing of the war. Varon, *Disunion!*, 2–4; Ayers, *What Caused the Civil War*, 131–42; Cook, Barney, and Varon, *Secession Winter*, 86–87. See McPherson, *Battle Cry of Freedom*; Foner, *Free Soil, Free Labor, Free Men*; Ashworth, *Slavery, Capitalism, and Politics*, vol. 2; Wilentz, *The Rise of American Democracy*; Cooper, *We Have the War upon Us*; Holt, *Political Crisis*; Gienapp, *The Origins of the Republican Party*; Freehling, *Road to Disunion*, vol. 1. Michael E. Woods similarly notes recent trends in the literature on the coming of the Civil War that reveal "an impatience with old interpretive categories." Woods, "What Twenty-First-Century Historians Have Said about the Causes of Disunion," 438. Frank Towers gives a slightly different interpretation of three successive "research agendas" that informed interpretations of the coming of the Civil War in "Partisans, New History, and Modernization."

14. I rely on the methods of collective biography and community studies to under-

stand the connection between social and political life. Two recent books on the American founding by Richard Beeman and Jack Rakove, and an earlier study of the French Revolution by Timothy Tackett, have particularly influenced my approach. All three scholars explore the ways in which political actors brought individual characteristics and ideals—in sum, their private lives—to political problems. See Beeman, *Plain, Honest Men*; Rakove, *Revolutionaries*; and Tackett, *Becoming a Revolutionary*. Work by John L. Brooke on the upper Hudson, Charlene Boyer Lewis on the Virginia Springs, Karen Hansen on New England, and Gregg D. Kimball on Richmond, Virginia, has similarly provided a road map for examining the cultural contours of individual communities. Brooke, *Columbia Rising*; Lewis, *Ladies and Gentlemen on Display*; Hansen, *A Very Social Time*; Kimball, *American City, Southern Place*.

15. As gender historians have shown, there was not one particular way of demonstrating masculinity in the mid-nineteenth century. Still, the fraternal experience of living in Washington would have been informed by antebellum conceptions of gender roles and behavior. See Berry, *All That Makes a Man*, 19–27; Carnes, "Middle Class Men," 45–49; Dorsey, *Reforming Men and Women*, 6–8; A. Greenberg, *Manifest Manhood*, 6–14;

16. Joseph H. Allen to Theodore Parker, Washington, May 22, 1848, Theodore Parker Papers, MHS.

Prologue

1. Quotations: Zevely, "Old Houses on C Street," 151–52, and Sunderland, "Washington as I First Knew It," 195; Leech, *Reveille in Washington*, 12; Dickens, *American Notes for General Circulation*, 1:283. For a history of L'Enfant's design and the status of the Capitol dome in the antebellum period, see Allen, *History of the United States Capitol*, 8–9; Bednar, *L'Enfant's Legacy*, 5–16; Green, *Washington, Village and Capital*, 4–10; Gugliotta, *Freedom's Cap*, 11–14.

2. Green, *Washington, Village and Capital*, 4; Leech, *Reveille in Washington*, 5–12; Ellet, *Court Circles of the Republic*, 425.

3. Leech, *Reveille in Washington*, p. 10–11; Haley, *Philip's Washington Described*, 221–22; Press, "South of the Avenue," 51:51; Gugliotta, *Freedom's Cap*, 26. For a thorough accounting of the free black population of the area, see Harrison, *Washington during the Civil War and Reconstruction*; Masur, *An Example for All the Land*; and Harrold, *Subversives*.

4. Clay, *A Belle of the Fifties*, 28; Green, *Washington, Village and Capital*, 160; Gugliotta, *Freedom's Cap*, 28.

5. See, for example, David Outlaw to his wife, February 12, 1848, David Outlaw Papers, SHC; Alexander Stephens to Linton Stephens, July 24, 1850, January 22, 1851, and January 11, 1854, Alexander Hamilton Stephens Papers, Manhattanville College Library, Purchase, N.Y.; *Harper's Weekly*, March 14, 1857; Windle, *Life in Washington*, 24–25. There was some controversy later in the nineteenth century about the hotel poisoning and whether the sickness came from "gaseous emanations from the sewer" instead. See James Ridgeway to George Schutt, November 11, 1907, National Hotel Research Documents, Historical Society of Washington, D.C.

6. Mackay, *The Western World*, 1:117; Windle, *Life in Washington*, 32, 67.

7. Robert Winthrop to John Clifford, June 20, 1841, Winthrop Family Papers, MHS.

Chapter 1

1. The Walker Tariff of 1846 altered the Whig-sponsored Tariff of 1842 by lowering the rates on most manufactured goods while simultaneously raising rates on a number of raw materials imported by American manufacturers. The Whig minority allowed a Democratic majority to pass this tariff with the hopes of regaining a political advantage when (in the Whigs' predictions) economic disaster followed. Michael Holt explains the political maneuvering in Congress in Holt, "Winding Roads to Recovery, 144–45, and Holt, *Rise and Fall*, 246–47.

2. For useful summaries of events leading up to the Mexican War, see Silbey, *Storm over Texas*; Hietala, *Manifest Design*; Pletcher, *The Diplomacy of Annexation*; and most recently A. Greenberg, *A Wicked War*.

3. For Democratic support for the war and westward expansion, see Ashworth, *Slavery, Capitalism, and Politics*, 1:340; M. Morrison, *Slavery and the American West*, 81–82; and Merk, *Manifest Destiny*, 95. For the Whig perspective, see Holt, *Rise and Fall*, 252, and M. Morrison, "'New Territory versus No Territory,'" 28.

4. Polk may have wanted the territory, in part, for slavery reasons. But he was motivated primarily by a belief in American superiority, a desire for American expansionism, and, ultimately, an interest in cheap land. See Sellers, *James K. Polk: Continentalist*, 213–66; Siegenthaler, *James K. Polk*, 132.

5. *Congressional Globe*, 29th Cong., 1st Sess., 1214. Michael Holt argues that the Democratic group was motivated to introduce the proviso as a result of a challenge by New York Whig Hugh Lawson White. White insisted that Polk's appropriation bill be amended so as to prevent slavery from entering the territories. This challenge, according to Holt, crystallized because "Northern Democrats feared that Polk's move would allow their Whig rivals to accuse them of supporting a southern-sponsored war for slavery extension." Holt, *Rise and Fall*, 251. Yet White made his challenge *after* the recess; by that point, the Democrats had already had their dinner meeting and decided on a course of action. See *Congressional Globe*, 29th Cong., 1st Sess., 1213.

The description of Wilmot can be found in the memoirs of one of Wilmot's friends, Indiana representative George W. Julian. See Julian, *Political Recollections*, 29. Historians have disagreed for generations over who was the original author of the Wilmot Proviso. Because Wilmot had been a supporter of the Polk administration during the tariff battle earlier that session, some of his contemporaries believed the Pennsylvanian was merely a pawn of the Van Buren coalition. Furthermore, Ohioan Jacob Brinkerhoff claimed he had come up with the idea and presented it to the group over dinner. Wilmot, however, insisted that Brinkerhoff was mistaken; it was called the Wilmot Proviso for a reason. Preston King would reintroduce the proviso in the next session, making it plausible that the New Yorker was, in fact, the brains of the operation. Ultimately, we will never know for sure who wrote the original, but as historian Eric Foner has remarked, it is probably irrelevant.

More important are the reasons behind introducing the bill and the eventual vote in its favor. Again, historians disagree. While Wilmot's biographer, Charles Buxton Going, suggests that Wilmot introduced the bill because of his moral opposition to slavery, others attribute the bill's introduction as well as its eventual passage to frustration over Polk's patronage policies, the tariff, the Oregon boundary line, and any of a number of other political reasons. In a recent book on the Free-Soil men, Jonathan Earle revives Going's thesis that Wilmot was far more interested in abolishing slavery than modern historians have given him credit for. In all likelihood, there was some combination of motives among the men at the dinner meeting (including Wilmot himself) and in the House that evening. Key works on the authorship controversy and motivational controversy include C. Morrison, *Democratic Politics and Sectionalism*; Going, *David Wilmot, Free-Soiler*; Stenberg, "The Motivation of the Wilmot Proviso"; Earle, *Jacksonian Antislavery*; and particularly Foner, "The Wilmot Proviso Revisited," and Richards, *The Slave Power*.

6. *Congressional Globe*, 29th Cong., 1st Sess., 1215. Other Southerners who spoke on the $2 million bill but did not broach the subject of Wilmot's amendment include Reuben Chapman of Alabama, Garrett Davis of Kentucky, Edwin Ewing of Tennessee, and Seaborn Jones of Georgia.

7. For a summary of the Gag Rule fight in Congress, see Freehling, *Road to Disunion*, 1:336. Statistical analysis of the sectional breakdown among Whigs during the gag rule fight can be found in Alexander, *Sectional Stress and Party Strength*, 42–45; and among Democrats in Silbey, *The Shrine of Party*, 59–63.

8. *Congressional Globe*, 29th Cong., 1st Sess., 1217–18. On Monday, August 10, the last day of the congressional term, antislavery senator John W. Davis attempted to speak on the $2 million measure until the last minute of debate, hoping the Senate would pass the appropriation with the Wilmot amendment intact. But the Massachusetts senator was unaware of an eight-minute difference between the Senate and House clocks, and by the time he finished speaking, the House had already adjourned. See *Congressional Globe*, 29th Cong., 1st Sess., 1220–21.

9. Because of the eventually polarizing impact of the Wilmot Proviso in congressional debate, nearly every historian of the antebellum era has analyzed the provision. William Cooper explains that while regular Democrats did not initially think that the introduction of Wilmot's amendment was particularly threatening to the health of the party, they had to account for South Carolinian John C. Calhoun's reaction the following session. He argues that Calhoun eventually saw the proviso as "a vehicle for his politics of confrontation," which, in turn, forced Southern Democrats to take a stronger stand against the amendment. Thus, the ultimate impact of Calhoun's influence was a delayed fury against David Wilmot and his proviso. Cooper, *The South and the Politics of Slavery*, 233–35. Freehling largely agrees with this point in *Road to Disunion*, 1:459–60.

Historians such as Eric Foner, Sean Wilentz, and Michael Morrison similarly see the Wilmot Proviso as a critical motivating factor in the fight against slavery in the North. Foner uses the proviso as an example of burgeoning Free-Soil ideology. Foner, *Free Soil, Free Labor, Free Men*, 308–11. Wilentz explains that the "Democratic antislavery argument embodied in the Wilmot Proviso was above all an attack on the authority of the aristocratic Slave Power." Wilentz, *The Rise of American Democracy*, 299. Morrison argues that "the basic parameters" of sectionalism that would cause the Civil War "were articulated and defined in the spring of 1847," when the Wilmot Proviso was reintroduced. M. Morrison, *Slavery and the American West*, 64. Furthermore, as Orville Vernon Burton has argued, Southerners' worst fears were realized by the introduction and reintroduction of the proviso. See Burton, *The Age of Lincoln*, 30.

10. *Washington Daily Union*, August 10, 1846. Some newspapers outside of Washington, D.C., did pick up on the Wilmot Proviso debate in the few weeks that followed. For

examples, see the *Boston Whig*, August 15, 1846, and the *Niles' National Register*, August 15, 1846. In one of the only monographs written specifically about the Wilmot Proviso, Chaplain Morrison explains that Northerners paid the amendment little attention, and Southerners even less, considering it a piece of temporary political strategy. He notes that South Carolinian John C. Calhoun, who eventually became the most vocal opponent of the proviso, did not voice any special concern about it in the months following the House's passage of the $2 million bill. Morrison, *Democratic Politics and Sectionalism*, 18. Stephen Maizlish makes a similar point in *The Triumph of Sectionalism*, 54.

Michael Holt has offered a compelling explanation for why many Northerners may have initially disregarded the proviso. As he explains, while antislavery Whigs in and out of Congress rejoiced at the amendment's introduction, they realized that the proviso did not offer a substantially different stance on the slavery issue from their Democratic colleagues. Because party differentiation was key to political success, a campaign that focused on the Wilmot Proviso would not substantially aid either Democrats or Whigs in 1846 campaigns in the North, nor would it help keep the coalition of Northerners and Southerners together for ensuing presidential elections. Only when the proviso was reintroduced in the following session would it begin to play more of an important role. Holt, *Rise and Fall*, 251–52. Holt's argument runs contrary to other historians who suggest that Free-Soilers thought that by supporting the amendment, they would unify Northern Democrats. See M. Morrison, *Slavery and the American West*, 42–44. Ultimately, each of these historians does much to show why Americans outside of Congress reacted the way that they did from August 1846 until the following spring of 1847. This chapter builds on their analysis by focusing on the politicians involved in the passage of the proviso itself. I investigate how such a bill could come to the floor, why it would pass, and why Washington politicians thought little of it at the time.

11. Voting numbers give us a good sense of who was present during the session, as one of the House rules stipulated that all members present must participate in votes unless excused by that body. A few of the members even asked to be excused from the vote but were denied by the rest of the House. See *Congressional Globe*, 29th Cong., 1st Sess., 1217–18; Cooper, *Jefferson Davis*, 135; Shalhope, *Sterling Price*, 54. The Twenty-Ninth Congress had a large number of single-term representatives. At least ten members, in addition to Price, were not renominated by their states.

12. Kinsley S. Bingham to his wife, February 11, 1849, Kinsley S. Bingham Papers, UM-B; Alpheus Felch to Henry B. Joy, January 25, 1850, Henry B. Joy Historical Research Collection, UM-B.

13. James K. Polk to Ezekiel P. McNeal, January 12, 1846, in Cutler, *Correspondence of James K. Polk*, 17–18; John A. Rockwell to unknown, June 7, 1852, Papers of John Arnold Rockwell, HUN. Emphasis is Rockwell's.

14. David Outlaw to his wife, December 7, 1848, David Outlaw Papers, SHC; John Fairfield to his wife, December 29, 1848, in Staples, *The Letters of John Fairfield*, 427; Artemas Hale diary entry, December 31, 1846, Artemas Hale Papers, LC.

15. James G. King to unknown, December 4, 1850, Ewing-King Papers, NYHS (quotation); Horace Mann to his wife, January 5, 1850, Horace Mann Papers, MHS. The House would lose a number of prominent ex-members in the winter of the second session, including favorites John Fairfield and Alexander Barrow.

16. David Outlaw to his wife, December 13, 1847, Outlaw Papers (quotation); Salmon P. Chase to "Belle," July 29, 1850, in J. McClure, Lamphier, and Kreger, *"Spur Up Your Pegasus,"* 81.

17. Horace Mann to his wife, Sunday, January 28, 1849, Mann Papers; Edward Everett to W. C. Dawson, Boston, May 20, 1854, Edward Everett Papers, MHS; Dixon H. Lewis to Lewis S. Coryell, May 1, 1847, in Lewis S. Coryell Papers, HSP; Sam Houston to his wife, May 21, 1846, in M. Roberts, *Personal Correspondence*, 2:76 (quotation).

18. Horace Mann to his wife, September 23, 1850, Mann Papers.

19. Henry A. Wise to Edward Everett, June 8, 1856, Everett Papers (quotation); Robert Hatton to his wife, Tuesday, April 24, 1860, in Drake, *Life of General Robert Hatton*, 273.

20. Alpheus Felch to his wife, July 5 and July 18, 1852, Alpheus Felch Papers, UM-B; Daniel M. Barringer to Lizzie, March 1, 1848, Daniel M. Barringer Papers, SHC (quotation).

21. John A. Rockwell to unknown, June 7, 1852, Rockwell Papers; Edward Everett diary entry, February 1, 1854, Everett Papers.

22. Jacob Collamer to Mary Collamer, January 24, 1847, Collamer Family Papers, University of Vermont Digital Collections; *Congressional Directory for 1846*; Edward Everett diary entry, March 3, 1854, Everett Papers (quotation).

23. David Outlaw to his wife, July 30, 1848, Outlaw Papers (quotation); Salmon P. Chase to Kate Chase, July 31, 1854, in J. McClure, Lamphier, and Kreger, *"Spur Up Your Pegasus,"* 142–43; Daniel M. Barringer to Lizzie Wethered, January 28, 1847, Barringer Papers; See, for example, *Washington Daily Union*, January 23, 1846, February 4, 1846, and March 16, 1846.

24. Horace Mann to his wife, January 18, 1850, Mann Papers.

25. David Outlaw to his wife, December 10, 1847, and February 15, 1848, Outlaw Papers (quotation).

26. David Outlaw to his wife, January 12, 1848, also see David Outlaw to his wife, January 18, 1848, Outlaw Papers; John Berrien to Major Harris, March 13, 1847, John Macpherson Berrien Correspondence, UGA; Charles Francis Adams diary entry, January 25, 1860, Adams Family Papers, MHS; Solomon Haven to James M. Smith, January 15, 1856, Solomon G. Haven Family Papers, UM-C (quotation).

27. Eckloff, *Memoirs of a Senate Page*, 7; Isaac Bassett Papers, NARA (quotation).

28. Willie P. Mangum to Asbury Dickins, September 12, 1852, Asbury Dickins Family Papers, LC (quotation); *Harper's Weekly*, June 12, 1858; Winthrop, *Memoir of Robert C. Winthrop*, 77 (quotation). According to Bassett, Daniel Webster kept a private room (called the "Wine Room") upstairs in the Capitol dedicated to all the wines and liquors he received as gifts. Bassett Papers.

29. Salmon P. Chase to Kate Chase, August 27, 1852, in J. McClure, Lamphier, and Kreger, *"Spur Up Your Pegasus,"* 123; Charles Francis Adams diary entry, June 6, 1860, Adams Family Papers.

30. Robert Hatton diary entry, December 27, 1859, in Drake, *Life of General Robert Hatton*, 190 (quotation); Julian, *Political Recollections*, 43; George M. Dallas diary entry, February 10, 1849, in Nichols, "The Library: II," 512–13.

31. Robert C. Winthrop to John Clifford, June 20, 1841, Winthrop Family Papers, MHS; Cox, *Eight Years in Congress*, 19–20.

32. Joshua Giddings diary entry, March 3, 1849, in Julian, *The Life of Joshua R. Giddings*; Jacob Collamer to Mary Collamer, February 24, 1856, Collamer Papers; David Outlaw to his wife, January 6, 1848, Outlaw Papers; Horace Mann to his wife, August 24, 1852, Mann Papers (quotation).

33. Julian, *Political Recollections*, 43; Henry A. Wise to Edward Everett, August 17, 1856, Everett Papers (quotation).

34. Sam Houston to his wife, August 17, 1852, in M. Roberts, *Personal Correspondence*, 3:458; *Congressional Globe*, 30th Cong., 2nd Sess., 690.

35. James K. Polk diary entry, August 8, 1846, in Quaife, *Diary of James K. Polk*, 2:74.

36. Alexander Stephens to Linton Stephens, February 1, 1845, Alexander Hamilton Stephens Papers, Manhattanville College Library, Purchase, N.Y. (quotation); David Outlaw to his wife, March 29, 1848, Outlaw Papers; Salmon Chase to Kate Chase, July 31, 1854, in J. McClure, Lamphier, and Kreger, *"Spur Up Your Pegasus,"* 142; Sam Houston to his wife, August 23, 1850, in M. Roberts, *Personal Correspondence*, 3:252 (quotation); Robert Winthrop to Edward Everett, April 11, 1846, Everett Papers; Poore, *Perley's Reminiscences*, 1:204; John Fairfield to his wife, April 1, 1846, in Staples, *Letters of John Fairfield*, 395.

37. John Fairfield to his wife, December 23, 1845, in Staples, *Letters of John Fairfield*, 369 (quotation); William H. Seward to his wife, August 9, 1856, in F. Seward, *Seward at Washington*, 1:286 (quotation).

38. *Harper's Weekly*, February 13, 1858; David Outlaw to his wife, January 10, 1848, and July 30, 1848 (quotation), Outlaw Papers.

39. Lanman, *Bohn's Handbook of Washington*, 16; Eckloff, *Memoirs of a Senate Page*, 4. Mark Summers has written extensively about the number of members who returned to Washington under lobbying contracts. See Summers, *The Plundering Generation*, 85–89.

40. Willie P. Mangum to Charity Mangum, February [17?], 1851, in Shanks, *Papers of Willie Person Mangum*, 5:204; Charles F. Adams diary entry, March 2, 1860, Adams Family Papers.

41. Several members described the new seat lottery in 1846. See Washington Hunt to Hamilton Fish January 29, 1846, Hamilton Fish Papers, LC; Artemas Hale diary entry, December 7, 1846, Artemas Hale Papers; David Outlaw to his wife, February 28, 1848, Outlaw Papers; Robert Winthrop to John Clifford, December 14, 1845, Winthrop Family Papers. Before conducting the lottery, the House usually let old, established members like John Quincy Adams, and ex-Speakers make their selections. See Gallaway, *History of the House of Representatives*, 48.

42. See, for example, Alpheus Felch to his wife, February 5, 1850, Felch Papers; Kinsley S. Bingham to his wife, January 6, 1848, Bingham Papers.

43. Charles Francis Adams diary entry, December 23, 1859, Adams Family Papers.

44. Jane Caroline North diary entry, August 11, 1852, in O'Brien, *An Evening When Alone*, 188; David Outlaw to his wife, July 20, 1848, Outlaw Papers; Frank McDowell to Mary McDowell, February 21, 1849, in James McDowell Papers, SHC; Charles Francis Adams diary entry, January 3, 1860, Adams Family Papers; Horace Mann to his wife, January 2, 1849, Mann Papers; Lincoln Clark to Julia Clark, May 14, 1852, Papers of Lincoln Clark, HUN; *Washington Daily Union*, March 5, 1846, 3 (quotation), August 10, 1846, 3.

The paper reported what Wilmot said during his speech on the proviso but made no note of the potential implications of a sectional vote.

45. The Constitution stipulated that each house of Congress was entitled to make its own rules. Typically, at the beginning of each Congress, the House and Senate accepted the rules of the previous session and added a few others. The result was that by the beginning of the Civil War, the House of Representatives had at least 150 rules, consuming some twenty pages of the House Journals. Each rule also tended to include several provisions. See Gallaway, *History of the House of Representatives*, 8–13, 49–50.

46. Robert Hatton diary entry, January 11, 1860, in Drake, *Life of General Robert Hatton*, 195.

47. Willie Mangum to Messrs. Gales & Seaton, June 6, 1846, in Shanks, *Papers of Willie Person Mangum*, 4:447; Robert Hatton diary entry, January 4, 1860, in Drake, *Life of General Robert Hatton*, 193–94.

48. *Harper's Weekly*, February 27, 1858. Historians such as Mark E. Neely Jr. have often pointed out the prevalence of "personal explanations" in Congress. See Neely, "The Kansas-Nebraska Act," 13–46.

49. James Buchanan to John J. Crittenden, [n.d.], in Coleman, *Life of John J. Crittenden*, 2:38.

50. William Seward to his wife, June 13, 1858, in F. Seward, *Seward at Washington*, 346. Joanne Freeman has written extensively on the impact of duels and other "affairs of honor." For her take on antebellum violence, see Freeman, "The Culture of Congress," in addition to her groundbreaking book on the Early Republic: *Affairs of Honor*.

51. Edward Everett diary entry, February 10, 1854, Everett Papers; David Outlaw to his wife, February 13, 1848, Outlaw Papers (Rayner's opinion).

52. Lincoln Clark to Julia Clark, May 24, 1852, Clark Papers.

53. Kinsley S. Bingham to his wife, January 10, 1848, Bingham Papers (quotation); David Outlaw to his wife, August 4, 1848 (continuation of a letter begun August 2, 1848), Outlaw Papers; Alexander H. Buel to John S. Bagg, April 26, 1850, Papers of John Sherman Bagg, HUN; Lincoln Clark to Julia Clark, March 7, 1852, Clark Papers (quotation).

54. David Outlaw to his wife, February 7, 1848, Outlaw Papers.

55. Robert Winthrop to John Clifford, September 13, 1850, Winthrop Family Papers; Jefferson Davis to Hamilton Fish, February 29, 1856, Fish Papers.

56. Emily Baldwin to her father, January 5, 1850, Roger Baldwin Papers, Yale University Manuscripts and Archives, New Haven, Conn.; *Congressional Globe*, 31st Cong., 1st Sess., 520; also see Wilson and Cook, *Papers of John C. Calhoun*, 27:232–33; and Poore, *Perley's Reminiscences*, 1:205. Among other friends, Seward regularly associated with Californian William Gwin and, ironically, was also intimate with Foote's Mississippi rival, Jefferson Davis. For Seward's relationship with Gwin, see Kushner, "Visions of the Northwest Coast," 295–306; for his relationship with Jefferson Davis, see Cooper, *Jefferson Davis*, 281, 309.

57. For background on the Foote-Benton relationship, see Chambers, *Old Bullion Benton*, 350. Foote also gives an explanation for their testy relationship in his memoir. See Foote, *Casket of Reminiscences*, 330, 338–39. I discuss the compromise measures in detail in chapter 3.

58. *Congressional Globe*, 31st Cong., 1st Sess., 761–63. Also see Chambers, *Old Bullion Benton*, 360–61.

59. On the dinner, see David Outlaw to his wife, July 7, 1850, Outlaw Papers, and Winthrop, *Memoir of Robert C. Winthrop*, 126. On the January speech, see David Outlaw to his wife, January 17, 1850, Outlaw Papers.

60. Holt, *Rise and Fall*, 615. Mark Stegmaier makes a similar suggestion that Foote purposely provoked the fight with Benton. See Stegmaier, *Texas, New Mexico, and the Compromise of 1850*, 114. Yet his hypothesis that Foote was trying to "galvanize the Senate into action on his resolution" seems less likely, as Foote was generally considered a blowhard. As Sam Houston explained, "If the Senate had to select its own members, he wou'd not be chosen one of them!" Sam Houston to his wife, December 23, 1851, in M. Roberts, *Personal Correspondence*, 3:356.

61. David Outlaw to his wife, April 27, 1850, Outlaw Papers. I discuss the prevalence of guns and other violent instruments in the Capitol and in Washington in general in chapter 5.

62. John A. Rockwell to unknown, June 7, 1852, Rockwell Papers (quotation); Kinsley S. Bingham to his wife, January 10, 1848, Bingham Papers.

63. Robert Hatton diary entry, December 6, 1859, in Drake, *General Robert Hatton*, p. 176; *Congressional Globe*, 35th Cong., 1st Sess., 418–19, 458–60, 502–4; *Harper's Weekly*, February 27, 1858.

64. Sam Houston to his wife, September 20, 1850, in M. Roberts, *Personal Correspondence*, 3:271; Henry A. Wise to Edward Everett, December 31, 1851 (quotation), and Edward Everett to Charles Eames, May 16, 1854, Everett Papers; Aaron V. Brown to David R. Atchison, March 1, 1846, David Rice Atchison Papers, Western Historical Manuscripts Collection, University of Missouri, Columbia.

65. James Polk diary entry, August 10, 1846, in Quaife, *Diary of James K. Polk* 2:75–76.

66. *Washington Daily Union*, August 10, 1846, and *Daily National Intelligencer*, August 11, 1846. The failure to note or be concerned with the sectional implications of the vote runs counter to the claims of some historians that the proviso was "a portent of things to come." Maltz, *Dred Scott and the Politics of Slavery*, 43. Also see Silbey, *Party over Section*, 36. A sectional vote on the proviso in 1846 did not particularly startle most of the members; only when the bill was reintroduced in 1847 did a significant number of Southern congressmen begin to become agitated.

67. Washington Hunt to Thurlow Weed, August 12, 1846, Thurlow Weed Papers, Rush Rhees Library, University of Rochester. Jonathan Earle argues that the Wilmot group was genuinely shocked that the proviso provoked little debate or interest during the 1846 campaign. See Earle, *Jacksonian Antislavery*, 134.

68. The House vote on the Wilmot Proviso on February 15, 1847, can be found in *Congressional Globe*, 29th Cong., 2nd Sess., 425. According to Chaplain Morrison, King actually spurned his fellow antislavery New York Democrats when deciding to take that step. See Morrison, *Democratic Politics*, 20–25. I fully agree with historians who suggest that much of the opposition to the Wilmot Proviso was about principle rather than practice. Southerners felt insulted by the Northern push to restrict slavery even though most believed slavery would never exist in the territories acquired from Mexico. William Freehling eloquently explains this point in *Road to Disunion*, 1:461.

69. *Congressional Globe*, 31st Cong., 2nd Sess., 28.

70. Salmon P. Chase to Edward S. Hamlin, December 15, 1849, in Niven, *Salmon Chase Papers*, 2:267. On Toombs's commitment to creating a compromise, see Robert Toombs to Linton Stephens, March 22, 1850, in Phillips, "Correspondence," 188. For Toombs's unionism in the winter of 1849–50, see Holt, *Rise and Fall*, 486, 612–13. Holt points out that Toombs was likely engaging in buncombe to neutralize an attempt by his Georgia rival, John M. Berrien, to outflank him on the slavery issue. For example, Don Fehrenbacher cites Toombs's speech as an example of Southern anger and frustration regarding the continued agitation over the Wilmot Proviso. See Fehrenbacher, *Sectional Crisis*, 25–26.

71. I am not the first to suggest that the House, in particular, was the scene of chaos during the antebellum years. Joel Silbey, for example, points out that accommodations in the Capitol were cramped, and members did not always handle themselves with propriety. Still, Silbey and others rely heavily on the debates in Congress to further their arguments about political ideology. These scholars do much to illustrate how congressional speeches spoke to constituent needs but do not fully explain how Congress operated in the mid-nineteenth century. See Silbey, "Congress in a Partisan Political Era," 139–52.

72. See Daniel Webster to Edward Everett, February 5, 1846, Everett Papers; Hamilton Fish to J. B. Ruggles, February 13, 1854, Fish Papers; Rowan F. Hopkins to William B. Campbell, January 6, 1849 (quotation, emphasis in original), Campbell Family Papers, DU.

73. Orasmus B. Matteson to Thurlow Weed, March 5, 1850, Weed Papers; William L. Marcy to Prosper M. Wetmore, January 18, 1846, William L. Marcy Papers, LC; Edward Stanly to John M. Clayton, February 3, 1852, John M. Clayton Papers, LC; Solomon Haven to his wife, February 7, 1854, Haven Family Papers (quotation).

74. Charles Francis Adams diary entry, January 28, 1860, Adams Family Papers.

Chapter 2

1. Holt, *The Rise and Fall*, 257–58.

2. *Congressional Globe*, 30th Cong., 1st Sess., 4–12.

3. David Outlaw to his wife, [n.d. but likely December 7, 1848], David Outlaw Papers, SHC; Thomas Jefferson Rusk to David Rusk, New York, May 7, 1848, Thomas Jefferson Rusk Papers, CAH. For example, possible Whig candidates included Senators John M. Clayton (Del.), Tom Corwin (Ohio), John J. Crittenden (Ky.), Willie P. Mangum (N.C.), and the Supreme Court's associate justice John McLean of Ohio.

4. Donald, *Lincoln*, 121. As Richard Carwardine points out, although contemporaries and historians have disagreed about many of Lincoln's characteristics, nearly all agree on his unquenchable ambition. Carwardine, *Lincoln*, 2. Perhaps because of scant primary sources, little has been written specifically on Lincoln's time in Congress. Two exceptions include Riddle, *Congressman Abraham Lincoln*, and Findley, *A. Lincoln, the Crucible of Congress*. Michael Burlingame's recent two-volume work on Lincoln also devotes considerable attention to Lincoln's time in Congress. In particular, he focuses on Lincoln's desire for effective speechmaking. See Burlingame, *Abraham Lincoln*, 1:264.

5. *Congressional Globe*, 30th Cong., 1st Sess., 64. The *Globe* substantially altered Lincoln's original resolutions. See "'Spot' Resolutions in the United States House of Representatives," in Basler, *Collected Works*, 1:420–22. Lincoln's resolutions accorded him the

nickname "Spotty Lincoln" by some unfriendly members of the press. See Donald, *Lincoln*, 123–24.

6. Abraham Lincoln to William H. Herndon, December 13, 1847, and February 1, 1848, in Basler, *Collected Works*, 1:420, 446–48. See Donald, *Lincoln*, 124. Polk reported in his diary on January 13 (the day after Lincoln's speech) that Whigs were speaking against him in Congress but did not mention Lincoln by name and talked generally about the opposition party. Quaife, *Diary of James K. Polk*, 3:299.

7. See chapter 1.

8. Historians disagree about whether the Young Indians organized in December 1847 or earlier. Stephens's biographer, Thomas E. Schott, places the organizational date in December 1847. Michael Holt argues that Lincoln was not an original member in Holt, "Winding Roads to Recovery," 132, citing an earlier date of formation. Stephens himself named Lincoln as an original member, which suggests that the group did not come together until Lincoln was present in Washington. See Schott, *Alexander H. Stephens of Georgia*, 82–83. Stephens claimed to have initiated the group specifically to promote Taylor's candidacy, yet some evidence suggests that members did more than simply discuss the upcoming election. Avary, *Recollections*, 21. At least one of Lincoln's early biographers suggests that the group was primarily dedicated to debating national questions. See Tarbell, *Boy Scouts' Life of Lincoln*.

9. In his recollections, Stephens claimed that Alabama Whig Henry W. Hilliard and Edward C. Cabell of Florida were not original members but later joined the group. Avary, *Recollections*, 22.

10. On the Calhoun argument, see Cooper, *The South and the Politics of Slavery*, 243–44, and Holt, *Rise and Fall*, 286. On Taylor's slaveholding credentials, see Bauer, *Zachary Taylor*, 320.

11. Holt, *Rise and Fall*, 285–88. For a detailed look at Lincoln's reasons for joining the pro-Taylor movement from an economic standpoint, see Boritt, *American Dream*, 137–47.

12. *Congressional Directory for 1848*. On the Toombs-Stephens relationship, see W. Davis, *The Union That Shaped the Confederacy*, 43–50. On Smith's role, see Holt, "Rethinking," 97–111.

13. See the seating chart in the *Congressional Directory for 1848*. Michael Burlingame has suggested that Lincoln shared a desk with North Carolina congressmen Daniel Barringer, but I have found no evidence in the *Congressional Directories* for this claim, and unless Lincoln swapped seats later in the session, their desk pairing is unlikely. Barringer sat between A. H. Shepard of North Carolina and Lewis Levin of Pennsylvania in the first session. A second empty seat marked in the *Congressional Directory* was directly behind Barringer, however, and it is possible Lincoln sat there. See Burlingame, *Abraham Lincoln*, 1:261.

14. *New York Tribune*, September 4, 1860, quoted in Burlingame, *Abraham Lincoln*, 1:263.

15. John J. Crittenden to William Ballard Preston, May 6, 1849, Preston Family Papers, VHS.

16. See, for example, Randall, *Lincoln the President*; Richard N. Current, *The Lincoln Nobody Knows*. In a more recent example, Richard Carwardine also omits any mention of Lincoln's involvement in the Young Indians in an otherwise outstanding biography; Car-

wardine, *Lincoln*. Biographers of other members of the Young Indians have been similarly silent. See Thompson, *Robert Toombs of Georgia*.

17. Burlingame has suggested that Lincoln received considerable praise and attention for his speeches. In order to demonstrate Lincoln's stature, he cites a Washington-based publisher named Charles Brainerd whose 1880 reminiscences proclaimed that whenever the Illinois representative "addressed the House, he commanded the individual attention of all present." Charles H. Brainard, "Reminiscences of Abraham Lincoln," *Youth's Companion*, Dec. 9, 1880, 435–36, in Burlingame, *Abraham Lincoln* 1:262. Because of the late date of Brainerd's letter, he likely fabricated (or improperly remembered) Lincoln's effect on the House.

18. See, for example, Varon, *We Mean to Be Counted*; Hahn, *A Nation under Our Feet*; and Wilentz, *Chants Democratic*.

19. To some extent, scholars' failure to discuss Washington associations may stem from a long-standing tradition of viewing antebellum reformers as acting in opposition to (rather than alongside) government. In other words, historians have argued that small groups formed to protect themselves from the interference of government in their community affairs. See, for example, Ryan, *Civic Wars*; Walters, *American Reformers*; and Bender, *Community and Social*. In the past decade, historians and political scientists have debunked the notion that small community organizations were typically antigovernment, painting a more complicated picture of associational relationships with political institutions. See Skocpol, Ganz, and Munson, "A Nation of Organizers"; Mintz, *Moralists and Modernizers*; Ginzberg, *Women and the Work of Benevolence*.

20. Dan Feller makes a similar point in "A Brother in Arms," 56, 61.

21. Abraham Lincoln to William H. Herndon, February 2, 1848, in Basler, *Collected Works*, 1:448; Avary, *Recollections*, 276, 61.

22. Young, *The Washington Community*, 52–59; Radomsky, "The Social Life of Politics," 363.

23. See, for example, Abraham Lincoln to William Herndon, December 5, 1847; December 13, 1847; January 19, 1848, in Basler, *Collected Works*, 1:416, 420, 445. The line between pursuing two professions and engaging in unethical or corrupt behavior was not always clear. For examples of conflicts of interest in economic professions, see Summers, *The Plundering Generation*, 113–15.

24. Busey, *Personal Reminiscences*, 25, 124–25.

25. *Cultivator* (Albany), August 1852, 284; *Chronicle* (Bellows Falls, Vt.), February 8, 1853, 23; *New York Times* January 17, 1859.

26. Carrier, "The United States Agricultural Society," 280. Members of the society subscribed to a particularly progressive vision of agricultural development and improvement. See Herrington, "Agricultural and Architectural Reform," 861–62, 867–68.

27. Ibid., 282; *Journal of the United States Agricultural Society* 5 (1857): 66; *Daily Cleveland Herald*, January 15, 1857.

28. Morrill's role in promoting the land-grant college legislation is well documented. Yet strangely his biographer has not drawn the connection between the Agricultural Society and the bill. See Cross, *Justin Smith Morrill*, 79–85.

29. The four Southerners who voted for the land-grant college legislation were Ameri-

can Party members John Bell (Tenn.), John J. Crittenden (Ky.), Anthony Kennedy (Md.), and John Thompson (Ky.). All but Kennedy were active members of the U.S. Agricultural Society. Members who were connected with the society but skipped the vote were Democrats Jesse Bright (Ind.), Stephen Douglas (Ill.), James Pearce (Md.), and Charles Stuart (Mich.). Opposition to the bill came entirely from Democrats. *Congressional Globe*, 35 Cong., 2nd Sess., 857; *Journal of the United States Agricultural Society* 5 (1857): 11.

30. *Annual Report of the Board of Regents of the Smithsonian for 1857*, 46.

31. Horace Mann to his wife, March 2, 1850, Horace Mann Papers, MHS; Robert Winthrop to Edward Everett, September 22, 1849, Edward Everett Papers, MHS (quotation).

32. *Annual Report of the Board of Regents of the Smithsonian for 1857*, 78. For regents lists, see *Annual Report of the Board of Regents of the Smithsonian for 1857*, 5, and *Annual Report of the Board of Regents of the Smithsonian for 1856*, 5; Joseph Henry to Robert Hare, May 14, 1848, in Rothernberg, *Papers of Joseph Henry*, 7:22. Pearce was a Whig until 1856 and then joined the Democratic Party.

33. Similar to historians who study antebellum associational life, religious historians have thoroughly investigated the role of religion in the lives of average Americans. Some have even explored the influence of religious observance on nineteenth-century American politics. For example, Richard Carwardine has argued that evangelical Christians were among the principle shapers of antebellum political culture. See Carwardine, *Evangelicals and Politics*, ix, xvi. Charles Irons similarly shows how evangelicals in the Upper South differed in their political behavior from those in the Lower South. Irons, *The Origins of Proslavery Christianity*, 213, 255. Such studies are important for understanding the behavior of average Americans but do not fully examine the role of religion in Washington politics and society.

34. Howe, *What Hath God Wrought*, 477–82; Noll, *America's God*, 367–68.

35. *Ten Eyck's Washington and Georgetown Directory for 1855*, 52–53. There were eight churches of varying denominations in Georgetown, as well as three African American churches advertised in the directory.

36. Alpheus Felch to his wife, May 22, 1848, Alpheus Felch Papers, UM-B (quotation); Thomas Ritchie to his wife, October 12, 1846, Papers of Thomas Ritchie, LC; Pryor, *Reminiscences of Peace and War*, 47; James K. Polk diary entry, February 1, 1846, in Quaife, *Diary of James K. Polk*, 1:206.

37. Smith Pyne to William W. Corcoran, April [n.d.], 1859, in Corcoran, *A Grandfather's Legacy*, 181; Edward Everett diary entry, November 21, 1852, Everett Papers; Lincoln Clark to Julia Clark, May 9, 1858, Lincoln Clark Papers, HUN; David Outlaw to Emily Outlaw, March 3, 1848, Outlaw Papers; Charles Francis Adams diary entry, January 22, 1859, Adams Family Papers, MHS; James G. King to his wife, August 11, 1850, Ewing-King Papers, NYHS. Also see Green, *The Church on Lafayette Square*, 26.

38. Jacob Collamer to his wife, February 13, 1859, Collamer Papers (quotation); Benjamin French diary entry, December 27, 1857, in French, *Witness to the Young Republic*, 288.

39. William V. H. Brown to David Settle Reid, March 1, 1859, in Butler, *Papers of David Settle Reid*, 2:288; David Outlaw to his wife, January 5, 1850, Outlaw Papers.

40. Lincoln Clark to Julia Clark, February 13, 1852, Clark Papers (quotation); Edward Everett to his wife, November 14, 1852, and March 27, 1853, Everett Papers; Bates diary

entry, March 3, 1861, in Beale, *The Diary of Edward Bates*, 176. Joseph Kennedy was superintendent of the Census Bureau in D.C.

41. Kinsley S. Bingham to his wife, January 16, 1848, Kinsley S. Bingham Papers, UM-B (quotation); Jane Caroline North diary entry, August 15, 1852, in O'Brien, *An Evening When Alone*, 191 (quotation). John Fairfield to his wife, February 22, 1846, in Staples, *The Letters of John Fairfield*, 390; David Outlaw to his wife, January [n.d.], 1851, Outlaw Papers.

42. Jacob Collamer to Mary Collamer, December 26, 1858, Collamer Family Papers, University of Vermont Digital Collections; Alpheus Felch to his wife, December 14, 1851, Felch Papers; David Outlaw to his wife, December 29, 1849, Outlaw Papers; Robert Hatton diary entry, March 25, 1860, in Drake, *Life of General Robert Hatton*, 255. Also see Robert M. T. Hunter to his wife, July 5, 1850, in Hunter, *A Memoir of Robert M. T. Hunter*, 104.

43. William Graham to James W. Bryan, January 27, 1851, in Hamilton, *The Papers of William Alexander Graham*. 4:15; Artemas Hale diary entry, January 2, 1848, Artemas Hale Papers, LC; Sam Houston to his wife, February 6, 1848, in M. Roberts, *Personal Correspondence*, 2:257; Charles Francis Adams diary entry, February 1, 1859, Adams Family Papers.

44. John Quincy Adams et al. to John Joseph Hughes, Washington, December 9, 1847, John Joseph Hughes Invitation, HUN; December 12, 1847, Outlaw Papers; Artemas Hale diary entry, December 12, 1847, Artemas Hale Papers.

45. William Hodges to Charles J. Faulkner, November 22, 1853, Faulkner Family Papers, VHS (quotation); Henry Slicer to Alpheus Felch, November 22, 1849, and Alpheus Felch to his wife, December 7, 1851, Felch Papers; Henry Slicer to David Settle Reid, February 26, 1853, in Butler, *Papers of David Settle Reid*, 21; Jesse D. Bright to Robert M. T. Hunter, November 16, 1856, Hunter Family Papers, VHS.

46. Robert Hatton diary entry, March 6, 1860, in Drake, *Life of General Robert Hatton*, 246; *Congressional Globe*, 36th Cong., 1st Sess., 1015.

47. Alexander Stephens to Linton Stephens, January 14, 1855, and June 15, 1856, Alexander Hamilton Stephens Papers, Manhattanville College Library, Purchase, N.Y.; Robert Hatton diary entry, January 1, 1860, in Drake, *Life of General Robert Hatton*, 192. Although he was a churchgoer in Illinois and also frequently read the Bible, Lincoln left no record of attending church in Washington. See Carwardine, *Lincoln*, 30–37; Barringer, *Lincoln Day by Day*, 1:296–330.

48. *Annual Reports of the American Bible Society for 1861*, 3, 7; *Eighth Annual Report of the Executive Committee of the Bible Society of Washington City* for 1844.

49. *Daily National Intelligencer*, June 2, 1848, and June 14, 1858; Managers of the Washington Bible Society to James McDowell, April 20, 1848, and Samuel J. Prime to James McDowell, March 2, 1849, James McDowell Papers, SHC.

50. Freehling, *Road to Disunion*, 1:157–58. Historians have disagreed about the true intentions of members of the American Colonization Society. For example, Eric Foner and George Fredrickson have argued that many colonizationists were more concerned with eliminating the black race from the United States rather than freeing slaves. Foner, *Free Soil, Free Labor, Free Men*, 276–79; Fredrickson, *The Black Image in the White Mind*, 9–12. Similarly, Ira Berlin points out that most African Americans strongly opposed coloniza-

tion. Berlin, *Slaves without Masters*, 168–71. Yet, in a recent study specifically of the ACS, Eric Burin successfully illustrates the extent to which the society was dedicated to subverting slavery. Burin, *Slavery and the Peculiar Solution*, 2–5. As Bruce Dorsey explains, colonization promoters tended to be male, and in fact the ACS promoted the idea of men as natural colonizers. See Dorsey, *Reforming Men and Women*, 139–43.

51. Numerous historians have documented the rise of a positive conception of slavery in the South. Peter Kolchin offers a useful summary in *American Slavery*, 184–99. For the "positive good" argument's effect on the colonization movement, see Ford, *Deliver Us from Evil*, 325–28, 535–36.

52. *Thirty-Fifth Annual Report of the American Colonization Society for 1852*, 32.

53. W. M. Sain to James McDowell, December 23, 1846, McDowell Papers; David Outlaw to Emily Outlaw, January 18, 1848, Outlaw Papers (quotation); *Daily National Intelligencer*, January 19, 1848; *New York Herald*, January 20, 1848. Although Lincoln was an ardent supporter of colonization, there is no evidence that Lincoln attended the American Colonization Society meeting that January.

54. Edward Everett diary entry, January 18, 1852, Everett Papers.

55. Horace Mann to his wife, February 10, 1852, Mann Papers; *Ten Eyck's Washington and Georgetown Directory*, 52–53.

56. Tyrrell, *Sobering Up*, 5. Also see Rorabaugh, *The Alcoholic Republic*, 219–20.

57. Sam Houston to his wife, January 20, 1849 (quotation); May 29, 1850; September 2, 1850; February 15, 1851; February 4, 1852, in M. Roberts, *Personal Correspondence*, 3:58, 202, 258, 303, 386.

58. Tyrrell, *Sobering Up*, 211–14; Pflugrad-Jackisch, *Brothers of a Vow*, 2.

59. *Daily National Intelligencer*, February 23, 1846. The Masonic movement played an important role in Washington politics during the Early Republic. See Brooke, "Ancient Lodges," 327–54. For an overview of the Antimasonic movement and its aftermath, see Bullock, *Revolutionary Brotherhood*, and Holt, *Political Parties*, 89–106.

60. Pflugrad-Jackisch, *Brothers of a Vow*, 2, 8. For more comprehensive membership lists, see A. Roberts, *House Undivided*, 333–44.

61. Benjamin French diary entry, December 30, 1849 (quotation), in French, *Witness to the Young Republic*, 211; Alpheus Felch to his wife, July 5, 1848, Felch Papers; "Laurie" to Willie P. Mangum, April 21, 1847, Willie P. Mangum Papers, LC; James K. Polk diary entry, February 26, 1848, in Quaife, *Diary of James K. Polk* 3:362. A schedule of chapter meetings for the Masons, Odd Fellows, Red Men, and other fraternal organizations can be found in the *Congressional Directories* for 1846–61.

62. The origin of the name "Know-Nothings" comes from the secret nature of the group. When a member was asked about his activities with the group, he was supposed to reply, "I know nothing." Several historians have documented the rise of Know-Nothingism and its impact on the Whig and Republican parties of the 1850s. See Holt, *Rise and Fall*, 846–908; Holt, *Political Parties*, 107–20; Maizlish, "The Meaning of Nativism," 166–98.

63. John McCalla to Brother William H. Hoon, December 20, 1854, and Chief Council of the District of Columbia Executive Committee Announcement, November 26, 1855, John Moore McCalla Papers, VHS.

64. Eyal, *The Young America Movement*, 11–13.

65. Circular, Pierce Club Rooms, Washington, June 21, 1852, John Bragg Papers, SHC;

New York Weekly Herald, July 15, 1854; *Kansas Herald of Freedom*, October 21, 1854; J. E. Goodrich to Hamilton Fish, June 24, 1854, Hamilton Fish Papers, LC.

66. Abraham Lincoln to Usher F. Linder, March 22, 1848, in Basler, *Collected Works*, 1:458. See *Congressional Directory for 1848*. I discuss boardinghouse arrangements in chapter 4.

67. Michael Holt explains the details of the "no territory" policy and the ramifications of the treaty in Holt, *Rise and Fall*, 310–16.

68. Robert Toombs to William Ballard Preston, May 18, 1849, Preston Papers.

69. Abraham Lincoln to William Ballard Preston, April 20, 1849, in Basler, *Collected Works* 1:42. According to Burlingame, Lincoln was not initially planning to ask for an office in the new administration, but he would eventually change his mind. See Burlingame, *Abraham Lincoln*, 1:296.

70. See chapter 7.

Chapter 3

1. Clay submitted the resolutions to the Senate on January 29, 1850. He spoke for another three hours the following day, February 6, 1850. *Congressional Globe*, 31st Cong., 1st Sess., 244–52. Alexander Stephens described the scene in the galleries and on the floor of the Senate in a letter to his brother, Linton Stephens, February 10, 1850, Alexander Hamilton Stephens Papers, Manhattanville College Library, Purchase, N.Y. Also see Horace Mann to his wife, February 6, 1850, Horace Mann Papers, MHS; Francis French diary entry, February 5, 1850, in French, *Growing Up on Capitol Hill*, 7.

2. Mark Stegmaier effectively demonstrates the importance of the boundary issue to disagreements over the Mexican Cession in *Texas, New Mexico, and the Compromise of 1850*, 2–3.

3. Cobb was elected after the House voted on a procedural motion to elect a Speaker by plurality (rather than majority), 113–6. Cobb won 102 votes to Robert Winthrop's 99.

4. Taylor had decided ahead of time not to submit the message until after Congress had organized itself.

5. John M. Berrien to C. M. Jenkins, December 10, 1849, John M. Berrien Papers, SHC; Richardson, *A Compilation of the Messages*, 23 (quotation), 5:26–30.

6. *Congressional Globe*, 31st Cong., 1st Sess., 945–56 and appendix, 401–556.

7. Historians David S. Heidler and Jeanne T. Heidler have recently argued that Clay was, in fact, responsible for the final compromise settlement. See *Henry Clay*, 477. Their argument runs counter to nearly all other accounts of the bill's passage, including those of Holman Hamilton, Michael F. Holt, Mark Stegmaier, and Sean Wilentz.

8. Only four senators voted for every provision of the Compromise of 1850; seven more voted for five of the bills but abstained on the sixth. Because of this voting pattern, several historians have asserted that the Compromise of 1850 was not really a compromise at all. Rather, it could be called an armistice or a truce. See Potter, *Impending Crisis*, 133, and Wilentz, *Rise of American Democracy*, 637. Ironically, Douglas's tactic of splitting up the bills and letting each section vote for its preferred bills was the same approach Clay had used when pushing through the Missouri Compromise in 1820. See Forbes, *The Missouri Compromise*, 69–120.

9. Knupfer, *The Union As It Is*, 90, 159.

10. Holt, *Political Crisis*, 90. While Holman Hamilton was the first to note the odd breakdown of Whig and Democratic votes during the compromise voting, Holt was the first to adequately explain the votes. See Hamilton, *Prologue to Conflict*, xiii, 162–64. Few historians disagree with Holt's analysis, but John Ashworth has provided an alternative explanation. He argues that Northern Democrats allied with Southern Whigs because of their mutual interest in capitalism: commercial and capitalist Northerners (Democrats) combined with Southerners who did not perceive a conflict between slavery and capitalism. See Ashworth, *Slavery, Capitalism, and Politics*, 1:478, 491.

11. Hamilton, *Prologue to Conflict*, 124–31.

12. George Fitzhugh, "Washington City," *De Bow's Review* 24 (1858): 507; Benjamin Ogle Tayloe to William W. Corcoran, September 27, 1856, William W. Corcoran Papers, LC.

13. *Boston Daily Atlas*, February 2, 1850.

14. Henry A. Wise to Edward Everett, January 4, 1855, Edward Everett Papers, MHS; William Seward to his wife, June 11, 1847, in F. Seward, *Seward at Washington*, 1:50.

15. *Etiquette at Washington*, 18–19; William L. Marcy to Samuel Marcy, February 25, 1851, William L. Marcy Papers, LC. Etiquette books that emphasized a commitment to good manners were widespread in American culture in the mid-nineteenth century. See Kasson, *Rudeness and Civility*, 23–69.

16. Kinsley Bingham to his wife, December 25, 1847, Kinsley S. Bingham Papers, UM-B; David Outlaw to his wife, December 21, 1847, David Outlaw Papers, SHC.

17. Judith Rives to Maria L. Gordon, January 7, 1842, in Clark, "Observations on Washington Society," 56; Mary Bingham to Lucina, January 6, 1860, Bingham Papers; Maria B. Ewing to Ellen Sherman, May 9, 1850, Ellen Ewing Sherman Correspondence, HUN; L. Burrows to Emmeline, December 17, 1850, Burrows Family Papers, UM-B; Julia G. Tyler to her mother, August 19, 1844, in Wallace, "'Letters of the Presidentess,'" 642.

18. Howell Cobb to his wife, January 1, 1856, Howell Cobb Papers, UGA; Alpheus Felch to his wife, December 22, 1847, Alpheus Felch Papers, UM-B.

19. Solomon Haven to Harriett Newell Haven, January 1, 1853, Solomon G. Haven Papers, UM-C; Jacob Collamer to Mary Collamer, January 2, 1859, Collamer Family Papers, University of Vermont Digital collections. *Daily National Intelligencer*, January 2, 1850; Howell Cobb to his wife, January 1, 1850, in Brooks, "Howell Cobb Papers," 35.

20. Busey, *Personal Reminiscences*, 87.

21. Kinsley Bingham to Mary Bingham, May 11, 1848, Bingham Papers (quotation). Seward, *Reminiscences of a War-Time Statesman*, 83. Ostrowski, *Books, Maps, and Politics*, 201–06. Thomas J. Brown catalogs Dorothea Dix's prison reform efforts in *Dorothea Dix*, 129–47. On Dix's daily trips to the library, see Horace Mann to his wife, July 18, 1850, Mann Papers. Dix also used the library as a place to conduct her political correspondence. See, for example, Dorothea Dix to Millard Fillmore, March 3, 1851, in Snyder, *The Lady and the President*, 99.

Dix is the perfect example of the type of woman who went beyond the traditional female sphere of politics that Janet Coryell describes in "Superseding Gender," 85–87. Coryell's article serves as a counterweight to the unique way that women participated in politics that Catherine Allgor describes in *Parlor Politics*. According to Allgor, women were able to engage in lobbying and other political activities that were taboo for men during the Early Republic. By the antebellum era, Washington saw a mix of the types of women that Allgor and Coryell describe.

22. Alexander H. H. Stuart to his wife, Tuesday Night [n.d. but probably November 1850], Stuart Family Papers, VHS; Poore, *Perley's Reminiscences*, 1:39.

23. *Daily National Intelligencer*, December 28, 1847; John L. Taylor to Alexander St. Clair Boys, December 20, 1848, Alexander St. Clair Boys Papers, Ohio Historical Society, Columbus. Many of the men elected to serve as managers received multiple terms. For example, Thomas B. King was also a manager in 1847. See A. L. McClure to Thomas B. King, December 11, 1846, Thomas Butler King Papers, SHC.

24. Sam Houston to his wife, February 22, 1847, in M. Roberts, *Personal Correspondence*, 2:218; diary entry, February 23, 1846, in Quaife, *Diary of James K. Polk*, 1,:243; Peter V. Daniel to his daughter, February 23, 1851, Daniel Family Papers, VHS.

25. Kinsley S. Bingham to his wife, December 12, 1847, Bingham Papers; Clay, *A Belle of the Fifties*, 29; David Outlaw to his wife, March 26, 1848, Outlaw Papers.

26. *Harper's Weekly*, January 30, 1858. See Allgor, *Parlor Politics*, and Wood, "'One Woman So Dangerous,'" 237–75.

27. Lincoln Clark to Julia Clark, January 27, 1852, Papers of Lincoln Clark, HUN (quotation); Windle, *Life in Washington*, 43–44; Peter V. Daniel to his daughter, February 7, 1852, Daniel Family Papers; Guy M. Bryan to Laura Bryan, January 12, 1858, Guy M. Bryan Papers, CAH (quotation).

28. *Etiquette at Washington*, 18 (quotation); Mrs. William M. Meredith to Willie, January 16, 1850, Meredith Family Papers, HSP.

29. Sam Houston to his wife, April 17, 1846, in M. Roberts, *Personal Correspondence*, 2:43; John Fairfield to his wife, January 21, 1846, in Staples, *Letters of John Fairfield*, 380; Jacob Collamer to Mary N. Collamer, February 3, 1856, Collamer Papers.

30. Alpheus Felch to his wife, December 24, 1849, Felch Papers; David Outlaw to his wife, December 21, 1849, Outlaw Papers; Peter V. Daniel to his daughter, January 3, 1850, Daniel Family Papers.

31. Nathan Sargent to John J. Crittenden, July 18, 1849, Papers of John Jordan Crittenden, LC (quotation); Henry Clay to Lucretia Hart Clay, March 16, 1850, in Hay, *Papers of Henry Clay*, 10:689; Daniel Webster to Jonathan Prescott Hall, May 18, 1850, in Wiltse and Birkner, *Papers of Daniel Webster*, 7:99; Mrs. William M. Meredith to Willie, January 16, 1850, Meredith Papers; Alexander Stephens to Linton Stephens, April 15, 1850, Stephens Papers.

32. Humphrey Marshall to John J. Crittenden, March 10, 1850, Crittenden Papers; John J. Crittenden to John M. Clayton, September 29, 1849, Clayton Papers; Alexander Stephens to Linton Stephens, April 17, 1850, Stephens Papers (on Clayton's reputation); Arthur Campbell to David Campbell, January 30, 1850, Campbell Family Papers, DU ("weak and inefficient"); D. F. Wiley to C. H. Caldwell, January 7, 1850, David F. Caldwell Papers, SHC ("illiterate . . ."). A number of major Washington players in the Whig Party had hoped that Crittenden himself would join Taylor's cabinet. See, for example, Garnett Duncan to John J. Crittenden, January 22, 1849, and Joseph Grinnell to John J. Crittenden, January 31, 1849, Crittenden Papers.

33. Francis French diary entry, January 1, 1850, in French, *Growing Up on Capitol Hill*, 2.

Francis French was the son of local politician Benjamin French; Francis was quoting his father. For information on Taylor's patronage issues, see Holt, *Rise and Fall*, 465. As Holt argues, Taylor's patronage policies, as well as his suggestions for adjusting the Mexican Cession, both came from his desire to broaden the base of Whig support, perhaps for a new party. See Holt, *Political Crisis*, 75–76.

34. Alexander H. H. Stuart to his wife, [December 1850], Stuart Family Papers, VHS; Lincoln Clark to Julia Clark, January 31, 1852, Clark Papers; Jacob Collamer to Mary N. Collamer, January 19, 1846, Collamer Papers.

35. Salmon Chase to Kate Chase, March 25, 1852, in J. McClure, Lamphier, and Kreger, *"Spur Up Your Pegasus,"* 116; Guy M. Bryan to Laura Bryan, January 26, 1858, Bryan Papers (quotation).

36. James K. Polk diary entries for March 4 and December 24, 1846, in Quaife, *Diary of James K. Polk*, 1:264, 2:292; David Outlaw to his wife, February 20, 1848, Outlaw Papers.

37. As Mark Stegmaier explains, Daniel Webster was the original author of this bill, but when Webster consulted with friends about his plan, they were so opposed that he never introduced it. Instead, Bell took the lead in supporting the proposal in Congress. Webster's name was never associated with his plan in the Senate. Webster did, however, remind Northerners in his March 7 speech that they were committed by the terms of Texas annexation to admit as many as four additional states out of the area Texas claimed. See Stegmaier, *Texas, New Mexico, and the Compromise of 1850*, 107.

38. Horace Mann to Mary Mann, March 2, 1850, Mann Papers.

39. James G. King to unknown, September 20, 1850, Ewing-King Papers, NYHS. For examples of cross-sectional dinners at the White House during Taylor's presidency, see David Outlaw to his wife, December 21, 1849, Outlaw Papers; *Trenton State Gazette*, January 12, 1850.

40. Muscoe R. H. Garnett to his mother, February 26, 1848, Hunter Garnett Family Papers, UVA; Benjamin Wade to Caroline, February 13, 1852, Benjamin F. Wade Papers, LC; *Harper's Weekly*, February 4, 1860; Horace Mann to his wife, February 3, 1850, Mann Papers.

41. Alexander Stephens to Linton Stephens, February 4, 1853, Stephens Papers.

42. Meredith P. Gentry to William A. Graham, January 6, 1851, Hamilton, *Papers of William Alexander Graham*, 3:6.

43. Diary entry, January 15, 1861, in Keyes, *Fifty Years*, 353; Robert Hatton to his wife, January 22, 1860, in Drake, *Life of General Robert Hatton*, 222; William Seward to his wife, January 1, 1858, in F. Seward, *Seward at Washington*, 333; *Harper's Weekly*, February 4, 1860.

44. Solomon Haven to James M. Smith, April 6, 1856, Haven Papers; Muscoe Garnett to his mother, February 4, 1857, Garnett Family Papers; Guy M. Bryan Autobiographical Sketch, Bryan Papers.

45. Townsend, *Historic Sketches at Washington*, 116; Peter V. Daniel to his daughter, January 15, 1851, Daniel Family Papers.

46. Lincoln Clark to his wife, January 26, 1852, Clark Papers; Sherrard Clemens to Charles J. Faulkner, November 8, 1852, Faulkner Family Papers, VHS.

47. Charles Francis Adams diary entries, December 27, 1859 (quotation), and March 5, 1860, in Adams Family Papers, MHS; Edward Everett to his wife, November 14, 1852,

and August 23, 1856, Everett Papers; David Outlaw to his wife, February 2, 1849, Outlaw Papers.

48. John Crampton to John Clayton, June 22, 1849, Clayton Papers (quotation); Henry A. Wise to Edward Everett, August 23, 1856, Everett Papers; Peter V. Daniel to his daughter, January 12, 1849, Daniel Papers.

49. *Etiquette at Washington*, 105; Charles Francis Adams diary entry, February 14, 1860, Adams Family Papers.

50. Amanda Foreman details the relationships between Napier, Lyons, and the Washington community in *A World on Fire*, 3–13.

51. Holt, *Rise and Fall*, 693–95.

52. Henry A. Wise to Edward Everett, December 29, 1851, Everett Papers; Peter V. Daniel to his daughter, January 8, 1852, Daniel Family Papers; *New York Times*, January 5, 1852.

53. Thomas Corwin to John J. Crittenden, [January 8, 1852], in Coleman, *Life of John J. Crittenden*, 2:38.

54. Peter V. Daniel to his daughter, January 8, 1852, Daniel Family Papers; Lincoln Clark to his wife, January 9, 1852, Clark Papers. Emphasis is Clark's. Wayne was rumored to be interested in the presidency before multiple elections, including the election of 1860. See Benjamin Rush to James M. Wayne, June 9, 1860, James Moore Wayne Papers, Georgia Historical Society, Savannah.

55. Edwin M. Stanton to Ellen Stanton, December 11, 1854, Edwin M. Stanton Correspondence, HUN; William Seward to his wife, December 16, 1853, in F. Seward, *Seward at Washington*, 1:212.

56. Diary entry, December 25, 1854, in Appleton, *Selections from the Diaries*, 173; Peter V. Daniel to his daughter, January 12, 1849, Daniel Family Papers; Varina Davis to her mother, December 16, 1857 (quotation), and January 6, 1850, in Strode, *Jefferson Davis*, 97 and 59.

57. Kinsley Bingham to his wife, January 20, January 25, and February 10, 1851, Bingham Papers; Mary Mann to Sophia [n.d.], 1851, Mann Papers (quotation).

58. Alexander Stephens to Linton Stephens, January 11, 1851, Stephens Papers.

59. Charles Sumner to Theodore Parker, January 3, 1854, Theodore Parker Papers, MHS; Henry A. Wise to Edward Everett, May 12, 1851, and January 25, 1852, Everett Papers; William Seward to Thurlow Weed, May 22, 1850, in F. Seward, *Seward at Washington*, 1:134. For some other examples of cross-sectional dinners, see Hamilton Fish to Stephen A. Douglas, January 13, 1857, and Albert G. Brown to Stephen A. Douglas, January 14, 1857, Stephen A. Douglas Papers, SCRC; Guy M. Bryan to Laura Bryan, March 16, 1858, Bryan Papers; John O. Sargent to Benjamin R. Curtis, March 22, 1879, in Curtis, *Memoir of Benjamin Robbins Curtis*, 1:166–67.

60. Hamilton Fish Dinner Books, 1852–56, Hamilton Fish Papers, LC.

61. Ibid.

62. Peter V. Daniel to his daughter, April 26, 1850, Daniel Family Papers; Solomon G. Haven to his wife, January 8, 1853, Haven Papers; Clay, *Belle of the Fifties*, 211–12; George Dallas to his wife, February 18, 1845, in Nichols, "Mystery of the Dallas Papers I," 362.

63. George Dallas to his wife, February 18, 1845, Nichols, *Disruption*, 362; Edward

Everett diary entry, December 17, 1853, Everett Papers. Also see Virginia Clay to her mother, February 14, 1856, Clement Clay Papers, DU.

64. Henry A. Wise to Edward Everett, February 14, 1856, Everett Papers; diary entry, April 27, 1860, Adams Family Papers; William H. Seward to his wife, December 24, 1853, in F. Seward, *Seward at Washington*, 1:213.

65. Cohen, *Business and Politics*, 15, 36, 118.

66. George Peabody to William Corcoran, January 13, 1854, in Corcoran, *A Grandfather's Legacy*, 121 (quotation); Cohen, *Business and Politics*, 26, 136.

67. Tayloe, *Our Neighbors*, 34; Edward Everett to William Corcoran, May 20, 1854, Corcoran Papers (quotation).

68. John McLean to William Corcoran, February 4, 1847, James Watson Webb to William Seward, November 27, 1849 (quotation), Jesse Bright to William Corcoran, April 10, 1855, Corcoran Papers.

69. Hamilton, *Prologue to Conflict*, 128–31; Cohen, *Business and Politics*, 131. According to Hamilton's research, only one congressman, Texas's David S. Kaufman, was a security holder, but several members had a variety of relatives and constituents with a financial interest in the settlement.

70. Benjamin O. Tayloe to William Corcoran, September 27, 1856, Corcoran Papers; Cohen, *Business and Politics*, 4. Corcoran did have friendly relationships with a number of bankers in New York and Boston. On the prominence of disunion discussion during the winter of 1849–50, see Varon, *Disunion!*, 213–16.

71. *North American Review* 71, no. 1 (July 1850): 229. Also see chapter 1.

72. Francis Grund to William D. Lewis, September 1, 1850, William D. Lewis Papers, HUN; Horace Mann to his wife, June 17, 1850, Mann Papers.

73. *Congressional Globe*, 31st Cong., 1st Sess., 451–55 and 481–84 (quotation); Daniel Webster to William W. Corcoran March 7, 1850, and March 9, 1850 (quotation), in Corcoran, *A Grandfather's Legacy*, 84–85; Hamilton, *Prologue to Conflict*, 81.

74. Foote, *Casket of Reminiscences*, 24–27; Charles S. Morehead to John J. Crittenden, March 30, 1850, Crittenden Papers; Edmund Ruffin diary entry, January 16, 1859, in Scarborough, *The Diary of Edmund Ruffin*, 1:267; Hamilton, *Prologue to Conflict*, 66, 120–22; Stephen A. Douglas to William W. Corcoran, September 10, 1850, Corcoran Papers. For a detailed description of the "corrupt bargain," see Wilentz, *Rise of American Democracy*, 255–56.

75. Lists of dinner company, 1847–50, Corcoran Papers; William R. King to Col. G. W. Gayle, January 15, 1850, William R. King Papers, Alabama Department of Archives and History, Montgomery. For Buchanan and King's relationship, see Robert C. Winthrop to John Clifford, June 4, 1848, Winthrop Family Papers, MHS.

76. Lists of dinner company, 1847–50, Corcoran Papers.

77. *Congressional Globe*, 31st Congress, 1 Sess., 1490–91, appendix, 1470–88; Hamilton, *Prologue to Conflict*, 102–17.

78. Poore, *Perley's Reminiscences*, 1:209 (quotation); Holt, *Rise and Fall*, 533; Alexander H. H. Stuart to his wife, [1850], Stuart Family Papers (quotation).

79. Edward Everett to his wife, February 28, 1851, Everett Papers; Tayloe, *In Memoriam*, 41.

80. Lists of dinner company, 1847–50, Corcoran Papers. For analyzing the votes, I have

relied heavily on Hamilton, *Prologue to Conflict*, 191–200. For surprise over Clarke's vote, see Hamilton, *Prologue to Conflict*, 142.

Chapter 4

1. *Harper's Weekly*, January 2, 1858; Eckloff, *Memoirs of a Senate Page*, 74. Huston, *Stephen A. Douglas*, 97–98; Johannsen, *Stephen A. Douglas*, 345–55. In the 1852 election, Douglas was the favorite of "Young America," a faction of the Democratic Party composed of young politicians who believed that an older generation of Democrats was producing political stagnation. See Eyal, *The Young America Movement*, 11–13.

2. Democrats had 38 of the 62 seats in the Senate and a whopping 157 seats out of 234 in the House.

3. Douglas first introduced legislation in 1844 to organize the remaining territories of the Louisiana Purchase. For Douglas's interest in the transcontinental railroad, see Potter, *Impending Crisis*, 145–54; Johannsen, *Stephen A. Douglas*, 304–17; Wilentz, *Rise of American Democracy*, 671.

4. For western Americans' interest in settling the territory, see Malin, *The Nebraska Question*, 208–87.

5. Varon, *Disunion!*, 227–31; M. Morrison, *Slavery and the American West*, 127. For Davis's opposition, see Cooper, *Jefferson Davis*, 220–21, 229. For Pierce's position, see Holt, *Franklin Pierce*, 41; Nichols, *Franklin Pierce*, 202.

6. *Congressional Globe*, 33rd Cong., 1st Sess., 44, 115.

7. Holt, *Rise and Fall*, 806–8. Christopher Childers gives a detailed description of the origins and meaning of "popular sovereignty" in "Popular Sovereignty."

8. Parrish, *David Rice Atchison*, 126–31. In addition to his proslavery leanings, Atchison was motivated in part by a state conflict with his Senate counterpart, Thomas Hart Benton. Benton wanted to keep slavery out of the new territories to reserve the area for whites. Wilentz, *Rise of American Democracy*, 671; Nichols, "The Kansas-Nebraska Act," 202.

9. Potter, *Impending Crisis*, 159. Vice President William R. King (D-Ala.) died in April 1853, giving Atchison the role.

10. Dixon proposed the repeal after discussing the matter with Tennessee Whig James Jones. Both Dixon and Jones were present at the dinner with Seward in December. William H. Seward to his wife, December 29, 1853, in F. Seward, *Seward at Washington*, 1:213. Seward specifically mentions discussing the slavery issue. Several historians have argued that Dixon and Jones needed no prodding from Seward to propose repealing the line. Both men needed to reaffirm their proslavery credentials to be reelected in 1854. See Freehling, *Road to Disunion*, 1:555; Holt, *Rise and Fall*, 809. While they are right to suggest that the two Southerners may have had their own reasons for promoting a repeal, there is a good chance that Seward was involved at least in a cursory discussion of the matter.

11. *Congressional Globe*, 33rd Cong., 1st Sess., 240; Holt, *Rise and Fall*, 809–10. Also see Cooper, *The South and the Politics of Slavery*, xi, 74, for the importance of promoting one's proslavery credentials at home. As Holt argues, Dixon's bill actually went beyond repealing the compromise line and declared that citizens had the right to take their slaves to any American territory now or in the future (p. 809).

12. Philip Phillips, "A Summary of the Principal Events of My Life, Written between the 10th and 20th June [1876]," 31, Philip Phillips Papers, LC.

13. Ibid., 30; Seward, *Reminiscences of a War-Time Statesman*, 68. Frederick Seward describes the house of his father, William H. Seward. William Seward and Phillips were neighbors in 1854. *Congressional Directory for 1854*. Mason, Butler, and Hunter had lived together since the mid-1840s. See *Congressional Directories for 1848–1853*.

14. Phillips, "A Summary," 33, Phillips Papers.

15. Ibid., 34; *Congressional Directory for 1854*. For Jefferson Davis's role in the meeting, see Cooper, *Jefferson Davis*, 286–87. Exactly what was said in the meeting is unclear, but a detailed account can be found in Nichols, *Franklin Pierce*, 321–24. For Pierce's concerns about the Missouri Compromise repeal and eventual submission, see Wallner, *Franklin Pierce*, 96–98; Holt, *Franklin Pierce*, 77. Pierce actually wrote the final language regarding the Missouri restriction contained in Douglas's Kansas-Nebraska bill.

16. *Congressional Globe*, 33rd Cong., 1st Sess., 353; Holt, *Rise and Fall*, 809.

17. Johannsen, *Stephen A. Douglas*, 434; Nichols, "The Kansas-Nebraska Act," 204; Potter, *Impending Crisis*, 161. Contemporary accounts are similarly contradictory. See Phillips, "A Summary," 31; Parker, *"The Missing Link,"* 14.

18. Freehling, *Road to Disunion*, 1:550. The only full-length treatment of congressional boarding arrangements is Young's *The Washington Community*. Although Young argues that his conclusions may be applied to the antebellum period (p. 98), the book focuses almost exclusively on the early national period.

19. *Congressional Directory for 1854*. For the New Year's festivities, see chapter 3. Also see Shelden, "Messmates' Union."

20. *Congressional Directory for 1847; Ten Eyck's Washington and Georgetown Directory; Department Directory and Register of Officers for 1861*. Numbers are necessarily rough estimates because members would sometimes move quarters after the congressional reporters took down residence information. Others did not provide their living information to the reporter or had not yet arrived in Washington. This evidence runs counter to Young's conclusions in *The Washington Community*; he erroneously argues that messes were generally sectionally organized until the Civil War. See Young, *The Washington Community*, 98–102, 104.

21. David Outlaw to his wife, January 18, 1848, and December 16, 1847 (quotation), David Outlaw Papers, SHC; *Congressional Directory for 1848*.

22. The 181 number includes 42 men who lived at a boardinghouse that did not include other federal politicians. See *Congressional Directories for 1846–1849* and *Congressional Directory for 1854*. Boardinghouses were not unique to Washington. Cities like Boston and New York also provided temporary lodgings for men and women of the middle and lower classes. Gamber, *The Boardinghouse in Nineteenth Century America*.

23. Busey, *Personal Reminiscences*, 45–46; Wilson Fairfax diary entries for November 27 and December 4, 1851, Wilson Miles Cary Fairfax Diary, 1834–57, VHS.

24. George Mifflin Dallas to his wife, February 22, 1845, in Nichols, "The Library: I," 363; Dallas diary entry, December 4, 1848, in Nichols, "The Library: II," 475; David Outlaw to his wife, December 10, 1847, and July 18, 1848, Outlaw Papers; Jacob Collamer to Mary N. Collamer, December 11, 1859, Collamer Family Papers, University of Vermont Digital collections; Edwin B. Morgan to his brothers, November 28, 1855, in Hollcroft, "A Congressman's Letters," 448; Robert Toombs to his wife, January 3, 1851, in Robert Toombs Letters, UGA.

25. George W. Bagby, "Washington City," *Atlantic Monthly* 7 (January 1861), 3–4; Dallas to his wife, November 30, 1845, in Nichols, "The Library: I," 367.

26. Horace Mann to his wife, July 28, 1850, Horace Mann Papers, MHS; *Weekly Wisconsin Patriot*, February 23, 1856 (quotation); Muscoe Garnett to his mother, February 21, 1857, Hunter Garnett Family Papers, UVA.

27. Clement Clay Jr. to his father, December 11, 1858, Clement Clay Papers, DU; David Outlaw to his wife, December 9, 1847 (quotation), December 17 1847, and December 7, 1848, Outlaw Papers; Alexander H. H. Stuart to his wife, June 2 [1841?], Stuart Family Papers, VHS; Mary Bingham to Lucina, May 11, 1848, Kinsley S. Bingham Papers, UM-B; Alpheus Felch to his wife, December 22, 1847, Alpheus Felch Papers, UM-B; Willie P. Mangum to his wife, December 1, 1850, in Shanks, *Papers of Willie Person Mangum*, 5:195.

28. Mary Bingham to Lucina, December 11, 1849, Bingham Papers; Horace Mann to his wife, January 3, January 28 (quotation), and May 13, 1849, Mann Papers; David Outlaw to his wife, January 13, 1848, Outlaw Papers.

29. *Congressional Directories for 1846–1850*; Robert C. Winthrop to John Clifford, June 4, 1848, Winthrop Family Papers, MHS.

30. Robert Schenck to Thomas Butler King, May 6, 1846, and October 25, 1846 (quotation), Thomas Butler King Papers, SHC; Robert Treat Paine to Caleb Blood Smith, November 10, 1850, Spooner-Smith Collection, HUN; Asbury Dixkins to Willie P. Mangum, January 13, 1849, in Shanks, *Papers of Willie Person Mangum*, 5:134–35; John M. Berrien to A. F. Owen, May 29, 1850, John Macpherson Berrien Papers, Georgia Historical Society, Savannah.

31. Arthur Campbell to David Campbell, January 20, 1847, Campbell Family Papers, DU; Alexander Stephens to Linton Stephens, December 14, 1844, and November 25, 1845, Alexander Hamilton Stephens Papers, Manhattanville College Library, Purchase, N.Y.

32. Stephen A. Douglas to David S. Reid, March 24, 1847, David S. Reid to James K. Polk, April 26, 1847, David S. Reid to Stephen A. Douglas, February 2, 1853 (quotation), in Butler, *Papers of David Settle Reid*, 1:188, 213, 2:13; Johannsen, *Stephen A. Douglas*, 207, 381.

33. Sarah B. Seddon to Sally, July 4, 1850, Bruce Family Papers, VHS; Alexander Stephens to Linton Stephens, January 28, 1848, Stephens Papers; Linn Boyd to Mrs. Anne Boyd, July 9, 1850, Boyd Family Papers, University of Kentucky, Lexington; Winthrop, *Memoir of Robert C. Winthrop*, 29.

34. *Congressional Directory for 1848*; Busey, *Personal Reminiscences*, 26.

35. The Giddings-Wilson-Green story is explained in detail in Harrold, *Subversives*, 108–11. Harrold argues that Green's proslavery interests were at the heart of the South Carolinian's behavior.

36. Alexander Stephens to Linton Stephens, November 30, 1855, Stephens Papers; Mary Mann to Rebecca Mann, December 19, 1850, and Horace Mann to Mr. Downer, December 22, 1850, Mann Papers.

37. Sam Houston to his wife, February 11, 1847, in M. Roberts, *Personal Correspondence*, 2:35, 212; Henry Clay to Lucretia Hart Clay, February 18, 1848, in Hay, *Papers of Henry Clay*, 10:403. Large and fashionable hotels were a relatively new phenomenon in Washington beginning in the late 1820s. See King, "The First-Class Hotel and the Age of the Common Man," 182–84.

38. Guy M. Bryan to Laura Bryan, February 15, 1858, Guy M. Bryan Papers, CAH.

39. David S. Reid to his wife, December 11, 1858, in Butler, *Papers of David Settle Reid*, 2:265; *Harper's Weekly*, December 18, 1858; Clay, *A Belle of the Fifties*, 43–44 (quotation). Also see Varina Davis to her mother, January 6, 1850, in Strode, *Jefferson Davis*, 59.

40. Alexander H. H. Stuart to his wife, December 8, 1849, Stuart Family Papers; Edward Everett to his wife, November 11, 1852, Edward Everett Papers, MHS; David Outlaw to his wife, February 15, 1848 (quotation), Outlaw Papers; Solomon Haven to James M. Smith, January 9, 1856, Solomon G. Haven Papers, UM-C.

41. *Times Dispatch* (Richmond), July 4, 1903. Also see Jacob, *Capital Elites*, 38. For the presence of abolitionists in Washington and a description of the runaways in this case, see Harrold, *Subversives*, 123–66. David Outlaw also describes the events surrounding Toombs's and Stephens's slaves' disappearance. See David Outlaw to his wife, July 29, 1850, and August 8, 1850, Outlaw Papers. In 1850, Toombs lived in Donahoo's building, and Stephens was still at Mrs. Carter's. *Congressional Directory for 1850*.

42. *Congressional Directories for 1846–1860*. See, for example, the Exchange Hotel listings for 1847 and 1848.

43. John S. Pendleton to William B. Preston, July 9, 1850, Preston Family Papers, VHS; Lizzie Burrows to her children, December 2, 1850, Burrows Family Papers, UM-B; Alpheus Felch to his wife, December 7, 1851, Felch Papers.

44. Clay, *Belle of the Fifties*, 35; Benjamin Robbins Curtis to his uncle, December 27, 1851, in Curtis, *Memoir of Benjamin Robbins Curtis*, 1:163–64; Samuel R. Curtis to his brother, December 15, 1857, Papers of Samuel Ryan Curtis, HUN.

45. John M. Berrien to Anne Charlotte Lynch, October 14, 1851, John Macpherson Berrien, Correspondence, UGA; *Congressional Directory for 1849*; Solomon Haven to James M. Smith, December 3, 1855, Haven Papers. For the rivalry between Berrien on the one hand and Toombs and Alexander Stephens on the other, see Holt, *Rise and Fall*, 222.

46. Alpheus Felch to his wife, December 12, 1852, Felch Papers; Salmon P. Chase to his wife, January 7, 1850, in Niven, *The Salmon P. Chase Papers*, 2:275; John A. Bryans to William L. Marcy, May 2, 1848, William L. Marcy Papers, LC.

47. *Congressional Directory for 1854*; Solomon G. Haven to his wife, December 5, 1853, and January 12, 1854, Haven Papers.

48. *Congressional Directory for 1854*; Colin M. Ingersoll to Howell Cobb, January 20, 1854, in Phillips, "Correspondence," 339.

49. William Seward to his wife, July 31, 1856, in F. Seward, *Seward at Washington*, 1:284.

50. H. A. Wise to Edward Everett, April 14, 1851, Everett Papers; Francis Markoe to W. T. Carroll, Washington, April 11, 1851, Hamilton Fish Papers, LC.

51. *Harper's Weekly*, May 9, October 3, and December 12, 1857; H. A. Wise to Edward Everett, March 21, 1857, and April 2, 1852, Everett Papers; Mrs. Robert J. Walker Receipt for a house owned by Mrs. Margaret Eaton, April 21, 1857, Margaret Eaton Papers, HUN.

52. Alexander H. H. Stuart to his wife, [n.d., 1850], Stuart Family Papers; Charles Francis Adams diary entry, December 1, 1859, Adams Family Papers, MHS; Edward Everett to John Mason, August 8 and September 27, 1853, Everett Papers.

53. Winthrop, *Memoir of Robert C. Winthrop*, 81; Alexander H. H. Stuart to his wife, September 15, [1850], Stuart Family Papers (quotation); William A. Graham to Susan

Graham, August 13, 1850, in Hamilton, *The Papers of William Alexander Graham*, 3:356; Helen Maria Jackson to Ann Maria Palmer [n.d.], 1853, Helen Maria Jackson Papers, HUN.

54. Pryor, *Reminiscences of Peace and War*, 42; Roger B. Taney to J. M. Carlisle, December 17, 1856, Lincoln Miscellaneous Manuscripts, SCRC; Roger Taney letter to James Mandeville Carlisle, December 18, 1856, Roger Taney Papers, HUN.

55. *Congressional Directory for 1854*; *Congressional Directories for 1850–1856*.

56. Tayloe, *Our Neighbors*, 6; *Congressional Directories for 1850–1859*.

57. Tayloe, *Our Neighbors*, 6. For Corcoran's role in Washington social life, see chapter 3. Jackson Place and Madison Place were called 16½ Street and 15½ Street, respectively, during the 1850s. The names were changed after the Civil War.

58. *Congressional Directory for 1854*. Henry Wise to Edward Everett, February 13, 1851, Everett Papers. For a list of residents of the Decatur House in the 1850s, including Appleton; James and John King, who were brothers from New Jersey and New York; and Louisiana senator Judah Benjamin, see Beale, *Decatur House*; and see Belohlavek, *Broken Glass*, 276, for Cushing's residence in Lafayette Square.

59. Henry Wise to Hamilton Fish, May 16 and May 22, 1860, Fish Papers.

60. Charlie Wise to Edward Everett, March 21, 1857 (quotation), Everett Papers; Montgomery Blair to Carlisle, December 23, 1858, Lincoln Miscellaneous Manuscripts; *Harper's Weekly*, December 12, 1857; J. P. Killer to William Bigler, August 31, 1860, William Bigler Papers, HSP.

61. Edward Everett to Charlie Wise, June 8, 1854, Henry A. Wise to Edward Everett, December 12, 1854, Charlie Wise to Edward Everett, January 18, 1856, and March 12, 1857, Everett Papers. Wise and Davis originally got off on the wrong foot, disagreeing about various amenities in the Everett house, but they managed to patch up any differences.

62. James G. King to his wife, August 11, 1850, Ewing-King Papers, NYHS; Alexander H. H. Stuart to his wife, [November 1850], Stuart Family Papers; Edward Everett diary entries for December 14, 1852, November 19, November 24, and December 3, 1853, Everett Papers; Edward Everett to Louise Corcoran, May 30, 1857, William W. Corcoran Papers, LC.

63. Virginia Clay to her father, December 25, 1855, Clay Papers; F. Seward, *Reminiscences of a War-Time Statesman*, 68. For Seward's relationship with Gwin, see Kushner, "Visions of the Northwest Coast," 295–306. William J. Cooper gives a detailed description of the Davis-Seward friendship in *Jefferson Davis*, 281, 309. Also see chapters 1 and 3 for the Seward-Davis friendship.

64. Reminiscences of Caroline Phillips Myers, Phillips-Myers Family Papers, SHC.

65. Edward Everett to Mrs. Charles Eames, November 2, 1857, Everett Papers.

66. Some historians believe the "Appeal" was a critical factor in causing Southern Whigs to eventually vote for the Kansas-Nebraska Act. Michael Holt argues that the Appeal "defined the purpose of Douglas's measure before he himself could do so," making opposition to the bill grounds for accusations of abolitionism. See Holt, *Rise and Fall*, 815. Others remain unconvinced. Mark Neely Jr. has recently argued that the "Appeal" received very little attention by newspapers outside of those already associated with the antislavery cause and may have had a more limited effect. See Neely, "The Kansas-Nebraska Act," 41–42.

67. Hamilton Fish to J. B. Ruggles, February 13, 1854, Fish Papers.

68. *Congressional Globe*, 33rd Cong., 1st Sess., 532, 550, 1195. Three Southern and three

Northern Whigs missed the vote in the Senate. In the House, thirteen Southern Whigs voted for the bill, while seven voted against, with four not voting. Stephen A. Douglas to Howell Cobb, April 2, 1854, in Johannsen, *Letters of Stephen A. Douglas*, 300. For Douglas's pride in passing the bill, see Johannsen, *Stephen A. Douglas*, 434.

69. Israel Washburn Jr. to John Wentworth, March 20, 1882, in Wentworth, *Congressional Reminiscences*. Dickinson originally lived at Willard's Hotel but moved to Crutchett's when Eliot arrived in the city in late April. Eliot replaced Massachusetts Whig Zeno Scudder on April 17 after Scudder resigned because of an accident that affected his health. *Congressional Directory for 1854*.

70. Quoted in Johannsen, *Stephen A. Douglas*, 451.

Chapter 5

1. Description of Brooks in Donald, *Charles Sumner*, 242. For Brooks's state of mind and lack of sobriety, see *New York Times*, January 29, 1857; Mathis, "Preston Smith Brooks," 303; Hoffer, *The Caning of Charles Sumner*, 7.

2. Fewer than 800 white settlers lived in Kansas when Congress passed the Kansas-Nebraska Act in May 1854. Over the next nine months, however, that number increased tenfold. Nicole Etcheson gives the fullest explanation of events on the ground in the territory in *Bleeding Kansas*, 29–30, 46–49, 89–112. Also see M. Morrison, *Slavery and the American West*, 161–67; Holt, *Political Crisis*, 192–94; Miner, *Seeding the Civil War*, 1–6. As Holt and Miner both point out, there was a difference between what was actually happening in Kansas and what political propagandists said was happening.

3. *Congressional Globe*, 34th Cong., 1st Sess., Appendix, 529–43. Other antislavery senators, including John P. Hale (R-N.H.), William Henry Seward (R-N.Y.), and Henry Wilson (R-Mass.), made speeches earlier in the session that mirrored several of Sumner's arguments. *Congressional Globe*, 34th Cong., 1st Sess., appendix, 89–407. A number of other senators, including some Northerners, opposed the speech. Bruns, "The Assault," 5.

4. Majority Report on the Sumner Caning Incident, House of Representatives, 34th Cong., 1st Sess., H.R. 182. Brooks's belief that he must act to avenge his cousin and state stemmed in part from a complex code of honor that was prominent throughout the United States in the mid-nineteenth century. Several historians, beginning with Bertram Wyatt-Brown's groundbreaking work, have argued that men from the slaveholding states had a peculiarly southern conception of honor. See Wyatt-Brown, *Southern Honor*, 14–15; K. Greenberg, *Honor and Slavery*, 51–53; Olsen, *Political Culture*, 17–18. Recently, other scholars have demonstrated that affairs of honor had more national characteristics, rather than sectional ones. See Freeman, "The Culture of Congress"; Freeman, *Affairs of Honor*, xvi; Bowman, *At the Precipice*, 84–111; A. Greenberg, *Manifest Manhood*, 139–40. Much of this code was tied up in conceptions of American manhood. As James Corbett David argues, Brooks's reaction stemmed in part from a belief that Sumner had emasculated his family and his state. See David, "The Politics of Emasculation," 327.

5. Preston Brooks to his brother, "Ham," May 23, 1856, in Meriwether, "Preston S. Brooks," 2; Majority Report on the Sumner Caning Incident; Benson, *The Caning of Senator Sumner*, 139; Donald, *Charles Sumner*, 244; Bruns, "The Assault," 4.

6. Minority Report on the Sumner Caning Incident, House of Representatives, 34th

Cong., 1st Sess., H.R. 182; "Alleged Assault on Senator Sumner," 34th Cong., 1st Sess., H.R.182; Benson, *The Caning of Senator Sumner*, 138.

7. Majority Report on the Sumner Caning Incident; Minority Report on the Sumner Caning Incident; Benson, *The Caning of Senator Sumner*, 138. In the Senate chamber, each chair was connected to its desk by a set of tracks. To dislodge the chair, the person seated had to push straight back. Hoffer, *The Caning of Charles Sumner*, 9; Bruns, "The Assault," 6.

8. "Alleged Assault on Senator Sumner"; Benson, *The Caning of Senator Sumner*, 135–36; Hoffer, *The Caning of Charles Sumner*, 71. The House committee included Lewis D. Campbell (Opp-Ohio), Howell Cobb (D-Ga.), Alfred B. Greenwood (D-Ark.), Alexander C. M. Pennington (Opp-N.J.), and Francis E. Spinner (D-N.Y.). The Senate committee included Phillip Allen (D-R.I.), Lewis Cass (D-Mich.), Henry Dodge (D-Wisc.), Henry Geyer (W-Mo.), and James A. Pearce (Opp-Md.).

9. "Alleged Assault on Senator Sumner"; *Congressional Globe*, 34th Cong., 1st Sess., 279, 317; Wilentz, *Rise of American Democracy*, 691.

10. Hoffer, *The Caning of Charles Sumner*, 81; Donald, *Charles Sumner*, 260; Potter, *Impending Crisis*, 210–11. Both Donald and Potter suggest that while Sumner did have some disabling physical injuries, he was primarily affected by post-traumatic stress syndrome and other psychological problems.

11. For a catalog of editorial reactions to the caning, North and South, see Benson, *Caning of Senator Sumner*, 161–75, as well as Benson's "Secession Era Editorials Project," http://history.furman.edu/.

12. A number of historians have illustrated the impact of the caning on various aspects of mid-nineteenth-century America, including politics, ideology, sectionalism, and even the prospects for civil war. These works have provided a better understanding of the way that journalists, political leaders, African Americans, and others used the event to galvanize sectional support. See Donald, *Charles Sumner*, 250–52; Gienapp, *Origins of the Republican Party*, 302–3, 362; Holt, *Political Crisis*, 195–96; Richards, *The Slave Power*, 195–96; Sinha, "The Caning of Charles Sumner," 235; Wilentz, *Rise of American Democracy*, 691–92.

13. William H. Seward to his wife, June 13, 1856, in F. Seward, *Seward at Washington*, 1:277; Henry A. Wise to Edward Everett, June 5, 1856, Edward Everett Papers, MHS; Charles Sumner to George William Curtis, April 24, 1858, in B. Palmer, *Selected Letters of Charles Sumner*, 1:504.

14. Solomon Haven to his wife, May 28, 1856, Solomon G. Haven Family Papers, UM-C.

15. *New York Herald*, May 14, 1848; Thomas Harding Ellis to Conway Robinson, September 5, 1856, Robinson Family Papers, VHS; H. F. Bullock to William S. Bodley, July 16, 1844, Bodley Family Papers, FIL; Asa Biggs to R. M. T. Hunter, March 27, 1860, in Ambler, *Correspondence of Robert M. T. Hunter*, 308.

16. Boston *Daily Atlas*, March 27, 1856; Julian, *Political Recollections*, 43; Zebulon Vance to his cousin, Jane, February 10, 1859, in Johnston, *Papers of Zebulon Baird Vance*, 1:40.

17. Horace Greeley to James S. Pike, February 15, 1856, in Pike, *First Blows of the Civil War*, 305; David Outlaw to his wife, March 21, 1848, David Outlaw Papers, SHC.

18. Julian, *Political Recollections*, 43 (quotation); Robert Hatton to his wife, December 16, 1859, in Drake, *Life of General Robert Hatton*, 182; Elizabeth Lomax diary entry,

July 1, 1859, Lomax Family Papers, VHS (quotation); Lincoln Clark to his wife, December 27, 1851, Papers of Lincoln Clark, HUN; Charles Sumner to Henry W. Longfellow, January 11, 1852, in B. Palmer, *Selected Letters of Charles Sumner*, 1:348.

Significant alcohol consumption was a nationwide phenomenon, and drinking among Washington's politicians generally reflected American trends. Although the percentage of Americans who were drinkers declined in the 1840s, alcohol was still popular both in and outside Washington during the 1840s and 1850s. See Rorabaugh, *The Alcoholic Republic*, x–xi, 7–11.

19. Alexander Stephens to Linton Stephens, December 14, 1844 (for Story), and December 3, 1854 (for Pierce), Alexander Hamilton Stephens Papers, Manhattanville College Library, Purchase, N.Y.; Horace Mann to C. Pierce, February 13, 1852 (Webster quotation), Horace Mann Papers, MHS; Amos Kendall to George Wood, July 1, 1852 (Pierce quotation), Amos Kendall Miscellaneous Papers, FIL.

20. *Weekly Wisconsin Patriot*, October 17, 1860.

21. Isaac Bassett Papers, NARA; *Harper's Weekly*, April 3, 1858.

22. Bill of Hon. W. P. Mangum "Bot" of John H. Buthmann for 1846 (totaling $37.75 and $46.50), Willie P. Mangum Papers, LC; James M. Wayne to Hamilton Fish, November 2, 1852, Hamilton Fish Papers, LC; Poore, *Perley's Reminiscences*, 1:237.

23. James G. King to his wife, August 11, 1850, Ewing-King Papers, NYHS; Benjamin Wade to Caroline, January 10, 1852, Benjamin F. Wade Papers, LC; Winthrop, *Memoir of Robert C. Winthrop*, 29.

24. Busey, *Personal Reminiscences*, 90 (McConnell quote); David Outlaw to his wife, February 20, 1848, Outlaw Papers (Jameson quote); Asbury Dickins to Willie P. Mangum, January 13, 1849, in Shanks, *Papers of Willie Person Mangum*, 5:134; David Outlaw to his wife, January 18, 1848, and February 18, 1848, Outlaw Papers; Willie P. Mangum and J. T. Morehead to John M. Clayton, March 25, 1844, John M. Clayton Papers, LC; William W. Morrison to William A. Graham, April 2, 1855, in Hamilton, *Papers of William Alexander Graham*, 4:596.

25. Henry A. Wise to Franklin Pierce, June 22, 1852, Wise Family Papers, VHS; Thomas Corwin to James A. Pearce, May 16, 1856, in Steiner, "Some Letters," 167.

26. A. S. Loughery to Orlando Brown, August 21, 1853 (quotation), and September 25, 1849, Orlando Brown Papers, FIL. For Westcott's notoriety, see David Outlaw to his wife, March 2, 1850, Outlaw Papers.

27. Henry A. Wise to Edward Everett, May 21, 1856, Everett Papers.

28. Charles Francis Adams diary entry, March 27, 1860, Adams Family Papers, MHS.

29. Alexander Stephens to Linton Stephens, August 24, 1856, Stephens Papers; Robert Toombs to Alexander Stephens, January 5, 1860, in Phillips, "Correspondence," 455; Thomas J. Rusk to David Rusk, May 7, 1848, Thomas Jefferson Rusk Papers, CAH.

30. *Harper's Weekly*, June 13, 1857; David Outlaw to his wife, January 30, 1849, Outlaw Papers.

31. Mileage was the refund that congressmen received for the expense of their travel to and from Washington. It was calculated by miles. *Congressional Directory for 1856*; Edward Everett to J. C. Spencer, February 15, 1854, Everett Papers; Samuel Ryan Curtis to Henry B. Curtis, December 15, 1857, Papers of Samuel Ryan Curtis, HUN; Clement Clay, Jr. to his mother, December 15, 1854, Clement Clay Papers, DU; Arthur Campbell to David Camp-

bell, November 25, 1845, Campbell Family Papers, DU; Benjamin Curtis to Millard Fillmore, September 1, 1857, in Curtis, *Memoir of Benjamin Robbins Curtis*, 1:250; D. H. Wood to Paulus Powell, October 8, 1857, Paulus Powell Papers, VHS; Edward Stanly to Schuyler Colfax, February 4, 1853, Schuyler Colfax Papers, LC; William Preston to Susan Christy, February 4, 1854, Preston Family Papers—Davie Collection, FIL.

While cabinet members were guaranteed their yearly salaries, congressmen had to rely on a quick organization of the House of Representatives in order to receive their daily pay. This became a problem at several points in the antebellum period because of long, drawn-out, speakership battles. See chapter 1, and Andrew J. Hamilton to his wife, January 16, 1860, Andrew Jackson Hamilton Papers, CAH; David Outlaw to his wife, December 11, 1849, Outlaw Papers.

32. See chapter 2.

33. Reverdy Johnson to John M. Clayton, January 3, 1855, Clayton Papers; Reverdy Johnson to William Corcoran, September 16, 1850, William W. Corcoran Papers, LC; William Preston to Willie P. Mangum, July 31, 1846, Willie P. Mangum Papers, LC; David Outlaw to his wife, December 5, 1850, Outlaw Papers; Jesse D. Bright to William English, December 7, 1854, in Bright, "Some Letters of Jesse Bright," 381; Jesse D. Bright to William Preston, October 30, 1854, Wickliffe-Preston Family Papers, University of Kentucky, Special Collections Division, Lexington.

34. Truman Smith to William B. Campbell, May 15, 1852, Campbell Family Papers (quotation); B. L. Boyan to John Letcher, January 10, 1857, John Letcher Papers, VHS; Edmund Ruffin diary entry, February 19, 1857, in Scarborough, *The Diary of Edmund Ruffin*, 1:37–38; *Congressional Globe*, 34th Cong., 3rd Sess., 275; Alexander Stephens to Linton Stephens, January 17, 1845, Stephens Papers; David Outlaw to his wife, January 14, 1850, Outlaw Papers. Mark W. Summers gives the fullest treatment of corruption in the antebellum period throughout the United States in *Plundering Generation*, especially 69–70, 85–97.

35. Brudnick, "Salaries of Members of Congress," 4; Sam Houston to his wife, August 21, 1856, in M. Roberts, *Personal Correspondence*, 4:238; *New York Herald*, February 12, 1857. Congressmen tried to raise their salaries again in the 1870s and were far less successful. During the famous "Salary Grab Act" of 1873, members passed a law that raised the president's and the Supreme Court justices' pay, with a 50 percent raise for themselves hidden in the bill. After a public outcry, Congress rescinded that part of the act. *Congressional Globe*, 42nd Cong., 3rd Sess., 2100.

36. David Outlaw to his wife, December 7, 1848, Outlaw Papers; Busey, *Personal Reminiscences*, 72; George M. Dallas diary entry, December 6, 1848, in Nichols, "The Library: II," 476.

37. John Y. Mason to William L. Marcy, September 9, 1847, William L. Marcy Papers, LC; Poore, *Perley's Reminiscences*, 1:244.

38. *Harper's Weekly*, December 4, 1858; *Daily Ohio Statesman*, October 8, 1859; *Weekly Wisconsin Patriot*, March 22, 1856.

39. *Harper's Weekly*, November 13, 1858; Poore, *Perley's Reminiscences*, 2:43; Busey, *Personal Reminiscences*, 89.

40. *Boston Post*, quoted in the *Weekly Raleigh Register*, November 17, 1858; *Daily Evening Bulletin* (San Francisco), April 30, 1856; Poore, *Perley's Reminiscences*, 2:44 (quotation).

41. *Congressional Directory for 1852*; *Weekly Wisconsin Patriot*, August 1, 1857; Poore, *Perley's Reminiscences*, 2:46; *Bangor Daily Whig & Courier*, February 3, 1860; Humphrey Marshall to Hunter, February 2, 1861, Humphrey Marshall Papers, FIL.

42. Henry Wise to Edward Everett, February 17, 1856, Everett Papers; *Harper's Weekly*, December 4, 1858; *Columbus Ledger-Enquirer*, December 6, 1858; *Mercury* (Charleston), December 24, 1858; *Weekly Wisconsin Patriot*, January 1, 1859; William P. Fessenden to Hamilton Fish, December 18, 1858, Fish Papers.

43. *Sun* (Baltimore), April 5, 1855, and April 5, 1856.

44. Poore, *Perley's Reminiscences*, 2:44; Townsend, *Historic Sketches at Washington*, 60; *North American* (Philadelphia), quoted in *Harper's Weekly*, November 27, 1858.

45. David Outlaw to his wife, January 30, 1848, and December 16, 1847, Outlaw Papers.

46. David Outlaw to his wife, January 27, 1849, February 15, 1848, February 23, 1848, Outlaw Papers.

47. Isaac Bassett Papers (quotation). Bassett was a poor speller, and I have changed some of the spelling and added punctuation to make the quote easier to read.

48. Guy M. Bryan to Laura Bryan, May 8, 1858, Guy M. Bryan Papers, CAH; *Harper's Weekly*, May 15 and June 17, 1858. See chapter 4 for a detailed picture of the Lafayette Square neighborhood.

49. *Harper's Weekly*, June 17 (quotation) and November 6, 1858.

50. For this and the previous paragraph: Fontaine, *Trial*, 3–4; *Harper's Weekly*, March 12, 1859; Poore, *Perley's Reminiscences*, 2, 25; Benjamin French diary entry, February 28, 1859, in French, *Witness to the Young Republic*, 309–10; Elizabeth Lomax diary entry, February 27, 1859, Lomax Family Papers.

51. Fontaine, *Trial*, 102–6. As Hendrig Hartog points out, the acquittal was, in many ways, a validation of common nineteenth-century beliefs about husband's rights. See Hartog, "Lawyering," 74. For a popular account of the Sickles murder and trial, see Brandt, *The Congressman Who Got Away with Murder*.

52. "A Composition. Washington. Telegraph-News," written by Harriot Appleton, December 3, 1856, Curtis-Stevenson Papers, MHS (quotation); David Outlaw to his wife, September 26, 1850, Outlaw Papers; Elizabeth Lomax diary entry, February 27, 1857, Lomax Family Papers; *Harper's Weekly*, March 7 and March 14, 1857.

53. Clement Clay to his father, March 14, 1854, Clay Papers; *Harper's Weekly*, March 6, 1858.

54. *Harper's Weekly*, December 25, 1858, and January 22, 1859.

55. *Trenton State Gazette*, August 15, 1856; *Harper's Weekly*, May 16, 1857.

56. *Sun* (Baltimore), May 9, 1856; *Daily National Intelligencer*, May 9, 1856.

57. Henry A. Wise to Edward Everett, May 9, 1856, Everett Papers; *Daily National Intelligencer*, May 9–10, 12–13, 1856; Holt, "Making and Mobilizing," 45.

58. John Fairfield to his wife, January 10, 1845, in Staples, *Letters of John Fairfield*, 355; Alexander Stephens to Linton Stephens, January 10, 1845, Stephens Papers; Sam Houston to his wife, December 25, 1846, in M. Roberts, *Personal Correspondence*, 2:174; *Harper's Weekly*, February 13, 1858.

59. David Settle Reid to his wife, February 8, 1858, in Butler, *Papers of David Settle Reid*, 2: 229; Alexander Stephens to Linton Stephens, February 5, 1858, Stephens Papers.

60. David Outlaw to his wife, March 10, 1848, Outlaw Papers (quotation); Artemas

Hale diary entry, March 10, 1848, Artemas Hale Papers, LC; *Harper's Weekly*, March 7, 1857 (quotation).

61. See David Outlaw to his wife, March 30, 1850, Outlaw Papers; *Harper's Weekly*, July 18, 1857; Alexander Stephens to Linton Stephens, March 24, 1850, Stephens Papers; John V. Wright, "Some Public Men I Have Known," address delivered at Selmer, Tenn., April 13, 1907, John Vines Wright Papers, SHC.

62. Clay, *A Belle of the Fifties*, 95; Benjamin French diary entry, February 1, 1857, in French, *Witness to the Young Republic*, 276. Robert Neil Mathis makes a similar point in "Preston Smith Brooks," 302.

63. Henry Wilson to Theodore Parker, May 31, 1858, Theodore Parker Papers, MHS. Also see a similar letter from Anson Burlingame to Theodore Parker, May 8, 1858, in the same collection.

Chapter 6

1. Albert D. Kirwan has written the only modern full-length biography of John J. Crittenden. Kirwan, *John J. Crittenden*, 283. Damon R. Eubank gives a larger (if limited) view of the Crittenden family as a whole in *In the Shadow of the Patriarch*, 3. Also see Coleman, *Life of John J. Crittenden*, 1:21. Coleman was Crittenden's eldest daughter. Michael Holt explains the reasons why the Whig Party died in Holt, *Rise and Fall*, 951–5.

2. Whigs and Democrats had disagreed on a number of ideological issues. Some of these included executive power, territorial expansion, and internal improvements. See Holt, *Rise and Fall*, 28–32; Howe, *Political Culture*, 299. For a discussion of the Kansas-Nebraska Act, see chapter 4. For Crittenden's opposition to the Kansas-Nebraska Act, see John J. Crittenden to Archibald Dixon, March 7, 1854, and John J. Crittenden to Presley Ewing, March 6, 1854, in Coleman, *Life of John J. Crittenden*, 1:61–63.

3. Crittenden had served as attorney general under Whig president Millard Fillmore, and in 1856 Fillmore ran on the American Party ticket for president. Crittenden's relationship with Fillmore undoubtedly influenced his switch to the Americans. In the Thirty-Fifth Congress, American Party senators included John Bell of Tennessee, Crittenden, Sam Houston of Texas, Anthony Kennedy of Maryland, and John Thompson of Kentucky. The Senate also included three "Opposition" Party members from the North and one Whig. Michael F. Holt describes the process by which many Whigs in the Border States joined the fledgling Know-Nothing movement beginning in 1855. Know-Nothingism grew out of a negative response to increasing immigration in the late 1840s. Nativists organized in secret societies that were not originally political, but by the mid-1850s, the group had developed a political arm that helped to disrupt Whig power. When their party disappeared, several former Whigs particularly in the North and the Border States, joined the political arm of the Know-Nothings, which was called the American Party. See Holt, *Rise and Fall*, 908, and Holt, *Political Parties*, 112–28.

4. One of the reasons why free-state men refused to participate in the referendum is that the Lecompton delegates did not submit the entire constitution for a vote. Rather, they gave voters a choice between allowing more slaves to come into the region after statehood or barring their entry. Voters did not have the option of making Kansas a free state. Etcheson, *Bleeding Kansas*, 142–47; Holt, *Political Crisis*, 203; Freehling, *Road to Disunion*, 2:138. Most historians believe that Buchanan supported Lecompton out of political neces-

sity; his actions were controlled by the 174 Southern electoral votes that made him president in 1856, and therefore he deferred to the Southern members of his cabinet including Secretary of the Treasury Howell Cobb of Georgia, Secretary of War John B. Floyd of Virginia, Postmaster General Aaron V. Brown of Tennessee, and Secretary of the Interior Jacob Thompson of Mississippi. See Potter, *Impending Crisis*, 299; Klein, *James Buchanan*, 302–3; J. Baker, *James Buchanan*, 102–6.

5. *Congressional Globe*, 35th Cong., 1st Sess., 501 and 1260.

6. *Congressional Globe*, 35 Cong., 1 Sess., 1880–1906; Potter, *Impending Crisis*, 324.

7. *Congressional Directory for 1848*; Kirwan, *John Crittenden*, 338. For background on the Young Indians, see chapter 2.

8. Abraham Lincoln to John J. Crittenden, July 7, 1858, in Coleman, *Life of John J. Crittenden*, 2:162. For Northerners' opposition to the Kansas-Nebraska Act and its relationship to the Republican Party, see Gienapp, *Origins of the Republican Party*, 76, 191–92, 358–65; Richards, *The Slave Power*, 2–16.

9. John J. Crittenden to Abraham Lincoln, July 29, 1858, in Coleman, *Life of John J. Crittenden*, 2;162–64.

10. Ibid. Buchanan and Douglas had harbored disdain for each other dating back at least to the 1852 Democratic nominating convention. Regardless of that personal animosity, in December 1857 Douglas tried to convince Buchanan that he should not support the Lecompton Constitution. But the president disagreed and threatened to excommunicate him from the Democratic Party. Buchanan went through with his threats in the summer of 1858, when his lieutenants did everything they could to defeat the Little Giant. For the December Buchanan-Douglas exchange, see Wilentz, *Rise of American Democracy*, 717. Douglas's motives in opposing the Lecompton Constitution were both political and ideological. See Johannsen, *Stephen A. Douglas*, 582; Huston, *Stephen A. Douglas*, 137–38; Guelzo, *Lincoln and Douglas*, 23–26. For the long-standing rivalry between Buchanan and Douglas, see Wells, *Stephen Douglas*, 25.

11. Stephen A. Douglas to John J. Crittenden, March 14, 1858, in Coleman, *Life of John J. Crittenden*, 2:145.

12. Johannsen, *Stephen A. Douglas*, 540–44; "The Death of Stephen Douglas," Crittenden speech in the House of Representatives, July 9, 1861, in Coleman, *Life of John J. Crittenden*, 2:323–24. Crittenden explained in his eulogy of Douglas that the two "were kept apart by our political differences for a considerable period of the time that we both served in the national councils" but that in the "last four or five years of Mr. Douglas's life we were associated personally and politically, and I had the opportunity of knowing him well."

13. Clay, *A Belle of the Fifties*, 84 (quotation); *The Mississippian*, January 12, 1858; *Trenton State Gazette*, February 2, 1858. Buchanan's closest friends were part of William Corcoran's social circle, and neither Crittenden nor Douglas was invited to most of the banker's dinner parties. See Lists of Dinner Company, 1857–58, William W. Corcoran Papers, LC.

14. Charles F. Adams diary entry, December 5, 1859, Adams Family Papers, MHS; Edward Everett diary entry, January 3, 1854, Edward Everett Papers, MHS; Alpheus Felch to his wife, December 8, 1847, Alpheus Felch Papers, UM-B (quotation). At the beginning of each session, there were always members who had not yet arrived.

15. See chapter 5.

16. Sam Houston to his wife, June 30, 1850, in M. Roberts, *Personal Correspondence*,

3:224; Thomas J. Rusk to General Ben Cleveland, December 18, 1847, Thomas Jefferson Rusk Papers, CAH; William Seward to his wife, August 10, 1856, in F. Seward, *Seward at Washington*, 1:286.

17. Guy M. Bryan to his wife, June 14, 1858, Guy M. Bryan Papers, CAH; David S. Reid to his wife, December 11, 1854, in Butler, *Papers of David Settle Reid*, 2:97; Howell Cobb to his wife, March 2, 1852, in Brooks, "Howell Cobb Papers," 45; Lincoln Clark to his wife, April 30, 1858, Papers of Lincoln Clark, HUN.

18. Daniel Webster to Charles Henry Warren, March 1, 1850, in Wiltse and Birkner, *Papers of Daniel Webster*, 7:20; Hale diary entry, December 31, 1846, Artemas Hale Papers, LC.

19. William Seward to Hamilton Fish, February 7, 1857, Hamilton Fish Papers, LC; John Reagan to William H. Seward, June 3, 1865, John H. Reagan Papers, CAH; W. Seward, *Remarks of William H. Seward*, 3 (quotations). For the Rusk-Seward exchange in 1850, see "A Friend in Truth" to [unknown], September 5, 1850, Burrows Family Papers, UM-B; Thomas J. Rusk to James Brooks, September 11, 1850, Rusk Papers.

20. *Daily National Intelligencer*, February 25, 1848, and April 5, 1848. Allan Bogue evaluated antebellum congressional eulogies systematically in Bogue, *Congressman's Civil*, 28.

21. William P. Fessenden to Hamilton Fish, December 18, 1858, Fish Papers; Alexander Stephens to Linton Stephens, December 11, 1855, Alexander Hamilton Stephens Papers, Manhattanville College Library, Purchase, N.Y.; Robert Winthrop to Edward Everett, September 19, 1857, Everett Papers.

22. Robert Winthrop to John P. Kennedy, October 18, 1850, Winthrop Family Papers, MHS; Charles Sumner to John Bigelow, August 30, 1852, in B. Palmer, *Selected Letters of Charles Sumner*, 1:370.

23. Robert Winthrop to John P. Kennedy, November 20, 1851, Winthrop Papers; Robert Toombs to his wife, December 2, 1851, "Robert Toombs Letters UGA; Charles Sumner to Charles Francis Adams, February 1, 1852, and January 26, 1853 (quotation), in B. Palmer, *Selected Letters of Charles Sumner*, 1:382.

24. Lists of Dinner Company, 1847–52 and 1857–58, Corcoran Papers; Sam Houston to his wife, June 10, 1854, in M. Roberts, *Personal Correspondence*, 4:138.

25. *Harper's Weekly*, December 26, 1857; Stephen A. Douglas to John A. McClernand, December 7, 1859, in Johannsen, *Letters of Stephen A. Douglas*, 479. For a complete list of Douglas's Republican guests, see Johannsen, *Stephen A. Douglas*, 593.

26. *Harper's Weekly*, January 29, 1859; Guy M. Bryan to his wife, May 7, 1858, Bryan Papers.

27. David Outlaw to his wife, March 12, 1848, David Outlaw Papers, SHC; William H. Seward to his wife, August 26, 1856, in F. Seward, *Seward at Washington*, 1:288 (quotation); Alpheus Felch to his wife, December 6, 1847, Felch Papers. The Supreme Court chamber was located in the Capitol building during the mid-nineteenth century.

28. Justice John McLean, for example, was frequently considered a nominee for the Whig Party. See *Congressional Directory for 1845* and *Congressional Directory for 1846*.

29. 60 U.S. (19 How.) 393 (1857). Benjamin Curtis to William T. Carroll, April 6, 1857, Roger B. Taney to Benjamin Curtis, April 28, 1857, Benjamin Curtis to Roger B. Taney, May 13, 1857, Benjamin Curtis to Millard Fillmore, September 1, 1857, and Benjamin Curtis to George Ticknor, July 3, 1857, in Curtis, *Memoir of Benjamin Robbins Curtis*, 1:212, 214, 218–19, 250, 246. For the cost of living issue in Washington in the 1850s, see

chapter 5. For a detailed description of the issues in the *Dred Scott* case, see Fehrenbacher, *The Dred Scott Case*, 335–64; Finkelman, *Dred Scott v. Sandford*, 2–52; and Maltz, *Dred Scott and the Politics of Slavery*, 101–39.

30. John Catron to Benjamin Curtis, September 8, 1857, and James M. Wayne to Benjamin Curtis, September 21, 1857, in Curtis, *Memoir of Benjamin Robbins Curtis*, 1:255–56.

31. *Congressional Directories for 1855–1858*; James A. Pearce to John M. Clayton, September 15, 1855, John M. Clayton Papers, LC.

32. *Congressional Directories for 1849–1853*.

33. *Chicago Herald*, February, 13, 1892, Felch Papers. For Lincoln's proximity to other Young Indians in the House seating arrangements, see chapter 2.

34. R. Davis, *Recollections of Mississippi*, 388–89.

35. Daniel Webster to Peter Harvey, October 2, 1850, in Wiltse and Birkner, *Papers of Daniel Webster*, 7:155; Daniel Webster to Daniel S. Dickinson, September 27, 1850, Daniel M. Barringer Papers, SHC.

36. John Catron to Benjamin Curtis, September 8, 1857 (quotation), and James M. Wayne to Benjamin Curtis, September 21, 1857, in Curtis, *Memoir of Benjamin Robbins Curtis*, 1:255–56; George Ashmun to Howell Cobb, October 11, 1851, in Phillips, "Correspondence," 261–62.

37. Daniel M. Barringer to John Bragg, January 15, 1852, John Bragg Papers, SHC; Robert Winthrop to Howell Cobb, in Phillips, "Correspondence," 357–58.

38. Robert Winthrop to Edward Everett, February 13, 1851, and April 14, 1854 (quotation), Everett Papers.

39. Henry Clay to Alexander H. H. Stuart, November 18, 1850, Henry Clay Papers, UVA; Edward Everett to R. B. Rhett, March 17, 1847 (quotation), January 17, 1848, and May 24, 1848, Everett Papers.

40. Henry Wise to Edward Everett, May 20 (quotation) and May 21, 1860, and Charlie Wise to Edward Everett, May 21, 1860, Everett Papers. Everett and these other men may have considered John Bell less prominent than the Massachusetts native, but Bell had been involved in politics for some time. See Fuller, "The Last True Whig," 105–13.

41. John M. Clayton to James Buchanan, April 14, 1849, and James Buchanan to John M. Clayton, April 17, 1849, Clayton Papers.

42. James Buchanan to John M. Clayton, May 30, 1856, Clayton Papers; Edward Everett to William L. Marcy, July 15, 1853, Everett Papers.

43. Millard Fillmore to Gilbert Davis, January 22, 1853, and Millard Fillmore to Franklin Pierce, August 11, 1854, Severance, "Millard Fillmore Papers, Volume 2," 337, 345; Solomon Haven to his wife, February 26, 1853, Solomon G. Haven Family Papers, UM-C. Also see Julia G. Tyler to Mrs. E. N. Horsford, March 6, 1845, in Wallace, "'Letters of the Presidentess,'" 644.

44. James Young to John A. Rockwell and others, December 22, 1847, and Abel Rathbone Corbin to John A. Rockwell, October 9, 1848, Papers of John Arnold Rockwell, HUN.

45. Abel Rathbone Corbin to John A. Rockwell, April 14, 1849, Rockwell Papers.

46. "Amos & John E. Kendall agreement with John A. Rockwell to prosecute claim against U.S. arising out of contract with the Western Cherokee Indians," January 9, 1850; "George W. Jones agreement with John A. Rockwell & Abel Rathbone Corbin that they shall aid in procuring grants of public land from Congress for the benefit of the railroad

companies incorporated by Iowa to build railroads from Du Buque to Keokuck & from Davenport to Council Bluffs," Washington, November 12, 1851; "Contract concerning E.G. Tinkham & Co's Bank & the Bank of the Republic," Sangamon Co., Ill., [n.d.], 1859, Rockwell Papers.

47. Thomas J. Rusk to John Stryker, May 12, 1854; Thomas J. Rusk to Truman Smith, March 7 and 8, 1855, and March 30, 1857, Thomas J. Rusk to O. B. Matteson, March 7, 1855, O. B. Matteson to Thomas J. Rusk, May 16, 1855, and April 17, 1857, Rusk Papers. It was not until 1855 that Congress appropriated $7.75 million dollars for a settlement (about 76.9 cents on the dollar owed). See Stegmaier, *Texas, New Mexico, and the Compromise of 1850*, 316.

48. Much of the evidence for this relationship comes from the Rusk Papers, and the paucity of Truman Smith's own correspondence has probably contributed to scholars' omission of their business dealings.

49. Thomas Hart Benton to John Clayton, June 11 and June 16 (quotation), 1851, and January 6, 1854, Clayton Papers.

50. Edward Everett diary entries for November 10, December 2 (quotation), and December 12, 1852, Everett Papers.

51. Abraham Lincoln to John J. Crittenden, November 4, 1858, in Coleman, *Life of John J. Crittenden*, 2:164; Abraham Lincoln Speech at Cincinnati Ohio, September 17, 1859, in Basler, *Collected Works*, 3:452. Historians have covered the Lincoln-Douglas debates that took place in cities throughout Illinois during the summer of 1858, in painstaking detail. Some useful accounts include Guelzo, *Lincoln and Douglas*; Fehrenbacher, *Prelude to Greatness*; and Jaffa, *Crisis of the House Divided*.

52. John A. Gilmer to William Graham, Washington, D.C., February 23, 1858, in Hamilton, *Papers of William Alexander Graham*, 5:38; [Unknown] to John J. Crittenden, Lexington, Ky., March 22, 1858, Papers of John Jordan Crittenden, LC; Crittenden to S. S. Nicholas, January 29, 1860, quoted in Kirwan, *John J. Crittenden*, 349; Cole, *The Whig Party in the South*, 331–36. For a discussion of the post-Lecompton efforts to organize a Union party and its relationship to Northern Republicans, see Crofts, "The Southern Opposition," 85–86, 98–101.

53. Abraham Lincoln to Nathan Sargent, June 23, 1859, Basler, *Collected Works*, 3:387; John Crittenden to Alexander Stephens, January 13, 1860, Crittenden Papers; Kirwan, *John J. Crittenden*, 354; Sargent, *Public Men and Events*, 2:330–31.

54. Once elected, Lincoln was encouraged by a number of moderates to appoint various Southerners to posts in his new administration as a show of good faith to people in the South. Lincoln was skeptical but did at least consider North Carolinian John A. Gilmer as one option, and Gilmer had supported the Constitutional Union Party in 1860. See Burlingame, *Abraham Lincoln*, 1:1962, 1970, 1973–74.

Chapter 7

1. Charlie Wise to Edward Everett, January 13 and January 20, 1861, Edward Everett Papers, MHS.

2. Varina Davis to Jefferson Davis, November 15, 1860, in Strode, *Jefferson Davis*, 115; Elizabeth Lee to Phil Lee, December 5, 1860, in Lee, *Wartime Washington*, 13; Charlie Wise to Edward Everett, January 13, 1861, Everett Papers (quotation); Cooper, *Jefferson Davis*, 347.

3. Charlie Wise to Edward Everett, January 20, 1861, Everett Papers; Jefferson Davis to Franklin Pierce, January 20, 1861, in Pierce, "Some Papers of Franklin Pierce," 367. Davis had served in Pierce's cabinet as secretary of war. The Davis family had spent some of the summer of 1860 visiting Northern states but had not quite made its way to Pierce's home in New Hampshire, to everyone's regret. Davis sent a similar letter to Iowa Democrat George W. Jones in which he explained, "I am sorry to be separated from many true friends at the North." Davis to George W. Jones, January 20, 1861, in Rowland, *Jefferson Davis*, 5:39.

4. Charlie Wise to Edward Everett, January 13, 1861 (quotation), and March 3, 1861, Everett Papers; Halsey Wigfall to Louly Wigfall, March 30, 1861, Lewis T. Wigfall Papers, CAH.

5. Taft diary entry, January 21, 1861, Diary of Horatio Taft, LC; *New York Times*, January 21, 1861.

6. Davis and other Southern Senators signed a statement "To our Constituents" on December 14, which said "the argument is exhausted" and recommended secession. See J. Davis, *Papers of Jefferson Davis*, 6:377; Cooper, *Jefferson Davis*, 342. For the compromise efforts in Congress, see *Congressional Globe*, 36th Cong., 2nd Sess., 71–76, 85–87, 99–104, 112–14, 211, 237, 264–67. As a number of historians have shown, prospects for settling the sectional conflict rose and fell a number of times during the second session of the Thirty-Sixth Congress. See Potter, *Impending Crisis*, 525, 534–36; Crofts, *Reluctant Confederates*, xvi–xix; McClintock, *Lincoln and the Decision*, 275–76; Ayers, *In the Presence of Mine Enemies*, xx, 109–10. Ayers focuses on the perspectives of average Americans during secession winter, but his conclusions can easily be applied to politicians as well.

7. Mississippi seceded January 9, 1861, followed the next day by Florida, and Alabama on January 11. Georgia declared secession on Saturday, January 19, which explains why Iverson had not received official word.

8. *Congressional Globe*, 36th Cong., 2nd Sess., 485–87; *New York Herald*, January 22, 1861; *Boston Daily Advertiser*, January 22, 1861; Underwood, *Stephen Russell Mallory*, 71.

9. *New York Herald*, January 22, 1861; Reminiscences of Caroline Phillips Myers, Phillips-Myers Family Papers, SHC. Newspaper accounts disagree as to whether all of the Republican senators participated in bidding goodbye to their Southern colleagues, but most of the original accounts and reminiscences insist that they did.

10. Stampp, *And the War Came*, 3 (quotation); Potter, *Lincoln and His Party*, viii; Freehling, *Road to Disunion*, 2:513. As Russell McClintock argues, Americans outside of Washington also looked to their representatives for a solution. See McClintock, *Lincoln and the Decision*, 5.

11. Gunderson, *Old Gentlemen's Convention*, 6. Russell McClintock makes the critical point that most Americans saw disunion as a *political* issue. See McClintock, *Lincoln and the Decision*, 5.

12. See Latimer, *1812*, 301–22.

13. Egerton, *Year of Meteors*, 217–18. A number of historians have made this point about Republican patronage. See Holt, *Political Crisis*, 255; Freehling, *Road to Disunion*, 2:454–55; Perman, *Pursuit of Unity*, 89.

14. *Semi-Weekly Mississippian*, June 26, August 14, August 17 (quotation), October 16,

and November 9 (quotation), 1860; *Charleston Courier*, September 13 and November 1, 1860; *Savannah Daily Morning News*, June 11, 1860.

15. W. T. Early to Abraham Lincoln, October 30, 1860, Abraham Lincoln Papers, LC; William Preston to his sister, November 9, 1860, Preston Family Papers—Davie Collection, FIL.

16. Alexander Stephens to J. Henly Smith, July 10, 1861, in Phillips, "Correspondence," 487. The emphasis is Stephens's. William J. Cooper Jr. has recently argued that describing Stephens and Lincoln as "friends" is "surely an exaggeration, for the two men had seen each other only during sessions of the Thirtieth Congress and had not been in contact since they left Washington in early 1849." See Cooper, "Critical Signpost," 14–15. Although the two men may not have been in contact for some years, I disagree with Cooper's conclusion that they could not have considered one another friends. The boundaries of friendship were clearly different in the nineteenth century, when men often went years and even decades without seeing each other but renewed their bonds easily when reunited or when corresponding. Stephens's contention that he knew Lincoln well illustrates this point; he did not assume that Lincoln had altered substantially since the two interacted in Washington.

17. Stephens's speech can be found in Freehling and Simpson, *Secession Debated*, 51–79. Abraham Lincoln to Alexander Stephens, November 30, 1860, in Basler, *Collected Works*, 4:146; Alexander Stephens to Abraham Lincoln, December 14, 1860, Lincoln Papers.

18. Abraham Lincoln to Alexander Stephens, December 22, 1860, in Basler, *Collected Works*, 4:160; Alexander Stephens to Abraham Lincoln, December 30, 1860, in Avary, *Recollections*, 60.

19. Robert Winthrop to John P. Kennedy, November 14, 1860, Winthrop Family Papers, MHS; Winthrop, *Memoir of Robert C. Winthrop*, 81.

20. Daniel M. Barringer to his wife, February 24, 1861, Daniel M. Barringer Papers, SHC; John Crisfield to his son, February 24, 1861, Henry Page Papers, SHC; Poore, *Perley's Reminiscences*, 2:65.

21. Anonymous to William H. Seward, January 22, 1850, in F. Seward, *Seward at Washington*, 1:130; *Semi-Weekly Mississippian*, August 24 and September 28, 1860; *Charleston Courier*, September 13, 1860.

22. Foote, *Casket of Reminiscences*, 126; *Harper's Weekly*, January 23, 1858; Willie P. Mangum Jr. to Willie P. Mangum, February 17, 1861, in Shanks, *Papers of Willie Person Mangum*, 5:384; V. Davis, *Jefferson Davis*, 1:180–81; Cooper, *Jefferson Davis*, 341. For more positive comments of Seward among Washington's political families, see Hatton diary entry, February 29, 1860, in Drake, *Life of General Robert Hatton*, 241; Clay, *A Belle of the Fifties*, 135; as well as previous chapters.

23. John Archibald Campbell to Mary Williamson Campbell, March 6, 1861 (quotation), Campbell to William Seward, April 13, 1861, and Campbell to Judge George Goldthwaite, April 20, 1861, Campbell Family Papers, SHC. Dan Crofts describes the exchanges between Seward and Gilmer in Crofts, *Reluctant Confederates*, 257–60, 310–11. Also see Crofts, "A Reluctant Unionist," 225–49, and Lankford, *Cry Havoc!*, 40–41.

24. *Department Directory and Register of Officers for 1861.*

25. Ibid.; Taft diary entry, February 11, 1861, Taft Diary; Daniel Barringer to his wife, February 4, 1861, Barringer Papers; *Louisville Journal*, August 14, 1860, quoted in Gunder-

son, *Old Gentlemen's Convention*, 23; Keene, *The Peace Convention of 1861*, 52; Chittenden, *Report of the Debates*, 9; *New York Herald*, February 17, 1861.

26. Abraham Lincoln to Elihu Washburne, February 15, 1861, in Basler, *Collected Works*, 4:217; Taft diary entry, February 23, 1861, Taft Diary; Poore, *Perley's Reminiscences*, 2:64–65.

27. *Department Directory and Register of Officers for 1861*; *Harper's Weekly*, March 14 and May 30, 1857; Abraham Lincoln to Elihu Washburne, February 15, 1861, in Basler, *Collected Works*, 4:217; Bates diary entry, February 1861, in Beale, *Diary of Edward Bates*, 175; Taft diary entries, January 25 (quotation) and March 27, 1861, 1861, Taft Diary.

28. *Harper's Weekly*, October 3 and December 12, 1857; Edward Everett to A. Hyde, February 16, 1859 (first quotation), January 12, 1861, and January 22, 1861 (second and third quotations), Everett Papers.

29. Charlie Wise to Edward Everett, March 3, 1861, Everett Papers; Pryor, *Reminiscences of Peace and War*, 47; Bates diary entry, March 3, 1861, in Beale, *Diary of Edward Bates*, 176.

30. *Daily National Intelligencer*, December 10, 1860; Robert Hatton to his wife, December 10, 1860 (quotation), and December 24, 1860, in Drake, *Life of General Robert Hatton*, 302.

31. Taft diary entry, January 4, 1861, Taft Diary; Stockton, *Address by Thomas H. Stockton*, 16.

32. See *Daily National Intelligencer*, December 3, 1860–April 15, 1861; William Seward to his wife, December 10, 1860, in F. Seward, *Seward at Washington*, 1:481; *Annual Report of the Board of Regents of the Smithsonian Institution for 1860*, 111–15.

33. Everett diary entry, January 28, 1861, Everett Papers; French diary entry, February 26, 1861, in French, *Witness to the Young Republic*, 343.

34. Henry Adams to Charles Francis Adams Jr., February 5, 1861, in Levenson et al., *Letters of Henry Adams*, 1:229 (quotation); *Daily National Intelligencer*, January 2, 1861; Robert Hatton to his wife, January 1, 1861, in Drake, *Life of General Robert Hatton*, 316.

35. Everett diary entries for January 29 and February 5, 1861, and Charlie Wise to Edward Everett, February 12, 1861, Everett Papers; Keyes diary entries for January 31 and February 2, 1861, and February 15, 1861, in Keyes, *Fifty Years*, 362, 365; Robert Hatton to his wife, January 31, 1861, in Drake, *Life of General Robert Hatton*, 323; Henry Adams to Charles Francis Adams Jr., February 5, 1861, in Levenson, *Letters of Henry Adams*, 1:229; Taft diary entries, February 12, 1861, February 14, 1861, and March 8, 1861, Taft Diary; Stephen Douglas to John Tyler, February 11, 1861, in Johannsen, *Letters of Stephen A. Douglas*, 507; *Harper's Weekly*, March 23, 1861; *New York Herald*, February 17, 1861.

36. Charles Francis Adams diary entry, December 22, 1860, Adams Family Papers, MHS; Keyes diary entries, December 26, 1860, and January 31, 1861, Keyes, *Fifty Years*, 347; Nevins, *The Emergence of Lincoln*, 2:360; Everett diary entry, February 5, 1861, Everett Papers; Robert Hatton to his wife, February 12, 1861, in Drake, *Life of General Robert Hatton*, 340–41.

37. William Appleton to Nathan Appleton, December 21, 1860, Nathan Appleton Papers, MHS; Mary Bingham to Lucina, December 30, 1860, Kinsley S. Bingham Papers, UM-B.

38. Elizabeth Lee to Phil, January 12, 1861, in Lee, *Wartime Washington*, 23; Keyes diary entry, January 7, 1861, in Keyes, *Fifty Years*, 350.

39. Horatio King to James Buchanan, November 7, 1860, and King to John A. Dix, November 25, 1860, in King, *Turning on the Light*, 24, 27; *Boston Daily Advertiser*, December 13, 1860, in Stegmaier, *Henry Adams in the Secession Crisis*, 16; John A. Gilmer to William A. Graham, December 5, 1860, in Hamilton, *Papers of William Alexander Graham*, 5:200.

40. *Congressional Directory for 1850*; *Congressional Directory for 1852*; *Congressional Directory for 1854*; *Congressional Directory for 1856*; Clay, *Belle of the Fifties*, 42–43; David Outlaw to his wife, February 15, 1848, in David Outlaw Papers, SHC.

41. Cohen, *Business and Politics*, 210–12.

42. Elbridge Gerry Spaulding to Thurlow Weed, December 23, 1860, Thurlow Weed Papers, University of Rochester, Rush Rhees Library. *Chicago Tribune*, December 27, 1860, January 16, 23, February 6, 13, 1861; *New York Times*, January 4, 23, February 9, 1861; *Daily National Intelligencer*, January 7 and February 9, 1861.

43. *Daily National Intelligencer*, January 4, 1861.

44. *Daily National Intelligencer*, January 21, 1861 (quotation), and December 3, 1860–April 1, 1861; Ames, *History of the* National Intelligencer, 327–31.

45. William Appleton diary entry, December 17, 1860, in Appleton, *Selections*, 231; Keyes diary entry, January 13, 1861, in Keyes, *Fifty Years*, 351; Benjamin O. Tayloe to Daniel Barringer, February 8, 1861, Barringer Papers.

46. Julia Tyler to Mrs. Gardiner, February 13, 1861, in Tyler, *Letters and Times of the Tylers*, 2:612–13; Gunderson, *Old Gentlemen's Convention*, 58; Charles Francis Adams diary entry, December 22, 1860, Adams Papers.

47. Hatton diary entry, December 16, 1860, in Drake, *Life of General Robert Hatton*, 306; Stephen Douglas and John J. Crittenden to William H. Polk, February 5, 1861, Stephen A. Douglas Papers, SCRC; Stephen Douglas to Alexander Stephens, December 25, 1860, Lincoln Miscellaneous Manuscripts, SCRC.

48. Philip Phillips to Stephen Douglas, January 8, 1861, Douglas Papers; "Interview of Duff Green with Mr. Lincoln on the Crisis, January 6, 1861," *New York Herald*, January 8, 1861; Abraham Lincoln to Duff Green, Springfield, Ill., December 28, 1860, and Abraham Lincoln to Lyman Trumbull, Springfield, Ill., December 28, 1860, in Basler, *Collected Works*, 4:162–63; Harrold, *Subversives*, 110; Belko, *Invincible Duff Green*, 444; Woodward, "Mysterious Trumbull Letter," 210–14.

49. John Gilmer to Abraham Lincoln, December 10, 1860, Thomas Corwin to Abraham Lincoln, December 10, 1860 (quotation), Elihu Washburne to Abraham Lincoln, December 9, 1860, John D. Defrees, December 15, 1860, and January 8, 1861, Lincoln Papers. Some Republicans were among the voices that begged Lincoln to speak out. See Sowle, "The Conciliatory Republicans," 46–52.

50. Alexander Stephens to Abraham Lincoln, December 30, 1860, in Avary, *Recollections*, 60; Wilentz, *Rise of American Democracy*, 780. Some historians have taken a positive view of Lincoln's policy of silence, particularly Michael Burlingame in *Abraham Lincoln*, 1:702–3, and Harold Holzer in *Lincoln President-Elect*, 114–47. Others continue to view Lincoln's behavior more skeptically. See, for example, McClintock, *Lincoln and the Decision*, 49–53.

51. McClintock, *Lincoln and the Decision*, 243; Burlingame, *Abraham Lincoln*, 1:704–6.

52. Abraham Lincoln to Alexander Stephens, December 22, 1860, in Basler, *Collected*

Works, 4:160; *Statutes at Large*, 36th Cong., 2nd Sess., 251; McClintock, *Lincoln and the Decision*, 79; Cooper, "Critical Signpost," 16.

53. *Congressional Globe*, 36th Cong., 2nd Sess., 1285; Crofts, *Reluctant Confederates*, 165–94.

54. Potter, *Lincoln and His Party*, xxvii, 47; Varon, *Disunion!*, 14. Also see McClintock, *Lincoln and the Decision*, 9–10.

55. Letter of Stephen F. Hale, Commissioner from Alabama, to Governor Beriah Magoffin of Kentucky, December 27, 1860, *Official Records*, ser. IV, vol. 1, 4–11, quoted in Dew, *Apostles of Disunion*, appendix, 100; Freehling, *Road to Disunion*, 2:xiii, 349, 367; Holt, *Political Crisis*, 220–21; Rable, *The Confederate Republic*, 21–23.

56. For the strong commitment to the Confederate cause among these men, as well as Southerners in general, see Gallagher, *The Confederate War*, 17, 27, 42–60; Rable, *The Confederate Republic*, 64–70; Rubin, *A Shattered Nation*, 3–4, 9–12. Clay was a member of the Confederate Senate, Mallory served as Confederate secretary of the navy, and Slidell was charged with a diplomatic mission to England and France as a representative of the Confederate government.

57. "Some Public Men I Have Known," April 13, 1907, John Vines Wright Papers, SHC.

Epilogue

1. Abraham Lincoln to William H. Seward, February 2, 1865, 9 a.m.; Abraham Lincoln to Lieutenant-General Grant, February 2, 1865, 9 a.m.; and Thomas T. Eckert to Lieutenant-General Grant, February 2, 1865, 11:30 a.m., *Official Records*, ser. I, vol. 46, part II, 352–53.

2. Memorandum of the Conversation at the Conference in Hampton Roads, signed by John Archibald Campbell, February 1865, Campbell Family Papers, SHC; Stephens, *A Constitutional View*, 2:599. Michael Vorenberg has expressed some skepticism of Stephens's accounts of other parts of meeting, particularly in relation to their discussion of freedmen. See Vorenberg, *Final Freedom*, 223–25.

3. Stephens, *A Constitutional View*, 2:601–2 (quotation), 619. The French army had overthrown the Mexican government and named Austrian archduke Maximilian as emperor of Mexico. John Quincy Adams crafted the Monroe Doctrine while serving as secretary of state. President James Monroe enunciated the principles of self-determination for countries in the Western Hemisphere in his State of the Union address of December 1823. See Howe, *What Hath God Wrought*, 111–15. The classic text on the history of the Monroe Doctrine is Perkins's *History of the Monroe Doctrine*. For a more recent take on the Monroe Doctrine that highlights the Civil War period, see Hendrickson, *Union, Nation, or Empire*, 201–34. For a look at the United States involvement in Mexico during the Civil War period, see Schoonover, *Dollars over Dominion*, 140–77.

4. Hunter, "The Peace Commission of 1865," 169. Wilfred Buck Yearns Jr. has argued that Blair may have even made unauthorized promises that Confederate lawmakers would be able to transfer their seats to the U.S. Congress. See Yearns, "The Peace Movement," 14. Blair had been a loyal Democrat since the Andrew Jackson administration. A journalist, Blair founded the *Washington Globe* in 1830 and edited the paper for fifteen years. In 1856 he was one of the critical organizers of the Republican Party. See E. Smith, *Francis Preston Blair*, 45–61, 215–37.

5. Although Foote represented Tennessee in the Confederacy, he had served as a senator from Mississippi in the U.S. Congress. On the growth of the Confederate peace movement, see Kirkland, *The Peacemakers*, 217–22; Wakelyn, *Confederates against the Confederacy*, 53–76; Yearns, *The Confederate Congress*, 178–79.

6. Memo of Conversation with Jefferson Davis on Thursday & Saturday January 12 & January 14, 1865, by Francis P. Blair of Silver Spring taken from his dictation by M. Blair, January 18, 1865, Blair Family Papers, LOC; J. Davis, *Rise and Fall*, 2:617–18. The presence of Blair in Richmond was the subject of much comment among Southerners, particularly because the Union representative seemed to converse freely with Confederate officials. See diary entries for January 14, 23, and 25, 1865, in Jones, *A Rebel War Clerk's Diary*, 2:386, 397; Stephens, *A Constitutional View*, II:589–90; and diary entry, January 13, 1865, in Younger, *Inside the Confederate Government*, 187.

On the Confederate push toward emancipation, see Durden, *The Gray and the Black*, 101; Levine, *Confederate Emancipation*, 110–28. Although a few Southerners had pushed for emancipation earlier in the war, the administration had only recently begun to consider the measure. Davis used his November 1864 message to Congress as an opportunity to begin a more serious conversation about emancipation in the Confederacy. When the peace commissioners visited Lincoln, no legislative action had yet passed. Finally, in March 1865, with the blessing of Confederate hero Robert E. Lee, the Confederate Congress adopted legislation to recruit and arm black slaves. Critically, the war ended before the small number of slaves could be mustered into service under the new law.

7. Davis's motive in agreeing to send peace commissioners has been the subject of some debate. Historians, such as Stephens's biographer Thomas Schott, have remarked that Davis agreed to the peace mission because of a desire to discredit the Confederate peace movement. See Schott, *Alexander H. Stephens*, 439. Charles W. Sanders Jr., however, argues convincingly that Davis's motives were pure. See Sanders, "Jefferson Davis," 812.

Scholars have similarly disagreed about Lincoln's motives for agreeing to the conference. Eric Foner has recently remarked that Lincoln was "impatient" with the discussion of the Mexican scheme, suggesting he was never really invested in the conference. Foner, *The Fiery Trial*, 315. David Donald argues that Lincoln was simply trying to discredit the Confederate commissioners and the Davis administration. See Donald, *Lincoln*, 559–60. William Harris takes issue with Donald's perspective, however. Rather, Harris suggests that, although Lincoln would not have accepted anything but unconditional surrender, he nonetheless wanted to explore all real possibilities for peace. See Harris, "Hampton Roads."

8. According to Stephens, Hunter was the first person to hear about the details of Mr. Blair's visit. The president then let Stephens in on the discussion before presenting the matter formally to his cabinet. Stephens, *A Constitutional View*, 2:590–91. Campbell later claimed that he first learned of the mission from Judah Benjamin, the Confederate secretary of state. See Campbell, *Reminiscences*, 3. It is possible, however, that Campbell had advance knowledge of the negotiations as well; according to John Jones, a Confederate clerk in the war department, Hunter and Campbell were close conspirators and were constantly speaking in Mr. Campbell's office behind closed doors. This may also explain, in part, why Davis selected these three men to serve as commissioners. See diary entries for January 15 and 23, 1865, in Jones, *A Rebel War Clerk's Diary*, 2:387, 395.

9. Stephens, *A Constitutional View*, 2:593–94; John Archibald Campbell to Samuel Nelson, December [n.d.], 1864, Campbell Family Papers, SHC.

10. J. Davis, "The Peace Commission," 208. Stephens was not pleased by this arrangement not because of an unwillingness to go, but because he thought the choices would be too conspicuous. If Stephens was missing from the Senate then Hunter, as pro tempore, was supposed to take the chair, but he too would be absent (a circumstance, according to Stephens, that had never before occurred). See Stephens, *A Constitutional View*, 2:595.

11. J. Davis, *Rise and Fall*, 2:617; Campbell, *Reminiscences*, 3–4; Alexander H. Stephens, J. A. Campbell, and R. M. T. Hunter to U. S. Grant, January 30, 1865, *Official Records*, ser. I, vol. 46, part II, 297.

12. Memorandum of Lincoln, January 18, 1865, and Edwin M. Stanton to Major General Ord, January 30, 1865, *Official Records*, ser. I, vol. 46, part II, 206 and 302; Kirkland, *The Peacemakers*, 236.

13. Only that evening did Grant come across the previous correspondence. Upon seeing that he did not follow Lincoln's wishes, Grant hastily wrote Secretary of War Edwin M. Stanton, "had I known of this correspondence in time these gentlemen would not have been received within our lines." U. S. Grant to Edwin M. Stanton, January 31, 1865, 7:30 p.m., Major-General J. G. Parke to Major-General Willcox, January 31, 1865, and Brevet-Major General O. B. Willcox to Brevet Major General A. S. Webb, January 31, 1865, *Official Records*, ser. I, vol. 46, part II, 311, 317; Grant, *Personal Memoirs*, 2:421–22; George Gordon Meade to his wife, February 1, 1865, in Meade, *Life and Letters*, 2:258–59; Stephens, *A Constitutional View*, 2:597.

14. Thomas T. Eckert to Edwin M. Stanton, February 1, 1865, 10 p.m., but delivered at 10:20 a.m. on February 2 via Fort Monroe (quotations), and Thomas T. Eckert to Abraham Lincoln, February 1, 1865, 10 p.m., *Official Records*, ser. I, vol. 46, part II, 341–42; Kirkland, *The Peacemakers*, 238.

15. U. S. Grant to Edwin M. Stanton, February 1, 1865, 10:30pm, in Grant, *Papers of Ulysses S. Grant*, 13:345 (quotations); A. Lincoln to William H. Seward, February 2, 1865, 9 a.m., A. Lincoln to Lieutenant-General Grant, February 2, 1865, 9 a.m., Lieutenant-General U. S. Grant to Secretary of State, February 2, 1865, 9 a.m., *Official Records*, ser. I, vol. 46, part II, 342–43, 352.

16. Seward to Stanton, February 7, 1865, *Official Records*, ser. I, vol. 46, part II, 472; Stephens, *A Constitutional View*, 2:608 (quotation), 621; John A. Campbell to R. M. T. Hunter, November 6, 1877, Hunter Family Papers, VHS. Stephens later attributed the failure of the conference to the significant publicity surrounding the meeting. See Sanders, "Jefferson Davis," 820.

17. William H. Seward to Edwin Stanton, February 7, 1865, *Official Records*, ser. I, vol. 46, part II, 471–73; F. Seward, *Seward at Washington*, 618. The Seward story is quoted in Donald, *"We Are Lincoln Men,"* 174–75.

18. Abraham Lincoln to William H. Seward, April 1, 1861, in Basler, *Collected Works*, 4:316–17; Sowle, "A Reappraisal," 234–35; Potter, *Lincoln and His Party*, 368–69.

19. Blair and Seward could actually be considered political enemies. Francis Preston Blair had even degraded the secretary of state in his discussions with Jefferson Davis. At least one historian has argued that the Blair family and its formerly Democratic allies tried to use the Seward "Some Thoughts" letter to discredit the New Yorker after the war. See

Ferris, "Lincoln and Seward." For Blair's disparagement of Seward during the meetings with Davis, see "Memo of Conversations with Jefferson Davis," Blair Family Papers. Yet the dispute between Blair and Seward may be somewhat overblown. A few months before the Hampton Roads conference, Seward had ingratiated himself to the elder Blair by supporting Blair's son (Montgomery Blair) for the vacant place on the Supreme Court owing to Chief Justice Roger Taney's death. Seward's motives here were mostly to prevent the ultimate replacement, Salmon Chase, from becoming Lincoln's choice. Still, the position was immensely important to Francis Preston Blair, and while he may not have trusted Seward, he appreciated the support. See W. Smith, *Blair Family*, 2:298.

20. Kirkland, *The Peacemakers*, 219–20; Avary, *Recollections*, 82–83.

21. F. Seward, *Seward at Washington*, 2:295–29; John Reagan to William H. Seward, June 3, 1865, John H. Reagan Papers, CAH.

22. Stephens, *A Constitutional View*, 2:661–62.

23. Jeremiah S. Black to Howell Cobb, April [n.d.], 1868, in Phillips, "Correspondence," 694; R. B. Rhett to James Buchanan, April 2, 1867, and James Buchanan to R. B. Rhett, April 8, 1867, in Moore, *Works of James Buchanan*, X:442–43.

24. Alexander Stephens to J. Glancy Jones, June 8, 1868, May 30, 1871, and June 19, 1872, Alexander Stephens Letters to J. Glancy Jones, UGA.

25. Joshua Fry to unknown, April 21, 1874, and Alexander Stephens to Truman Smith, December 1, 1878, Truman Smith Collection, Connecticut State Library, Hartford.

BIBLIOGRAPHY

Manuscript Collections
Allendale, Mich.
    Grand Valley State University, Special Collections and University Archives
        Nathan Sargent Collection (digital)
Ann Arbor, Mich.
    University of Michigan, Bentley Historical Library
        Kinsley S. Bingham Papers (microfilm)
        Burrows Family Papers
        Thomas McIntyre Cooley Papers
        Alpheus Felch Papers
        George D. Hill Papers
        William Alanson Howard Papers
        Henry B. Joy Historical Research Collection
        Robert McClelland Papers
        Francis Ranna Stebbins Papers
    University of Michigan, Clements Library
        Lewis Cass Papers
        William Pitt Fessenden Papers
        Solomon G. Haven Family Papers
Athens, Ga.
    University of Georgia, Hargrett Rare Book and Manuscript Library
        John Macpherson Berrien Correspondence (microfilm)
        John Archibald Campbell Collection
        Howell Cobb Papers
        Alexander Stephens–Howell Cobb Correspondence
        Alexander Stephens Letters to J. Glancy Jones
        Robert Toombs Letters (digital)
        Robert Toombs Papers
Austin, Tex.
    University of Texas, Center for American History
        Guy M. Bryan Papers
        Andrew Jackson Hamilton Papers
        Sam Houston Papers
        John H. Reagan Papers
        Thomas Jefferson Rusk Papers
        George W. Smyth Papers
        Louis T. Wigfall Papers
Baltimore, Md.
    Enoch Pratt Free Library

John Pendleton Kennedy Papers (microfilm)
Boston, Mass.
   Massachusetts Historical Society
      Adams Family Papers (microfilm)
      Nathan Appleton Papers
      Curtis-Stevenson Papers
      Edward Everett Papers (microfilm)
      Horace Mann Papers (microfilm)
      Theodore Parker Papers (microfilm)
      Winthrop Family Papers (microfilm)
Burlington, Vt.
   University of Vermont, Special Collections Library
      Collamer Family Papers (digital)
Chapel Hill, N.C.
   University of North Carolina, Southern Historical Collection
      Daniel M. Barringer Papers
      John M. Berrien Papers
      John Bragg Papers
      David F. Caldwell Papers
      Campbell Family Papers
      Clingman and Puryear Family Papers
      Edward Everett Papers
      Benjamin Fitzpatrick Papers
      George Washington Jones Papers
      Thomas Butler King Papers
      Stephen R. Mallory Papers (microfilm)
      James McDowell Papers
      Orr-Patterson Papers
      David Outlaw Papers
      Henry Page Papers
      Robert Treat Paine Papers
      Phillips-Myers Family Papers
      John Vines Wright Papers
Charlottesville, Va.
   University of Virginia, Albert and Shirley Small Special Collections
      Henry Clay Papers
      Hunter Garnett Family Papers
Chicago, Ill.
   Chicago Historical Society
      Stephen A. Douglas Papers
      John Wentworth Papers
   University of Chicago, Special Collections Research Center
      Butler-Gunsaulus Miscellaneous Manuscripts Collection
      Stephen A. Douglas Papers

      Lincoln Miscellaneous Manuscripts

      Miscellaneous Manuscripts Collection

Columbia, Mo.

  University of Missouri, Western Historical Manuscripts Collection

      David Rice Atchison Papers

Columbus, Ohio

  Ohio Historical Society

      Alexander St. Clair Boys Papers

Durham, N.C.

  Duke University, William R. Perkins Special Collections Library

      Campbell Family Papers

      Clement Clay Papers

      Herschel V. Johnson Papers

Frankfort Ky.

  Kentucky Historical Society

      John J. Crittenden Papers

      Charles Haskell Collection

      Thomas Metcalfe Collection

Hartford, Conn.

  Connecticut State Library

      Truman Smith Collection

Lexington, Ky.

  University of Kentucky, Special Collections Division

      Boyd Family Papers (microfilm)

      Wickliffe-Preston Family Papers

Louisville, Ky.

  Filson Historical Society

      Bodley Family Papers

      Orlando Brown Papers

      John J. Crittenden Miscellaneous Papers

      Norvin Green Papers

      Richard Mentor Johnson Miscellaneous Papers

      Josiah Stoddard Johnston Papers

      Jones Family Papers

      Amos Kendall Miscellaneous Papers

      Humphrey Marshall Papers

      George D. Prentice Miscellaneous Papers

      Preston Family Papers—Davie Collection

      Preston Family Papers—Joyes Collection

      James Fowler Simmons Miscellaneous Papers

      Speed Family Papers

      Alexander H. H. Stuart Miscellaneous Papers

      Todd Family Papers

      Charles Anderson Wickliffe Miscellaneous Papers

Montgomery, Ala.
  Alabama Department of Archives and History
    William R. King Papers
New Haven, Conn.
  Yale University Manuscripts and Archives
    Roger Sherman Baldwin Papers
New York, N.Y.
  New-York Historical Society
    Ewing-King Papers
    King Family Papers
Philadelphia, Pa.
  Historical Society of Pennsylvania
    William Bigler Papers
    Lewis S. Coryell Papers
    Meredith Family Papers
Purchase, N.Y.
  Manhattanville College Library, Rare Books and Manuscripts
    Alexander Hamilton Stephens Papers (microfilm)
Richmond, Va.
  Virginia Historical Society
    Bruce Family Papers
    Daniel Family Papers
    Wilson Miles Cary Fairfax Diary
    Faulkner Family Papers
    Hunter Family Papers
    John Letcher Papers
    Lomax Family Papers
    MacLeod Family Papers
    John Moore McCalla Papers
    Paulus Powell Papers
    Preston Family Papers
    Rives Family Papers
    Robinson Family Papers
    Seddon Family Papers
    William Selden Papers
    Stuart Family Papers
    Tayloe Family Papers
    Wise Family Papers
Rochester, N.Y.
  University of Rochester, Rush Rhees Library
    Thurlow Weed Papers
San Marino, Calif.
  Huntington Library, Munger Research Center
    Papers of John Sherman Bagg
    Papers of Lincoln Clark

John J. Crittenden Papers

Papers of Samuel Ryan Curtis

George M. Dallas Correspondence

Daniel Family Papers

Margaret Eaton Papers

Joseph Holt Papers

John Joseph Hughes Invitation

Helen Maria Jackson Papers

Lewis Levin Papers

William D. Lewis Papers

James K. Polk Papers

Papers of Rodman Price

Papers of John Arnold Rockwell

Ellen Ewing Sherman Correspondence

Smith-Spooner Collection

Edwin M. Stanton Correspondence

Charles Sumner Correspondence

Roger Taney Papers

Savannah, Ga.

  Georgia Historical Society

    John MacPherson Berrien Papers

    James Moore Wayne Papers

Washington, D.C.

  Historical Society of Washington, D.C.

    Agg Family Papers

    Blair-Janin Family Papers

    National Hotel Research Documents

  Library of Congress, Manuscript Division

    Lucian Barbour Papers

    Blair Family Papers

    Zachariah Chandler Papers (microfilm)

    John M. Clayton Papers

    Schuyler Colfax Papers

    William W. Corcoran Papers

    Papers of John Jordan Crittenden (microfilm)

    Asbury Dickins Family Papers

    Dunlop Family Papers

    George Eustis Papers

    Ewing Family Papers

    Hamilton Fish Papers

    Artemas Hale Papers

    Papers of Joseph Holt

    Horatio King Papers

    Abraham Lincoln Papers (digital)

    Willie P. Mangum Papers

William L. Marcy Papers
Philip Phillips Family Papers
Papers of Thomas Ritchie
Diary of Horatio Taft (digital)
Benjamin F. Wade Papers (microfilm)
National Archives and Records Administration
Isaac Bassett Papers

Government Documents, Directories, and Official Reports

Annual Reports of the American Bible Society with an Account of Its Organization, List of Its Officers, of Life Directors and Life Members, Extracts of Correspondence, &c &c. Vol. 3. New York: American Bible Society, 1861.

Annual Report of the Board of Regents of the Smithsonian Institution Showing the Operations, Expenditures, and Condition of the Institution Up to January 1, 1856 and the Proceedings of the Board Up to March 22, 1856. Washington, D.C.: Cornelius Wendell, Printer, 1856.

Annual Report of the Board of Regents of the Smithsonian Institution Showing the Operations, Expenditures, and Condition of the Institution for the Year 1856 and the Proceedings of the Board Up to January 28, 1857. Washington, D.C.: Cornelius Wendell, Printer, 1857.

Annual Report of the Board of Regents of the Smithsonian Institution, Showing the Operations, Expenditures, and Condition of the Institution for the Year 1860. Washington, D.C.: George E. Bowman, Printer, 1861.

Biographical Directory of the American Congress, 1774–1996. Alexandria, Va.: CQ Staff Directories, 1997.

Congressional Directories, 29th–36th Congresses. Washington, D.C.: J. & G. S. Gideon, Printers, 1845–61.

Congressional Globe, 29th–36th Congresses, 1845–61.

Department Directory and Register of Officers in the Service of the United States in the City of Washington. Washington, D.C.: W. H. Moore, Printer, 1861.

Eighth Annual Report of the Executive Committee of the Bible Society of Washington City, Presented February 26, 1844. Washington, D.C.: J. & G. S. Gideon, Printers, 1844.

Journal of the Congress of the Confederate States of America, 1861–1865. 7 vols. Washington, D.C.: Government Printing Office, 1905.

Journal of the United States Agricultural Society. Vol. 5 (1857).

Official Records of the War of the Rebellion: A Compilation of the Official Records of the Union and Confederate Armies. 128 vols. Washington, D.C.: Government Printing Office, 1880–1901.

Records of the Columbia Historical Society, Washington, D.C. Vols. 5 and 51. Washington, D.C.: Published by the Society, 1902, 1984.

Ten Eyck's Washington and Georgetown Directory, with a Complete Congressional and Department Directory. Washington, D.C.: Henry Polkinhorn, Printer, 1855.

Thirty-Fifth Annual Report of the American Colonization Society, with the Proceedings of the Board of Directors and of the Society; and the Addresses Delivered at the Annual Meeting, January 20, 1852 . . . Washington, D.C.: C. Alexander Printer, 1852.

Newspapers and Contemporary Periodicals

Atlantic Monthly

Bangor Daily Whig and Courier

Boston Daily Advertiser

Boston Daily Atlas

Boston Post

Boston Whig

Charleston Courier

Chicago Herald

Chicago Tribune

Chronicle (Bellows Falls, Vt.)

Columbus Ledger-Enquirer

Cultivator (Albany)

Daily Cleveland Herald

Daily Evening Bulletin (San Francisco)

Daily National Intelligencer

Daily Ohio Statesman

De Bow's Review

Fayetteville Observer

Harper's New Monthly Magazine

Harper's Weekly

Kansas Herald of Freedom

Mercury (Charleston)

Mississippian

New York Herald

New York Times

New York Tribune

New York Weekly Herald

Niles National Register

North American (Philadelphia)

North American Review

Savannah Daily Morning News

Semi-Weekly Mississippian

Sun (Baltimore)

Times Dispatch (Richmond)

Trenton State Gazette

Washington Daily Union

Washington Evening Star

Weekly Raleigh Register

Weekly Wisconsin Patriot

Published Correspondence, Diaries, Memoirs, and Public Papers

Adams, Charles Francis. *Charles Francis Adams, 1835–1915: An Autobiography*. Boston: Houghton Mifflin, 1916.

Adams, Henry. *The Letters of Henry Adams*. Edited by J. C. Levenson, Ernest Samuels, Charles Vandersee, and Viola Hopkins Winner. 6 vols. Cambridge, Mass.: Harvard University Press, 1982.

Ambler, Charles Henry, ed. *Correspondence of Robert M. T. Hunter, 1826–1876*. New York: Da Capo Press, 1971.

Appleton, William. *Selections from the Diaries of William Appleton*. Boston: privately printed, 1922.

Avary, Myrta Lockett, ed. *Recollections of Alexander H. Stephens: His Diary Kept When a Prisoner at Fort Warren, Boston Harbour, 1865*. New York: Doubleday, Page, 1910.

Barnes, Thurlow Weed. *Memoir of Thurlow Weed*. Boston: Houghton Mifflin, 1884.

Basler, Roy P., ed. *The Collected Works of Abraham Lincoln*. 9 vols. New Brunswick, N.J.: Rutgers University Press, 1955.

Beale, Howard K., ed. *The Diary of Edward Bates, 1859–1866*. Washington, D.C.: Government Printing Office, 1933.

Belmont, August. *Letters, Speeches and Addresses of August Belmont*. Privately published, 1890.

Benton, Thomas Hart. *Thirty Years' View: A History of the Working of the American Government for Thirty Years, from 1820 to 1850*. 2 vols. New York: D. Appleton, 1857.

Biggs, Asa. *Autobiography of Asa Biggs: Including a Journal of a Trip from North Carolina to New York in 1832*. Raleigh: Edwards & Broughton Printing, 1915.

Brainard, Charles Henry. *John Howard Payne: A Biographical Sketch of the Author of "Home, Sweet Home."* Washington, D.C.: G. A. Coolidge, 1885.

Bright, Jesse. "Some Letters of Jesse Bright to William H. English (1842–1863)." *Indiana Magazine of History* 30 (December 1934): 370–92.

Brooks, Robert P., ed. "Howell Cobb Papers." *Georgia Historical Quarterly* 5 (June 1921): 50–61.

Busey, Samuel C. *Personal Reminiscences and Recollections of Forty-Six Years Membership in the Medical Society of the District of Columbia, and Residence in This City, with Biographical Sketches of Many of the Deceased Members.* Washington, D.C., 1895.

Butler, Lindley S., ed. *The Papers of David Settle Reid.* 2 vols. Raleigh, N.C.: Department of Cultural Resources Division of Archives and History, 1993.

Campbell, John A. *Reminiscences and Documents Relating to the Civil War during the Year 1865.* Baltimore: John Murphy, 1887.

Carson, James Petigru, ed. *Life, Letters, and Speeches of James Louis Petigru, the Union Man of South Carolina.* Washington, D.C.: W. H. Lowdermilk, 1920.

Chittenden, L. E. *Report of the Debates and Proceedings in the Secret Session of the Conference Convention, for Proposing Amendments to the Constitution of the United States, Held at Washington, D.C., in February, A.D. 1861.* New York: D. Appleton, 1864.

Claiborne, John F. H. *Life and Correspondence of John A. Quitman: Major-General, U.S.A., and Governor of the State of Mississippi.* 2 vols. New York: Harper and Brothers, 1860.

Clark, Raymond B., Jr., ed. "Observations on Washington Society: Mrs. W. C. Rives—Miss Maria L. Gordon Letters, 1842." *Albemarle County Historical Society Papers* 11 (1950–51): 53–61.

Clay, Virginia. *A Belle of the Fifties: Memoirs of Mrs. Clay, of Alabama Covering Social and Political Life in Washington and the South, 1853–66.* New York: Doubleday, Page, 1905.

Coleman, Mary Chapman, ed. *The Life of John J. Crittenden, with Selections from His Correspondence and Speeches.* 2 vols. Philadelphia: J. B. Lippincott, 1871.

Colton, Calvin, ed. *The Private Correspondence of Henry Clay.* New York: A. S. Barnes, 1855.

Corcoran, William Wilson. *A Grandfather's Legacy; Containing a Sketch of His Life and Obituary Notices of Some Members of His Family Together with Letters from His Friends.* Washington, D.C.: Henry Polkinhorn, Printer, 1879.

Cox, Samuel Sullivan. *Eight Years in Congress from 1857–1865.* New York: D. Appleton, 1865.

Crittenden, H. H. *The Crittenden Memoirs.* New York; G. P. Putnam's Sons, 1936.

Curtis, Benjamin R., ed. *Memoir of Benjamin Robbins Curtis, LL.D., with Some of his Professional and Miscellaneous Writings.* Boston: Little, Brown, 1879.

Cutler, Wayne, ed. *Correspondence of James K. Polk.* Vol. 11. Knoxville: University of Tennessee Press, 2009.

Davis, Jefferson. *The Papers of Jefferson Davis.* Edited by Lynda Lasswell Crist et al. 12 vols. Baton Rouge: Louisiana State University Press, 1991–2008.

———. "The Peace Commission—Letter from Ex-President Davis." *Southern Historical Society Papers* 4 (1877): 208–14.

———. *Rise and Fall of the Confederate Government.* 2 vols. New York: D. Appleton, 1912.

Davis, Reuben. *Recollections of Mississippi and Mississippians*. Boston: Houghton, Mifflin, 1890.

Davis, Varina Howell. *Jefferson Davis Ex-president of the Confederate States: A Memoir by His Wife*. 2 vols. New York: Belford, 1890.

Dickens, Charles. *American Notes for General Circulation*. 2nd ed. 2 vols. London: Chapman and Hall, 1842.

Drake, James Vaulx. *Life of General Robert Hatton Including His Most Important Public Speeches; Together with Much of His Washington and Army Correspondence*. Nashville, Tenn.: Marshall & Bruce, 1867.

Eckloff, Christian F. *Memoirs of a Senate Page (1855–1859)*. New York: Broadway, 1909.

Ellet, Elizabeth Fries. *Court Circles of the Republic*. Hartford, Conn.: Hartford Publishing, 1870.

Etiquette at Washington: Together with the Customs Adopted by Polite Society, in the Other Cities of the United States. 3rd ed. Baltimore: Murphy, 1857.

Foote, Henry S. *Casket of Reminiscences*. Washington, D.C.: Chronicle, 1874.

Fontaine, Felix G. *Trial of the Hon. Daniel E. Sickles for Shooting Philip Barton Key, Esq. . . .* New York: R. M. DeWitt, 1859.

French, Benjamin Brown. *Witness to the Young Republic: A Yankee's Journal, 1828–1870*. Edited by Donald B. Cole and John J. McDonough. Hanover, N.H.: University Press of New England, 1989.

French, Francis O. *Growing Up on Capitol Hill: A Young Washingtonian's Journal, 1850–1852*. Edited by John J. McDonough. Washington, D.C.: Library of Congress, 1998.

Graf, Le Roy P., and Ralph W. Haskins, eds. *The Papers of Andrew Johnson*. 16 vols. Knoxville: University of Tennessee Press, 1967–2000.

Grant, Ulysses S. *The Papers of Ulysses S. Grant*. Edited by John Y. Simon. 29 vols. Carbondale: Southern Illinois University Press, 1967–2008.

———. *Personal Memoirs of U. S. Grant*. 2 vols. New York: Charles L. Webster, 1886.

Haley, William D., ed. *Philip's Washington Described: A Complete View of the American Capital, and the District of Columbia, with Many Notices Historical, Topographical, and Scientific of the Seat of Government*. New York: Rudd & Carleton, 1861.

Hamilton, J. G. De Roulhac, ed. *The Papers of William Alexander Graham*. 8 vols. Raleigh: State Department of Archives and History, 1957–92.

Hay, Melba Porter, ed. *The Papers of Henry Clay*. 11 vols. Lexington: University Press of Kentucky, 1992.

Herr, Pamela, and Mary Lee Spence, eds. *The Letters of Jesse Benton Frémont*. Urbana: University of Illinois Press, 1993.

Hollcroft, Temple R., ed. "A Congressman's Letters on the Speaker Election in the Thirty-Fourth Congress." *Mississippi Valley Historical Review* 43 (1956–57): 444–58.

Hunter, Martha T. *A Memoir of Robert M. T. Hunter*. Washington, D.C.: Neale, 1903.

Hunter, Robert M. T. "The Peace Commission of 1865." *Southern Historical Society Papers* 3 (1877): 168–76.

Johannsen, Robert W., ed. *The Letters of Stephen A. Douglas*. Urbana: University of Illinois Press, 1961.

Johnston, Frontis W., ed. *The Papers of Zebulon Baird Vance*. 2 vols. Raleigh: State Department of Archives and History, 1963.

Jones, John B. *A Rebel War Clerk's Diary at the Confederate State Capital*. 2 vols. Philadelphia: J. B. Lippincott, 1866.

Julian, George Washington. *The Life of Joshua R. Giddings*. Chicago: A. C. McClurg, 1892.

———. *Political Recollections, 1840 to 1872*. Chicago: Janson, McClurg, 1884.

Keyes, Erasmus Darwin. *Fifty Years Observation of Men and Events, Civil and Military*. New York: Charles Scribner's Sons, 1884.

King, Horatio. *Turning on the Light*. Philadelphia: J. B. Lippincott, 1895.

Lanman, Charles. *Bohn's Handbook of Washington*. Washington, D.C.: Casmir Bohn, 1858.

Lee, Virginia Jeans, ed. *Wartime Washington: The Civil War Letters of Elizabeth Blair Lee*. Urbana: University of Illinois Press, 1991.

Leech, Margaret. *Reveille in Washington, 1860–1865*. New York: Harper Brothers, 1941.

Levenson, J. C., et al., eds. *The Letters of Henry Adams*. 3 vols. Cambridge, Mass.: Harvard University Press, 1982.

Mackay, Alex. *The Western World; or, Travels in the United States in 1846–1847: Exhibiting them in their latest development, social, political, and industrial; including a chapter on California*. 2 vols. Philadelphia: Lea & Blanchard, 1849.

Meade, George Gordon, ed. *Life and Letters of George Gordon Meade, Major General United States Army*. 2 vols. New York: Charles Scribner's Sons, 1913.

Meriwether, Robert L. "Preston S. Brooks on the Caning of Charles Sumner." *South Carolina Historical and Genealogical Magazine* 52 (January 1951): 1–4.

McClure, Alexander K. *Colonel Alexander K. McClure's Recollections of a Half Century*. Salem, Mass.: Salem Press, 1902.

McClure, James P., Peg A. Lamphier, and Erika M. Kreger, eds. *"Spur Up Your Pegasus": Family Letters of Salmon, Kate, and Nettie Chase, 1844–1873*. Kent, Ohio: Kent State University Press, 2009.

Moore, John Bassett, ed. *The Works of James Buchanan, Comprising His Speeches, State Papers, and Private Correspondence*. Philadelphia: J. B. Lippincott, 1909.

Morrison, O. H. *Morrison's Stranger's Guide and Etiquette for Washington City and Its Vicinity*. Washington, D.C.: W. H. & O. H. Morrison, 1860.

Nichols, Roy F., ed. "The Library: The Mystery of the Dallas Papers I." *Pennsylvania Magazine of History and Biography* 73 (July 1949): 349–92.

———. "The Library: The Mystery of the Dallas Papers II; Diary and Letters of George M. Dallas, December 4, 1848–March 6, 1849." *Pennsylvania Magazine of History and Biography* 73 (October 1949): 475–517.

Niven, John, ed. *The Salmon P. Chase Papers*. 3 vols. Kent, Ohio: Kent State University Press, 1993–1996.

O'Brien, Michael, ed. *An Evening When Alone: Four Journals of Single Women in the South, 1827–1867*. Charlottesville: Published for the Southern Texts Society by the University Press of Virginia, 1993.

Palmer, Beverly Wilson, ed. *The Selected Letters of Charles Sumner*. Boston: Northeastern University Press, 1990.

Palmer, George Thomas, ed. "Letters from Lyman Trumbull to John M. Palmer, 1854–1848." *Journal of the Illinois State Historical Society* 16 (1923–24): 20–41.

Parker, John A. *"The Missing Link": What Led to the War, or the Secret History of the Kansas-Nebraska Bill*. Washington, D.C.: Gray & Clarkson, Printers and Publishers, 1886.

Phillips, Ulrich B., ed. "The Correspondence of Robert Toombs, Alexander Stephens, and Howell Cobb." *Annual Report of the American Historical Association for 1911.* Vol. 2. Washington, D.C., 1913.

Pierce, Franklin. "Some Papers of Franklin Pierce, 1852–1862." *American Historical Review* 10 (January 1905): 350–70.

Pike, James S. *First Blows of the Civil War: The Ten Years of Preliminary Conflict in the United States.* New York: American News, 1879.

Poore, Ben Perley. *Perley's Reminiscences of Sixty Years in the National Metropolis.* 2 vols. Philadelphia: Hubbard Brothers, 1886.

Pryor, Mrs. Roger A. *Reminiscences of Peace and War.* New York: Macmillan, 1905.

Quaife, Milo Milton, ed. *The Diary of James K. Polk during his Presidency, 1845 to 1849.* Repr. ed. 4 vols. New York: Kraus Reprint, 1970.

Richardson, James D., ed. *A Compilation of the Messages and Papers of the Presidents, 1789–1897.* 10 vols. Washington, D.C.: Bureau of National Literature and Art, 1900.

Roberts, Madge Thornall, ed. *The Personal Correspondence of Sam Houston.* 4 vols. Denton: University of North Texas Press, 1998.

Rothernberg, Marc, ed. *The Papers of Joseph Henry.* 12 vols. Washington, D.C.: Smithsonian Institution, 1972–2007.

Rowland, Dunbar, ed. *Jefferson Davis, Constitutionalist: His Letters, Papers and Speeches.* 10 vol. Jackson: Mississippi Department of Archives and History, 1923.

Sargent, Nathan. *Public Men and Events from the Commencement of Mr. Monroe's Administration, in 1817, to the Close of Mr. Fillmore's Administration, in 1853.* 2 vols. Philadelphia: J. B. Lippincott, 1875.

Scarborough, William Kauffman, ed. *The Diary of Edmund Ruffin.* 2 vols. Baton Rouge: Louisiana State University Press, 1972.

Severance, Frank H., ed. "Millard Fillmore Papers, Volume Two." *Publications of the Buffalo Historical Society* 11 (1907).

Seward, Frederick W., ed. *Reminiscences of a War-Time Statesman and Diplomat, 1830–1915.* New York: G. P. Putnam's Sons, 1916.

———. *Seward at Washington, Senator and Secretary of State: A Memoir of His Life with Selections from His Letters, 1846–1861.* New York: Derby and Miller, 1891.

Seward, William H. *Remarks of William H. Seward in Memory of Thomas J. Rusk, Deceased, Late Senator from Texas, in the Senate of the United States, January 19, 1858.* Washington, D.C.: Buell & Blanchard, Printers, 1858.

Shanks, Henry Thomas, ed. *The Papers of Willie Person Mangum.* 5 vols. Raleigh, N.C.: State Department of Archives and History, 1950.

Snyder, Charles M. *The Lady and the President: The Letters of Dorothea Dix and Millard Fillmore.* Lexington: University Press of Kentucky, 1975.

Staples, Arthur G., ed. *The Letters of John Fairfield, a Representative in Congress from 1835 to 1837; A Member of the Senate of the United States from 1843 to 1847.* Lewiston, Maine: Lewiston Journal, 1922.

Stegmaier, Mark J. *Henry Adams in the Secession Crisis: Dispatches to the "Boston Daily Advertiser," December 1860–March 1861.* Baton Rouge: Louisiana State University Press, 2012.

Steiner, Bernard C., ed. "Some Letters from the Correspondence of James Alfred Pearce." *Maryland Historical Magazine* 16 (1921): 150–78.

Stephens, Alexander H. *A Constitutional View of the Late War between the States; Its Causes, Character, Conduct and Results. Presented in a Series of Colloquies at Liberty Hall.* 2 vols. Philadelphia: National, 1870.

Stockton, Thomas H. *Address by Thomas H. Stockton, Chaplain U.S.H.R. Delivered in the Hall of the House of Representatives on the Day of National Humiliation, Fasting and Prayer, Friday, January 4, 1861.* Washington, D.C.: Printed by Lemuel Towers, 1861.

Strode, Huston, ed. *Jefferson Davis: Private Letters, 1823–1889.* New York: Harcourt Brace Jovanovich, 1966.

Sunderland, Byron. "Washington as I First Knew It." *Records of the Columbia Historical Society, Washington, D.C.* Washington, D.C.: Published by the Society, 1902.

Tayloe, Benjamin O. *In Memoriam: Benjamin Ogle Tayloe.* Philadelphia: Sherman & Co., Printers, 1872.

———. *Our Neighbors on La Fayette Square.* Washington, D.C.: Junior League of Washington, 1872.

Thorndike, Rachel Sherman, ed. *The Sherman Letters: Correspondence between General and Senator Sherman from 1837 to 1891.* New York: Charles Scribner's Sons, 1894.

Townsend, George Alfred. *Historic Sketches at Washington. Containing a Full Record of the Origin and Early History of Washington City and Its Founders, Together with a Detailed Account of Its Growth, Its Public Buildings, the Style and Extravagance of Living There, and a Description of the Inside Workings of the Lobby, and the Various Departments of the Government.* Hartford, Conn.: James Betts, 1877.

Tyler, Lyon Gardiner. *The Letters and Times of the Tylers.* 2 vols. Richmond, Va.: Whittet & Shepperson, 1885.

Wallace, Sarah Agnes, ed. "'Letters of the Presidentess': Julia Gardiner Tyler, 1844–1845." *Daughters of the American Revolution Magazine* 87 (1953): 641–46.

Welles, Gideon. *Diary of Gideon Welles, Secretary of the Navy under Lincoln and Johnson.* 2 vols. Boston: Houghton Mifflin, 1911.

Wentworth, John. *Congressional Reminiscences, Adams, Benton, Calhoun, Clay, and Webster: An Address.* Chicago: Fergus Printing Company, 1882.

Wilson, Clyde N., and Shirley Bright Cook, eds. *The Papers of John C. Calhoun.* 18 vols. Columbia: University of South Carolina Press, 1969–2003.

Wiltse, Charles M., and Michael J. Birkner, eds. *The Papers of Daniel Webster.* 7 vols. Hanover, N.H.: University Press of New England, 1986.

Windle, Mary J. *Life in Washington, and Life Here and There.* Philadelphia: J. B. Lippincott, 1859.

Winthrop, Robert C., Jr. *A Memoir of Robert C. Winthrop.* Boston: Little Brown, 1897.

Wyeth, S. D. *The Federal City; or, Ins and Abouts of Washington.* Washington, D.C.: Gibson Brothers, 1865.

Younger, Edward. *Inside the Confederate Government: The Diary of Robert Garlick Hill Kean.* New York: Oxford University Press, 1957.

Zevery, Douglas. "Old Houses on C Street and Those Who Lived There." *Records of the Columbia Historical Society, Washington D.C.* Washington, D.C.: Published by the Society, 1902.

Secondary Sources

Alexander, Thomas. *Sectional Stress and Party Strength: A Study of Roll-Call Voting Patterns in the United States House of Representatives, 1836–1860*. Nashville: Vanderbilt Press, 1967.

Allen, William C. *History of the United States Capitol: A Chronicle of Design, Construction, and Politics*. Sen. Doc. 106-29, 106th Cong., 2nd Sess. Washington, D.C.: Government Printing Office, 2001.

Allgor, Catherine. *Parlor Politics: In Which the Ladies of Washington Help Build a City and a Government*. Charlottesville: University of Virginia Press, 2000.

Ames, William E. *History of the* National Intelligencer. Chapel Hill: University of North Carolina Press, 1972.

Ashworth, John. *Slavery, Capitalism, and Politics in the Antebellum Republic*. Vol. 1, *Commerce and Compromise, 1820–1850*. New York: Cambridge University Press, 1995.

———. *Slavery, Capitalism, and Politics in the Antebellum Republic*. Vol. 2, *The Coming of the Civil War 1850–1861*. New York: Cambridge University Press, 2007.

Ayers, Edward L. *In the Presence of Mine Enemies: The Civil War in the Heart of America, 1859–1863*. New York: W. W. Norton, 2003.

———. *What Caused the Civil War: Reflections on the South and Southern History*. New York: W. W. Norton, 2005.

Baker, Jean H. *Affairs of Party: The Political Culture of Northern Democrats in the Mid-Nineteenth Century*. Ithaca, N.Y.: Cornell University Press, 1983.

———. *James Buchanan*. New York: Henry Holt, 2004.

Baker, Paula. "The Domestication of Politics: Women and American Political Society, 1780–1920." *American Historical Review* 89 (June 1984): 620–47.

Bauer, K. Jack. *Zachary Taylor: Soldier, Planter, Statesman of the Old Southwest*. Baton Rouge: Louisiana State University Press, 1985.

Barney, William L. *The Secessionist Impulse: Alabama and Mississippi in 1860*. Tuscaloosa: University of Alabama Press, 1974.

Barringer, William E. *Lincoln Day by Day: A Chronology, 1809–1848*. 3 vols. Washington, D.C.: Lincoln Sesquicentennial Commission, 1960.

Beale, Marie. *Decatur House and Its Inhabitants*. Washington, D.C.: National Trust for Historic Preservation, 1954.

Bednar, Michael. *L'Enfant's Legacy: Public Open Spaces in Washington, D.C.* Baltimore: Johns Hopkins University Press, 2006.

Beeman, Richard. *Plain, Honest Men: The Making of the American Constitution*. New York: Random House, 2010.

Belko, Stephen. *The Invincible Duff Green: Whig of the West*. Columbia: University of Missouri Press, 2006.

Belohlavek, John M. *Broken Glass: Caleb Cushing and the Shattering of the Union*. Kent, Ohio: Kent State University Press, 2005.

Bender, Thomas. *Community and Social Change in America*. Baltimore: Johns Hopkins University Press, 1978.

Bensel, Richard. *The American Ballot Box in the Mid-Nineteenth Century*. New York: Cambridge University Press, 2004.

Benson, T. Lloyd. *The Caning of Senator Sumner*. Belmont, Calif.: Thompson Learning, 2004.

Berlin, Ira. *Slaves without Masters: The Free Negro in the Antebellum South*. New York: Pantheon Books, 1974.

Berry, Stephen W., II. *All That Makes a Man: Love and Ambition in the Civil War South*. New York: Oxford University Press, 2003.

Bogue, Allan. *The Congressman's Civil War*. New York: Cambridge University Press, 1989.

Bogue, Allan, and Mark Paul Marlaire. "Of Mess and Men: The Boardinghouse and Congressional Voting, 1821–1842." *American Journal of Political Science* 19, no. 2 (May 1975).

Boritt, Gabor S. *Lincoln and the Economics of the American Dream*. Memphis, Tenn.: Memphis State University Press, 1978.

Bowman, Shearer Davis. *At the Precipice: Americans North and South during the Secession Crisis*. Chapel Hill: University of North Carolina Press, 2010.

Brandt, Nat. *The Congressman Who Got Away with Murder*. Syracuse, N.Y.: Syracuse University Press, 1991.

Brooke, John L. "Ancient Lodges and Self-Created Societies: Voluntary Association and the Public Sphere in the Early Republic." In *Launching the "Extended Republic": The Federalist Era*, edited by Ronald Hoffman and Peter J. Albert, 273–359. Charlottesville: University Press of Virginia, 1996.

———. *Columbia Rising: Civil Life on the Upper Hudson from the Revolution to the Age of Jackson*. Chapel Hill: University of North Carolina Press, 2010.

Brown, Thomas J. *Dorothea Dix: New England Reformer*. Cambridge, Mass.: Harvard University Press, 1998.

Brudnick, Ida A. "Salaries of Members of Congress: A List of Payable Rates and Effective Dates, 1789–2008." *Congressional Research Service Report for Congress*, February 2008.

Bruns, Roger A. "The Assault on Charles Sumner 1856." In *Congress Investigates: A Documented History 1792–1974*, edited by Arthur M. Schlesinger Jr. and Roger Bruns, 2:3–102. New York: Chelsea House, 1983.

Bullock, Steven C. *Revolutionary Brotherhood: Freemasonry and the Transformation of the American Social Order, 1730–1840*. Chapel Hill: University of North Carolina Press, 1996.

Burin, Eric. *Slavery and the Peculiar Solution: A History of the American Colonization Society*. Gainesville: University Press of Florida, 2005.

Burlingame, Michael. *Abraham Lincoln: A Life*. 2 vols. Baltimore: Johns Hopkins University Press, 2008.

Burton, Orville Vernon. *The Age of Lincoln*. New York: Hill and Wang, 2007.

Carmichael, Peter S. *The Last Generation: Young Virginians in Peace, War, and Reunion*. Chapel Hill: University of North Carolina Press, 2005.

Carnes, Mark C. "Middle Class Men and the Solace of Fraternal Ritual." In *Meanings for Manhood: Constructions of Masculinity in Victorian America*, edited by Mark C. Carnes and Clyde Griffen, 37–66. Chicago: University of Chicago Press, 1990.

Carrier, Lyman. "The United States Agricultural Society, 1852–1860: Its Relation to the Origin of the United States Department of Agriculture and the Land Grant Colleges." *Agricultural History* 2 (October 1937): 278–88.

Carwardine, Richard J. *Evangelicals and Politics in Antebellum America*. Knoxville: University of Tennessee Press, 1997.

———. *Lincoln*. London: Pearson Education, 2003.

Chambers, William Nisbet. *Old Bullion Benton, Senator from the New West: Thomas Hart Benton, 1782–1858*. Boston: Little, Brown, 1956.

Childers, Robert Christopher. "Popular Sovereignty, Slavery in the Territories, and the South, 1785–1860." Ph.D. diss., Louisiana State University, 2010.

Cohen, Henry. *Business and Politics in America from the Age of Jackson to the Civil War: A Career Biography of W. W. Corcoran*. Westport, Conn.: Greenwood, 1971.

Cole, Arthur C. *The Whig Party in the South*. Washington, D.C.: American Historical Association, 1914.

Cook, Robert J., William L. Barney, and Elizabeth R. Varon, *Secession Winter: When the Union Fell Apart*. Baltimore: Johns Hopkins University Press, 2013.

Cooper, William J., Jr. "The Critical Signpost on the Journey toward Secession." *Journal of Southern History* 67 (February 2011): 3–16.

———. *Jefferson Davis, American*. New York: Alfred A. Knopf, 2000.

———. *The South and the Politics of Slavery, 1828–1856*. Baton Rouge: Louisiana State University Press, 1978.

———. *We Have the War upon Us: The Onset of the Civil War, November 1860–April 1861*. New York: Alfred A. Knopf, 2012.

Coryell, Janet L. "Superseding Gender: The Role of the Woman Politico in Antebellum Partisan Politics." In *Women and the Unstable State in Nineteenth-Century America*, edited by Alison M. Parker and Stephanie Cole, 84–112. College Station: Texas A&M University Press, 2000.

Crofts, Daniel W. *Reluctant Confederates: Upper South Unionists in the Secession Crisis*. Chapel Hill: University of North Carolina Press, 1989.

———. "A Reluctant Unionist: John A. Gilmer and Lincoln's Cabinet." *Civil War History* 24 (September 1978): 225–49.

———. "The Southern Opposition and the Crisis of Union." In *A Political Nation: New Directions in Mid-Nineteenth-Century American Political History*, edited by Gary W. Gallagher and Rachel A. Shelden, 85–111. Charlottesville: University of Virginia Press, 2012.

Cross, Coy F. *Justin Smith Morrill: Father of the Land Grant Colleges*. East Lansing: Michigan State University Press, 1999.

Current, Richard N. *The Lincoln Nobody Knows*. New York: Hill and Wang, 1958.

David, James Corbett. "The Politics of Emasculation: The Caning of Charles Sumner and Elite Ideologies of Manhood in the Mid-Nineteenth Century United States." *Gender and History* 19 (August 2007): 324–45.

Davis, William C. *The Union That Shaped the Confederacy: Robert Toombs and Alexander Stephens*. Lawrence: University Press of Kansas, 2001.

Dew, Charles B. *Apostles of Disunion: Southern Secession Commissioners and the Causes of the Civil War*. Charlottesville: University of Virginia Press, 2001.

Donald, David Herbert. *Charles Sumner and the Coming of the Civil War*. New York: Alfred A. Knopf, 1960.

———. *Lincoln*. New York: Simon & Schuster, 1996.

———. *"We Are Lincoln Men": Abraham Lincoln and His Friends*. New York: Simon & Schuster, 2003.

Donald, David Herbert, Jean Harvey Baker, and Michael F. Holt. *The Civil War and Reconstruction*. New York: W. W. Norton, 2001.

Dorsey, Bruce. *Reforming Men and Women: Gender in the Antebellum City*. Ithaca, N.Y.: Cornell University Press, 2002.

Durden, Robert F. *The Gray and the Black: The Confederate Debate on Emancipation*. Baton Rouge: Louisiana State University Press, 1972.

Earle, Jonathan. *Jacksonian Antislavery and the Politics of Free Soil, 1824–1854*. Chapel Hill: University of North Carolina Press, 2004.

Egerton, Douglas E. *Year of Meteors: Stephen Douglas, Abraham Lincoln, and the Election That Brought on the Civil War*. New York: Bloomsbury Press, 2010.

Egnal, Marc. *Clash of Extremes: The Economic Origins of the Civil War*. New York: Hill and Wang, 2009.

Etcheson, Nicole. *Bleeding Kansas: Contested Liberty in the Civil War Era*. Lawrence: University Press of Kansas, 2004.

Eubank, Damon R. *In the Shadow of the Patriarch: The John J. Crittenden Family in War and Peace*. Macon, Ga.: Mercer University Press, 2009.

Eyal, Yonatan. *The Young America Movement and the Transformation of the Democratic Party, 1828–1861*. New York: Cambridge University Press, 2007.

Fehrenbacher, Don E. *The Dred Scott Case, Its Significance in American Law and Politics*. New York: Oxford University Press, 1978.

———. *Prelude to Greatness: Abraham Lincoln in the 1850s*. Stanford, Calif.: Stanford University Press, 1962.

———. *Sectional Crisis and Southern Constitutionalism*. Baton Rouge: Louisiana State University Press, 1995.

Feller, Daniel. "A Brother in Arms: Benjamin Tappan and the Anti-slavery Democracy." *Journal of American History* 88 (June 2001): 48–74.

Ferris, Norman B. "Lincoln and Seward in Civil War Diplomacy: Their Relationship at the Outset Reexamined." *Journal of the Abraham Lincoln Association* 12 (Spring 1991): 21–42.

Findley, Paul. *A. Lincoln, the Crucible of Congress: The Years Which Forged His Greatness*. Fairfield, Calif.: James Stevenson, 1979.

Finkelman, Paul. *Dred Scott v. Sandford: A Brief History with Documents*. Boston: Bedford Books, 1997.

Finkelman, Paul, and Donald Kennon, eds. *In the Shadow of Freedom: The Politics of Slavery in the National Capital*. Athens: Ohio University Press, 2011.

Fleche, Andrew M. *The Revolution of 1861: The American Civil War in the Age of Nationalist Conflict*. Chapel Hill: University of North Carolina Press, 2012.

Fogel, Robert William. *Without Consent or Contract: The Rise and Fall of American Slavery*. New York: W. W. Norton, 1989.

Fogel, Robert William, and Stanley L. Engerman. *Time on the Cross: The Economics of American Negro Slavery*. New York: Little Brown, 1974.

Foner, Eric. *The Fiery Trial: Abraham Lincoln and American Slavery*. New York: W. W. Norton, 2010.

———. *Free Soil, Free Labor, Free Men: The Ideology of the Republican Party before the Civil War*. New York: Oxford University Press, 1970.

———. "The Wilmot Proviso Revisited." *Journal of American History* 56, no. 2 (September 1969): 262–79.

Forbes, Robert Pierce. *The Missouri Compromise and Its Aftermath: Slavery and the Meaning of America*. Chapel Hill: University of North Carolina Press, 2007.

Ford, Lacy K. *Deliver Us from Evil: The Slavery Question in the Old South*. New York: Oxford University Press, 2009.

Foreman, Amanda. *A World on Fire: Britain's Crucial Role in the American Civil War*. New York: Random House, 2010.

Formisano, Ronald. *The Transformation of American Political Culture: Massachusetts Parties, 1790s-1840s*. New York: Oxford University Press, 1983.

Fredrickson, George M. *The Black Image in the White Mind: The Debate on Afro-American Character and Destiny, 1817–1914*. New York: Harper & Row, 1971.

Freehling, William W. *The Road to Disunion*. Vol. 1, *Secessionists at Bay, 1776–1854*. New York: Oxford University Press, 1990.

———. *The Road to Disunion*. Vol. 2, *Secessionists Triumphant, 1854–1861*. New York: Oxford University Press, 2007.

Freehling, William W., and Craig M. Simpson, eds. *Secession Debated: Georgia's Showdown in 1860*. New York: Oxford University Press, 1992.

Freeman, Joanne. *Affairs of Honor: National Politics in the New Republic*. New Haven, Conn.: Yale University Press, 2001.

———. "The Culture of Congress in the Age of Jackson." *History Now* 22 (December 2009), http://www.gilderlehrman.org/history-by-era/jackson-lincoln/essays/culture-congress-age-jackson.

Fuller, A. James. "The Last True Whig: John Bell and the Politics of Compromise in 1860." In *The Election of 1860 Reconsidered*, edited by A. James Fuller, 103–39. Kent, Ohio: Kent State University Press, 2013.

Gallagher, Gary W. *The Confederate War*. Cambridge, Mass.: Harvard University Press, 1997.

———. *The Union War*. Cambridge, Mass.: Harvard University Press, 2011.

Gallaway, George B. *History of the House of Representatives*. New York: Thomas Y. Croswell, 1962.

Gamber, Wendy. *The Boardinghouse in Nineteenth Century America*. Baltimore: Johns Hopkins University Press, 2007.

Gienapp, William E. *The Origins of the Republican Party, 1852–1856*. New York: Oxford University Press, 1987.

Ginzberg, Lori D. *Untidy Origins: A Story of Woman's Rights in Antebellum New York*. Chapel Hill: University of North Carolina Press, 2005.

———. *Women and the Work of Benevolence: Morality, Politics, and Class in the 19th-Century United States*. New Haven, Conn.: Yale University Press, 1990.

Glendzel, Glen. "Political Culture: Genealogy of a Concept." *Journal of Interdisciplinary History* 28 (Autumn, 1997): 225–50.

Going, Charles Buxton. *David Wilmot, Free-Soiler: A Biography of the Great Advocate of the Wilmot Proviso*. New York: D. Appleton, 1924.

Grant, Susan-Mary. *North over South: Northern Nationalism and American Identity in the Antebellum Era*. Lawrence: University Press of Kansas, 2000.

Green, Constance M. *The Church on Lafayette Square: A History of St. John's Church, Washington, D.C., 1815–1970*. Washington, D.C.: Potomac Books, 1970.

———. *Washington, Village and Capital, 1800–1878*. Princeton, N.J.: Princeton University Press, 1962.

Greenberg, Amy S. *Manifest Manhood and the Antebellum American Empire*. New York: Cambridge University Press, 2005.

———. *A Wicked War: Polk, Clay, Lincoln, and the 1846 U.S. Invasion of Mexico*. New York: Alfred A. Knopf, 2012.

Greenberg, Kenneth S. *Honor and Slavery: Lies, Duels, Noses, Masks, Dressing as Women, Gifts, Strangers, Humanitarianism, Death, Slave Rebellions, the Proslavery Argument, Baseball, Hunting, and Gambling in the Old South*. Princeton, N.J.: Princeton University Press, 1996.

Guelzo, Allen C. *Lincoln and Douglas: The Debates That Defined America*. New York: Simon & Schuster, 2004.

Gugliotta, Guy. *Freedom's Cap: The United States Capitol and the Coming of the Civil War*. New York: Hill and Wang, 2012.

Gunderson, Robert Gray. *Old Gentlemen's Convention: The Washington Peace Conference of 1861*. Madison: University of Wisconsin Press, 1961.

Gutman, Herbert. *Slavery and the Numbers Game: A Critique of Time on the Cross*. Urbana: University of Illinois Press, 1975.

Hahn, Steven. *A Nation under Our Feet: Black Political Struggles in the Rural South from Slavery to the Great Migration*. Cambridge, Mass.: Belknap Press of Harvard University Press, 2003.

Hamilton, Holman. *Prologue to Conflict: The Crisis and Compromise of 1850*. 2nd ed. Lexington: University Press of Kentucky, 2005.

Hansen, Karen. *A Very Social Time: Crafting Community in Antebellum New England*. Berkeley: University of California Press, 1994.

Harris, William C. "The Hampton Roads Peace Conference: A Final Test of Lincoln's Presidential Leadership." *Journal of the Abraham Lincoln Association* 21 (Winter 2000): 31–61.

Harrison, Robert. *Washington during the Civil War and Reconstruction: Race and Radicalism*. New York: Cambridge University Press, 2011.

Harrold, Stanley. *Subversives: Antislavery Community in Washington, D.C., 1828–1865*. Baton Rouge: Louisiana State University Press, 2003.

Hartog, Hendrig. "Lawyering, Husbands' Rights, and 'the Unwritten Law' in Nineteenth-Century America." *Journal of American History* 84 (June 1997): 67–96.

Heidler, David S., and Jeanne T. Heidler. *Henry Clay: The Essential American*. New York: Random House, 2010.

Hendrickson, David. *Union, Nation, or Empire: The American Debate over International Relations, 1789–1941*. Lawrence: University Press of Kansas, 2009.

Herrington, Philip Mills. "Agricultural and Architectural Reform in the Antebellum South: Fruitland at Augusta, Georgia." *Journal of Southern History* 78 (November 2012): 855–86.

Hess, Earl J. *Liberty, Virtue, and Progress: Northerners and Their War for the Union*. New York: Fordham University Press, 1997.

Hietala, Thomas R. *Manifest Design: American Exceptionalism and Empire*. Ithaca, N.Y.: Cornell University Press, 1985.

Hitchcock, William S. "Southern Moderates and Secession: Senator Robert M. T. Hunter's Call for Union." *Journal of American History* 59 (March 1973): 871–84.

Hoffer, Williamjames Hull. *The Caning of Charles Sumner: Honor, Idealism, and the Origins of the Civil War*. Baltimore: Johns Hopkins University Press, 2010.

Holt, Michael F. *Franklin Pierce*. New York: Times Books, 2010.

———. "Making and Mobilizing the Republican Party, 1854–1860." In *The Birth of the Grand Old Party: The Republicans First Generation*, edited by Robert F. Engs and Randall M. Miller, 29–59. Philadelphia: University of Pennsylvania Press, 2002.

———. *The Political Crisis of the 1850s*. New York: W. W. Norton, 1978.

———. *Political Parties and American Political Development: From the Age of Jackson to the Age of Lincoln*. Baton Rouge: Louisiana State University Press, 1992.

———. "Rethinking Nineteenth-Century American Political History." *Congress and the Presidency* 19 (Autumn 1992): 97–111.

———. *Rise and Fall of the American Whig Party: Jacksonian Politics and the Onset of the Civil War*. New York: Oxford University Press, 1999.

———. "Winding Roads to Recovery: The Whig Party from 1844 to 1848." In *Essays on American Antebellum Politics, 1840–1860*, edited by Stephen E. Maizlish and John J. Kushma, 121–65. College Station: Texas A&M University Press, 1982.

Holzer, Harold. *Lincoln President-Elect*. New York: Simon & Schuster, 2008.

Howe, Daniel Walker. *The Political Culture of the American Whigs*. Chicago: University of Chicago Press, 1984.

———. *What Hath God Wrought: The Transformation of America, 1815–1848*. New York: Oxford University Press, 2007.

Huston, James L. *Stephen A. Douglas and the Dilemmas of Democratic Equality*. Lanham, Md.: Rowman & Littlefield, 2007.

Irons, Charles F. *The Origins of Proslavery Christianity: White and Black Evangelicals in Colonial and Antebellum Virginia*. Chapel Hill: University of North Carolina Press, 2008.

Jacob, Kathryn Allamong. *Capital Elites: High Society in Washington, D.C. after the Civil War*. Washington, D.C.: Smithsonian Institution Press, 1995.

Jaffa, Harry V. *Crisis of the House Divided*. New York: Doubleday, 1959.

Johannsen, Robert W. *Stephen A. Douglas*. New York: Oxford University Press, 1973.

John, Richard. "Affairs of Office: The Executive Departments, the Election of 1828, and the Making of the Democratic Party." In *The Democratic Experiment: New Directions in American Political History*, edited by Meg Jacobs, William J. Novak, and Julian E. Zelizer, 50–84. Princeton University Press, 2003.

Kasson, John F. *Rudeness and Civility: Manners in Nineteenth-Century Urban America*. New York: Hill and Wang, 1990.

Keene, Jesse Lynn. *The Peace Convention of 1861*. Tuscaloosa, Ala.: Confederate Publishing, 1961.

Kimball, Gregg D. *American City, Southern Place: A Cultural History of Antebellum Richmond*. Athens: University of Georgia Press, 2000.

King, Doris Elizabeth. "The First-Class Hotel and the Age of the Common Man." *Journal of Southern History* 23 (May 1957): 173–88.

Kirkland, Edward Chase. *The Peacemakers of 1864*. New York: Macmillan, 1927.

Kirwan, Albert D. *John J. Crittenden: The Struggle for the Union*. Lexington: University Press of Kentucky, 1974.

Klein, Philip S. *James Buchanan: A Biography*. University Park: Pennsylvania State University Press, 1962.

Knupfer, Peter B. *The Union As It Is: Constitutional Unionism and Sectional Compromise, 1787–1861*. Chapel Hill: University of North Carolina Press, 1991.

Kolchin, Peter. *American Slavery, 1619–1877*. New York: Hill and Wang, 1993.

———. "More Time on the Cross? An Evaluation of Robert William Fogel's *Without Consent or Contract*." *Journal of Southern History* 58, no. 3 (August 1992): 491–502.

———. "Toward a Reinterpretation of Slavery." *Journal of Social History* 9 (Fall 1975): 99–113.

Kushner, Howard I. "Visions of the Northwest Coast: Gwin and Seward in the 1850s." *Western Historical Quarterly* 4 (July 1973): 295–306.

Lankford, Nelson D. *Cry Havoc! The Crooked Road to Civil War, 1861*. New York: Viking, 2007.

Latimer, Jon. *1812: War with America*. Cambridge, Mass.: Harvard University Press, 2007.

Lawson, Melinda. *Patriot Fires: Forging a New American Nationalism in the Civil War North*. Lawrence: University Press of Kansas, 2002.

Levine, Bruce. *Confederate Emancipation: Southern Plans to Free and Arm Slaves during the Civil War*. New York: Oxford University Press, 2006.

Lewis, Charlene Boyer. *Ladies and Gentlemen on Display: Planter Society at the Virginia Springs, 1790–1860*. Charlottesville: University of Virginia Press, 2001.

Maizlish, Stephen E. "The Meaning of Nativism and the Crisis of the Union: The Know-Nothing Movement in the Antebellum North." In *Essays on American Antebellum Politics, 1840–1860*, edited by Stephen E. Maizlish and John J. Kushma, 166–98. College Station: Texas A&M University Press, 1982.

———. *The Triumph of Sectionalism: The Transformation of Ohio Politics, 1844–1856*. Kent, Ohio: Kent State University Press, 1983.

Malin, James C. *The Nebraska Question, 1852–1854*. Lawrence, Kans.: n.p., 1953.

Maltz, Earl M. *Dred Scott and the Politics of Slavery*. Lawrence: University Press of Kansas, 2007.

Masur, Kate. *An Example for All the Land: Emancipation and the Struggle over Equality in Washington, D.C.* Chapel Hill: University of North Carolina Press, 2010.

Mathis, Robert Neil. "Preston Smith Brooks: The Man and His Image." *South Carolina Historical Magazine* 79 (October 1978): 296–310.

McClintock, Russell. *Lincoln and the Decision for War*. Chapel Hill: University of North Carolina Press, 2008.

McCurry, Stephanie. *Masters of Small Worlds: Yeoman Households, Gender Relations and the Political Culture of the Antebellum South Carolina Low Country*. New York: Oxford University Press, 1995.

McPherson, James M. *Battle Cry of Freedom: The Civil War Era*. New York: Oxford University Press, 1988.

Merk, Frederick. *Manifest Destiny and Mission in American History*. New York: Alfred A. Knopf, 1963.

Miner, Craig. *Seeding the Civil War: Kansas in the National News, 1854–1858*. Lawrence: University Press of Kansas, 2008.

Mintz, Steven. *Moralists and Modernizers: America's Pre–Civil War Reformers*. Baltimore: Johns Hopkins University Press, 1995.

Morrison, Chaplain. *Democratic Politics and Sectionalism: The Wilmot Proviso Controversy*. Chapel Hill: University of North Carolina Press, 1967.

Morrison, Michael A. "'New Territory versus No Territory': The Whig Party and the Politics of Western Expansion, 1846–1848." *Western Historical Quarterly* 23 (February 1992): 25–51.

———. *Slavery and the American West: The Eclipse of Manifest Destiny and the Coming of the Civil War*. Chapel Hill: University of North Carolina Press, 1997.

Nagel, Paul C. *One Nation Indivisible: The Union in American Thought, 1776–1861*. New York: Oxford University Press, 1964.

Neely, Mark E., Jr. *The Boundaries of American Political Culture in the Civil War Era*. Chapel Hill: University of North Carolina Press, 2005.

———. "The Kansas-Nebraska Act in American Political Culture: The Road to Bladensburg and the *Appeal of the Independent Democrats*." In *The Nebraska-Kansas Act of 1854*, edited by John R. Wunder and Joann M. Ross, 13–46. Lincoln: University of Nebraska Press, 2008.

———. *The Union Divided: Party Conflict in the Civil War North*. Cambridge, Mass.: Harvard University Press, 2002.

Nevins, Allan. *The Emergence of Lincoln*. 2 vols. New York: Charles Scribner and Sons, 1950.

Nichols, Roy F. *The Disruption of American Democracy*. New York: Free Press, 1948.

———. *Franklin Pierce, Young Hickory of the Granite Hills*. Philadelphia: University of Pennsylvania Press, 1958.

———. "The Kansas-Nebraska Act: A Century of Historiography." *Mississippi Valley Historical Review* 43 (September 1956): 187–212.

Noll, Mark A. *America's God: From Jonathan Edwards to Abraham Lincoln*. New York: Oxford University Press, 2002.

Olsen, Christopher J. *Political Culture and Secession in Mississippi: Masculinity, Honor, and the Antiparty Tradition, 1830–1860*. New York: Oxford University Press, 2005.

Onuf, Nicholas, and Peter Onuf. *Nations, Markets, and War: Modern History and the American Civil War*. Charlottesville: University of Virginia Press, 2006.

Ostrowski, Carl. *Books, Maps, and Politics: A Cultural History of the Library of Congress, 1783–1861*. Amherst: University of Massachusetts Press, 2004.

Parrish, William E. *David Rice Atchison: Border Politician*. Columbia: University of Missouri Press, 1961.

Pasley, Jeffrey L., Andrew W. Robertson, and David Waldstreicher, eds. *Beyond the Founders: New Approaches to the Political History of the Early American Republic*. Chapel Hill: University of North Carolina Press, 2004.

———. *"The Tyranny of Printers": Newspaper Politics and the Early American Republic*. Charlottesville: University of Virginia Press, 2001.

Perkins, Dexter. *A History of the Monroe Doctrine*. New York: Little Brown, 1963.

Perman, Michael. *Pursuit of Unity: A Political History of the American South*. Chapel Hill: University of North Carolina Press, 2001.

Pflugrad-Jackisch, Ami. *Brothers of a Vow: Secret Fraternal Orders and the Transformation of White Male Culture in Antebellum Virginia*. Athens: University of Georgia Press, 2010.

Pierce, Katherine Anna. "Networks of Disunion: Politics, Print Culture, and the Coming of the Civil War." Ph.D. diss., University of Virginia, 2006.

Pletcher, David M. *The Diplomacy of Annexation: Texas, Oregon, and the Mexican War*. Columbia: University of Missouri Press, 1973.

Potter, David M. "The Historian's Use of Nationalism and Vice Versa." *American Historical Review* 67 (1962): 924–50. Reprinted in Potter, *The South and the Sectional Conflict* (Baton Rouge: Louisiana State University Press, 1968), 34–83.

———. *The Impending Crisis, 1848–1861*. New York: Harper & Row, 1976.

———. *Lincoln and His Party in the Secession Crisis*. New Haven, Conn.: Yale University Press, 1942.

Press, Donald E. "South of the Avenue from Murder Bay to the Federal Triangle." *Records of the Columbia Historical Society*. Washington, D.C.: Historical Society of Washington, 1984.

Quigley, Paul D. H. "Patchwork Nation: Sources of Confederate Nationalism, 1848–1865." Ph.D. diss., University of North Carolina at Chapel Hill, 2006.

Rable, George C. *The Confederate Republic: A Revolution against Politics*. Chapel Hill: University of North Carolina Press, 1994.

Radomsky, Susan. "The Social Life of Politics: Washington's Official Society and the Emergence of a National Political Elite, 1800–1876." Ph.D. diss., University of Chicago, 2005.

Rakove, Jack N. *Revolutionaries: A New History of the Invention of America*. Boston: Houghton Mifflin, 2010.

Ramsdell, Charles W. "The Natural Limits of Slavery Expansions." *Mississippi Valley Historical Review* 16 (1929): 151–71.

Randall, James G. "The Blundering Generation." *Mississippi Valley Historical Review* 27 (June 1940): 3–28.

———. *Lincoln the President*. 2 vols. New York: Dodd, Meade, 1946.

Remini, Robert V. *The House: The History of the House of Representatives*. Washington, D.C.: Smithsonian Books, 2006.

Richards, Leonard L. *The Slave Power: The Free North and Southern Domination, 1780–1860*. Baton Rouge: Louisiana State University Press, 2000.

Riddle, Donald W. *Congressman Abraham Lincoln*. Urbana: University of Illinois Press, 1957.

Roberts, Allen B. *House Undivided: The Story of Freemasonry and the Civil War*. Richmond, Va.: Macoy Publishing and Masonic Supply, 1961.

Robertson, Andrew W. *The Language of Democracy: Political Rhetoric in the United States and Britain, 1790–1900*. Charlottesville: University of Virginia Press, 2005.

Rorabaugh, W. J. *The Alcoholic Republic: An American Tradition*. New York: Oxford University Press, 1979.

Rubin, Anne Sarah. *A Shattered Nation: The Rise and Fall of the Confederate Nation, 1861–1868*. Chapel Hill: University of North Carolina Press, 2005.

Ryan, Mary P. *Civic Wars: Democracy and Public Life in the American City during the Nineteenth Century*. Berkeley: University of California Press, 1997.

Sanders, Charles W., Jr. "Jefferson Davis and the Hampton Roads Peace Conference: 'To secure Peace to the two countries.'" *Journal of Southern History* 63 (November 1997): 803–26.

Schoonover, Thomas D. *Dollars over Dominion: The Triumph of Liberalism in Mexican–United States Relations, 1861–1867*. Baton Rouge: Louisiana State University Press, 1978.

Schott, Thomas E. *Alexander H. Stephens of Georgia, a Biography*. Baton Rouge: Louisiana State University Press, 1988.

Sellers, Charles. *James K. Polk: Continentalist, 1843–1846*. Princeton, N.J.: Princeton University Press, 1966.

Shalhope, Robert E. *Sterling Price: Portrait of a Southerner*. Columbia: University of Missouri Press, 1971.

Shelden, Rachel A. "Messmates' Union: Friendship, Politics, and Living Arrangements in the Capital City, 1845–1861. *Journal of the Civil War Era* 1 (December 2011): 453–80.

Siegenthaler, John. *James K. Polk*. New York: Henry Holt, 2003.

Silbey, Joel. "Congress in a Partisan Political Era." In *The American Congress: The Building of Democracy*, edited by Julian E. Zelizer, 139–52. New York: Houghton Mifflin, 2004.

———. *Party over Section: The Rough and Ready Presidential Election of 1848*. Lawrence: University Press of Kansas, 2009.

———. *The Shrine of Party: Congressional Voting Behavior, 1841–1852*. Pittsburg: University of Pittsburgh Press, 1967.

———. *Storm over Texas: The Annexation Controversy and the Road to Civil War*. New York: Oxford University Press, 2005.

Sinha, Manisha. "The Caning of Charles Sumner: Slavery, Race, and Ideology in the Age of the Civil War." *Journal of the Early Republic* 23 (Summer 2003): 233–62.

Skocpol, Theda, Marshall Ganz, and Ziad Munson. "A Nation of Organizers: The Institutional Origins of Civic Voluntarism in the United States." *American Political Science Review* 94 (September, 2000): 527–46.

Smith, Elbert B. *Francis Preston Blair*. New York: Macmillan, 1980.

Smith, William E. *The Francis Preston Blair Family in Politics*. 2 vols. New York: Macmillan, 1933.

Sowle, Patrick M. "The Conciliatory Republicans during the Winter of Secession." Ph.D. diss., Duke University, 1963.

———. "A Reappraisal of Seward's Memorandum of April 1, 1861." *Journal of Southern History* 33 (May 1967): 234–39.

Stampp, Kenneth M. *And the War Came: The North and the Secession Crisis, 1860–1861*. Baton Rouge: Louisiana State University Press, 1950.

———. "The Concept of a Perpetual Union." In *The Imperiled Union: Essays on the Background of the Civil War*, 3–36. New York: Oxford University Press, 1980.

Stegmaier, Mark. *Texas, New Mexico, and the Compromise of 1850*. Kent, Ohio: Kent State University Press, 1996.

Stenberg, Richard R. "The Motivation of the Wilmot Proviso." *Mississippi Valley Historical Review* 108 (March 1932): 532–41.

Summers, Mark. *The Plundering Generation: Corruption and the Crisis of Union, 1849–1861*. New York: Oxford University Press, 1988.

Tackett, Timothy. *Becoming a Revolutionary: The Deputies of the French National Assembly and the Emergence of a Revolutionary Culture, 1789–1790*. University Park: Pennsylvania State University Press, 1996.

Tarbell, Ida. *Boy Scouts' Life of Lincoln*. New York: Macmillan, 1922.

Thompson, William Y. *Robert Toombs of Georgia*. Baton Rouge: Louisiana State University Press, 1966.

Torget, Andrew. "Unions of Slavery: Slavery, Politics, and Secession in the Valley of Virginia." In *Crucible of the Civil War: Virginia from Secession to Commemoration*, edited by Edward L. Ayers, Gary W. Gallagher, and Andrew Torget, 9–34. Charlottesville: University of Virginia Press, 2006.

Towers, Frank. "Partisans, New History, and Modernization: The Historiography of the Civil War's Causes, 1861–2011." *Journal of the Civil War Era* 1, no. 2 (July 2011): 237–64.

Tyrrell, Ian R. *Sobering Up: From Temperance to Prohibition in Antebellum America, 1800–1860*. Westport, Conn.: Greenwood Press, 1979.

Underwood, Rodman L. *Stephen Russell Mallory: A Biography of the Confederate Navy Secretary and United States Senator*. Jefferson, N.C.: McFarland, 2005.

Varon, Elizabeth R. *Disunion! The Coming of the American Civil War, 1789–1859*. Chapel Hill: University of North Carolina Press, 2008.

———. *We Mean to Be Counted: White Women and Politics in Antebellum Virginia*. Chapel Hill: University of North Carolina Press, 1998.

Vorenberg, Michael. *Final Freedom: The Civil War, the Abolition of Slavery, and the Thirteenth Amendment*. Cambridge: Cambridge University Press, 2004.

Wakelyn, Jon L. *Confederates against the Confederacy: Essays on Leadership and Loyalty*. Westport, Conn.: Praeger Press, 2002.

Waldstreicher, David. *In the Midst of Perpetual Fetes: The Making of American Nationalism, 1776–1820*. Chapel Hill: University of North Carolina Press, 1997.

Wallner, Peter A. *Franklin Pierce: Martyr for the Union*. Concord, N.H.: Plaidswede, 2007.

Walters, Ronald G. *American Reformers, 1815–1860*. New York: Hill and Wang, 1978.

Wells, Damon. *Stephen Douglas: The Last Years, 1857–1861*. Austin: University Press of Texas, 1971.

White, G. Edward. *The Marshall Court and Cultural Change, 1815–1835*. Abridged edition. New York: Oxford University Press, 1991.

White, Jonathan W. *Abraham Lincoln and Treason in the Civil War: The Trials of John Merryman*. Baton Rouge: Louisiana State University Press, 2011.

Wiebe, Robert. *Self Rule: A Cultural History of American Democracy*. Chicago: University of Chicago Press, 1995.

Wilentz, Sean. *Chants Democratic: New York City and the Rise of the American Working Class, 1788–1850*. New York: Oxford University Press, 1984.

———. *The Rise of American Democracy: Jefferson to Lincoln*. New York: W. W. Norton, 2005.

Wongsrichanalai, Kanisorn. "The Burden of Their Class: College-Educated New Englanders and Leadership in the Civil War Era." Ph.D. diss., University of Virginia, 2010.

Wood, Kirsten. "'One Woman So Dangerous to Public Morals': Gender and Power in the Eaton Affair." *Journal of the Early Republic* 17 (Summer 1997): 237–75.

Woods, Michael E. "What Twenty-First-Century Historians Have Said about the Causes of Disunion: A Civil War Sesquicentennial Review of the Recent Literature." *Journal of American History* 99 (September 2012): 415–39.

Woodward, David E. "Abraham Lincoln, Duff Green, and the Mysterious Trumbull Letter." *Civil War History* 42 (September 1996): 211–19.

Wyatt-Brown, Bertram. *Southern Honor: Ethics and Behavior in the Old South*. New York: Oxford University Press, 1982.

Yearns, Wilfred B. *The Confederate Congress*. Athens: University of Georgia Press, 1960.

———. "The Peace Movement in the Confederate Congress." *Georgia Historical Quarterly* 41 (March 1957): 1–18.

Young, James Sterling. *The Washington Community, 1800–1828*. New York: Columbia University Press, 1966.

INDEX

Georgetown, 11, 114
Giddings, Joshua, 25, 61, 107–8
Gilmer, John, 177, 184, 188, 190
Gossip. *See* Rumor
Graham, William A., 80, 87, 112, 113, 127, 184
Grant, Ulysses S., 195–96
Greeley, Horace, 111, 153
Green, Duff, 107–8, 187–89
Grow, Galusha, 141
Grund, Francis, 90–91
Gwin, William, 31–33, 71, 113, 116, 117, 156, 160; as dinner guest, 85, 87

Hale, Artemas, 54, 150
Hale, John P., 8, 49, 111, 156, 178
Hamilton, James A., 90–92
Hamlin, Hannibal, 70, 110, 156, 157
Hammond, James Henry, 151, 156
Hampton Roads, 192–98
Hannegan, Edward, 106, 127, 128
Haskell, William T., 128
Hatton, Robert, 30, 37, 54–55, 80, 180; on liquor, 24, 125, 182–83
Haven, Solomon, 23, 40, 71, 80, 111, 124
Henry, Joseph. *See* Smithsonian Institution
Herbert, Philemon, 140–41
Hole in the Wall, 23–25
Holmes, Isaac, 87, 127
Hotels (Washington, D.C.), 10–11, 40, 51, 69, 73, 82, 142, 169, 191; and boarding arrangements, 2, 101–13, 153, 177–79; and secession crisis, 171–72, 174, 182–84; and Washington vices, 118, 124, 126, 133–34, 136, 139–40, 143. *See also* Brown's Hotel; Gambling; National Hotel; Willard's Hotel
House chamber, 24, 27–32, 39, 158
Houston, Sam, 13, 20, 27, 37, 63, 74–75, 79, 108–9, 131, 149, 153, 155–57; as dinner guest, 111–12; on liquor, 25–26, 58
Hülsemann, J. G., 83. *See also* Diplomats; Kossuth, Lajos
Hunt, Washington, 38, 151

Hunter, Robert M. T., 13, 156, 198–99; and F Street Mess, 54–55, 99–101; as dinner guest, 84, 92, 186; at Hampton Roads, 192–97

Iverson, Alfred, 156, 169

Johnson, Andrew, 110, 156
Johnson, Reverdy, 84, 130, 175, 182
Jones, George W. (Iowa), 156, 157, 160, 163
Jones, George W. (Tennessee), 88, 142
Jones, J. Glancy, 112–13, 200
Julian, George W., 125

Kansas-Nebraska Act of 1854, 3, 6, 20, 21, 60, 95, 114–15, 151, 187; consequences of, 120–23, 144–47, 153; and Democratic Party, 110–12, 117–19; and F Street Mess, 96–101
Keating, Thomas, 140–41
Keitt, Laurence, 121–23, 141
Kennedy, Anthony, 155–56
Kennedy, John P., 87, 152, 174
Kennedy, Joseph C. G., 53, 180
Key, Philip Barton, 137–40
Keyes, Erasmus, 186
King, James G., 19, 52, 79, 117, 127
King, John, 52, 117, 127
King, Preston, 38, 60, 156–57, 206–7 (n. 5)
King, Thomas Butler, 72, 106
King, William R., 81, 87, 92, 106, 160
Know-Nothings, 59–60, 145
Kossuth, Lajos, 83–84

Lafayette Square, 52, 67, 101, 112–18, 127, 179; and Corcoran, 89, 92, 136–38
Lecompton Constitution, 7, 37, 151, 153, 155, 187; moderate opposition to, 144–49, 165–66; origins of, 120–21
Library of Congress, 71–72, 104–5
Lincoln, Abraham, 6, 54, 56–59, 104, 107, 157, 163, 200; as congressman, 22, 41–48, 60–62; and 1858 senatorial campaign, 146–49; at Hampton Roads, 192–98; as president, 5, 172;

as president-elect, 167–90; and secession winter, 187–88; relationship with
Crittenden, 146–47, 165–66
Liquor, 2, 6, 14, 40, 58, 84–86, 108, 117,
133–35, 142, 153, 171, 178–81, 191, 193;
abuse of, 124–30; in Capitol building,
23–28; and violence, 120–21, 139
Lobbying, 11, 18, 39, 73, 80, 108, 129–30,
136, 163; and gambling, 134–35; and
Texas bonds, 67, 89–92

Mallory, Stephen R., 156, 160, 169–70, 190
Mangum, Willie, 30, 102, 106, 135, 176;
and alcohol, 24, 127, 130, 142
Mann, Horace, 19, 20, 22, 29, 50, 58, 91,
108; as dinner guest, 78, 85, 105
Marcy, William L., 69, 111, 114, 132, 142,
161
Marshall, Humphrey, 76, 134
Marshall, Tom, 25
Mason, James M., 51, 55, 87, 91, 132, 156,
181; and F Street Mess, 99–101
Mason-Dixon line. See Missouri Compro-
mise
McLean, John, 28, 56, 106, 180
Meredith, William, 74, 117, 127
Mexican Cession, 63–66, 76, 78, 90. See
also Compromise of 1850; Mexican War
Mexican War, 8, 15, 22, 41–44, 46, 63–65,
78; appropriation for, 14–15; Treaty
of Guadalupe-Hidalgo, 61. See also
Wilmot Proviso
Missouri Compromise, 78, 98–100, 108,
118–19
Mrs. Selden's boardinghouse, 44–45, 107,
146
Mrs. Sprigg's boardinghouse, 22, 48, 61,
107–8, 187
Montgomery, William, 140
Morehead, James T., 128
Morrill, Justin S., 49

Napier, Lord William, 82, 116. See also
Diplomats
Napoleon III, 193

National Hotel, 109–11, 133–34, 142,
178–79
Navy Yard, 11, 55
Nebraska Bill. See Kansas-Nebraska Act
of 1854
Nullification Crisis, 65

Odd Fellows, 6, 46, 58–59
Opposition party, 55, 155
Orr, James L., 52, 109, 114, 184
Outlaw, David, 19, 22, 27–28, 33, 36,
53–54, 57, 69, 75, 130, 135–36; and
boarding choices, 102–5

Paine, Robert Treat, 106, 131
Pairing off, 19–20
Palace of Fortune, 133–35
Parker, Theodore, 8, 143
Patronage, 62, 76–77, 85, 129–30, 135, 172,
176; and Democratic Party, 15, 100, 112
Peace Conference (Hampton Roads,
1865). See Hampton Roads
Peace Conference (Washington, D.C.,
1861), 171–78, 182, 185–86, 189
Pearce, James, 51, 93, 128, 134, 156–57, 181
Pendleton, Edward, 133–35
Pendleton, John C., 44–45, 54, 61–62
Pennington, William, 129, 158, 182, 186
Pennsylvania Avenue, 11–12, 71, 94,
121, 133, 157, 170, 174, 191; as central
housing location, 102–3, 109, 184
Phillips, Philip, 99–100, 114, 117–18, 170,
187
Pierce, Franklin, 60, 95–96, 111–12, 121,
161–62, 168; and alcohol, 126, 128; and
Kansas-Nebraska Act, 100, 118
Polk, James K., 18, 26, 37–38, 51, 77–78,
132, 162; cabinet, 74–75, 161; and
Mexican War, 15–16, 41–43, 61
Popular sovereignty, 97–99, 145
Pratt, Thomas, 82, 134
Presidential election: of 1848, 42–44,
61–62; of 1852, 83, 95; of 1860, 166,
167, 171–73, 184, 188
Preston, William (Kentucky), 130, 173

Preston, William B., 44, 54, 61–62, 117, 127, 173, 192
Price, Sterling, 18
Pugh, George, 27, 109, 156

Quorum, 14, 18, 20–22

Reid, David Settle, 52, 55, 107, 109, 150, 156
Republican Party, 126, 129, 144, 148, 198; and Crittenden compromise, 188–89; and election of 1860, 62, 172–73; and Lecompton Constitution debate, 145, 153–55, 158; reaction to Sumner caning, 123–24, 142
Rhett, Robert Barnwell, 160, 199
Rice, Henry M., 112
Richardson, William, 112, 140
Riggs, Elisha, 87–88, 184–85
Ritchie, Thomas, 52, 72, 91–92, 115, 117, 127, 132
Rockwell, John, 162–64
Rockwell, Julius, 151
Rumor, 23, 27, 88, 121, 126, 146, 167, 172, 185; within Washington community, 125, 134, 136–37
Rusk, Thomas, 42, 49, 129, 149, 151, 199; relationship with Truman Smith, 163–64

St. John's Church, 52–53, 179
Schenck, Robert, 106, 114
Schermerhorn, Abraham, 106
Scott, Winfield, 183, 186
Seaton, William, 53, 71, 185
Secession crisis, 4–5, 90, 166, 167–90
Senate Chamber, 28, 99, 149–50, 160, 168–70, 181; and attack on Sumner, 120–22; and Compromise of 1850, 29, 35, 63–65; as escape from House Chamber, 14, 22, 26–27; seating arrangements in, 155–57
Sergeant-at-Arms, 22–23, 69, 165
Seward, William H., 27, 52, 69, 79, 89, 124, 126, 128, 149–50, 154, 156–57, 179; and April 1861 memo to Lincoln,

197–98; as dinner guest, 78, 82, 84–88; at Hampton Roads, 192, 194–97; house in Washington, 112, 114, 117; on Kansas-Nebraska Act, 98, 117–18; relationship with Southerners, 31–32, 34, 88, 151, 176–77, 198–99; reputation outside Washington, 172, 176; and secession winter, 181, 188, 190
Shields, James, 86, 94, 152
Sickles, Daniel, 137–40
Slavery, 2, 56–57, 59, 61, 88, 103, 107–8, 117–19, 143, 151–52, 190, 193, 199; and caning of Charles Sumner, 120–23; as cause of the Civil War, 5–6; Lincoln's views on, 107, 172, 174, 187–89; in Mexican Cession, 3, 15–17, 38–39, 62, 64–66, 68, 78, 90; and popular sovereignty, 97–99; and Washington churches, 52, 180
Slidell, John, 37, 114, 117, 156, 168, 186, 190
Smith, Caleb Blood, 106
Smith, Truman, 44–45, 57, 60–61, 84, 151, 192, 200; relationship with Rusk, 163–64
Smithsonian Institution, 46, 48–51, 56, 181
Soulé, Pierre, 74, 152, 157
Southern Convention, 65, 90
Speaker of the House, 19, 24, 28–29, 37, 52, 61, 69, 102, 126, 148; Banks as, 122, 143; Cobb as, 71, 92, 159; Pennington as, 129, 158, 182, 186; Winthrop as, 24, 64, 159, 174
Stanton, Benjamin, 51, 58, 181
Stanton, Edwin, 59, 84, 139, 194, 196
Stephens, Alexander H., 26, 56, 61, 79–80, 85, 106–8, 110, 129, 141, 151–52, 165, 199; cornerstone speech, 190; frustration with Taylor, 65, 75–76; and Hampton Roads, 192–97; relationship with Lincoln, 46–47, 62, 173–74, 188–89, 196–98; as Young Indian, 44–47, 200
Story, Joseph, 106, 126
Stuart, Alexander H. H., 72, 87, 94, 113, 117, 160